W9-DJE-299

CONTEMPORARY PERSPECTIVES ON

STRATEGIC

MARKET

PLANNING

CONTEMPORARY PERSPECTIVES ON

Strategic

Market

Planning

ROGER A. KERIN
Southern Methodist University

VIJAY MAHAJAN
Southern Methodist University

P. RAJAN VARADARAJAN
Texas A & M University

ALLYN AND BACON
Boston London Sydney Toronto

Production Administrator: Susan McIntyre
Series Editor: Henry Reece
Series Editorial Assistant: Katherine Grubbs
Editorial-Production Service: Editing, Design & Production, Inc.
Cover Administrator: Linda Dickinson
Manufacturing Buyer: Tamara Johnson

Copyright © 1990 by Allyn and Bacon
A Division of Simon & Schuster, Inc.
160 Gould Street
Needham Heights, MA 02194

Library of Congress Cataloging-in-Publication Data
Kerin, Roger A.
     Contemporary perspectives on strategic market planning / Roger A.
Kerin, Vijay Mahajan, P. Rajan Varadarajan.
          p.   cm.
     ISBN 0-205-12301-5
     1. Marketing—Planning.   2. Strategic planning.   I. Mahajan,
Vijay.   II Varadarajan, P.   III. Title.
HF5415.13.K46   1989   89-36587
658.8'01—dc20   CIP

Printed in the United States of America
10 9 8 7 6 5 4 3 2 1   94 93 92 91 90 89

TO OUR PARENTS

Joseph and Mary Kerin

Lajwanti (mother) and Shiv Saran Gupta (father)

Saroja (mother) and Poondi Venkatadri (father)

CONTENTS

Preface   ix

PART I. CURRENT PERSPECTIVES ON STRATEGIC
         MARKET PLANNING PRACTICES   1
Chapter 1. Foundations of Strategic Market Planning   3
Chapter 2. Portfolio Models: Foundations   30
Chapter 3. Multifactor Portfolio Matrix Models and Competitive
            Strategy Models   71
Chapter 4. Business Strategy and the Experience Curve   114
Chapter 5. Analysis of Pooled Business Experience:
            The PIMS Program   140
Appendix: Selected Questions from PIMS Forms   188

PART II. PERSPECTIVES FROM INDUSTRIAL
          ORGANIZATION ECONOMICS   221
Chapter 6. Intensive, Integrative and Diversification
            Growth Strategies   223
Appendix: Measurement of Firm Diversity   270
Chapter 7. Assessment of Industry Competition and
            Competitors   282

PART III. PERSPECTIVES FROM CORPORATE
           FINANCE   339
Chapter 8. Sustainable Growth   341
Chapter 9. Value-Based Planning   358

PART IV. PERSPECTIVES FROM THE ORGANIZATIONAL
          SCIENCES   385
Chapter 10. A Quest for Organizational Excellence   387
Chapter 11. Organization Renewal: The Role of Corporate Culture,
            Leadership, and Entrepreneurship   409

Index   443

PREFACE

Strategic market planning is a recent addition to the lexicon of business concepts. Popularized in the late 1970s, strategic market planning became the subject of serious study by academics. At the same time, strategy consultants and corporate executives embraced and contributed to the concept. This healthy interplay between the theory and practice of strategic market planning created an extensive and diverse body of knowledge over the past decade.

Contemporary Perspectives on Strategic Market Planning appears exactly ten years after Derek Abell and John Hammond introduced the concept with their seminal text, *Strategic Market Planning: Problems and Analytical Approaches* (Prentice-Hall, 1979). In the ensuing decade, literally hundreds of conceptual and empirically based works have been published examining one or more aspects of strategic market planning. During this period, new ideas and viewpoints surfaced that may influence how strategic market planning is studied and practiced.

The purpose of this book is two-fold:

1. To review in depth concepts, analytical techniques, empirical findings, and paradigms that collectively form the foundation for strategic market planning as it is known and practiced today.
2. To introduce emerging concepts, analytical techniques, empirical findings, and paradigms that are likely to alter the nature, scope, and practice of strategic market planning in the foreseeable future.

Contemporary Perspectives on Strategic Market Planning is designed to provide a comprehensive review and assessment of present knowledge, as well as of new developments that may become germane to future research on and implementation of strategic market planning at the corporate and business unit level of the organization. As such, the contents are designed to provide a context and perspective for the thoughtful scholar, graduate student, and corporate planning executive. The reader will not find prescriptions for how to engage in strategic market planning or prepare a strategic market plan. Rather, the book is descriptive in the sense that it delineates what is known or often unknown in the study and practice of strategic market planning.

The book is divided into four parts and contains eleven chapters. Part One provides an overview of strategic market planning. Issues, important concepts, and planning tools and processes are emphasized. Specific topics address generally accepted facets of strategic market planning, including such topics as portfolio analysis, experience curves, and insights from the PIMS research program.

The remainder of the book explores recent developments and potentially controversial topics that may influence the nature, scope, and practice of strategic market planning in the near future. Most of the topics draw on work developed outside the traditional marketing literature. Coverage of these diverse literatures is in keeping with the interdisciplinary development of strategic market planning as a scholarly and practical concept. Part Two examines perspectives from the industrial organization economics literature. Specific perspectives on understanding the role of competition and competitors and insights from the work on diversification and integration are highlighted. Part Three introduces perspectives from corporate finance. Two major topics are reviewed: sustainable growth and value-based planning. Part Four provides perspectives from the organizational sciences. The literature on corporate excellence, culture, leadership, and entrepreneurship is assessed with reference to strategic market planning.

Multiple chapters benefited from the critical comments made by David Gardner, University of Illinois, Bruce Henderson, Vanderbilt University, John Quelch, Harvard Business School, Robert Ruekert, University of Minnesota, and Robin Wensley, University of Warwick, England. Individual chapters benefited from the insights provided by Yoram Wind, University of Pennsylvania, Richard Bettis, Southern Methodist University and Jeffrey Kerr, University of Miami. Comprehensive comments on the entire manuscript were provided by James Ginter, Ohio State University, Bernard Joworski, University of Arizona, and Ajay Kohli, University of Texas. The suggestions of all reviewers were invaluable in shaping the final manuscript. Notwithstanding the contributions of these many people, the authors bear full responsibility for all errors of omission and commission in the final product.

Roger A. Kerin
Vijay Mahajan
P. Rajan Varadarajan

PART **I**

CURRENT PERSPECTIVES ON

STRATEGIC MARKET

PLANNING PRACTICES

FOUNDATIONS OF

STRATEGIC MARKET PLANNING

Introduction
   Strategic Market Planning Defined

The Concept of Strategy
   Distinctive Competence
   Competitive Advantage
   Strategy Levels

Evolution of Planning Systems
   Financial Planning
   Long-range Planning
   Strategic Planning
   Strategic Management

The Strategic Market Planning Process

Dominant Themes in Strategic Market Planning
   Business Portfolio Matrices
   Analysis of Pooled Business Experience
   Application of Modern Industrial
      Organization Economics Framework to
      Competitive Analysis
   McKinsey Excellence Studies
   Organizational Renewal

A Concluding Note

References

INTRODUCTION

The 1970s brought a new dawn for American business. Executives awoke to an escalation in interest rates and inflation, slowed economic growth, deregulation, rapid development and diffusion of new technologies, the unexpected presence and success of foreign competitors, and changing

3

demographics of consumers, who demanded better products and services. The clash between the rapidly changing and often hostile environment and the lumbering corporation of the 1970s produced a cry for new perspectives and practices to meet these new challenges. Achieving and sustaining competitive advantage emerged as the cornerstones of strategic thinking and a focus on strategic market planning became a means to attain these goals.

The emphasis on competitive advantage raised a variety of questions:

- What are the firm's core markets and products?
- What new businesses or product-markets should the firm enter?
- Should the company be in a particular business?
- What businesses or product-markets should be divested or repositioned?
- How could a leadership position be achieved and sustained in a particular product-market?
- How should resources be allocated among product-markets?

The search for answers to such questions during the ensuing decades produced an extensive body of literature offering new concepts, analytical techniques, empirical findings, and paradigms that collectively formed the foundation for strategic market planning as it is known and practiced today.

This chapter sets the stage for the book by first providing a definition of strategic market planning. The remainder of the chapter further comments on the nature and scope of strategic market planning by elaborating on (1) the concept of strategy, (2) the types of planning systems, and (3) the process of strategic market planning. The chapter concludes with an overview of contemporary perspectives on strategic market planning and of the organization of the book.

Strategic Market Planning Defined

Corporate executives continuously seek an effective match or fit between the organization and its changing market environment. They carefully monitor and assess the marketplace, competition, laws and regulations, taxes and interest rates, business cycles, customer needs and desires, and any other pertinent factors to identify threats and locate opportunities. An example of such behavior is found in the strategic attempts made by Walt Disney Pictures to effectively match the organization to changing customer demographics (see Box 1.1). Contrary to its image, the firm formed a separate entity (Touchstone Pictures) to create and market pictures to the emerging twenty-five to forty year-old segment of the moviegoing market, enabling it to reestablish itself in the movie industry.

An organization develops strategies to cope with environmental threats and opportunities. The process of developing and evaluating strategies is called strategic market planning. The inclusion of the term *market* in strategic planning serves to emphasize that strategy development needs to be driven by the forces of the market environment rather than by internal factors. The following definition of *strategic market planning* is suggested:

> Strategic market planning is the managerial process that entails analysis, formulation and evaluation of strategies that would enable an organization to achieve its goals by developing and maintaining a strategic fit between the organization's capabilities and the threats and opportunities arising from its changing environment.

Strategic market planning needs to be distinguished from strategic marketing planning. Strategic market planning prepares a firm to develop a strategic response to its changing market environment. It involves the formulation and development of strategies to cope with the increased rate and abruptness of changes emerging from its market environment. Strategic marketing planning, on the other hand, is concerned with functional decisions related to marketing-mix elements, including price, distribution, and advertising. In that capacity, marketing competes with other functional areas for resources and forms an important input into the functionally integrative strategic market planning process (Biggadike 1981; Anderson 1982; Day and Wensley 1983; Wind and Robertson 1983; Yip 1985). Marketing, however, does play a key role in establishing a strategic fit between an organization and its changing market environment. The following from Day (1984, p. 3) articulates the strategic role played by marketing in establishing this interface:

> The primary responsibility of strategic planning is to look continuously outward and keep the business in step with the anticipated environment. The lead role in meeting this responsibility is played by marketing, for this is the boundary function between the firm and its customers, distributors, and competitors. As a general management responsibility, marketing embraces the interpretations of the environment and the crucial choices of customers to serve, competitors to challenge, and the product characteristics with which the business will compete. Strategic market planning is broader than marketing, however, for strategies that start with the analysis of market responses will not be effective unless they are fully integrated with other functional decisions.

That is, as a general management responsibility, marketing plays the lead role in achieving a productive match or fit with a firm's market environment, and, hence, in the conduct and practice of strategic market planning. Understanding strategic market planning, however, requires a delineation of the concept of strategy. This is done in the next section.

BOX **1.1**

STRATEGIC RESPONSE TO MARKET CHANGES
RESULTING FROM CUSTOMER DEMOGRAPHICS:
WALT DISNEY PICTURES

A major source of market discontinuities is customer demographics. The aging of the U.S. population, the emergence of dual-income households, and the increase in the number of single-person households are the major shifts in customer demographics that are requiring firms to develop strategic responses to cope with these changes.

The median age of the U.S. population in 1980 was thirty years; by the end of the 1990s it will be almost forty years. Today, more than fifty-five percent of all women have a job or career away from the home. By the end of the 1990s, this figure is expected to be at least sixty-five percent. There is also a rise in the number of single-person households. Such households currently constitute about twenty-five percent of the total households in the U.S. and should rise even more by the end of this century. The traditional family, comprising the homemaker, the breadwinner, and the children, now constitutes only seven percent of all U.S. households.

Understanding shifts in customer demographics and their impact is essential in maintaining the viability of a firm. Consider, for example, the movie market. In the early 1980s, the Motion Picture Association of

THE CONCEPT OF STRATEGY

Strategy is the means an organization uses to achieve its objectives. The evolution of the concept of strategy is portrayed in Table 1.1, which documents ten different definitions that have been proposed by various authors over the past twenty-five years. One of the earlier definitions was proposed by Chandler (1962:13) who defined strategy as "the determination of the basic long-term goals of an enterprise and the adoption of courses of actions and the allocation of resources necessary to carry out these goals." Critical to a better appreciation of the concept of strategy is an understanding of certain related concepts. These include:

- *Distinctive Competence:* those things that an organization is capable of doing especially well in comparison to its competitors;

America estimated that seventy-six percent of first-run theatrical film viewers were between the ages of twelve and twenty-four. In recent years, the teen bloc, which still accounts for a significant portion of the movie-going population, lost its percentage contribution to yuppies and their elders. In 1987, for example, according to the Motion Picture Association of America, movie attendance by those forty and older rose fifty-six percent over the 1986 figures. Not one of 1987 top ten hits was aimed primarily at the youth market.

Given the market discontinuities caused by customer demographics, Walt Disney Pictures created a separate entity—Touchstone Pictures—in 1981, charged with marketing pictures to the twenty-five- to forty year-old segment of the moviegoing market. The parent company formed the new film studio to produce films that were not consistent with the Walt Disney image, but fulfilled its creative and marketing requirements through Walt Disney Pictures. This action allowed the company to capitalize on its strengths, yet overcome the threats posed by market discontinuities of customer demographics. Touchstone Pictures has been successful in producing box-office hits such as "Three Men and a Baby" and "Good Morning, Vietnam."

Sources: *Broadcasting* (1982), "Moving Those Movies," (March 19), p. 133; *Business Week* (1987), "Disney's Magic: A Turnaround Proves Wishes Can Come True," (March 19), p. 65; *Fortune* (1987), "Putting Magic Back Into the King-dom," (January 5), p. 165; *Time* (1988), "Adults Also Permitted," (March 7), p. 72.

- *Competitive Advantage:* the unique position an organization develops *vis-a-vis* its competitors through its pattern of resource deployment and/or its product-market scope decisions; and
- *Strategy Levels:* strategy development generally takes place at multiple levels within an organization.

Distinctive Competence

Distinctive competence describes the special or unique capabilities of an organization. Day and Wensley (1988), identify two sources of distinctive competence for an organization: (1) the skills of its personnel and (2) its resources. Superiority in these two dimensions allows a firm to do more or better (or both) than its competitors.

Superior skills arise from an ability to perform certain functions more effectively than competitors. Superior engineering and technical skills, for

TABLE 1.1
DIMENSIONS OF THE CONCEPT OF STRATEGY

Definition Proposed by	Definition of Strategy	Key Strategy Dimension Identified in the Definition(s)
Chandler (1962)	Strategy is the determination of the basic, long-term goals of an enterprise and the adoption of courses of actions and the allocation of resources necessary to carry out these goals.	Strategy is a means of establishing the organizational purpose (in terms of its long-term objectives, action programs, and resource allocation priorities).
Schendel and Hatten (1972)	Strategy is the basic goals and objectives of the organization, the major programs of action chosen to reach these goals and objectives, and the major pattern of resource allocation used to relate the organization to its environment.	
Learned, Christensen, Andrews, and Guth (1965)	Strategy is the pattern of objectives, purposes, or goals and major policies and plans for achieving these goals, stated in such a way as to define what businesses the company is in or should be in and the kind of company it is or will be.	Strategy defines the competitive domain of the firm. That is, one of the central concerns of strategy is defining the businesses the firm is in or should be in.
Argyris (1985)	Strategy formulation and implementation include identifying opportunities and threats in the organization's environment, evaluating the strengths and weaknesses of the organization, designing structures, defining roles, hiring appropriate people, and developing appropriate rewards to keep those people motivated to make contributions.	Strategy is a response (continuous and adaptive) to external opportunities and threats and internal strengths and weaknesses that affect the organization.
Mintzberg (1979)	Strategy is a mediating force between the organization and its environment; there are consistent patterns of streams of organizational decisions to deal with the environment.	
Steiner and Miner (1977)	Strategy is the forging of company missions, setting objectives for the organization in light of external and internal forces, formulating specific policies and strategies to achieve objectives, and ensuring their proper implementation so that the basic purposes and objectives of the organization will be achieved.	

TABLE 1.1
DIMENSIONS OF THE CONCEPT OF STRATEGY, *continued*

Definition Proposed by	Definition of Strategy	Key Strategy Dimension Identified in the Definition(s)
Porter (1985)	Strategy (competitive) is the search for a favorable competitive position in an industry, the fundamental arena in which competition occurs. Competitive strategy aims to establish a profitable and sustainable position against the forces that determine industry competition.	Strategy is a central vehicle for achieving competitive advantage.
Andrews (1980)	Corporate strategy defines the businesses in which a company will compete, preferably in a way that focuses resources to convert distinctive competence into competitive advantage. Business strategy is the determination of how a company will compete in a given business and position itself among its competitors.	Strategy engages all the hierarchical levels of the firm: corporate, business, and functional.
Andrews (1980)	Corporate strategy is the pattern of decisions in a company that determines and reveals its objectives, purposes, or goals, produces the principal policies and plans for achieving those goals, and defines the range of businesses the company is to pursue, the kind of economic and human organization it is or intends to be, and the nature of the economic and noneconomic contribution it intends to make to its shareholders, employees, customers, and communities.	Strategy is a motivating force for the stakeholders (such as shareholders, debt-holders, managers, employees, customers, communities, government, and so forth) who directly or indirectly receive the benefits or costs derived from the actions of the firm.
Chaffee (1985)	Strategy is defined as orienting "metaphors" or frames of reference that allow the organization and its environment to be understood by organizational stakeholders. On this basis, stakeholders are motivated to believe and to act in ways that are expected to produce favorable results for the organization.	

Source: Derived from Hax, A. C. and N. S. Majluf (1988), "The Concept of Strategy and the Strategy Formation Process," *Interfaces*, 18 (May–June), pp. 99–109.

example, allow a firm to produce a better quality product than its competitors. Similarly, superior marketing skills permit a firm to better understand its customer's needs and execute marketing programs that are superior to those of its competitors. Skill at producing products involving few parts (disposable razors, disposable pens) at low cost in very large quantities by using highly automated facilities is one of the distinctive competences of the Bic Corporation. A distribution infrastructure that has an almost one hundred percent penetration in various types of retail outlets (food stores, drug stores, discount stores, mass merchandisers, etc.) is a resource as well as a distinctive competence possessed by this organization. These and other competencies provide Bic with a competitive advantage for its present product offerings, and also constitute a potential source of competitive advantage with respect to related product-markets (frequently purchased, inexpensive, convenience goods) that the firm might choose to enter.

Superior resources are tangible requirements that provide a firm with an ability to develop an advantage over its competitors. These abilities arise from sophisticated plant and equipment, the nature and scope of its distribution network, its production capabilities, unique sourcing of raw materials and financial funds, and an established brand name. Computerized reservation systems used by American Airlines and United Airlines have been described as superior resources created by these airlines to gain market dominance over their competitors in the airline industry (Petre, 1985).

Competitive Advantage

Competitive advantage arises from a firm's choice of markets to serve, its distinctive competences, and pattern of resource deployment that give it an edge over its competitors in chosen markets. In each market, a firm chooses to compete with other firms given the opportunities available. It does so by competing based on the value its product offers and the relative (to competitors) cost of delivering it to its customers.

Two basic alternatives available to a firm to achieve and sustain a competitive advantage over its competitors are: cost leadership and differentiation.

A firm can gain a competitive advantage by offering the same value to its customers at a lower delivered cost than its competitors'. The lower delivered cost can be realized through economies of scale, economies of scope, production efficiencies realized through investment in state-of-the-art equipment, favorable access to raw materials, a low-cost labor force, etc. For example, firms in several industries have attempted to gain a cost advantage over their competitors by sourcing parts from countries such as Malaysia, Singapore, and Taiwan, where labor costs are relatively lower. However, such sources of competitive cost advantage often erode as competitors follow suit. For a firm to achieve a *sustainable* competitive advantage, a capability (distinctive competence) must be unique to the firm.

That is, it must be based on a capability gap that separates the firm from its competitors. This point is discussed in greater detail in chapter seven.

A firm can also gain an edge over its competitors by differentiating and establishing perceived value for its customers along one or more dimensions, such as superior performance, innovative features, superior service, and brand prestige. IBM products, for example, are differentiated in terms of superior performance and service backup.

Strategy Levels

A multiproduct, multimarket firm competes in more than one business arena or market. That is, it manages a portfolio of businesses variously termed Strategic Business Units (SBU), Business Units, Strategic Business Groups, Strategic Business Segments, Natural Business Units, or Product-Market Units (PMU). Ideally, an SBU has the following characteristics (Hall, 1978; Abell and Hammond, 1979):

1. It has its own mission.
2. It produces and markets a well-defined set of related products and/ or services.
3. It serves a clearly defined customer group.
4. It competes with a well-defined set of competitors.

A strategic business unit can have a different meaning for different companies (Haspeslagh, 1982; Wind and Mahajan, 1981). Thus a strategic business unit can include one or more divisions, a product line within a division, or sometimes a single product or brand. Given the distribution, production, manufacturing, technology and other synergies between strategic business units, SBUs can be aggregated into sectors or what are referred to as strategic business families (Chakravarthy, 1984).

Originally pioneered by General Electric in the 1970s (Springer, 1973), a large number of multiproduct, multimarket firms have restructured themselves to facilitate the management of their portfolio of SBUs (Haspeslagh, 1982). Figure 1.1, for example, depicts how Bayer AG (West Germany) organized its various worldwide businesses and subsidiaries into six sectors. Formalized in 1984, the new organization structure contained six Business Sectors comprised of several Business Groups. As reported by Bayer AG:

All business activities of Bayer World are now grouped in six Business Sectors, each of which comprises several Business Groups with independent activities. A number of central staff and service functions are now combined in a new Corporate Staff Division, which serves the Company worldwide. The remaining service functions have been regrouped in five new Service Divisions.

Management of Business Sectors has been assigned to the Sector Heads, a newly created tier of management. Their main task is to coor-

FIGURE 1.1
BAYER AG ORGANIZATION

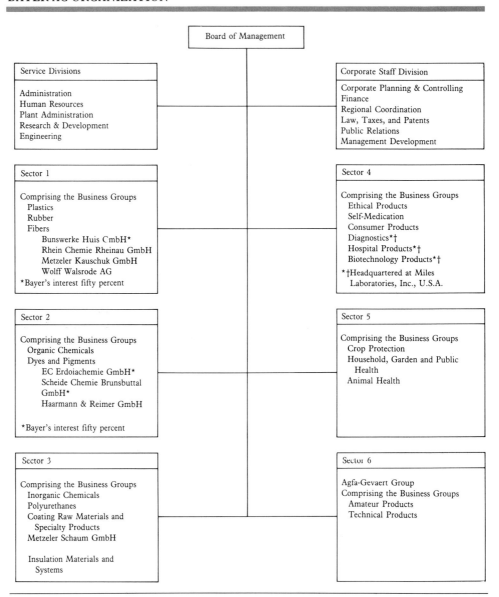

Source: Based on Vossberg, H. (1985), "Bayer Reorganizes in Response to Growth," *Long-Range Planning*, Vol. 18, p. 17.

dinate and monitor the business activities of the Business Groups within their Sectors; they are also responsible for developing corporate policy concepts in their Sectors. Like the former Operating Divisions, the Business Groups are largely independent operating units within the

Bayer organization and, as "profit centers," are responsible for the development and expansion of their respective fields of activity (Vossberg 1985, pp. 15–16).

Structuring organizations into SBUs is conducive to developing a more responsive posture for dealing with emerging threats and opportunities. It also disciplines the organization to think in terms of developing strategies at multiple levels within the organization, namely, the corporate, business, and functional levels.

Corporate Strategy   Andrews (1980) describes the scope of strategy at the corporate level by noting:

> Corporate strategy defines the businesses in which a company will compete, preferably in a way that focuses resources to convert distinctive competence into competitive advantage (pp. 18–19).

At the corporate level, a corporate strategy addresses two major questions:

1. What set of businesses should the firm compete in?
2. How should individual businesses be integrated?

Therefore, a major concern at the corporate strategy level is what businesses to enter, which businesses to hold, and which businesses to divest. Decisions involving new product-market entry (diversification), exiting from one or more product-markets where a firm presently competes (divestitures), type of entry (acquisition, internal development, joint ventures), and mode of exit (spin-offs, sell-offs, liquidation) are some of the major concerns here. These decisions determine the current and future composition of a firm's business portfolio, how the businesses complement or reinforce one another, and how corporate level resources are allocated to the various businesses. The nature of such decisions is illustrated in reference to Johnson & Johnson, Inc. in Box 1.2. These decisions indicate how Johnson & Johnson, Inc. has managed its worldwide portfolio of one hundred and sixty-five operating "companies" to retain and strengthen its competitive advantage in the health care industry.

It should be noted that a single business firm also pursues a corporate level strategy by choosing to compete in only one business rather than several. A case in point is McDonald's Corporation, which competes in the fast food market.

Business Unit Strategy   Corporations do not compete with each other in the marketplace. Rather, their individual businesses compete with each other (Porter, 1985). The following definition by Andrews (1980) highlights the scope of strategy at the business-unit level:

> Business strategy is the determination of how a company will compete in a given business and position itself among its competitors (p. 18).

BOX **1.2**

THE SCOPE OF CORPORATE STRATEGY:
JOHNSON & JOHNSON

Johnson and Johnson (J&J), comprised of about one hundred sixty-five operating "companies," generates most of its worldwide sales from a variety of health care related businesses: surgical and first-aid supplies, pharmaceuticals, sanitary napkins and tampons, baby products, diagnostic equipment, over-the-counter analgesic products, hospital supplies, and dental products. These businesses have been grouped by J&J into three distinct business families: consumer, professional, and pharmaceutical. The three families of businesses vary in terms of their product offerings, the target markets served, and the dominant channels of distribution.

Consumer businesses market their products, such as toiletries and hygienic products, first-aid products, and nonprescription drugs, to consumer markets (households) through wholesalers and independent and chain retail outlets. Professional businesses market their products to institutional markets (health care organizations and health care professionals) directly and through surgical supply dealers. Pharmaceutical businesses market prescription drugs to both consumers and institutional markets both directly and through wholesalers and independent and chain retail outlets.

J&J, however, is best known to its consumers for such brands as Band-Aid, Baby Shampoo, and Tylenol. In addition to consumer brands, J&J holds powerful and profitable positions in the hospital supply and prescription drug markets. For years, these product lines flourished under a marketing-dominated management structure and leadership. In fact, the majority of J&J's sales (about fifty-five percent) come from products that are number one in their markets. This dominance has helped J&J to maintain a thirteen percent average annual growth in its earnings.

For each business unit comprising the corporate portfolio, a strategy must be developed that focuses on how to compete most effectively in the product-market served by the business unit. Since each business unit operates in its own unique market environment and deals with a specific set of customers and competitors, it needs to allocate its resources across its functional areas (e.g., product design, manufacturing and marketing) to compete effectively. Superior performance, in terms of market share

Although J&J's core businesses remain solidly profitable, they are mostly in mature markets. Efforts to effectively manage the various product lines have included: (1) the *introduction* of new products to appeal to new market segments (e.g., the introduction of products such as shampoo for women over forty years of age with more brittle hair), (2) the *deletion* of certain products from certain markets (e.g., withdrawal from the U.S. disposable-diaper market), (3) the *repositioning* of certain products (e.g., the repositioning of J&J Baby Shampoo for the adult market), and (4) the *expansion* of certain product lines to appeal to the current or new market segments (e.g., the introduction of Junior Strength Tylenol for six-to fourteen-year-olds and a capsule-shaped Tylenol tablet).

Faced with mature markets, J&J has ventured into sophisticated medical technologies. Its chairman believes that maturing markets limit long-term growth, and since scientific and technological advances promise to revolutionize health care, entering high-tech markets is essential to the future of J&J. Since 1980, J&J has acquired several high-tech companies, thus positioning itself in markets ranging from introcular lenses and surgical lasers to magnetic-resonance scanners for diagnostic imaging.

Given J&J's strength in making and marketing consumer products, industry experts have questioned J&J's ability to successfully enter high-tech businesses and face well-entrenched competitors such as General Electric. The senior executives at J&J, however, feel that J&J's move into medical technologies gives its various "companies" an opportunity to share R&D and marketing resources. They believe this should enable J&J to speed product development, regain market share in such traditional markets as hospital supplies, and exploit new opportunities created by the movement toward preventive health care. For example, they believe that combining J&J's expertise in magnetic resonance and biotechnology could revolutionize diagnostics. However, the entry into high-tech markets has not yet been generally profitable for J&J.

Adapted from "Changing a Corporate Culture," *Business Week*, (May 14), 1984, pp. 130–138, and *1984, 1985 and 1986 Annual Reports*, New Brunswick, NJ: Johnson & Johnson.

dominance and above-average profitability in the industry, requires a business to achieve an advantage over its competitors by developing distinctive competences and lower delivered cost or by differentiating through superior customer value (Day and Wensley, 1988).

Functional Strategy Functional areas such as marketing, manufacturing, personnel, R&D, and so forth determine a business-unit strategy's success or failure. Functional strategy, therefore, involves decisions regarding the determination of how resources allocated to the various functional areas can be used most efficiently to support the business-unit strategy. For example, a business unit pursuing a market share building strategy needs to determine how its resources can be used most efficiently to take advantage of the various means of stimulating sales, such as advertising, promotion, and sales force development, and how such decisions affect other functions, such as manufacturing, finance, personnel, and so forth.

EVOLUTION OF PLANNING SYSTEMS

A *planning system* is a formalized and systematic approach to developing and implementing strategies. As shown in Table 1.2, planning systems can be characterized in terms of their (1) emphasis on creativity and control, (2) reliance on analytical techniques, (3) attention to resource auditing, (4) efforts at environmental scanning, (5) functional coverage, (6) resources provided for in planning, and (7) resistance to planning within a firm. Of these, the three characteristics that differentiate the most between more are less effective planning systems are: (1) management's resistance to planning within the firm, (2) the resources provided for planning, and (3) the emphasis on creativity and control (Ramanujam, Venkatraman, and Camillus, 1986). That is, no planning system can be effective if it faces resistance or if it is denied sufficient resources, including support from top management. Also, an effective planning system balances its emphases on capabilities encompassing creativity (anticipating surprises and crises) and on those ensuring control (upward and downward communication within an organizational hierarchy).

Although an organization should develop a planning system tailored to suit its structure and environmental context, attempts have been made in recent years to categorize planning systems. One such attempt has been reported by Gluck, Kaufman, and Walleck at McKinsey and Company (1980, 1982). In their review of one-hundred-twenty formal planning systems in mostly industrial goods companies in seven countries, the authors report that planning systems are likely to exist in one of four evolutionary states: financial planning, long-range planning, strategic planning, and strategic management (see Table 1.3). Since planning is a learning process, organizations typically progress through these four common stages in developing a planning system of their own. The type of planning system employed by organizations will also depend upon assumptions made about the nature of the market environment and its organizational context in terms of the nature of its business (Chakravarthy, 1987). Commentaries by Ansoff (1980), Chakravarthy and Lorange (1984) and Chakravarthy (1987), among others, provide additional insights into the distinguishing features and origination of these systems.

TABLE 1.2
CHARACTERISTICS OF PLANNING SYSTEMS

Characteristics	Description
Creativity and control	The creative ability of a system is its ability to anticipate surprises and crises, to adapt to unforeseen changes, and so forth. The control aspect refers to the degrees of emphasis given to managerial motivation, upward and downward communication within an organizational hierarchy, the integration of diverse operational areas, and the like.
Use of techniques	The degree of emphasis given to the use of planning techniques to structure ill-defined, messy, strategic problems.
Resource audit	The degree of attention to internal (organizational) factors, past performance, and the analysis of strengths and weaknesses.
Environmental scanning	The level of emphasis given to monitoring environmental trends.
Functional coverage	The extent of coverage given to different functional areas with a view to integrating different functional requirements into a general management perspective.
Resources provided for planning	The degree of organizational support in the form of number of planners, involvement of top management in planning, etc.
Resistance to planning within the firm (anti-planning bias)	The need to anticipate and overcome resistance to planning and to create a favorable climate for effective planning.

Source: Ramanujam, V., N. Venkatraman, and J. C. Camillus (1986), "Multi-objective Assessment of Effectiveness of Strategic Planning: A Discriminant Analysis Approach," *Academy of Management Journal*, 29 (June), p. 350.

The Financial Planning System

Under a financial planning system, planning mainly comprises the annual budgeting process. Financial considerations related to forecasting revenue, cost, and capital needs on an annual basis dominate the formalization of the system. Considerable emphasis is placed on conforming to the annual budget developed. Any deviations from the budget are monitored for possible explanations and remedial actions. Strategies are rarely formalized, but are implicitly worked out among the company's top management and corporate staff. Consequently, planning is centralized and top-down. The basic assumption is that the past will repeat itself. Although developed in

TABLE 1.3
TYPES OF PLANNING SYSTEMS

Feature	Budgeting/Control	Long-Range Planning	Strategic Market Planning	Strategic Market Management
Purpose	Control budget deviations	More effective planning for growth	Increasing response to markets and competition	Orchestration of all resources to create competitive advantage and to cope with strategic surprises
Assumptions about market environment	The past repeats	Past trends will continue in future	New trends and discontinuities are predictable	Planning cycles inadequate to deal with rapid changes
Direction of goal-setting	Top-down	Bottom-up	Mixed mode (leaning to top-down)	Mixed mode (leaning to bottom-up)
Linkage between action plans and budget	Very tight	Very loose, as long as budget is met	Loose for some divisions, tight for others	Simultaneously loose-tight for all divisions
Role of corporate planner in strategy formulation	Strategist	Catalyst	Mixed role	Catalyst
Planning time frame	Periodic	Periodic	Periodic	Real time
Value system	Meet the budget	Predict the future	Think strategically	Create the future
Time period associated with its origination	From 1900s	From 1950s	From 1960s	From mid-1970s

Source: Ansoff, H. I. (1980), "Strategic Issue Management," *Strategic Management Journal*, 1 (April–June), pp. 131–148; Gluck, F., S. Kaufman and A. S. Walleck (1982), "The Four Phases of Strategic Management," *Journal of Business Strategy*, 3 (Winter), pp. 9–21; B. S. Chakravarthy (1987), "On Tailoring a Strategic Planning System to its Context: Some Empirical Evidence," *Strategic Management Journal*, 3 (November–December), pp. 517–534; Aaker, D. A. (1984), *Strategic Market Management*, New York: John Wiley, p. 11.

the first half of the twentieth century, according to Gluck, Kaufman, and Walleck (1982, p. 11), in well over half of the business enterprises surveyed by them (including a number of highly successful companies), formal planning has never evolved beyond "meeting the numbers."

The Long-Range Planning System

In contrast to the financial planning system, the long-range planning system covers a longer time frame (e.g., five years) and is more future-oriented. Regarding market-environment forces, it is assumed that the past can be projected and extrapolated into the future. Therefore, most of strategic analyses included in this system are static in the sense that they do not anticipate, explore, or create future opportunities. Current capabilities of business units in a firm's portfolio are assumed as given (rather than something that can be affected) and, hence, resource allocation is based on current strengths and weaknesses and market performance.

Compared to financial planning, long-range planning represents a decentralized system. Each business unit is responsible for setting its own goals and strategies. That is, goal-setting is bottom-up, and the linkage between the five-year plan and budget is loose. Top management monitors the short-term performance of the various business units. Each business unit is treated as a profit center.

Although this type of system seems to have originated in the 1950s and early 1960s, Gluck, Kaufman, and Walleck (1982, p. 13) report that most planning systems today do not go much beyond this type of planning.

The Strategic Planning System

Although an extension of the long range-planning system, strategic planning is market-environment driven. Consequently, all strategic analyses are dynamic, emphasizing the anticipation, exploration, and creation of opportunities. Resource allocation is also dynamic, emphasizing the exploration and evaluation of options and alternatives. Current strengths and weaknesses of the businesses and their market conditions are not assumed to be given, but rather something that can be altered. Consequently, business units are not expected to perform in the same way and each have assigned missions. Depending upon the assigned missions, business units are monitored differently in terms of their profitability expectations. Although business units develop their own strategies, these strategies have to conform to a corporate level portfolio plan.

The Strategic Management System

According to Gluck, Kaufman, and Walleck (1982, p. 16), this planning system has been used in recent years by a few multinational diversified manufacturing companies, often involved in electrical and electronic products. Firms that use this type of planning system attempt to merge the scenario-based approach of strategic planning system with the management of the firm into a single system. The system, therefore, prepares an organization to respond to the market and environmental changes that occur rapidly or unexpectedly (in real time) to minimize damage to the firm. That is, instead of reacting to changes, the firm creates its own future. The system involves planning at all levels in the organization and rewards entrepreneurial thinking. The system encourages bottom-up planning, and is loosely coupled with the budgeting process.

STRATEGIC MARKET PLANNING PROCESS

In any planning system, and particularly in strategic planning and management systems, the strategic market planning process generally involves (1) analysis (e.g., environmental analysis; competitor and industry analysis; customer and market analysis; internal firm analysis) (2) the formulation and evaluation of alternative strategies, (3) the selection of a strategy, and (4) the development of detailed plans for implementing the strategy. The strategic market planning process focuses on three interrelated questions:

1. What do we want to achieve? (The statement of objectives).
2. Where are we? (The situation analysis).
3. How can we get from our current position to the desired position? (Strategy formulation and evaluation; strategy selection; and the development of detailed plans for strategy implementation.)

Alternative strategic market planning process frameworks are built around the various aspects of the above three questions. Figure 1.2 presents such a framework. The nine basic and interrelated phases describe this process, with phase five focusing on the corporate strategy, and phases six, seven, and eight focusing on the business unit strategy.

The nine phases of the frameworks are:

1. *Determination of corporate objectives:* The determination of the organization's objectives requires two major steps: (1) an identification of relevant objectives and (2) a determination of their relative importance. The objectives can be organized hierarchically to link decisions at the various levels of the organization. The objectives (at any level of the portfolio hierarchy) can include explicit portfolio objectives in terms of performance expectations (e.g., profits, market share, etc.) or the relative desired portfolio composition of the types of businesses.

2. *Monitoring the current and anticipated environment:* Chief among the environmental forces that should be monitored and projected are: (1) market demand; (2) competitive structure and actions; (3) the marketing (e.g., channel) environment; and (4) technological/social/cultural/political/legal regulatory environments. The exogenous environmental conditions are complex and difficult to monitor. Yet, a

FIGURE 1.2
A MARKETING-ORIENTED STRATEGIC PLANNING MODEL★

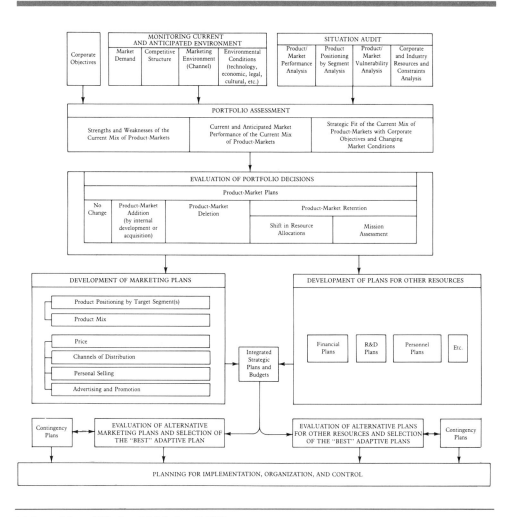

★Adapted from Wind and Mahajan (1982)

careful monitoring and projection of these forces, their interrelations, directions and magnitude of change, and likely effect on the organization's operations are essential inputs to the strategic market planning process.

3. *Situation audit:* A situation audit is an attempt to answer two questions: "Where are we?" and "Where are we going, assuming no changes in our marketing strategies, competitive actions, or environmental conditions?" It involves:

    a. Product-market analysis to assess the current and anticipated changes in the product's sales, profits, and market share positions by market segment (based on actual sales and profit data),

    b. Product positioning by market segment analysis to assess how various consumer segments and other relevant publics perceive and evaluate the firm's products *vis-a-vis* those of competitors,

    c. Product vulnerability/opportunity analysis to identify the firm's consumers who are vulnerable to competitors and potential consumers who can be attracted by the firm, and

    d. Corporate and industry analyses to assess the relative strengths and weaknesses of the firm with respect to its competitors along various dimensions, such as technology and production facilities, financial resources, management style, and marketing capabilities.

4. *Portfolio assessment:* The portfolio assessment profiles the organization's current mix of businesses, their current performance, and their anticipated performance under a set of relevant scenarios. The assessment determines the strategic fit of the current mix with the corporate objectives and changing market conditions.

5. *Portfolio decisions:* Analyses here relate to the evaluation and determination of the organization's portfolio from the available choices of the current as well as new businesses. What businesses to retain, add to, and delete from the portfolio are the focal issues. The allocation of resources among retained businesses and assignment of specific missions to individual businesses is another important aspect of this phase.

6. *Generation of alternative marketing programs:* To achieve the organization's objectives through the effective management of its portfolio of businesses, alternative marketing-mix programs need to be evaluated under various scenarios and contingencies. A marketing program should include (a) product decisions involving the determination of desired positioning by segment and (b) interrelated decisions regarding price, distribution, personal selling, advertising, and promotion.

7. *Generation of alternative programs for other functional areas:* Understandably, other functional area programs that complement marketing programs must be developed for the business unit strategy to come to fruition. These include programs related to manufacturing, R&D, finance, personnel and other functional areas needed to manage the desired portfolio of businesses. The scope of these programs include the funding, human resources, and capital resources (plant, equipment, technology) required to manage the desired portfolio.

8. *Evaluation of alternative programs:* The selection of any specific strategic plan should be congruent with: (a) the achievement of the corporate objectives, including target sales, profit, and market share,

(b) corporate resources and competitive advantage, and (c) the most likely future scenarios (including competitive reactions).

9. *Planning for implementation, organization, and control:* This phase entails the development of implementation plans, the design of an appropriate organizational structure (including communication, work flow, and reward systems), and control mechanisms for monitoring performance.

DOMINANT THEMES IN STRATEGIC MARKET PLANNING

In the late 1970s, writers introducing Business Week's new feature, "Corporate Strategies," raised the question, "What is the business concept that has become the major thrust and emphasis in the management of U.S. corporations today?" Their answer: strategic planning. The reason articulated for this answer was: "The discipline helps corporate officers anticipate and cope with a variety of forces beyond their control" (*Business Week,* 1979).

Since the early 1970s, a metamorphosis has taken place in strategic market planning. Beginning in about 1972, with the first of several "strategy briefs" prepared by the Boston Consulting Group, strategic market planning has evolved into a subject of serious study and debate among marketing consultants, practitioners, and academicians in a variety of disciplines (e.g., marketing, business policy, organizational behavior, and industrial organization economics). A retrospective glimpse at the past twenty years reveals five themes that have spawned most of the research and commentary on the theory and practice of strategic market planning (Mahajan, Varadarajan, and Kerin, 1987). Table 1.4 summarizes the strategy concerns of these themes and the various chapters of this book that include a relevant discussion of the conceptual and analytical contributions of each. Introductory comments on these themes are provided below.

Business Portfolio Matrices

The pioneering work of the Boston Consulting Group (1972) relating to experience curves and the growth share matrix, and the joint efforts of General Electric Co. and McKinsey & Company relating to portfolio matrices (Rothschild, 1976) have been instrumental in producing an extensive body of literature and research interest in the strategic analysis of a firm's portfolio of businesses. The continuing contributions of this literature stream are included in chapters two, three, and four.

These contributions have also evoked interest in (1) an examination of the alternative growth strategies available to a firm to diversify its portfolio of businesses (the focus of chapter six), and (2) analytical frameworks taken from the discipline of finance that measure the growth a firm can

TABLE 1.4
ORGANIZATION OF THE BOOK

Strategy Scope	Strategy Concerns	Perspectives	Analytical Input
Corporate Level	1. What product-markets should the firm compete in?	Quest for Organizational Excellence (chapter ten)	Intensive, Integrative, and Diversification Growth Strategies (chapter six)
	Decisions in the following realms would lead to a change in the firm's product-market scope of activities: a. Diversification into new product-markets (related and/or unrelated) b. Integration (horizontal and/or vertical) c. Product-market retention/deletion decisions	Organizational Renewal (chapter eleven)	Concept of Sustainable Growth (chapter eight) Value Based Planning (chapter nine)
	2. What specific objectives should the firm assign to the various business units in its portfolio? How should resources be optimally allocated among the business units commensurate with the objectives assigned to them?		Portfolio Models (chapters two and three) Concept of Sustainable Growth (chapter eight) Value Based Planning (chapter nine)
Business Unit Level	How should the firm compete in a specific product-market? 1. Sources of competitive advantage; 2. Linkages between business unit strategy, competitive environment, and performance.	Quest for Organizational Excellence (chapter ten) Organizational Renewal (chapter eleven) Assessment of Industry Competition and Competitors (chapter seven)	Portfolio Models and Competitive Strategy Models (chapter three) Experience Curves and Cost Leadership (chapter four) Analysis of Pooled Business Experience (chapter five) Assessment of Industry Competition and Competitors (chapter seven)

sustain with its available financial resources that provide financial-market-based performance models to allocate corporate resources to the various business units. Such contributions from the finance literature are included in chapters eight and nine.

The Analysis of Pooled Business Experience

The PIMS (Profit Impact of Market Strategies) data base, originated in the early seventies, provided a valuable source of cross-sectional and time series data for strategy researchers (Buzzell and Gale, 1987). The data base contains information on a number of environment-, strategy-, perform-ance-, competition-, and firm-related variables for approximately three thousand businesses (strategic business units or SBUs) collected from over four hundred and fifty participating member companies. The data base contains strategic information about individual businesses dating back to the early seventies. This information is available at the annual level, as well as in the form of averages for various four-year periods. Researchers have capitalized on the richness of the PIMS data base to examine a wide range of questions that have a direct impact on the practice of strategic market planning. Insights and perspectives emerging from the PIMS data base are examined in chapter five.

The Application of the Modern Industrial Organization Economics Framework to Competitive Analysis

Porter's (1980, 1985) seminal work relating to strategic groups within in-dustries, mobility barriers, extended rivalries, competitor analysis (whose scope extends beyond direct competitors), and the exposition of how var-ious competitive forces shape a firm's competitive strategy exemplifies this stream of research. To a large degree, the shift in emphasis and movement of issues relating to achieving and sustaining competitive advantage to the center stage of strategic market planning can be attributed to this body of literature. Chapter seven presents the key contributions of this literature.

The McKinsey Excellence Studies

A shift in emphasis from all-consuming focus on the analytic approaches to strategy formulation and toward the study of organizational factors that jointly determine corporate success in a competitive environment is ex-emplified by Peters and Waterman's (1982) study of excellent companies and the McKinsey 7-S framework (Waterman, Peters, and Phillips, 1980). These studies provide practical guidelines for the conduct and practice of strategic market planning. The main contributions of these studies are the focus of chapter ten.

Organizational Renewal

Among the most visible signs of the broadened scope of strategic market planning is the growing interest in the themes and paradigms that assist in creating product-markets rather than merely analyzing them. In addition to organizational renewal (Waterman, 1987; Peters, 1987), a number of related themes have been the focus of recent attention—strategic thinking (Morrison and Lee, 1979; Gluck, Kaufman and Walleck, 1980), strategic vision (Gluck, 1984), strategic leadership (Hosmer, 1980), marketing imagination (Levitt, 1983), and transformational management (Kozmetsky, 1985). Chapter eleven reviews the contributions of this literature and new questions it has raised.

A CONCLUDING NOTE

The management of an organization continuously attempts to effectively match or fit the organization with its changing market environment. To cope with threats and opportunities emerging from its market and environment, the organization develops strategies. Strategy is a means of achieving the organization's objectives. Strategic market planning encompasses the formulation, evaluation, and selection of strategies, as well as a multifaceted analysis (e.g., environmental analysis; industry and competitor analysis; internal analysis) that precedes and provides the analytical foundation for these activities.

Strategy development occurs at multiple levels—the corporate level, the business unit level, and the functional level—within the organization. At the corporate level, strategic market planning focuses on issues such as what businesses to delete, what businesses to retain, and what businesses to add to the firm's portfolio. "How should a business compete in a particular market?" is the primary focus of strategic market planning at the business unit level.

Marketing is the most boundary spanning of all organizational functions, and marketers continuously interface and interact with the environment, competitors, customers, and the marketplace. Several scholars have emphasized the importance of and need for the marketing function to contribute to strategy formulation at the corporate and business unit level (Day, 1986; Wind, 1982; Wind and Robertson, 1983). The emerging and evolving body of literature on strategic market planning addresses this need. This book deals with the emerging contributions of this literature. The book is not about the process of strategy formulation itself, nor is it about how its various phases should be analyzed. Rather, it focuses on new concepts, analytical techniques, empirical findings, and paradigms that have collectively affected our thinking about the conduct and practice of strategic market planning.

REFERENCES

Aaker, D. A. (1984), *Strategic Market Management*, New York: John Wiley.

Abell, D. F. and J. S. Hammond (1979), *Strategic Market Planning*. Englewood Cliffs, NJ: Prentice Hall.

Anderson, P. F. (1982), "Marketing, Strategic Planning and the Theory of the Firm," *Journal of Marketing*, 46 (Spring), pp. 15–26.

Andrews, K. R. (1980), *The Concept of Corporate Strategy*. Homewood, IL: Richard D. Irwin.

Ansoff, H. I. (1980), "Strategic Issue Management," *Strategic Management Journal*, 1 (April–June), pp. 131–148.

Argyris, C. (1985), *Strategy Change and Defensive Routines*. Marshfield, MA: Pitman Publishing.

Biggadike, E. R. (1981), "The Contributions of Marketing to Strategic Management," *Academy of Management Review*, 6 (October), pp. 621–632.

Boston Consulting Group (1972), *Perspectives on Experience*. Boston, MA: Boston Consulting Group.

Broadcasting (1982), "Moving Those Movies," (March 19), p. 133.

Business Week (1979), "Publishers Memo," (January 9), p. 5.

Business Week (1984), "Changing a Corporate Culture," (May 14), pp. 130–138.

Business Week (1987), "Disney's Magic: A Turnaround Proves Wishes Can Come True," (March 19), p. 65.

Buzzell, R. D. and B. T. Gale (1987), *The PIMS Principles: Linking Strategy to Performance*, New York: The Free Press.

Chaffee, E. E. (1985), "Three Models of Strategy," *Academy of Management Review*, 10, pp. 89–98.

Chakravarthy, B. S. (1984), "Strategic Self-Renewal: A Planning Framework for Today," *Academy of Management Review*, 9, pp. 536–547.

Chakravarthy, B. S. (1987), "On Tailoring a Strategic Planning System to its Context: Some Empirical Evidence," *Strategic Management Journal*, 8 (November–December), pp. 517–534.

Chakravarthy, B. S. and P. Lorange (1984), "Managing Strategic Adaptation: Options in Administrative Systems Design," *Interfaces*, 14, pp. 34–46.

Chandler, A. A., Jr. (1962), *Strategy and Structure: Chapters in the History of American Industrial Enterprise*. Cambridge, MA: The MIT Press.

Day, G. S. (1984), *Strategic Market Planning: The Pursuit of Competitive Advantage*. St. Paul, MN: West Publishing Co.

Day, G. S. (1986), *Analysis for Strategic Market Decisions*. St. Paul, MN: West Publishing Co.

Day, G. S. and R. Wensley (1983), "Marketing Theory with a Strategic Orientation," *Journal of Marketing*, 47 (Fall), pp. 79–89.

Day, G. S. and R. Wensley (1988), "Assessing Advantage: A Framework for Diagnosing Competitive Superiority," *Journal of Marketing*, 52 (April), pp. 1–20.

Fortune (1987), "Putting Magic Back Into Kingdom," (January 5), p. 165.

Gluck, F. W., S. P. Kaufman, and A. S. Walleck (1980), "Strategic Management for Competitive Advantage," *Harvard Business Review*, 58 (July–August), pp. 154–161.

Gluck, F. W. (1984), "Vision and Leadership," *Interfaces*, 14 (January–February), pp. 10–18.

Gluck, F. W., S. P. Kaufman, and A. S. Walleck (1982), "The Four Phases of Strategic Management," *Journal of Business Strategy*, 3 (Winter), pp. 9–21.

Glueck, W. F. (1976), *Business Policy, Strategy Formation, and Management Action*. New York: McGraw-Hill.

Hall, W. K. (1978), "SBUs: Hot New Topic in the Management of Diversification," *Business Horizons*, (February), pp. 17–25.

Haspeslagh, P. (1982), "Portfolio Planning: Limits and Uses," *Harvard Business Review*, 60 (January–February), pp. 58–73.

Hax, A. C. and N. S. Majluf (1988), "The Concept of Strategy and the Strategy Formation Process," *Interfaces*, 18 (May–June), pp. 99–109.

Hosmer, L. (1980), "The Importance of Strategic Leadership," *Journal of Business Strategy*, 1, pp. 47–57.

Johnson and Johnson (1986), *Annual Report*. New Brunswick, NJ: Johnson & Johnson.

Kozmetsky, G. (1985), *Transformational Management*, Cambridge, MA: Ballinger.

Learned, E. P., C. R. Christensen, K. R. Andrews, and W. D. Guth (1965), *Business Policy: Text and Cases*. Homewood, IL: Richard D. Irwin.

Levitt, T. (1983), *The Marketing Imagination*, New York: The Free Press.

Mahajan, V., R. Varadarajan and R. A. Kerin (1987), "Metamorphosis in Strategic Market Planning," in G. L. Frazier and J. N. Sheth (eds.), *Contemporary Views on Marketing Practice*, Lexington, MA: Lexington Books.

Mintzberg, H. (1979), *The Structure of Organizations*. Englewood Cliffs, NJ: Prentice-Hall.

Morrison, J. R. and J. G. Lee (1979), "The Anatomy of Strategic Thinking," *Financial Times*, July 27, p. 21.

Peters, T. J. (1987), *Thriving on Chaos: Handbook for a Management Revolution*, New York: Knopf.

Peters, T. J. and R. H. Waterman, Jr. (1982), *In Search of Excellence: Lessons from America's Best Run Companies*, New York: Harper and Row.

Petre, P. (1985), "How to Keep Customers Happy Captives," *Fortune*, (September 2), pp. 42–46.

Porter, M. E. (1980), *Competitive Strategy: Techniques for Analyzing Industries and Competitors*, New York: The Free Press.

Porter, M. E. (1985), *Competitive Advantage: Creating and Sustaining Superior Performance*. New York: The Free Press.

Ramanujam, V., N. Venkatraman, and J. C. Camillus (1986), "Multi-Objective Assessment of Effectiveness of Strategic Planning: A Discriminant Analysis Approach," *Academy of Management Journal*, 29 (June), pp. 347–372.

Rothschild, W. E. (1976), *Putting It All Together: A Guide to Strategic Thinking*. New York: AMACOM.

Schendel, D. E. and K. J. Hatten (1972), "Business Policy on Strategic Management: A View for an Emerging Discipline," in *Academy of Management Proceedings*, V. F. Mitchell, R. T. Berth and F. H. Mitchell (eds.).

Springer, C. H. (1973), "Strategic Management in General Electric," *Operations Research*, November–December, pp. 1177–1184.

Steiner, G. A. and J. B. Miner (1977), *Management Policy and Strategy*. New York: Macmillan.

Time (1988), "Adults Also Permitted," (March 7), p. 72.

Vossberg, H. (1985), "Bayer Reorganizes in Response to Growth," *Long Range Planning*, 18, pp. 13–20.

Waterman, Jr., R. H. (1987), *The Renewal Factor*, New York: Bantam Books.

Waterman, Jr., R. H., T. J. Peters, and J. R. Phillips (1980), "Structure is not Organization," *Business Horizons*, 23 (June), pp. 14–26.

Wind, Y. and V. Mahajan (1981), "Designing Product and Business Portfolios," *Harvard Business Review*, 59 (January–February), pp. 155–165.

Wind, Y. (1982), "Marketing and Corporate Strategy," *The Wharton Magazine*, 6 (Summer), pp. 38–45.

Wind, Y. and V. Mahajan (1982), "An Integrated Approach to Portfolio Analysis," Working Paper, The Wharton School, University of Pennsylvania.

Wind, Y. and R. S. Robertson (1983), "Marketing Strategy: New Directions for Theory and Research," *Journal of Marketing*, 47 (Spring), pp. 12–25.

Yip, G. S. (1985), "Who Needs Strategic Planning?," *Journal of Business Strategy*, 6 (Fall), pp. 30–43.

CHAPTER 2

PORTFOLIO MODELS:

FOUNDATIONS

Introduction
The Problem

Portfolio Analysis Concepts
The Strategic Business Unit (SBU)
Served Market
The Organizational Context
The Underlying Logic
The Conceptual Framework

The Growth-Share Matrix
Matrix Dimensions
Representation of SBUs
Grouping SBUs
Market Growth Rate
Relative Market Share
Market Share Measurement Can Be Elusive
Assumptions

Strategic Implications
SBU Retention/Deletion, Mission
Assignment and Resource Allocation
Decisions

Supporting Analysis
Share Momentum Analysis
Product Portfolio Trajectory Analysis
Analysis of Portfolio Imbalances
Analysis of Major Competitors' Portfolios

SBU Retention/Deletion Decisions:
Additional Considerations
Cost and Demand Interrelationships

Market Share Decisions and Cash Flow
Outlook: Additional Considerations
Sales Volume Growth Implications of Market
Share Growth Aspirations

Matching Market Share Growth Objectives
with Financial Goals and Policies
Validity of Assumptions

A Concluding Note

References

Introduction

THE PROBLEM

Allied-Signal, Inc., is a U.S. based, diversified company with annual sales in excess of $10 billion.[1] In the past decade, the company has added a number of businesses and deleted others. In 1978, chemicals, oil and gas, and mining and industrial products constituted its major businesses. Attracted by growth prospects in the health care and electronics industries, the company spent over $1.2 billion to acquire Eltra Corp., a maker of typesetting equipment and other electronic equipment, Bunker Ramo Corp., an information services company, and Fisher Scientific Co., a laboratory equipment maker. In 1983, its $1.8 billion acquisition of Bendix Corp. thrust Allied into the aerospace and automotive businesses. Allied's position in the aerospace and automotive businesses was further bolstered by its acquisition of the Signal Cos. in 1986.

During this period, Allied also exited from a number of businesses through divestitures and spinoffs. Health care, information systems, and oil and gas were among the lines of business Allied chose to divest itself from during the eighties. In 1986, Allied spun off to its shareholders the underperforming assets of 35 mostly unprofitable chemical and engineering companies into a separate company, the Henley Group, Inc.

As shown in Table 2.1, Allied's mix and scope of operations have undergone major changes over the years. The company's present plans are to grow by concentrating its efforts in: (1) the aerospace business by venturing further into missiles, antisubmarine warfare, and command control systems; (2) the automotive business by capitalizing on car makers' desire to buy more goods from fewer suppliers; and (3) the engineered materials business by focusing on developing specialty products for high-growth industries, such as lightweight aluminum for the aerospace industry.

TABLE 2.1
THE CHANGING BUSINESS MIX OF ALLIED-SIGNAL: 1978–1987

Lines of Business	Percent of Sales Accounted for by Major Lines of Business		
	1978	1984	1987
1. Chemicals	57%	23%	—
2. Chemicals and engineered materials	—	—	24%
3. Oil and Gas	29%	19%	—
4. Mining and industrial products	14%	—	—
5. Aerospace	—	17%	39%
6. Automotive parts	—	25%	24%
7. Electronic health care	—	16%	—
8. Electronics and instrumentation	—	—	13%
	100%	100%	100%

Source: Based on information presented in: *Business Week* (1987), "Will All That Restructuring Ever Pay Off For Ed Hennessy's Allied?," February 2, 78–80.

From 1978 to 1987, Allied spent more than $8 billion on acquisitions and sold operations with sales of more than $7 billion. Although asset redeployments are commonplace, the case of Allied-Signal, Inc., is unique in scope. The case of Allied-Signal illustrates the kinds of decisions multibusiness firms are required to make. These include:

1. What strategic business units (SBUs) should a firm *retain* and which should it *delete* from its portfolio?
2. What mission or objectives should the firm assign to these SBUs, such that successful realization of objectives by individual SBUs would collectively lead to the realization of the firm's corporate objectives?
3. How should resources be optimally allocated among individual units within the constraints of a given level of cash availability to facilitate realization of the objectives set for individual SBUs, as well as corporate objectives?

Product portfolio analysis techniques that address the above questions are the focus of this chapter as well as Chapter 3. This chapter first describes what is meant by a strategic business unit, and the organizational context, logic, and conceptual framework underlying portfolio matrix approaches to strategic market planning. This discussion is followed by a detailed review of the earliest and simplest portfolio analysis approach—the Boston Consulting Group (BCG) growth-share matrix. A discussion of the multifactor portfolio matrices appears in Chapter 3.

PORTFOLIO ANALYSIS CONCEPTS

Strategic Business Unit SBU

A strategic business unit (SBU) denotes a division, product line, or other profit center within a company that produces and markets a well-defined set of related products and/or services, serves a clearly defined set of customers, and competes with a distinct set of competitors. Often, the terms product-market unit (PMU), strategic business unit (SBU), strategic business segment (SBS), and planning and control unit (PCU) are used interchangeably in the strategic market planning literature.[2] The strategic business unit represents the smallest unit within the company for which it would be meaningful to undertake strategic planning. Ideally, an SBU should be able to stand alone from the rest of the company, and has a manager who is responsible for strategic planning and profit performance who controls most of the factors affecting the SBU's performance [Buzzell and Gale 1987; Kotler 1988].

Served Market

Served market is a second concept in the strategic market planning literature and forms the basis for measuring a SBU's market growth rate. The *served market* refers to those market sectors or segments of the total market within which a business actively competes.

From an analytical standpoint, determining the scope and boundaries of a market requires simultaneous consideration of multiple dimensions. Viewed in terms of customer functions served, customer groups served, and technologies utilized, a market can either be defined narrowly as a single market cell, or more broadly as a combination of adjacent cells (Figure 2.1). For planning purposes a single market cell (Figure 2.1, A), or a combination of adjacent cells (Figure 2.1, B-E) may be viewed as an SBU. Here, the term product refers to the physical manifestation of the application of a particular technology to the satisfaction of a particular function for a particular customer group (Abell, 1980).[3]

The Organizational Context

Broadly speaking, firms can be categorized into three groups: (1) single business firms; (2) multibusiness firms with a single dominant business; and (3) diversified firms with a product portfolio consisting of multiple businesses with no dominant business. The term "dominant" is used to denote a SBU that accounts for a disproportionately large percentage of the firm's sales revenues and/or profits. The various portfolio matrix concepts discussed in this and the next chapter are mostly relevant to diversified firms.

The emergence and widespread use of alternative portfolio approaches to strategic market planning is generally viewed as a corporate response to the problems and challenges of managing complexity in large multibusiness organizations (Haspeslagh, 1982). Table 2.2 characterizes the degree

FIGURE 2.1
ALTERNATIVE PERSPECTIVES OF A STRATEGIC BUSINESS UNIT

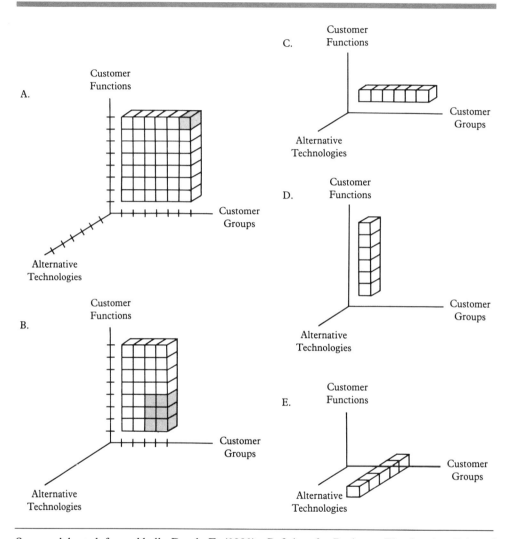

Source: Adapted from Abell, Derek F. (1980), *Defining the Business: The Starting Point of Strategic Planning*, Englewood Cliffs, NJ: Prentice-Hall.

of complexity of an organization in terms of ten variables grouped under three broad classifications: products, market/operating complexity, and environmental complexity. When complexity is low, a company is likely to be managed informally through personal knowledge and intensive individual involvement. However, with increasing complexity, the scope and magnitude of the tasks top management faces also increase substantially.

TABLE 2.2
INDICATORS OF COMPLEXITY OF A FIRM'S OPERATING UNIT

Product Complexity	*Degree of Complexity*			
	Low (1)	Moderate (2)	Substantial (3)	High (4)
1. Number of products	Single line	Several related	Several related, some unrelated	Diverse and complex
2. Complexity of technology/ individual products	Simple design	Multiple components	Highly intricate, technically sensitive	Complex systems
3. Degree of forward/ backward integration	None	Partial, one step	Extensive, more than one step	Highly integrated
4. Rate of innovation— technology, product, process	Slow	Slow to moderate	Moderate to rapid	Rapid
Market/Operating Complexity				
5. Geographic scope— Production	Single location	2–3 locations	Many domestic, some overseas	International
6. Geographic scope— Marketing	Regional	National	National, signifi-cant export	International
7. Distribution channels	Single	2–3	Several	Multiple, complex
8. End-user groups	Single, well defined	2–3	Several, distinct	Multiple, diverse
Environmental Complexity				
9. Competitive intensity (price, product, marketing)	Low	Low to moderate	Moderate to intense	Very intense
10. External pressures (economic, governmen-tal, societal)	Stable	Stable to moderate	Moderate to heavy	Volatile major threats, rapid changes, major penalties

Source: Reprinted with permission from: Clifford, Jr., D. K., and R. E. Cavanaugh (1986), *The Winning Performance*, New York: Bantam Books, p. 29.

The number of decisions that must be made and the number of activities that must be implemented, coordinated, and controlled grow geometrically as organizational complexity increases. Hence, the need for formalized approaches to portfolio management.

Several studies indicate that portfolio approaches to strategic market planning are pervasive in large diversified companies (Bettis and Hall, 1981; Coe, 1981; Haspeslagh, 1982; Farquhar and Shapiro, 1983; Canada Consulting Group, 1984; Hamermesh, 1986). For instance, one study reports that as of 1979, 36 percent of the *Fortune* 1000 and 45 percent of the *Fortune* 500 industrial companies had adopted some form of portfolio analysis as a planning mechanism (Haspeslagh, 1982).

The Underlying Logic

A number of portfolio analysis approaches base their normative recommendations on the following line of thinking:

1. The attractiveness of market opportunities differs among SBUs.
2. SBUs differ in their competitive ability to exploit opportunities for growth and profitability.
3. Growth and profitability are major considerations in a firm's SBU retention/deletion decision.
4. For those SBUs the firm chooses to retain, the assignment of a mission or objectives to individual SBUs should be commensurate with the market opportunities available to individual SBUs and their competitive abilities to capitalize on these opportunities. Collectively, the missions assigned to the various SBUs should help the firm realize its corporate objectives.
5. Resource allocation among SBUs should be in accordance with the missions assigned. The mission assignment and resource allocation problem generally tends to be a lengthy process involving several iterations. The process involves a careful analysis of various sources of cash and the cash needed by the SBUs to achieve the set objectives.

The Conceptual Framework

Two broad sets of factors—(1) factors *external* to the firm, and (2) factors *internal* to the firm—determine, respectively, the attractiveness of market opportunities available to individual SBUs, and their competitive ability to exploit these opportunities. Other things being equal, a firm is more likely to retain SBUs that compete in attractive markets and consider for possible deletion SBUs competing in less attractive markets. Similarly, a firm is more likely to retain SBUs that are in a strong competitive position and consider for possible deletion SBUs that are in a weak competitive position in their respective markets.

Proceeding a step further, a firm may be in a position to arrive at better SBU retention/deletion decisions by jointly considering both external and internal factors, rather than basing its decision on just one of the two. For example, joint consideration of both the relative market attractiveness and relative competitive position enables a firm to group SBUs into four clusters:

Cluster Number	Relative Attractiveness of Served Market	Relative Competitive Position of SBU in the Served Market
1	High	Strong
2	Low	Strong
3	High	Weak
4	Low	Weak

Most firms are likely to be inclined towards retaining SBUs in clusters 1 and 2, and deleting all or most of the SBUs in cluster 4. Firms are likely to retain SBUs in cluster 3 that can be moved into cluster 1, and consider for possible deletion SBUs that hold limited prospects for a change for the better in their relative competitive position. Resources available and resources needed to move various SBUs from cluster 3 to cluster 1 will also be major factors influencing the firm's decision.

To make further refinements, a firm could attempt to group its SBUs into nine (or perhaps even sixteen) rather than four strategic clusters, as summarized below.

Cluster Number	Relative Attractiveness of Served Market	Relative Competitive Position of SBU in the Served Market
1	High	Strong
2	High	Moderate
3	Average	Strong
4	Average	Moderate
5	Low	Strong
6	High	Weak
7	Average	Weak
8	Low	Moderate
9	Low	Weak

With this approach, a firm is likely to retain *all* or *most* of the SBUs that fall in clusters 1, 2, and 3 and consider for possible deletion *most* of the SBUs in clusters 7, 8, and 9. In regard to SBUs in clusters 4, 5, and 6, the firm is likely to be more selective in the decision-making process. The retention/deletion decision is likely to be made on a case-by-case basis rather than at the level of whole clusters.

Cluster Number	Relative Attractiveness of Served Market	Relative Competitive Position of SBU in the Served Market
1	High	Strong
2	High	Moderate
3	Average	Strong
4	Average	Moderate
5	Low	Strong
6	High	Weak
7	Average	Weak
8	Low	Moderate
9	Low	Weak

However, before the SBUs in a firm's portfolio are grouped into four or nine (or any number of) strategic subgroups, the company must address an important issue—namely, "What should be the basis for assessing the relative attractiveness of the markets in which a firm competes and its competitive ability to exploit the opportunities presented by these markets?" In its attempts to answer this question, a firm could develop two extensive lists (A and B) of variables/factors that provide insights into:

A. The relative attractiveness of the various markets in which it competes.
B. Its relative competitive position in these markets.

Once accomplished, it could choose between two broad approaches:

1. Select one factor/variable from *each* of the above lists that constitutes the best indicator of relative market attractiveness (list A) and relative competitive position (list B).
2. Select a subset of factors from list A and combine them in an appropriate manner to develop composite scores of the attractiveness of various markets in which the firm competes. Similarly, select a second subset of factors from list B and combine them to develop composite scores of the relative competitive position of the firm's SBUs in the markets in which they compete.

Based on the pairs of composite scores that uniquely describe the relative market attractiveness and competitive position of each SBU, the firm can make its SBU retention/deletion, mission assignment, and resource allocation decisions. This logic and framework constitute the building blocks of the various portfolio analysis approaches currently used.

The section that follows describes the BCG growth-share matrix approach to product portfolio analysis, which is based on the logic outlined above. The factors employed as indicators of relative market attractiveness and competitive position, and the underlying assumptions, normative recommendations, and limitations are discussed.

THE GROWTH-SHARE MATRIX

Classifying a firm's SBUs into homogeneous subgroups or clusters, allocating resources differentially among SBUs in the various clusters, and setting different objectives and/or pursuing different strategies are established business practices that have been extensively discussed in business and marketing literature. For instance, more than a quarter century ago, Peter Drucker (1963) proposed classifying a firm's products into the following six categories:

1. Tomorrow's breadwinners: New products; today's breadwinners modified and improved.
2. Today's breadwinners: The innovations of yesterday.
3. Products capable of becoming net contributors if something drastic is done.
4. Yesterday's breadwinners: Typically products with high volume, but badly fragmented into specials, small orders, and the like.
5. The also-rans: Typically the high hopes of yesterday that, while they did not work out well, nevertheless did not become outright failures.
6. The failures.

Similarly, an extensive body of literature in the marketing discipline has focused on appropriate competitive strategies for businesses in the introductory, growth, maturity, and decline stages of the product life cycle.[4] In comparison to these approaches, the BCG growth-share matrix approach and other multifactor approaches to portfolio analysis discussed in chapter 3 bring a greater degree of rigor, objectivity, and structure to the strategic market planning process.

Matrix Dimensions

In the BCG growth-share matrix approach, the SBUs that constitute a firm's portfolio of businesses are classified into four homogeneous subgroups. The basis for classification is the growth rate of the markets in which the SBUs compete and their relative market shares in these markets. Market growth rate is viewed as an indicator of relative market attractiveness and relative market share is viewed as an indicator of the relative competitive position of the SBUs in their served markets. As shown in Figure 2.2, the labels assigned to SBUs in the various quadrants are: (1) stars, (2) cash cows, (3) question marks (wildcats and problem children

FIGURE 2.2
THE BCG GROWTH-SHARE MATRIX

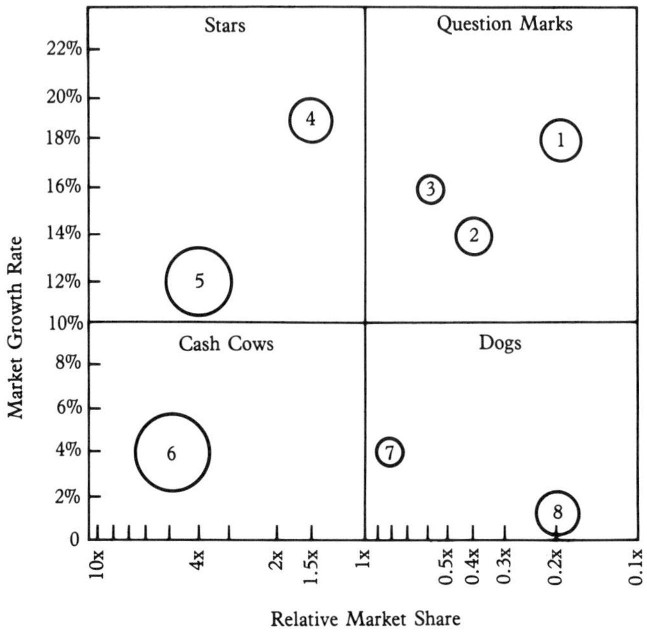

Source: B. Heldey, "Strategy and the Business Portfolio," *Long Range Planning*, February 1977, p. 12. Reprinted with permission from *Long Range Planning*, copyright 1977. Pergamon Press, Ltd.

are the other labels assigned to SBUs in this quadrant), and (4) dogs. A number of writers have questioned the wisdom underlying the use of barnyard language to describe SBUs in various quadrants as well as the organizational morale implications of assigning somewhat demeaning labels such as "dogs." Some organizations that have employed the growth-share matrix have coined their own names for SBUs in the various quadrants to avoid labels that could be viewed as demeaning.

Representation of SBUs

The SBUs in a firm's portfolio are represented as circles in the matrix. The areas of the circles are assigned in proportion to the SBUs' relative sizes, expressed as annual sales in dollars or appropriate currency.[5] The centers of the circles representing the SBUs (coordinate values along the X and Y axes) correspond to the SBUs' relative market shares and market growth rates.

Grouping SBUs

Grouping SBUs into homogeneous subgroups is accomplished by using somewhat arbitrary cutoff points to differentiate between high and low market growth rate, and high and low relative market share. Markets characterized by growth rates of 10% or higher are generally viewed as high growth markets, and those with growth rates lower than 10 percent, as low growth markets. In a sense, the high and low categories along the market growth rate dimension are proxies for the growth and maturity stages of the product-market life cycle. A relative market share of 1.0 or 1.5 is generally used as a cutoff point to differentiate between high- and low-relative-market-share SBUs.

However, there are no hard and fast rules for determining values that are employed as cutoff points for the horizontal and vertical dimension of the BCG matrix. Since cutoff points are judgmental and arbitrary, it is advisable to repeat the analysis by using different values as cutoff points. In addition, the central importance of market growth rate and relative market share in the growth-share matrix necessitates further examination of both dimensions.

Market Growth Rate   *Industry or market growth rate* (IGR) is defined as:

$$\text{IGR} = \frac{\begin{array}{c}\text{Total industry/market}\\ \text{sales during time}\\ \text{period } t+1\end{array} - \begin{array}{c}\text{Total industry/market}\\ \text{sales during time}\\ \text{period } t\end{array}}{\text{Total industry/market sales during time period } t} \qquad (1)$$

IGR figures greater than zero, equal to zero, and less than zero are indicative of a growing market, a static market, and a shrinking market, respectively. Given the diversity of a firm's product offerings, the industry/market growth rate is generally expressed as sales growth rate in constant dollars. The appropriate frames of reference are market growth rate during the most recent period, and the projected market growth rate for the immediate planning period.

The BCG approach views a market characterized by a higher growth rate as more desirable than one with a relatively lower growth rate. However, markets characterized by high growth rates may not always be the most desirable markets. Sometimes, high-growth markets may be characterized by intense competition. For instance, during the early 1980s, over 100 firms were competing for a share of the U.S. personal computer market. Furthermore, while a high-growth market may be attractive from the standpoint of some firms, this may not necessarily be true for other firms (Wernerfeldt and Montgomery, 1986). Also, the timing of market entry has a bearing on the attractiveness of a market opportunity in a high-growth market (Abell, 1980). The organizational and environmental conditions that favor a firm's entry into high-growth markets, as well as the perils of high-growth markets, are addressed in greater depth in the next chapter.

Relative Market Share *Relative market share* (RMS) is defined as the ratio of the market share of an SBU to that of its leading competitor:

$$RMS = \frac{\text{Market share of SBU "i"}}{\text{Market share of SBU i's leading competitor}} \tag{2}$$

Regarding the BCG definition of relative market share, the question "Why is relative market share a better indicator of a firm's relative competitive position than absolute market share?" is briefly discussed next.

Consider an industry dominated by four major competitors with market shares as follows:

A—50 percent; B—25 percent; C—20 percent; D—5 percent.

These market shares provide some idea of the relative competitive position of the four firms. Hence, unless relative market share provides an even better picture of their relative competitive positions, there is little justification for computing this number.

According to the BCG definition, the relative market shares of the competing firms are:

A—2.0; B—0.50; C—0.40; and D—0.10.

The relative market share figures indicate that A's market share is *twice* as large as that of its leading competitor, while D's is *one-tenth* that of the industry leader (Term A). This observation reveals that absolute market share in itself does not provide a clear picture of a critical factor, namely: *how much stronger* is the industry leader's competitive position relative to the next largest firm in the industry, or *how weak* the industry followers are, as compared to the industry leader.

The conceptual superiority of the relative market share measure can be further clarified with the hypothetical market share and relative market share data presented in Table 2.3. The focus here is on firm A competing in six different industries facing three competitors in each of the industries. These competitors are not necessarily the same firms. That is, competitor B in industry 1 could be different from the firm identified as competitor B in industry 2. From both market share and relative market share data, it is evident that firm A is the industry leader in three of the industries (I_1, I_2, and I_3) and a follower in three industries (I_4, I_5, and I_6). Additionally, based on relative market share data, it can be inferred that firm A's competitive position is very strong, somewhat strong, and marginally strong in industries 1, 2, and 3, respectively. Similarly, its relative competitive position in industries 4, 5, and 6 can be described as marginally weak, somewhat weak, and very weak, respectively.

TABLE 2.3
COMPETITIVE PROFILE OF A FIRM COMPETING IN SIX INDUSTRIES.

Firm	Industry 1		Industry 2		Industry 3		Industry 4		Industry 5		Industry 6	
	Market Share	Relative Market Share	Market Share	Relative Market Share	Market Share	Relative Market Share	Market Share	Relative Market Share	Market Share	Relative Market Share	Market Share	Relative Market Share
A	80	10.000	50	2.00	30	1.07	36	0.90	25.0	0.50	16	0.33
B	8	0.100	25	0.50	28	0.93	40	1.11	50.0	2.00	48	1.50
C	6	0.075	20	0.40	24	0.80	20	0.50	12.5	0.25	32	0.67
D	6	0.075	5	0.10	18	0.60	4	0.10	12.5	0.25	4	0.08

Note: Firm A is the focus of discussion in the text of the chapter.

Market Share Measurement Can Be Elusive   A clear explication of the frame of reference used to determine such variables as market share and relative market share is crucial. As Table 2.4 shows, the computed value of market share depends upon the unit of measurement, product definition, time frame, market definition, and nature of the denominator. Different frames of reference yield different market share values. For instance, market share can be computed as the ratio of an SBU's sales to the total sales of a *broadly defined industry* such as computers or automobiles. Alternatively, market share can be computed in relation to the SBU's *served market*, defined as that part or segment of an industry in which the SBU actively competes. Since the served market is a part of the overall industry in which the SBU competes, market share computed using the former approach in most instances will be smaller in comparison to the market share measure based on the latter approach. In a similar vein, the overall growth rate of a broadly defined industry in which the SBU participates and the growth rate of the served market in which a SBU actively competes

TABLE 2.4
MULTIDIMENSIONAL NATURE OF MARKET SHARE

1. *Units of Measurement*
    (a) dollar sales
    (b) unit sales
    (c) units purchased
    (d) users
2. *Product Definition*
    (a) product lines
    (b) brands in various sizes, forms, and positionings
3. *Time*
    short vs. long term
4. *Definition of Market*
    Served market defined in terms of
    (a) geography
    (b) customer segment
    (c) channel
    (d) usage occasion
5. *Nature of Denominator*
    (a) all brands in the given market
    (b) a selected number of brands (e.g., top three)
    (c) all products perceived as or actually serving the same need or solving the same problem

Source: Based on text of Wind, Y., and V. Mahajan (1981), "Market Share: Concepts, Findings and Directions for Future Research," in B. M. Enis and K. J. Roering (eds.), *Annual Review of Marketing*, Chicago American Marketing Association, 31–42.

may be different. Hence, it is important for the firm to carefully address issues relating to the "market" that would form the basis for computation of the market growth rates and market shares of various SBUs. Additional insights into the problems confronted are provided in Box 2.1 on market share measurement.

Assumptions

The portfolio problem as viewed from the BCG growth-share matrix perspective is one of developing a target portfolio balanced with respect to cash generation and cash use. The BCG portfolio approach strives for a state of internal cash balance in which the firm's total cash needs equal the total cash generation potential of the various SBUs. The cash flow outlook of individual SBUs is assumed to be determined by their position in the portfolio matrix and the intended market share strategy—build, maintain, or harvest market share. The key assumptions are:

1. Cash *generated* is a function of relative market share due to scale and experience effects (see Chapter 4 for a discussion of scale and experience effects).
2. Cash *required* is a function of market growth rate and market share strategy.
3. *Net* cash flow is a function of relative market share, market growth rate, and market share strategy (Abell and Hammond, 1979).

These assumptions further highlight the need for a careful definition of the market that forms the basis for the computation of the SBU's relative market share and estimation of market growth rate. The market should be defined such that: (1) relative market share bears some relationship to relative costs and (2) markets that are different in terms of competitors, strategies, growth rates, and current share are viewed as distinct. While the need to relate share to costs favors a relatively broad definition, the need to treat strategically different market segments as distinct entities favors a narrow definition. In practice, the product and market definitions employed tend to reflect a compromise between these conflicting demands (Abell and Hammond, 1979).

In addition, the BCG matrix approach implicitly assumes that the effect of the marketing effort of any single firm on market growth rate (or total industry sales or total size of the market) is negligible. Although this assumption might be valid in a number of situations, the marketing literature generally distinguishes between the "primary demand" stimulating marketing efforts of a firm (i.e., a firm's attempts to increase the size of the market), and its "secondary demand" or "selective demand" stimulating marketing efforts (a firm's attempts to increase its share of the total market).

There are a number of case histories of companies successfully stimulating primary demand through concerted marketing efforts. Furthermore, firms with a dominant share of their served markets (e.g., Arm & Hammer

BOX **2.1**

MARKET SHARE MEASUREMENT CAN BE ELUSIVE

The following excerpt from an article on competition in the U.S. soft drink industry succinctly summarizes the market share measurement problem:

"There are as many ways to analyze market share as bubbles in a pop can . . . Generally, Coke likes to play up its strongest suit: Its showing in the *total* soft drink market. Pepsi likes to talk up its strongest: its place in the food-store market—significant, it says, because, there consumers have a true vote (Morris, 1987).

Table 1 below shows the 1986 market shares of the top eleven brands in the U.S. soft drink market. For illustrative purposes, let us exclude the brands other than these and examine some of the problems pertaining to market share measurement. In Table 2.1.1, Coke Classic's market share is expressed as a percentage of the total quantity of soft drinks consumed in the United States during 1986. Other relevant market share measures include:

1. Coke's total share of the *soft drink market:*
   $1 + 3 + 6 + 9 + 10B = 33.6$ percent
2. Share of Coke brand cola beverages:
   $1 + 3 + 9 + 10B = 30.0$ percent
3. Coke Classic's share of the *cola market*
4. Coke Classic's share of the soft drinks sold through: (a) retail stores; (b) restaurants; and (c) vending machines.

Although market share measures 3 and 4 cannot be computed based on the information provided in Table 2.1.1, these could be very valuable to the decision makers in the organization.

Another relevant market share measure would be based on the firm's viewpoint on who its competitors are. In other words, a firm such as Coca Cola, Inc., not only competes with other soft drink firms, but also with a number of other companies whose beverages substitute for soft drinks to varying degrees. A strategy statement along the lines of "making the product available to consumers at an arm's length" has for long guided the marketing-channels-development effort of Coca Cola, Inc. Table 2.1.2 provides estimates of U.S. per capita consumption of various beverages. The

TABLE 2.1.1
RANKING THE BRANDS

Rank	Brand	Market Share
1	Coke Classic	18.9%
2	Pepsi	18.5
3	Diet Coke	7.1
4	Diet Pepsi	4.3
5	Dr. Pepper	4.1
6	Sprite	3.6
7	7 Up	3.5
8	Mountain Dew	2.6
9	Coke	2.3
10A	RC	1.7
10B	Cherry Coke	1.7

changes in per capita consumption of various forms of beverages between 1976 and 1986 suggest that it would be a fruitful exercise for Coca Cola, Inc., to compute its share of the total beverage market.

TABLE 2.1.2
U.S. LIQUID CONSUMPTION

Beverage	Estimated Per Capita Consumption in Gallons
Soft drinks	42.1
Coffee	25.4
Beer	23.9
Milk	20.3
Tea	7.4
Juices	6.3
Powdered drinks	6.1
Bottled water	5.7
Wine	2.5
Distilled spirits	1.6

Source: Morris, Betsy (1987), "Coke vs. Pepsi: Cola War Marches On," *Wall Street Journal*, June 3, p. 31.

baking soda; Lysol disinfectant spray; Kodak photographic film; Johnson & Johnson baby powder) might be better off focusing their marketing efforts on stimulating primary rather than selective demand for the following reasons. First, firms with a very large share (80 percent plus) of their served markets stand to benefit most by initiating actions designed to stimulate primary demand by promoting new uses, more frequent usage, more varied usage, larger quantity usage, usage in new places or on new occasions, and so forth. Second, the return on investment from secondary demand stimulation achieved by encouraging users of competitors' brands to switch to the firm's brands is likely to reveal a pattern of diminishing returns as a firm's market share gets increasingly larger. This occurs because it will cost more for a firm to convert extremely loyal users of competing brands than what it costs the firm to convert less brand-loyal users of competing brands.

In summary, although there are several reported case histories of firms successfully pursuing primary demand stimulation strategies, assuming that the market growth rate is an exogenous variable is reasonable in most product-market contexts. However, no firm can afford to overlook the feasibility, and the profit and growth potential, of primary demand stimulation strategies in the context of its various SBUs (Varadarajan, 1989).

STRATEGIC IMPLICATIONS

If the movement of an SBU is traced over time, assuming that the market growth rate is exogenous implies that the *vertical movement* of SBUs within the matrix is beyond the control of individual firms. The portfolio strategy problem in the BCG approach then reduces to charting a SBU's *horizontal movement* or specifying the market share objectives to be achieved by each of the N strategic business units that constitute the firm's portfolio.

In effect, subsets of SBUs will be assigned the mission to *build* market share, *maintain* market share, or *harvest* market share. With respect to a fourth subset of SBUs, the firm's decision might be liquidation, spinoff, or divestiture. Furthermore, at the individual SBU level, a strategic, objective statement such as *build* share must be more specific—for example, increase market share from x to $x + y$ over the time period t to $t + 1$ at a uniform rate.

According to the proponents of the BCG approach, a SBU's current competitive position, the growth rate of its market, and the assigned market share will have a predictable effect on cash flows and profitability. For example, an SBU in the cash cow quadrant pursuing a market share maintenance strategy will generate far more cash than it can profitably reinvest. On the other hand, a SBU in the question mark quadrant assigned a mission to build share will need a cash infusion. In summary, the cash needs of some of the SBUs will far exceed their cash generating ability, while the cash needs of other SBUs will be far less than their cash generating ability. A third group of SBUs will be in a state of self sustenance, with cash needs about equal to their cash generating ability. Hence, the financial feasibility of the market share objectives tentatively set for the various SBUs have to be evaluated from the standpoint of the firm's total cash needs and cash generating ability.

SBU Retention/Deletion, Mission Assignment and Resource Allocation Decisions

A firm's SBU retention/deletion decisions and mission assignment decisions should be based on an analysis of: (1) the market opportunities available to individual SBUs and their ability to capitalize on these opportunities; and (2) the resource requirements and cash flow implications of mission assignments, that is, whether a SBU would be a net cash user or a net cash generator. The desired directions of movement of the SBUs and cash flow are indicated in Figure 2.3 and discussed in greater detail next.

A. *Stars: SBUs in the high-market-growth-rate/high-relative-market-share quadrant.*

   1. *Deletion/Retention Decision.* SBUs in this quadrant should be preferably retained in the firm's portfolio.

   2. *Market Share Strategy Decision:*[6] For an SBU in this quadrant with a very high relative market share (substantially greater than 1.0 or close to the vertical axis), market share maintenance may be an appropriate strategy. On the other hand, for an SBU whose relative market share is only marginally greater than 1.0, an appropriate market share strategy may be to build share.

   3. *Cash Flow Outlook:* An SBU with a high relative market share in a high-growth market will produce a high level of cash owing to scale and experience effects and the resultant high profit margins. However, maintaining market share will require considerable cash to support increased expenditures on working capital and plant and equipment. Building market share in such a market will require even larger cash outlays to support the increased scale of operation. For the most part, SBUs in the high-market-growth-rate/high-relative-market-share quadrant will be self-sustaining. Their high relative market share, coupled with relatively high profit margins and low costs owing to scale and experience effects, makes them a major generator of cash. However, a strategy of share building or share maintenance in a high growth market also makes them a major user of cash. SBUs in this quadrant tend to be either in a state of cash balance (cash outflow = cash inflow), marginal cash surplus, or marginal cash deficit.

B. *Cash Cows: SBUs in the low-market-growth-rate/high-relative-market-share quadrant.*

FIGURE 2.3
PRODUCT FLOW AND CASH FLOW IN THE BCG GROWTH-SHARE MATRIX

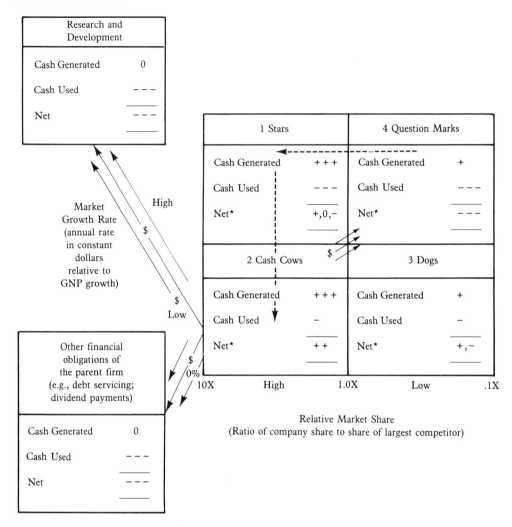

*1. Modest positive or negative cash flow, or cash balance
 2. Large positive cash flow
 3. Nominal positive or negative cash flow
 4. Large negative cash flow

——→ Principal cash flows

---→ Desired movement of SBUs over time

Note: Sources and uses of cash shown are illustrative and not exhaustive. For example, other sources of cash available to the firm include divestitures (of SBUs in dog and question mark quadrants) and acquisition (of cash cows in a merger involving exchange of shares).

Source: Adapted from: Day, G. (1977), "Diagnosing the Product Portfolio," *Journal of Marketing,* 41(April), 29–38.

1. *Deletion/Retention Decision:* SBUs in this quadrant should be retained in the firm's portfolio.
2. *Market Share Strategy Decision:* A strategy of market share maintenance is commonly advocated for SBUs in this quadrant in view of the low rate of their market's growth. Investments in capacity expansion may not be desirable. However, investments made to improve manufacturing processes that might lead to lower costs and/or better quality products should not be neglected.
3. *Cash Flow Outlook:* An SBU in this quadrant will be a net cash generator given its high relative market share, relatively lower costs vis-a-vis competitors because of scale and experience effects, and high profit margins. The sizeable net cash surplus will be a major source of cash to the parent corporation. It may be used to:
   a. finance the growth (share building strategy) of selected SBUs in the high-market-growth-rate/low-relative-market-share quadrant,
   b. finance corporate R&D efforts oriented towards the development of new SBUs,
   c. finance the acquisition of new SBUs, and
   d. meet other financial obligations of the parent company, such as debt servicing and dividend payments.
   Other sources of cash available to a firm include:
   a. cash generated from the sale of businesses judged as expendable and in the long-term interests of the organization, and
   b. acquisition of cash cow(s) (preferably in a merger involving an exchange of shares).
C. *Question Marks: SBUs in the high-market-growth-rate/low-relative-market-share quadrant.*
   1. *Retention/Deletion Decision:* The SBU retention/deletion decision in this quadrant should ideally be made on a case-by-case basis. For some SBUs, a firm's competitors might hold such commanding positions that the firm might have to invest heavily to build market share and move the SBU into the star quadrant. The viability of a market-share-building strategy based on identifiable sources of sustainable competitive advantage should be a major consideration in deciding which SBUs should be retained or deleted.
   2. *Market Share Strategy Decision:* A share-building strategy for SBUs retained in the portfolio and a share harvesting or liquidation strategy for SBUs earmarked for deletion is generally advocated.
   3. *Cash Flow Outlook:* SBUs in this quadrant will need sizeable cash infusions to finance share-building strategies and make investments in plant and equipment. A source of cash to finance the share-building strategy of SBUs in this quadrant earmarked for

retention would be the cash surplus generated by SBUs in the diagonally opposite quadrant—the cash cows.

D. *Dogs: SBUs in the low-market-growth-rate/low-relative-market-share quadrant.*

    1. *Retention/Deletion Decision:* Deletion of SBUs in this quadrant is generally advocated. However, cost and demand interrelationships with SBUs in other quadrants, barriers to exit, competitive considerations, and other considerations might influence a firm to retain certain SBUs in this quadrant.

    2. *Market Share Strategy Decision:* A market-share-harvesting strategy is generally advocated if for some reason (e.g., exit barriers, lack of buyers) a firm is unable to divest some of the SBUs in this quadrant.

    3. *Cash Flow Outlook:* With the benign neglect of top management, PMUs in this quadrant will become either marginal cash producers or marginal cash users. However, minimal investment in running the day-to-day operations of these SBUs and pursuing a share harvesting strategy could lead to the generation of a substantial cash surplus by these SBUs.

SUPPORTING ANALYSIS

Recommended retention/deletion decisions and market share strategies for SBUs in the various quadrants of the matrix are only suggestive, and not prescriptive. Additional insights into the desirability of pursuing these suggestions can be gained through four additional kinds of analysis:

1. share momentum analysis
2. product portfolio trajectory analysis
3. analysis of portfolio imbalances
4. analysis of major competitors' portfolios

Share Momentum Analysis

Share momentum analysis examines the relationship between the growth rate of an SBU and its served market. Three possibilities exist:

1. share growth
2. share maintenance
3. share erosion

For an SBU to increase its market share in a market characterized by a positive rate of growth, its unit sales volume should grow at a higher rate than the market growth rate. For an SBU to maintain its market share in a market characterized by positive rate of growth, its unit sales volume should grow at a rate equal to the total market's sales growth rate. When an SBU's rate of sales growth is less than the rate of market sales growth, its market share declines. Figure 2.4 summarizes the interrelationship

FIGURE 2.4
MARKET SHARE MOMENTUM ANALYSIS

SBU Sales Growth Rate

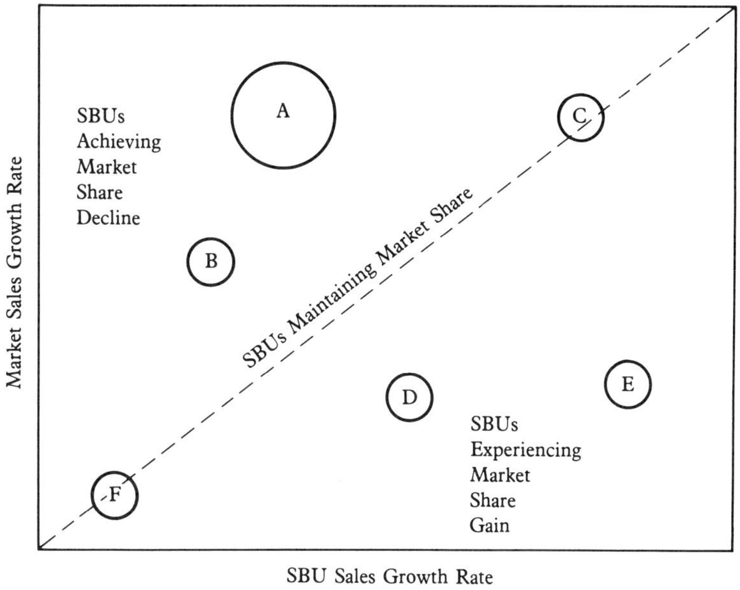

between the SBU sales growth rate and the total market sales (total industry sales) growth rate.

Product Portfolio Trajectory Analysis

Product portfolio trajectory analysis builds on share momentum analysis and involves tracking past and projected movements of SBUs over time to gain strategic insights. Analysis of a firm's portfolio at a given point in time provides only a static perspective. Development of portfolio matrices for previous time periods using historical data to track the portfolio trajectory (the progression or movement of SBUs over a period of time) may be warranted to analyze trends and gain a dynamic perspective. *Portfolio matrix scenarios* can be developed for future years on the basis of projected market growth rates and tentative decisions regarding the market share strategies for the various SBUs. This type of dynamic analysis is illustrated in Figure 2.5.

Tracing the trajectory of individual SBUs in years past and for future years could provide insights into:

1. past successful and disastrous paths taken by SBUs,
2. prospects for maintaining a balanced portfolio in future years, and
3. the need to develop new SBUs to overcome present imbalances and the likelihood of future portfolio imbalances.

FIGURE 2.5
THE PORTFOLIO TRAJECTORY: PRESENT AND PROJECTED
POSITIONS OF STRATEGIC BUSINESS UNITS

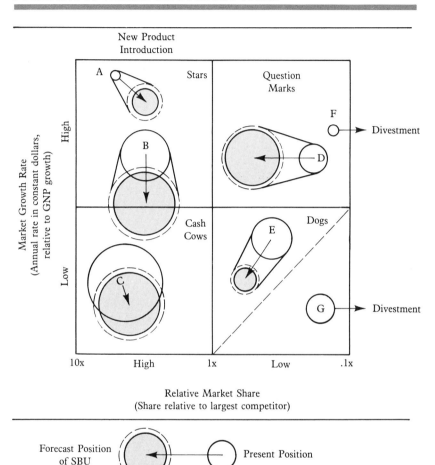

Diameter of circle is proportional to products contribution to total company
sales volume

Source: George S. Day, "Diagnosing the Product Portfolio," *Journal of Marketing,* 41 (April), 34.

A successful trajectory would be an SBU in the "star" quadrant pursuing
a market share buildup or maintenance strategy and later evolving into a
"cash cow" as the market growth rate slows down. A disastrous trajectory
would be an SBU in the "star" quadrant evolving into a "question mark"

FIGURE 2.6
SUCCESS AND DISASTER TRAJECTORIES

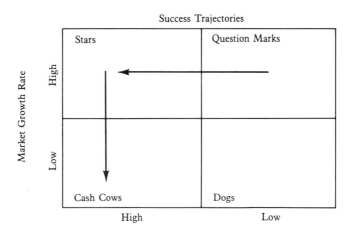

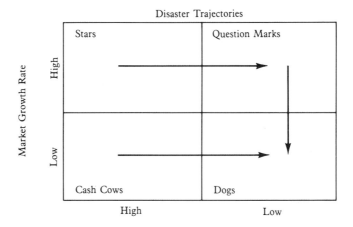

(losing market share) in a fast-growing market and later into a "dog" as market growth slows owing to poor cash management and poor market share management. This trajectory would occur when a "star" is milked for cash flow rather than allowed to reinvest most of its earnings to maintain or increase its market share. Figure 2.6 provides additional insights into success and disaster trajectories.

Analysis of Portfolio Imbalances

Firms strive for a balanced portfolio of SBUs under the BCG approach. The presence of a fair number of SBUs in the "star" and "cash cow" quadrants is a sign of a healthy and balanced portfolio. Indicators of an unbalanced portfolio include:

1. *A large number of SBUs in the "star" and "question mark" quadrants and very few in the "cash cow" quadrant.* A firm in this position might find itself short of cash to funnel into those "question marks" that have the potential to be stars. Tapping the capital market through an issue of "new equities" and/or "borrowing" is a possibility. However, other things being equal, a firm with an unbalanced portfolio might be viewed less favorably by the capital market as compared to one with a more healthy portfolio. This in turn would be reflected in the price at which the firm can sell new equity and/or the rate at which it can borrow.

2. *A large number of SBUs in the "cash cow" quadrant, but very few in the "star" quadrant.* This could be an indication that the firm is having a glorious present, but an uncertain future. As the market evolves over time, declining market growth rates would shrink the size of the market for today's "cash cows." As high-growth markets become mature, low-growth markets over time, a firm presently without SBUs in the "star" quadrant will find itself without "cash cows" in the future.

Examples of balanced and unbalanced portfolios are seen in Figure 2.7.

Analysis of Major Competitors' Portfolios

A firm should not base its market share strategy decisions solely on its portfolio of businesses. Every attempt should be made to develop similar matrices for major competitors. Imbalances in the portfolios of some competitors and strengths in the portfolios of others may provide insights into the strategies they are likely to pursue. For example, a competitor whose portfolio has few "cash cows" may lack the financial resources to pursue a share-building strategy to improve the competitive position of its SBUs in the "question mark" quadrant. Such signs of a competitor's vulnerability suggests that it will be easier for the firm to capture share from a cash-poor competitor than from another competitor with substantial resources.

SBU RETENTION/DELETION DECISIONS: ADDITIONAL CONSIDERATIONS

Early writings on the BCG matrix advocated that the company should divest itself of all SBUs in the Dog quadrant. This prescription has come under severe criticism (Sheth, 1985). A hasty decision to divest an SBU

FIGURE 2.7
BALANCED AND UNBALANCED PORTFOLIOS

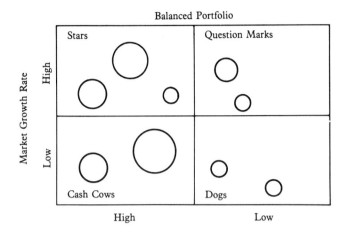

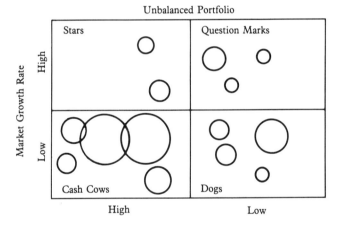

with a low relative market share that could have been turned around with the right strategy is one type of error. Likewise, a decision to retain an SBU with a low relative market share in a low growth market and investing heavily in it in the hope of turning it around is another kind of error. However, the most serious error firms could commit is making a sweeping decision such as "let's get rid of all SBUs in the dog quadrant over a period of time by harvesting, divesting, liquidating, or spinning-off."

Cost and Demand Interrelationships

The ramifications of overlooking cost and demand interrelationships among SBUs in the various quadrants when making deletion decisions could be severe. For instance, an examination of the portfolios of large, diversified firms reveals that most of these firms tend to diversify into related areas.[7] For these firms, cost and demand interrelationships exist among their SBUs owing to commonalities in markets served, manufacturing processes and equipment employed, and technologies utilized. The potential for synergies in these areas is also a major influence on a firm's SBU addition-retention-deletion decisions. These interrelationships are a key to a firm's realization of economies of *scope* in the areas of marketing, manufacturing, R&D, purchasing, and so forth.

When product-market-technology interrelationships exist among the SBUs, the company's decision to divest itself of one or more SBUs will have an effect on the costs of and demand for the offerings of the SBUs retained in the firm's portfolio. For example, in the area of marketing, the deletion of certain SBUs could lead to underutilization of certain shared resources (sales force, physical distribution facilities, and channel capacity) and increase the cost of certain acquired resources (advertising, sales promotion, etc.). Hence, some of the economies of scope the firm was realizing as a result of marketing synergies would be lost.

Similarly, some shared manufacturing facilities would be underutilized unless the manufacturing resources resulting from the deletion of certain SBUs could be effectively utilized to increase the level of output of other SBUs. Underutilization of manufacturing resources could lead to the loss of economies of scope that arise from manufacturing synergies. Hence, it is conceivable that a simple, four-group classification of SBUs may not always provide the insights needed to make the right retention/deletion decisions. This is especially true when there is diversity across SBUs and the number of SBUs in a firm's portfolio is quite large.

Also, if most firms in an industry define their served market in a similar manner, the strategic guidelines from use of the BCG approach could be potentially misleading. Under the highly unlikely scenario in which all competing firms use the BCG approach to portfolio analysis, in view of the value of relative market share (usually 1.0 or 1.5) used to differentiate between strong and weak competitive position, only one firm in any industry would fall into the cash cow or star quadrant depending upon the market growth rate (low versus high). In addition, the corresponding SBUs of all the firm's competitors will fall either in the dog or question mark quadrants.

Hence, considerable thought should be given to the feasibility of turning around an SBU with a low relative market share before deciding to harvest or divest an SBU. Several recent works (Sheth, 1985; Levitt, 1983) have focused on a variety of marketing strategies that firms could employ to turn around problem products. This point is further elaborated on in the next chapter.

MARKET SHARE DECISIONS AND CASH
FLOW OUTLOOK: ADDITIONAL CONSIDERATIONS

A firm should address a number of questions before embarking on a share-building strategy for one or more of its SBUs. Among the issues that merit deliberation from a *marketing perspective* are:

1. What strategy will help the firm achieve such a share gain?
2. From which competitors will the share come?
3. What competitive reactions can be expected?
4. What will be the magnitude of marketing investment required to realize the stated market share objectives over the planning horizon and maintain the share at the level during the post planning period?
5. For a given industry growth rate G, what is the SBU growth rate g required for it to realize the stated market share increase objectives in the prescribed time frame?

From a *corporate perspective*, some of the issues that need to be addressed include:

1. What are the manufacturing capacity expansion and total incremental capital requirements (both fixed and working capital) implications of the stated share-building objectives for the various SBUs?
2. Can the required SBU sales growth rates be sustained consistent with the firm's established financial policies?
3. If not, what steps can be taken to resolve the inconsistency between targeted growth rate and sustainable sales growth rate? (Varadarajan 1983.)

The discussion that follows highlights the relevance of some of these questions.

Sales Volume Growth Implications of Market Share Growth Aspirations

In reference to a specific SBU in the firm's portfolio, let S_{Lt}, the share of the market leader, be 40%, S_{Ct}, the share of the firm's SBU (the market challenger), be 20%, and S_{Ot}, the share of the other competitors, be 40% in the year t.

Suppose the objective of the challenger is to attain market share parity with the leader by the end of the year $t + 4$. Successful implementation of this market share strategy will depend in part on the reactions of the firm's competitors. Thus, an estimate of key competitors' decision processes is invaluable in planning competitive interaction. For example, the challenger may be inclined to believe that the leader will pursue a share maintenance strategy in view of legal and antitrust considerations (Bloom and Kotler, 1975), or because of the strategic role assigned to a business unit (cash flow maximization via market share maintenance), and/or other reasons.

If the challenger estimates that the market will grow at an annual rate of 10 percent, then its sales will have to grow at an annual rate of 31 percent over the next four years, or more than three times the projected market growth rate, for the challenger to realize its market share objectives. Furthermore, it will have to expand total manufacturing capacity by 193 percent over the next four years to accommodate the targeted higher level of sales. The share gain itself has to be realized at the expense of the lagging competitors and not the market leader (Varadarajan, 1983).[8]

Table 2.5 provides additional insights into the *annual* product sales/ manufacturing capacity growth rate implications of the market-share-building objectives set for an SBU. For a given market growth rate, the cell entries in Table 2.5 indicate the annual rate at which an SBU's sales and manufacturing capacity have to grow for the SBU to realize its market share growth objective over the specified time frame assuming that the present capacity is being fully utilized to meet the current level of sales.

Table 2.6 provides estimates of the *total* increase in sales and manufacturing capacity required during the time frame over which the SBU is to realize its market share objective.

Matching Market Share Growth Objectives with Financial Goals and Policies

A portfolio is considered balanced when the cash needs of SBUs assigned a mission to build or maintain share in high growth markets are about equal to (1) the cash surpluses generated through pursuit of market share maintenance strategies by SBUs in dominant competitive positions in mature markets, (2) the cash surpluses generated through the pursuit of harvesting strategies for SBUs in nondominant competitive positions, and (3) the cash generated through divestitures of certain SBUs in weak competitive positions. Although the BCG approach does not explicitly consider the capital market as a source of debt and equity capital, the underlying message is quite clear. Decisions to pursue market share growth, maintenance, and harvesting strategies should be based on a sound understanding of the short-term and long-term cash flow implications of these decisions. In an environment of rapid growth, maintaining market share in itself will require considerable cash to support increased expenditures on working capital and plant and equipment. Building market share in a high growth market will require even larger cash outlays to support an increased scale of operation.[9]

Based on the cash flow implications stemming from tentative market share objectives, SBUs can be broadly classified into three groups.

1. **Cash User SBUs:** SBUs that require cash infusion by the corporate parent to realize their market share objectives.
2. **Net Cash Generating SBUs:** SBUs that generate far more cash than they can profitably reinvest.

TABLE 2.5
ANNUAL SALES GROWTH RATE (CAPACITY EXPANSION) IMPLICATIONS OF STATED MARKET SHARE OBJECTIVES[a]

	T: Timeframe Over Which Firm Aspires to Achieve its Market Share Objective									
T	1	2	3	4	5	6	7	8	9	10
K: market share multiplication factor (= Target market share/ present market share)										
1.05	17.6	14.8	13.8	13.4	13.1	12.9	12.8	12.7	12.6	12.5
1.10	23.2	17.5	15.6	14.7	14.2	13.8	13.5	13.3	13.2	13.1
1.15	28.8	20.1	17.3	16.0	15.2	14.6	14.3	14.0	13.8	13.6
1.20	34.4	22.7	19.0	17.2	16.2	15.5	15.0	14.6	14.3	14.1
1.25	40.0	25.2	20.6	18.4	17.1	16.2	15.6	15.2	14.8	14.5
1.30	45.6	27.7	22.2	19.6	18.0	17.0	16.3	15.7	15.3	15.0
1.35	51.2	30.1	23.8	20.7	18.9	17.7	16.9	16.3	15.8	15.4
1.40	56.8	32.5	25.3	21.8	19.8	18.5	17.5	16.8	16.3	15.8
1.45	62.4	34.9	26.8	22.9	20.6	19.2	18.1	17.3	16.7	16.2
1.50	68.0	37.2	28.2	23.9	21.5	19.8	18.7	17.8	17.2	16.6
1.55	73.6	39.4	29.6	25.0	22.3	20.5	19.2	18.3	17.6	17.0
1.60	79.2	41.7	31.0	26.0	23.0	21.1	19.8	18.8	18.0	17.4
1.65	84.8	43.9	32.3	26.9	23.8	21.7	20.3	19.2	18.4	17.8
1.70	90.4	46.0	33.7	27.9	24.5	22.4	20.8	19.7	18.8	18.1
1.75	96.0	48.2	35.0	28.8	25.3	22.9	21.3	20.1	19.2	18.4
1.80	101.6	50.3	36.2	29.7	26.0	23.5	21.8	20.5	19.6	18.8
1.85	107.2	52.3	37.5	30.6	26.7	24.1	22.3	21.0	19.9	19.1
1.90	112.8	54.4	38.7	31.5	27.3	24.6	22.8	21.4	20.3	19.4
1.95	118.4	56.4	39.9	32.4	28.0	25.2	23.2	21.8	20.6	19.7
2.00	124.0	58.4	41.1	33.2	28.7	25.7	23.7	22.1	21.0	20.0

[a]Cell entries are in percent and are computed for a projected market growth rate of 12 percent.
☐ Interpretation of cell entries: In a market growing at an annual rate of 12 percent, for the SBU to realize its market share objective (1.30 times its present share by the end of year 5), its sales would have to grow at an annual rate of 18 percent. If the present manufacturing capacity is being fully utilized, its manufacturing capacity will also have to grow at the same annual rate.

Source: Adapted from Varadarajan, P. Rajan (1983), "The Sustainable Growth Model: A Tool for Evaluating the Financial Feasibility of Market Share Strategies," *Strategic Management Journal* 4(October–December), p. 356.

TABLE 2.6
TOTAL PERCENT SALES INCREASE (CAPACITY EXPANSION) IMPLICATIONS[a] OF STATED MARKET SHARE OBJECTIVES

	T: Timeframe Over Which Firm Aspires to Achieve its Market Share Objective									
	1	2	3	4	5	6	7	8	9	10
K: market share multiplication factor (= Target market share/ present market share)										
1.05	17.6	31.7	47.5	65.2	85.0	107.3	132.1	160.0	191.2	226.1
1.10	23.2	38.0	54.5	73.1	93.9	117.1	143.2	172.4	205.0	241.6
1.15	28.8	44.3	61.6	81.0	102.7	127.0	154.2	184.7	218.9	257.2
1.20	34.4	50.5	68.6	88.8	111.5	136.9	165.3	197.1	232.8	272.7
1.25	40.0	56.8	75.6	96.7	120.3	146.7	176.3	209.5	246.6	288.2
1.30	45.6	63.1	82.6	104.6	129.1	156.6	187.4	221.9	260.5	303.8
1.35	51.2	69.3	89.7	112.4	137.9	166.5	198.4	234.3	274.4	319.3
1.40	56.8	75.6	96.7	120.3	146.7	176.3	209.5	246.6	288.2	334.8
1.45	62.4	81.9	103.7	128.2	155.5	186.2	220.5	259.0	302.1	350.3
1.50	68.0	88.2	110.7	136.0	164.3	196.1	231.6	271.4	316.0	365.9
1.55	73.6	94.4	117.8	143.9	173.2	205.9	242.7	283.8	329.8	381.4
1.60	79.2	100.7	124.8	151.8	182.0	215.8	253.7	296.2	343.7	396.9
1.65	84.8	107.0	131.8	159.6	190.8	225.7	264.8	308.5	357.6	412.5
1.70	90.4	113.2	138.8	167.5	199.6	235.5	275.8	320.9	371.4	428.0
1.75	96.0	119.5	145.9	175.4	208.4	245.4	286.9	333.3	385.3	443.5
1.80	101.6	125.8	152.9	183.2	217.2	255.3	297.9	345.7	399.2	459.0
1.85	107.2	132.1	159.9	191.1	226.0	265.2	309.0	358.0	413.0	474.6
1.90	112.8	138.3	166.9	199.0	234.8	275.0	320.0	370.4	426.9	490.1
1.95	118.4	144.6	174.0	206.8	243.7	284.9	331.1	382.8	440.7	505.6
2.00	124.0	150.9	181.0	214.7	252.2	294.8	342.1	395.2	454.6	521.2

[a] Cell entries are in percent and are computed for a projected market growth rate of 12 percent.

☐ Interpretation of cell entries: In a market growing at an annual rate of 12 percent, for the SBU to realize its market share objective (1.30 times its present share by the end of year 5), its total sales would have to grow by 129 percent. If the present manufacturing capacity is being fully utilized, its total manufacturing capacity will also have to be increased by the same amount.

Source: Adapted from: Varadarajan, P. Rajan (1983), "The Sustainable Growth Model: A Tool for Evaluating the Financial Feasibility of Market Share Strategies," *Strategic Management Journal* 4(October–December), p. 357.

3. **Self-Sustaining SBUs:** SBUs whose cash generation potential and cash needs are in a state of balance (Varadarajan, 1990).

Hence, there is a need to evaluate the market-share objectives set for the various SBUs in the context of a firm's financial goals and policies. One approach to evaluating the consistency of a firm's growth aspirations with its financial policies and goals involves the concept of *sustainable growth.* Sustainable growth represents the maximum sales or asset growth that a firm can support using internally generated funds and incremental debt commensurate with its stated target debt-equity ratio. According to this concept, of the four fundamental financial goals and policies commonly established by firms—target return on total assets employed, target debt-equity ratio, target dividend payout ratio, and target growth rate—only three can be set independently and the fourth is uniquely determined. These four fundamental goals and policies define the boundaries within which management can arrive at a consistent set of growth objectives and financial goals and policies. A detailed discussion of the sustainable growth concept is presented in chapter 8.

Validity of Assumptions

The BCG approach is based on two key assumptions: (1) the cash flow from products with a high relative market share will be higher than that for those with smaller shares and (2) cash needs for products in rapidly growing markets will be greater than they are for those in slower growing ones. A number of authors have pointed out that actual cash flow patterns can deviate from these assumptions for a variety of reasons (Day, 1977; Abell and Hammond, 1979). These include

1. The supposed relationship between relative market share and cash flow may be weak. This can occur when:

   - experience or scale effects are insignificant
   - value added is relatively low
   - a competitor has a low-cost source of purchased materials unrelated to relative-share position
   - a competitor has moved to a lower, but parallel, experience curve by shifting production to low-labor-cost countries
   - low-share competitors are on steeper experience curves than high-share competitors by virtue of superior production technology
   - differences in experience have little impact on costs because innovations in production technology are quickly adopted by all suppliers
   - capacity utilization rates differ and
   - strategic factors other than relative market share (e.g., product quality or other forms of competitive differentiation) affect profit margins; for example, while certain product categories are charac-

terized by a high level of price competition (e.g., microprocessor chips), this is not the case in certain other product categories (e.g., watches, cosmetics).

2. The supposed relationship between industry growth rate and cash flow may be weak. This can occur when:

- capital intensity is low
- entry barriers are high enough so that even in rapid growth markets margins are large enough to finance growth and produce positive cash flow
- price competition depresses margins during the low growth maturity stage such that, even though financing needs decline, cash flow deteriorates
- legal/regulatory intervention holds down profits during maturity with the same result as above and
- seasonal or cyclical factors produce short-run supply/demand imbalances that affect profit and cash flow.

When one or more of the above assumptional limitation seems to be valid, they must be taken into consideration in using the growth-share matrix.

Studies by the Strategic Planning Institute utilizing Profit Impact of Market Strategy (PIMS) data also lend credence to the concerns expressed regarding the strength of the relationships between relative market share, competitive position, and cash flow. PIMS studies reveal that while market growth rate and relative share are linked to cash flows, other factors also influence cash flow. An analysis of a large sample of PIMS businesses, revealed that more than half of the SBUs in the question mark and dog quadrants were net cash generators, while about one quarter of the SBUs in the star and cash cow quadrants were net cash users (Buzzell and Gale, 1987). The results of this study are summarized in Table 2.7. Box 2.2, which focuses on why so called "cash cows" may not live up to their label, provides additional insights into this issue.

In effect, the BCG growth-share matrix might prove an appropriate diagnostic aid in analyzing a firm's portfolio of businesses only under certain conditions. These are that:

1. The relative market growth rate is the primary determinant of the relative industry attractiveness in most or all of the markets/industries in which the firm competes.
2. The relative market share is the primary determinant of the relative business strengths in most or all of the markets in which the firm competes owing to scale and experience effects.
3. Scale and experience effects are a major determinant of total costs with respect to most or all of the SBUs in a firm's portfolio.
4. Low costs and low prices are critical to achieving market dominance.

TABLE 2.7
CASH FLOW PATTERN OF PIMS BUSINESSES IN VARIOUS
GROWTH-SHARE QUADRANTS

Growth-Share Quadrant[a]	Market Growth Rate	Market-Share Rank	Percent of SBUs Generating Positive Cash Flows[b]
Stars	Positive	Leader	72%
Cash Cows	Negative	Leader	74%
Question Marks	Positive	Follower	54%
Dogs	Negative	Follower	59%

[a]The operational definition employed by PIMS researchers to classify SBUs as Stars, Cash Cows, etc., differs in certain respects from the BCG growth-share matrix conceptualization.
[b]Net cash flow is computed as after-tax income, plus depreciation plus or minus the net change in a unit's investment base.
Source: Adapted from: Buzzell, R. D., and B. T. Gale (1987), *The PIMS Principles: Linking Strategy to Performance*, New York: Free Press, p. 12.

A CONCLUDING NOTE

Missions assigned to individual SBUs and the allocation of resources among SBUs should be based on a careful analysis of market opportunities, company capabilities, the interdependence among the various SBUs, overall corporate objectives, and the future cash flow projections at the individual SBU level and the aggregate firm level. The BCG growth-share matrix provides diversified firms with a conceptual framework and guidelines for making decisions pertaining to (1) SBU retention/deletion, (2) the assignment of specific missions to individual SBUs, and (3) the optimal allocation of resources among the SBUs. However, a SBU's position in a portfolio matrix should not be the sole basis for such decisions. While the portfolio analysis techniques discussed in this chapter and the next chapter constitute a valuable strategic market planning tool, firms should guard against falling into a trap that might be labelled as a "mechanistic" numbers and formulas-driven approach to strategic decision-making. For example, a decision rule such as *all* SBUs in clusters *P, Q, and R* will be retained and *all* SBUs in clusters *X, Y, and Z* will be deleted is a sign of a numbers and formulas-driven mechanistic approach to strategic market planning. The use of portfolio analysis as a *prescriptive* strategic tool contrary to its intended use as a *diagnostic* tool should therefore be avoided.

NOTES

1. This example is adapted from *Business Week* (1987).
2. However, some authors draw a distinction between a product-market unit and a strategic business unit (e.g., Day, 1981).

BOX **2.2**

BUSINESSES IN THE "CASH COW" QUADRANT MAY NOT ALWAYS LIVE UP TO THEIR IMAGE

An SBU that is the market leader in a low-growth market may not always turn out to be a "cash cow." For instance, General Electric Co., (GE), was the industry leader in the U.S. television market. Its RCA and GE brands of televisions combined had the largest market share. However, during 1986, the consumer electronics division of GE barely broke even, although it posted $3.5 billion in revenue accounting for more than 10 percent of the firm's total revenue. Among the reasons attributed to the poor profitability of GE's consumer electronics division were the product innovations and price reductions initiated by overseas competitors (Guyon, 1987).

In July 1987, General Electric Co. agreed to sell its consumer electronics business to the French electronics giant Thomson S.A. in return for Thomson's medical equipment business and a cash sum estimated to be "significantly more than $500 million and less than $1 billion." Horizontal integration through acquisition of competitors and/or through exchange of assets such as the above are on the ascendance. For GE, already a leader in the medical equipment business with $1.6 billion in world-wide revenue, the Thomson operations constituted "an excellent fit" in a business GE views as among its fastest-growing. For Thomson, which has no consumer-electronics operation in the U.S., the move catapults it into the ranks of Phillips N.V. of the Netherlands and Japan's Matsushita Electric Industrial Co. as a world leader in consumer electronics. Thomson's 1986 revenues from consumer electronics and appliances were $3.3 billion (Landro and Sease, 1987).

Sources: Guyon, Janet (1987), "GE Gives Consumer Electronics a Chance to Change," *Wall Street Journal*, June 3, p. 6.
Landro, Laura and Douglas R. Sease (1987), "General Electric to Sell Consumer-Electronic Lines to Thomson SA for its Medical Gear Business, Cash," *Wall Street Journal*, July 23, p. 3.

3. A more detailed discussion of the nature of analysis a firm should undertake to satisfactorily address issues such as when it is appropriate for a firm to treat a single market cell as an SBU, and which adjacent market cells should be combined and treated as a single SBU is beyond the scope of this study. The scholarly works of a number of authors

(Abell, 1980; Buzzell, 1979; Day, 1981; Day, Shocker, and Srivastava, 1979; Srivastava, Leone, and Shocker, 1981) provide valuable insights into the underlying factors.

4. For additional insights into the product life cycle concept, see the special section on product life cycle published in the Fall, 1981 issue of the *Journal of Marketing* (pp. 60–132).

5. Unit sales would not be an appropriate basis for determining the area of the circles representing the various SBUs. For instance, a diversified firm such as General Electric might have annual sales of only a few hundred units of jet engines, and refrigerator sales of a couple of hundreds of thousands, but its annual light bulb sales might run into several millions.

6. Market share is generally viewed as one of the basic marketing objectives and a measure of product performance. In this context, market shares are not decisions, but outcomes of decisions relating to product, positioning, price, distribution, advertising, etc. (see for example, Buzzell and Wiersema's 1981 study of successful share-building *strategies*). However, in the context of achieving certain higher level objectives, such as growth, profitability and cash flow, one of the *strategic* decisions firms must make is whether a particular SBU should be assigned a mission to build share or directed to maintain share or harvest share. It is in this context that the term "market share strategy decision" is used here. As Buzzell and Gale note, ". . . pursuit of market share in itself is not a strategy. It is often an important *strategic* objective (1986, p. 23)."

7. A discussion of related versus unrelated diversification is presented in Chapter 6.

8. See Kotler (1988) for a discussion of market leader and challenger strategies.

9. Quantitative frameworks for projecting the marketing and manufacturing investment requirements of proposed portfolio strategies are discussed in a number of sources (Hax and Majluf, 1978; Larréché and Srinivasan, 1981, 1982).

REFERENCES

Aaker, David A. and George S. Day (1986), "The Perils of High-Growth Markets," *Strategic Management Journal*, 7 (September–October), 409–421.

Abell, Derek F. (1980), *Defining the Business: The Starting Point of Strategic Planning*, Englewood Cliffs, NJ: Prentice-Hall.

Abell, Derek F. and John S. Hammond (1979), *Strategic Market Planning: Problems and Analytical Approaches*, Englewood, NJ: Prentice-Hall.

Bettis, Richard A. and William K. Hall (1981), "Strategic Portfolio Management in the Multibusiness Firm," *California Management Review*, 24 (Fall), 23–38.

Bloom, Paul N. and Philip Kotler (1975), "Strategies for High Market Share Firms," *Harvard Business Review*, 53 (November–December), 63–72.

Boston Consulting Group (1972), *Perspectives on Experience*, Boston: The Boston Consulting Group.

Business Week (1987), "Will All That Restructuring Ever Pay Off For Ed Hennessy's Allied?," February 2, 78–80.

Buzzell, Robert D. and Fredrik D. Wiersema (1981), "Successful Share Building Strategies," *Harvard Business Review*, 59 (January–February), 135–144.

_____and Bradley T. Gale (1986), *"Does Market Share Still Matter?,"* Cambridge, Massachusetts: Strategic Planning Institute.

_____and _____(1987), *The PIMS Principles: Linking Strategy to Performance*, New York: Free Press.

Canada Consulting Group (1984), *Portfolio Planning in Canada*, Ontario: Canada Consulting Group.

Capon, N. and J. R. Spogli (1977), "Strategic Marketing Planning: A Comparison and Critical Examination of Two Contemporary Approaches," *Proceedings of the Annual Marketing Educators' Conference*, Chicago: American Marketing Association, 219–223.

Chakravarty, Balaji S. (1984), "Strategic Self-Renewal: A Planning Framework for Today," *Academy of Management Review*, 9 (July), 536–547.

Clifford, D. K., Jr. and R. E. Cavanagh (1985), *The Winning Performance: How America's High Growth Midsize Companies Succeed*, New York: Bantam Books.

Coe, Barbara J. (1981), "Use of Strategic Planning Concepts by Marketers," *Proceedings of the Annual Marketing Educators' Conference*, Chicago: American Marketing Association, 13–16.

Day, George S. (1977), "Diagnosing the Product Portfolio," *Journal of Marketing*, 41 (April), 29–38.

_____, Allan D. Shocker and Rajendra K. Srivastava (1979), "Customer Oriented Approaches to Identifying Product-Markets," *Journal of Marketing*, 43 (Fall), 8–19.

_____(1981), "Analytical Approaches to Strategic Market Planning," in B. M. Enis and K. M. Roering (eds.), *Annual Review of Marketing*, Chicago: American Marketing Association, 89–105.

_____(1986), *Analysis for Strategic Market Decisions*, St. Paul, MN: West Publishing.

Donaldson, G. (1984), *Managing Corporate Wealth*, New York: Prager Publishing.

Drucker, Peter (1963), "Managing for Business Effectiveness," *Harvard Business Review*, 41 (May–June), 53–60.

Faraquhar, Carolyn R., and Stanley J. Shapiro (1983), *Strategic Business Planning in Canada*, Ottawa: The Conference Board of Canada.

Fruhan, Jr. W. E. (1972), "Pyrrhic Victories in Fights for Market Share," *Harvard Business Review*, 50 (January–February), 97–106.

Guyon, Janet (1987), "GE Gives Consumer Electronics a Chance to Change," *Wall Street Journal*, June 3, 6.

Hall, William K. (1978), "SBU's: Hot, New Topic in the Management of Diversification," *Business Horizons*, 22 (February), 17–25.

Hamermesh, Richard G. (1986), "Making Planning Strategic," *Harvard Business Review*, 64 (July–August), 115–120.

Haspeslagh, Philippe (1982), "Portfolio Planning: Uses and Limits," *Harvard Business Review*, 60 (January–February), 58–72.

Hax, A. C. and N. S. Majluf (1978), "A Methodological Approach for the Development of Strategic Planning in Diversified Corporations," in A. C. Hax (ed.) *Studies in Operations Management*, Amsterdam, Holland: North-Holland Publishing Company, 41–98.

Hedley, Barry (1976), "A Fundamental Approach to Strategy Development," *Long Range Planning*, 9 (December), 2–11.

_____(1977), "Strategy and the Business Portfolio," *Long Range Planning*, 10 (February), 9–15.

Henderson, Bruce D. (1970), "The Product Portfolio," Boston: The Boston Consulting Group (*Perspectives*).

_____(1979), *Henderson on Corporate Strategy*. Cambridge, Massachusetts: Abt Books.

Kotler, Philip (1988), *Marketing Management: Analysis, Planning, and Control*, 6th ed., Englewood Cliffs, NJ: Prentice-Hall.

Landro, Laura and Douglas R. Sease (1987), "General Electric to Sell Consumer Electronics License to Thomson SA for Its Medical Gear Business, Cash," *Wall Street Journal*, (July 23), 3.

Larréché, Jean-Claude, and V. Srinivasan (1981), "STRATPORT: A Decision Support System for Strategic Planning," *Journal of Marketing*, 45 (Fall), 39–52.

_____and _____(1982), "STRATPORT: A Model for the Evaluation and Formulation of Business Portfolio Strategies," *Management Science*, 29 (September), 979–1001.

Levitt, Theodore (1983), *The Marketing Imagination*, New York: The Free Press.

Morris, Betsy (1987), "Coke vs. Pepsi: Cola War Marches On," *Wall Street Journal*, (June 3), 31.

Sheth, Jagdish N. (1985), *Winning Back Your Market*, New York: John Wiley and Sons.

Srivastava, Rajendra K., Robert P. Leone and Allan D. Shocker (1981), "Market Structure Analysis: Hierarchical Clustering of Products Based on Substitution in Use," *Journal of Marketing*, 45 (Summer), 38–48.

Varadarajan, P. Rajan (1983), "The Sustainable Growth Model: A Tool for Evaluating the Financial Feasibility of Market Share Strategies," *Strategic Management Journal*, 4 (October–December), 353–367.

_____(1990), "Product Portfolio Analysis and Market Share Objectives: An Exposition of Certain Underlying Relationships," *Journal of the Academy of Marketing Science* 18 (Winter) 1990.

Wensley, Robin (1981), "Strategic Marketing: Betas, Boxes or Basics," *Journal of Marketing*, 45 (Summer), 173–182.

_____(1982), "PIMS and BCG: New Horizons or False Dawns," *Strategic Management Journal*, 3 (April–June), 117–127.

Wernerfelt, Birger and Cynthia A. Montgomery (1986), "What Is an Attractive Industry?," *Management Science*, 32 (October), 1223–1230.

Wind, Yoram and Vijay Mahajan (1981a), "Designing Product and Business Portfolios," *Harvard Business Review*, 59 (January–February), 155–165.

_____and _____(1981b), "Market Share: Concepts, Findings, and Directions for Future Research," in B. M. Enis and K. J. Roering (eds.), *Annual Review of Marketing*, Chicago: American Marketing Association, 31–42.

CHAPTER

MULTIFACTOR PORTFOLIO

MATRIX MODELS AND

COMPETITIVE

STRATEGY MODELS

Introduction

Multifactor Portfolio Matrix Models
The Business Screen
The Life Cycle Portfolio Matrix
The Directional Policy Matrix

Product Portfolio Analysis: Extensions and Refinements

Using Portfolio Matrix Approaches: Caveats
Caveat: Realize Perils of High-Growth Markets
Caveat: Explore All Possible Strategic Options for Turning Around Poor Performers

Limitations of Portfolio Matrix Approaches

Competitive Strategy Models
Sustainable Competitive Advantage
The Competitive Advantage Matrix
The Strategic Gameboard
The Generic Strategies Matrix

Towards a Contingency Perspective of Product-Market Strategy

A Concluding Note

References

INTRODUCTION

The BCG growth-share matrix employs market growth rate and relative market share as *surrogates* for industry attractiveness and the firm's competitive position in that industry, respectively. While there seems to be little disagreement that market growth rate and relative market share are *indicators* of industry attractiveness and competitive position, there has been considerable disagreement over the adequacy of using single factors as indicators of industry attractiveness and a firm's competitive position across diverse industry settings. As a consequence, multifactor portfolio matrix approaches that use multiple factors to assess the relative attractiveness of industries in which a firm competes and its relative competitive position in those industries have been proposed.

This chapter is divided into two parts. Part one reviews three multifactor portfolio matrix approaches for strategic marketing planning: (1) the business screen, (2) the life cycle portfolio matrix, and (3) the directional policy matrix. Part two provides an overview of matrix conceptualizations that focus on the scope of competition, mode of competition, and sources of competitive advantage.

MULTIFACTOR PORTFOLIO MATRIX MODELS

Multifactor portfolio matrix models reveal certain similarities as well as differences in perspective, methodology, assumptions, data, conclusions, and implications.

1. These approaches attach great importance to rigorous analysis of relevant data. Collection and analysis of data pertaining to (a) the general market and political, economic, and social conditions affecting business; (b) the particular industry and served markets in which the business participates, including industry growth rates, basis of competition and strengths and weaknesses of competitors; and (c) the firm's business units' strengths and weaknesses, its technological resources, and the effectiveness of the strategies it pursues, provide the foundation for all portfolio approaches to strategic market planning.

2. They entail delineating the firm's diverse operations in terms of Strategic Business Units (SBUs). As noted earlier, a firm's SBUs are business areas with an external marketplace for goods or services for which one can determine objectives and execute strategies independent of other business areas. Clues for determining SBUs include:

(a) whether the firm can divest itself of the business without affecting other businesses, (b) whether the business can stand alone if divested from the corporation, (c) whether the business serves a distinct customer group, and (d) whether the business faces a distinct set of competitors.

3. They view the strategic conditions in which an SBU competes as a major factor influencing strategy choice.

4. The guidelines they offer are based on the premise that, given the strategic conditions under which an SBU operates, there exist a finite set of generic strategies from which an SBU can select a strategy to pursue.

Despite the commonalities, the approaches differ in the following respects:

1. the dimensions employed to define the strategic conditions under which various SBUs in a firm's portfolio operate,
2. the factors underlying these strategic conditions
3. generic strategic options that are available to an SBU operating under specific strategic conditions.

The Business Screen

The GE/McKinsey business screen portfolio matrix, along with indicators of industry attractiveness and business competitive position, is shown in Figure 3.1. The circles in the figure represent SBUs in the firm's portfolio. The sizes of the circles are in proportion to the sizes of the industries and the shaded portions of the circles are in proportion to the SBU's share of the industries in which they compete. The suggested strategy options to be pursued for SBUs in the various cells (invest/grow; selectivity/earning; or harvest/divert) are also indicated in the matrix. As with the BCG matrix, the proposed strategic guidelines are intended to be suggestive and not prescriptive.

The checklist of factors developed by McKinsey & Co. to develop a multifactor portfolio matrix are listed at the far right of the matrix (Figure 3.1). A more extensive list of factors considered indicative of market attractiveness and the business' competitive position are presented in Table 3.1. However, not all the factors listed in Table 3.1 are relevant in a particular context. By considering the characteristics of the industries, the characteristics of the firm, and its portfolio of businesses, a firm's management may be in a position to identify two smaller subsets of factors (indicative of relative market attractiveness and competitive position, respectively) from among the factors listed in Table 3.1.

The steps involved in identifying subsets of factors and computing pairs of composite scores (industry attractiveness score and competitive position score) for each of the SBUs in the firm's portfolio are summarized in Table 3.2. Based on pairs of composite scores for all of the SBUs in a firm's

FIGURE 3.1
THE BUSINESS SCREEN

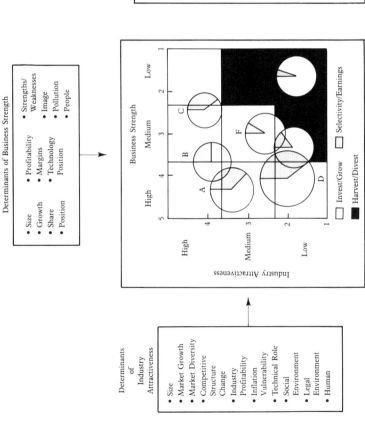

Determinants of Business Strength

- Size
- Growth
- Share
- Position

- Profitability
- Margins
- Technology
- Position

- Strengths/ Weaknesses
- Image
- Pollution
- People

Determinants of Industry Attractiveness

- Size
- Market Growth
- Market Diversity
- Competitive Structure Change
- Industry Profitability
- Inflation Vulnerability
- Technical Role
- Social Environment
- Legal Environment
- Human

Business Strength

High — Medium — Low

5 — 4 — 3 — 2 — 1

Industry Attractiveness

High — 4
Medium — 3
Low — 2 — 1

A B C
F
D

☐ Invest/Grow ☐ Selectivity/Earnings ■ Harvest/Divest

McKinsey's Checklist of Factors for Developing a Multifactor Portfolio Matrix

- Market Size (Domestic/Global)
- Market Growth (Domestic/Global)
- Price Trend
- Captive Market
- Cyclicality
- Concentration
- Competitive Characteristics
- Top Group Strength
- Replacement Threats Possibility
- Market Leader's Profits Trend
- Sociopolitical and Economic Environment
- Labor Situation
- Legal Issues
- Etc.

Source: This figure is a composite of matrices from several sources including the following:
1. Hofer, C. W., and D. Schendel (1979), *Strategy Formulation: Analytical Concepts,* St. Paul, Minn.: West Publishing, p. 83.
2. Koller, P. (1984), *Marketing Management: Analysis, Planning and Control,* 5th ed. Englewood Cliffs, NJ: Prentice-Hall, p. 55.
3. "Market Share and Return on Investment: A Popular Decision," *Management Practice,* New York: Main, Jackson and Garfield, Inc. (Fall 1978).

TABLE 3.1
FACTORS CONTRIBUTING TO MARKET ATTRACTIVENESS AND BUSINESS
POSITION

Attractiveness of Your Market	Status/Position of Your Business
Market factors	
Size (dollars, units, or both)	Your share (in equivalent terms)
Size of key segments	Your share of key segments
Growth rate per year:	Your annual growth rate:
Total	Total
Segments	Segments
Diversity of market	Diversity of your participation
Sensitivity to price, service features, and external factors	Your influence on the market
Cyclicality	Lags or leads in your sales
Seasonality	
Bargaining power of upstream suppliers	Bargaining power of your suppliers
Bargaining power of downstream suppliers	Bargaining power of your customers
Competition	
Types of competitors	Where you fit, how you compare in terms of products, marketing capability, service, production strength, financial strength, management
Degree of concentration	
Changes in type and mix	
Entries and exits	Segments you have entered or left
Changes in share	Your relative share change
Substitution by new technology	Your vulnerability to new technology
Degrees and types of integration	Your own level of integration
Financial and economic factors	
Contribution margins	Your margins
Leveraging factors, such as economies of scale and experience	Your scale and experience
Barriers to entry or exit (both financial and nonfinancial)	Barriers to your entry or exit (both financial and nonfinancial)
Capacity utilization	Your capacity utilization
Technological factors	
Maturity and volatility	Your ability to cope with change
Complexity	Depths of your skills
Differentiation	Types of your technological skills
Patents and copyrights	Your patent protection
Manufacturing process technology required	Your manufacturing technology
Sociopolitical factors in your environment	
Social attitudes and trends	Your company's responsiveness and flexibility
Laws and government agency regulations	Your company's ability to cope

(continued)

TABLE 3.1   (*continued*)

Attractiveness of Your Market	Status/Position of Your Business
Influence with pressure groups and government representatives	Your company's aggressiveness
Human factors, such as unionization and community acceptance	Your company's relationships

Source: Derek F. Abell and John S. Hammond, *Strategic Market Planning: Problems and Analytical Approaches,* © 1979, p. 214. Reprinted by permission of Prentice-Hall, Inc., Englewood Cliffs, New Jersey.

TABLE 3.2
ASSESSING RELATIVE INDUSTRY ATTRACTIVENESS AND BUSINESS
STRENGTH: AN EXPOSITION

A Industry Attractiveness Criteria	B Criteria Weight[1]	C Rating[2,3]	D = B × C Weighted Score[6]
Size	.15	4	.60
Growth	.12	3	.36
Pricing	.05	3	.15
Market diversity	.05	2	.10
Competitive structure	.05	3	.15
Industry profitability	.20	3	.60
Technical role	.05	4	.20
Inflation vulnerability	.05	2	.10
Cyclicality	.05	2	.10
Customer financials	.10	5	.50
Energy impact	.08	4	.32
Social	GO	4	—
Environmental	GO	4	—
Legal	GO	4	—
Human	.05	4	.20
	1.00		3.38

[1]The weights assigned should add up to 1. Some criteria may be of a GO/NO GO type and are not weighted. For most large firms, industries viewed negatively by the society would fall in the NO GO category.
[2]The hypothetical ratings are reported for a particular industry 'j' in which the firm's SBU 'i' competes. All other industries in which the firm's various SBUs compete should be rated along similar lines.
[3]A rating of '1' denotes "very unattractive," and a rating of '5' denotes "highly attractive."

portfolio, a portfolio matrix such as that shown in Figure 3.1 can be developed.

The Life Cycle Portfolio Matrix[1]

The life cycle portfolio matrix was developed by Arthur D. Little, Inc., a management consulting firm (see: Patel and Younger, 1978; Arthur D. Little, Inc., 1980). It builds on the premise that industries, like products, have life cycles. The life cycle approach distinguishes between four phases of industry maturity (embryonic, growing, maturing, and aging) and five levels of competitive position (dominant, strong, favorable, tenable, and weak). The resulting 4 × 5, two-dimensional matrix and proposed strategic guidelines for SBUs in various cells are shown in Table 3.3.[2]

Factors determining the stage of industry maturity, the horizontal dimension in the matrix are:

E Business Strength Determinants	F Determinant Weight[1]	G Rating[4,5]	H = F × G Weighted Score[6]
Market share	.10	5	.50
Breadth of product line	.05	4	.20
Sales distribution effectiveness	.20	4	.80
Advertising and promotion effectiveness	.05	4	.20
Facilities location and newness	.05	5	.25
Experience curve effects	.15	4	.60
Raw materials cost	.05	4	.20
Relative product quality	.15	4	.60
R and D advantages/position	.05	4	.20
Cash throw-off	.10	5	.50
General image	.05	5	.25
	1.00		4.30

[4]The hypothetical ratings reported are for a particular SBU in the firm's portfolio. All SBUs in the firm's portfolio should be rated along similar lines.
[5]A rating of '1' denotes "very weak competitive position," and a rating of '5' denotes "very strong competitive position."
[6]Together, the values (3.38, 4.30) describe the relative attractiveness of the industry 'j' in which the firm's SBU 'i' competes and the relative competitive position of the SBU in this industry. Similar pairs of composite scores describing relative industry attractiveness and business strength should be computed for all SBUs in the firm's portfolio. Based on these pairs of scores, the SBUs would be assigned to one of the nine cells in Figure 3.1.

Adapted from C. W. Hofer and D. Schendel, *Strategy Formulation: Analytical Concepts* (West, St. Paul, Minnesota, 1978), p. 73, 76.

- market growth rate
- market growth potential
- breadth of product lines
- number of competitors
- market share stability
- customer purchase patterns
- entry barriers
- technology

The characteristics of each stage of industry maturity are as follows (Hax and Majluf, 1984):

Embryonic Industry: rapid growth, changes in technology, vigorous pursuit of new customers, and fragmented and unstable market shares.

Growth Industry: rapid growth, clear trends in customer purchase patterns, competitors' market shares, and technological developments, and increasing barriers to entry.

Mature Industry: stable purchase patterns, technology, and market shares (however the industries themselves may be highly competitive).

Aging Industry: falling demand, a declining number of competitors, and a narrowing product line.

The competitive position of a business unit is not based on a numerical value such as market share, or a composite score based on multiple factors. Instead, a qualitative approach to assessing competitive position is adopted:

Dominant: Only one firm, if any at all, can be dominant in an industry. Kodak in color films, Boeing in commercial aircrafts, and IBM in mainframe computers are cases in point. A quasimonopoly or a well protected technological lead is often the key to dominance.

Strong: Firms that are industry leaders with respect to market share, but have not reached the absolute dominance of the former category, are classified as strong competitors (e.g., Kellogg in cereals, General Motors in passenger cars).

Favorable: This level describes the competitive position achieved in a fragmented industry by pursuing a differentiation strategy or exploiting a particular niche where the firm excels.

Tenable: A position that can be maintained profitably through geographic or product specialization in a narrow or protected market niche.

Weak: A position that cannot be sustained in the long run given the competitive economics of the industry. The choice is between striving to improve the position or leaving the industry.

TABLE 3.3
THE LIFE CYCLE PORTFOLIO MATRIX

Competitive Position	Stage of Industry Maturity			
	Embryonic	Growing	Mature	Aging
Dominant	All out push for share / Hold position	Hold position / Hold share	Hold position / Grow with industry	Hold position
Strong	Attempt to improve position / All out push for share	Attempt to improve position / Push for share	Hold position / Grow with industry	Hold position or Harvest
Favorable	Selective or all out push for share / Selectively attempt to improve competitive position	Attempt to improve position / Selective push for share	Custodial or maintenance / Find niche and attempt to protect	Harvest / Phased withdrawal
Tenable	Selectively push for position	Find niche and protect it	Find niche and hang on or Phased withdrawal	Phased withdrawal or Abandon
Weak	Up or Out	Turnaround or Abandon	Turnaround or Phased withdrawal	Abandon

Source: Patel, P., and M. Younger (1978), "A Frame of Reference for Strategy Development," *Long Range Planning*, 11 (April), 6–12. Reprinted by permission of Pergamon Press. Ltd., Oxford, England.

Proponents of the life cycle portfolio matrix advocate a three-step approach to identifying an appropriate strategy. Step one entails classifying business units into four broad categories—develop naturally, develop selectively, prove viability, and withdraw. The strategic guidelines associated with these categories labelled as *families of strategic thrusts* are as follows (Hax and Majluf, 1984):

Develop naturally: Businesses that merit strong support to assure industry-wide growth given their strong competitive position and industry maturity.

Develop selectively: Businesses that merit selective support in light of the attractiveness of the industry or because the firm has unique competitive skills that it can exploit.

Prove viability: A transitory situation that cannot be sustained and calls for immediate action to change the state of affairs.

Withdraw: Businesses from which the firm should withdraw.

The next step is to select a *specific strategic thrust* for each strategy center. The range of specific strategic thrusts available to the strategy centers in the four categories are different. The final step involves choosing a *generic strategy* to implement a specific strategic thrust. Table 3.4 illustrates the linkage between the three stages of the strategy identification process.

In certain respects, insights provided by the life cycle portfolio matrix are similar to those provided by the BCG growth-share matrix. For example, if a disproportionately large number of strategy centers fall into the dominant, strong, or favorable cells of the industry maturity stage, then the firm's current performance is likely to be quite good. However, unless corrective action is taken, over the long term the firm's performance might decline. Conversely, if a firm's portfolio has a large number of strategy centers in the embryonic stage, the firm would lack the internal resources needed to consolidate or strengthen the competitive positions of these businesses. Table 3.5 presents the distribution of strategy centers (in terms of number of business units and percentage of corporate assets) of a hypothetical firm over the various stages of industry maturity and competitive position. The distribution of assets across: (a) embryonic, growth, mature, and aging businesses, and (b) businesses in the dominant and strong categories are indicative of a sound portfolio.

The Directional Policy Matrix

The Directional Policy Matrix (DPM) approach to strategic market planning was developed by Shell Chemicals U.K. (Robinson, Hichens, and Wade, 1978; Hussey, 1978; Hughes, 1981). This matrix is based on two composite dimensions: (1) business sector prospects—the profit and growth potential of the sector (market segment) in which the business unit operates; and (2) the competitive position of the business in that sector. The DPM matrix differentiates between three levels of business sector

TABLE 3.4

GUIDELINES FOR IDENTIFYING APPROPRIATE STRATEGIES: THE LIFE CYCLE PORTFOLIO MATRIX

I. Families of Strategic Thrusts	II. Preferred Strategic Thrust	III. Preferred Generic Strategies
A. Natural Development	1. Start up	I. Marketing Strategies 1. Export/Same Product
	2. Growth with industry	2. Initial Market Development 3. Market Penetration 4. New Products/New Markets
	3. Gain position gradually	5. New Products/Same Markets 6. Same Products/New Markets
		II. Integration Strategies
	4. Gain position aggressively	1. Backward Integration 2. Forward Integration
		III. Go Overseas Strategies
	5. Defend position	1. Development of an Overseas Business
	6. Harvest	2. Development of Overseas Production Facilities
B. Selective Development	1. Find niche	3. Licensing Abroad
		IV. Logistics Strategies
	2. Exploit niche	1. Distribution Rationalization 2. Excess Capacity
	3. Hold niche	3. Market Rationalization 4. Product Rationalization
C. Prove Viability	1. Catch up	5. Product Line Rationalization
		V. Efficiency Strategies
	2. Renew	1. Methods and Functions Efficiency 2. Technological Efficiency
	3. Turn around	3. Traditional Cost Cutting
		VI. Harvest Strategies
	4. Prolong existence	1. Hesitation 2. Little Jewel
D. Withdrawal	1. Withdraw	3. Pure Survival 4. Maintenance
	2. Divest	5. Unit Abandonment
	3. Abandon	

Source: Adapted from Hax, A. E. and N. S. Majluf, *Strategic Management: An Integrated Perspective*, Englewood Cliffs, NJ: (1984), Figure 9.14 (p. 199) and Figure 9.15 (p. 200).

Note: 1. See Figure 9.15, p. 200 of Hax and Majluf (1984) for a more detailed mapping of generic strategies that are feasible in the context of various preferred strategic thrusts.

2. The generic strategies list developed by Arthur D. Little, Inc., which is shown column III of the figure, should be viewed as extensive and not comprehensive.

TABLE 3.5
COMPOSITION OF FIRM'S PORTFOLIO BY STAGE OF INDUSTRY MATURITY AND COMPETITIVE POSITION

| | Stage of Industry Maturity | | | | | | | | Row Totals | |
| | Embryonic | | Growth | | Mature | | Aging | | | |
Competitive Position	Number of units	Corporate assets (percent)	Number of units	Corporate assets (percent)	Number of units	Corporate assets (percent)	Number of units	Corporate assets (percent)	Number of units	Corporate assets (percent)
Dominant	2	15	2	8	1	2	1	10	6	35
Strong	1	5	1	3	4	40	—	—	6	48
Favorable	—	—	1	2	—	—	1	4	2	6
Tenable	1	3	—	—	1	1	—	—	2	4
Weak	1	3	—	—	1	4	—	—	2	7
Column Totals	5	26	4	13	7	47	2	14	18	100

Source: Adapted from: Patel, P., and M. Younger (1978), "A Frame of Reference for Strategy Development," *Long Range Planning*, 11 (April), 6–12.

prospects (attractive, average, and unattractive) and three levels of the company's competitive capabilities (strong, average, and weak). The proposed DPM matrix and suggested strategic guidelines for business units in the various cells are shown in Figure 3.2. Table 3.6 provides additional insights into the rationale underlying the proposed strategic options and the activities involved in implementing these options.

Like the business screen, a desirable feature of the DPM is the flexibility it offers in selecting factors relevant to the specific industry to assess business sector prospects and competitive position. The DPM approach employs four sets of factors to assess business sector prospects—market growth rate, market quality, industry situation, and environmental aspects. Competitive position is assessed based on market position, product research and development, and production capability. The industry context in which the matrix is employed plays a major role in the choice of subfactors employed to relate business sector prospects and competitive

FIGURE 3.2
THE DIRECTIONAL POLICY MATRIX

Business Sector Prospects

	Unattractive	Average	Attractive
Weak	Disinvest	Phased Withdrawal Custodial	Double or Quit
Average	Phased Withdrawal	Custodial Growth	Try Harder
Strong	Cash Generation	Growth Leader	Leader

Company's Competitive Capabilities

Source: Robinson, S. J. Q., R. E. Hichen and D. P. Wade, (1978), "The Directional Policy Matrix—Tool for Strategic Planning," *Long Range Planning*, 11 (June), 8–15. Reprinted by permission of Pergamon Press, Ltd., Oxford, England.

TABLE 3.6
ALTERNATIVE STRATEGIC OPTIONS FOR BUSINESS SECTORS:
THE DPM APPROACH

Disinvestment. Businesses falling in this area will probably be losing money—not necessarily every year, but losses in bad years will outweigh the gains in good years.

Phased withdrawal. Businesses in this category are unlikely to earn any significant amounts of cash. The recommended strategy is designed to help realize the value of the assets on a controlled basis to make the resources available for redeployment elsewhere.

Cash generator. A typical situation in this matrix area is when the company has a business which is moving towards the end of its life cycle, and is being replaced in the market by others. As long as the business is profitable, it should be used as a source of cash for other areas. Every effort should be made to maximize profits. Investments in expansion may not be appropriate.

Proceed with care. Some investment may be justified but major investments should be made with extreme caution.

Growth. Investment should be made to allow the business to grow with the market. Generally, the business will generate sufficient cash to be self-financing.

Double or quit. Tomorrow's breadwinners among today's R&D projects may come from this area. Businesses with the best prospects should be selected for full backing and development. The rest should be abandoned.

Try harder. Through judicious application of resources, businesses in this cell can be moved toward the leadership cell. It may be desirable for the firm to make available resources to these businesses in excess of what they can internally generate.

Leader. The strategy should be to maintain this position. Despite above average earnings, in certain situations, businesses in this cell may need resources in excess of their internal cash generating ability.

Source: Adapted from: Hussey, D. E. (1978), "Portfolio Analysis: Practical Experience with the Directional Policy Matrix," *Long Range Planning,* 11 (August), 2–8.

position. Table 3.7 sheds additional insights into this approach. The key factors relevant to assessing the two dimensions of the matrix are listed first. Additional details regarding subfactors relevant to an assessment of market quality and market position are described next.

As in the GE/McKinsey portfolio matrix approach, the position of a business in the DPM matrix is based on its composite scores for business sector prospects and company's competitive capabilities. However, unlike

TABLE 3.7
FACTORS UNDERLYING ANALYSIS OF BUSINESS SECTOR PROSPECTS AND
COMPANY'S COMPETITIVE CAPABILITIES

Factors Relevant to Analysis of Business Sector Prospects	Factors Revelant to Analysis of Company's Competitive Capabilities
1. Market growth 2. Market quality 3. Environmental aspects	1. Market position 2. Production capability 3. Product R&D

Guidelines for Assessing Market Quality

A sector for which the answers to all or most of the following questions are yes would attract a four or five point market quality rating.

The following questions may be relevant in a particular industry context.

(a) Has the sector a record of high, stable profitability?

(b) Can margins be maintained when manufacturing capacity exceeds demand?

(c) Is the product resistant to commodity pricing behavior?

(d) Is the technology of production freely available or is it proprietary?

(e) Is the market free from domination by a small group of powerful customers?

(f) Has the product high added value when converted by the customer?

(g) In the case of a new product, is the market destined to remain small enough not to attract too many producers?

(h) Is the product one where the customer has to change his formulation or even his machinery if he changes suppliers?

(i) Is the product free from the risk of substitution by an alternative product?

Guidelines for Assessing Market Position

Primary factor: percent share of total market.

Secondary factor: degree to which market-share is secured.

Rating Associated with Alternative Competitive Positions:

*Current position negligible.

**Minor market share. Less than adequate to support R&D and other services in the long run.

***A company with a strong viable stake in the market, but below the top league. Usually when one producer is a leader the next level of competition will be comprised of producers who merit a three point rating.

****Major producer. The position where, as in many businesses, no one company is a leader, but two to four competitors may merit a four point rating.

*****Leader. A company in a preeminent market position, likely to be followed by others, and also the acknowledged technological leader. The market share associated with this position may vary from case to case. A company with 25 percent share in a field of ten competitors may be regarded as a leader. However, a company with 50 percent in a field of two competitors may not be.

Source: Adapted from: Hussey, D. E. (1978), "Portfolio Analysis: Practical Experience with the Directional Policy Matrix," *Long Range Planning*, 11 (August), 2–8.

the GE/McKinsey approach, the DPM approach focuses on the attractiveness of a sector (market segment) rather than of an entire industry.

PRODUCT PORTFOLIO ANALYSIS: EXTENSIONS AND REFINEMENTS

Product portfolio analysis techniques have undergone numerous refinements in the last two decades, and continue to be the focus of further refinements. True to the evolutionary process in an emerging discipline, Table 3.8 summarizes some of the illustrative refinements that have occurred in portfolio analysis over time.

An extension of product portfolio analysis is the technology portfolio concept, which provides a tool for evaluating the particular mix of technologies in a firm's asset base and analyzing how they complement one another as part of the overall corporate strategy (Capon and Glazer, 1987; Harris, Shaw, and Sommers, 1981; Nemec, 1981). By developing a technology portfolio matrix, a firm gains insight into how its resources are distributed across its mix of technologies and the current standing of these technologies with respect to development/market exploitation and competitive strength. The eight-cell technology portfolio matrix proposed by Capon and Glazer (1987) is presented in Figure 3.3. Here, the vertical axis is a time dimension incorporating both technology and product life cycles. The axis is divided into two intervals reflecting the premarket and postmarket phases of technology exploitation. The premarket phase is further divided into the research and development stages of technology genera-

TABLE 3.8
ILLUSTRATIVE DEVELOPMENTS IN PORTFOLIO ANALYSIS

From Analysis Based On		To Analysis Based On
• One or two specified dimensions	$- - - \longrightarrow$	Management selected dimensions
• Single-measure dimensions	$- - - \longrightarrow$	Composite dimensions
• · Unweighted dimensions	$- - - \longrightarrow$	Weighted dimensions
• Single respondent's objective data	$- - - \longrightarrow$	Multiple respondents', and integrative and objective data
• Historical data	$- - - \longrightarrow$	Projected data
• Single-level analysis	$- - - \longrightarrow$	Multi-level hierarchical analysis

FIGURE 3.3
THE TECHNOLOGY PORTFOLIO MATRIX

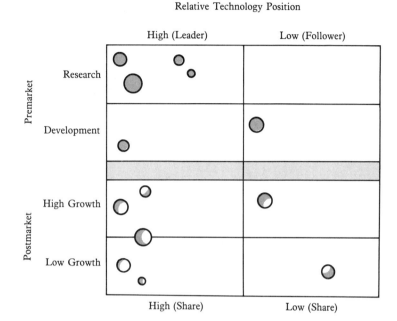

Relative Technology Position

Key

Circle = technology
Size of circle = relative resource flow associated with the technology
Shaded segment = cash user
Open segment = cash generator

Source: Capon, Noel and Rashi Glazer (1987), "Marketing and Technology: A Strategic Coalignment," *Journal of Marketing*, 51 (July), 1–14.

tion, and the postmarket phase, into the low and high growth stages of the technology life cycle. The horizontal dimension corresponding to the premarket phase indicates whether the firm is a leader or follower in the research and/or development of various technologies. The horizontal dimension corresponding to the postmarket phase indicates the relative competitive position of a firm with regard to the technologies in use. Each of the technologies represented in the postmarket cells has its own corresponding product portfolio. Table 3.9 provides additional insights into guidelines for managing the technology portfolio of the firm.

TABLE 3.9
GUIDELINES FOR TECHNOLOGY DEVELOPMENT AND COMMERCIALIZATION[1,2]

Technology Portfolio Matrix	Strategic Dimension A *Relative technology position*	Strategic Dimension B *Technology importance*	Normative Recommendation *Technology development strategy*
1. Booz, Allen & Hamilton's technology portfolio development matrix (Harris, Shaw, and Sommers 1981)	High	High	Best-invest to sustain and increase competitive advantage
	High	Low	Cash in
	Low	High	Draw-bet against competition and invest to attain a leadership position or develop a plan to disengage from that technology
	Low	Low	Fold
	Market opportunity	*Technical opportunity*[3]	*R&D effort strategy*
2. McKinsey's R&D effort portfolio (Foster 1981)	High	High	Heavy emphasis
	High	Moderate	Heavy emphasis
	Moderate	High	Heavy emphasis
	High	Low	Selective opportunistic development
	Moderate	Moderate	Selective opportunistic development
	Low	High	Selective opportunistic development
	Moderate	Low	Limited defensive support
	Low	Moderate	Limited defensive support
	Low	Low	Limited defensive support

	Relative technology position	Technology business position	Technology commercialization strategy
3. Booz, Allen & Hamilton's technology commercialization strategy matrix (Nemec 1981)	High	High	Preempt competitors by maintaining business and technology leadership
	High	Low	Preempt competitors by investing to build business or sell technology
	Low	High	Leverage market position by investing in technology or harvest business
	Low	Low	Withdraw

[1]The focus of these matrix conceptualizations is the *portfolio of technologies underlying* the firm's present product offerings and proposed future product offerings. In matrices 1 and 2 the primary concern is *technology development* strategy, while in matrix, 3 the concern is *technology commercialization* strategy.

[2]Also see Capon and Glazer (1987) for additional insights into technology development and commercialization strategies, and the marketing-technology interface.

[3]Measured in terms of the "technology gap"—the difference between the best anybody is able to do today, and the best that's theoretically possible, given the laws of nature.

USING PORTFOLIO MATRIX
APPROACHES: CAVEATS

Caveat: Realize Perils of High-Growth Markets

A trait common to all portfolio matrix approaches is the importance they attach to market growth rate as an indicator of industry attractiveness. It should be noted, however, that high market growth in itself does not make a market attractive. Rather, it is the firm's ability to exploit the opportunities presented by market growth to gain a competitive advantage that's critical. Table 3.10 provides a summary of the major premises underlying the argument that firms should invest in high-growth markets since they are relatively more attractive, and the limitations of these premises. Nevertheless, a number of organizational and environmental conditions do favor early entry in high-growth markets. They are (Aaker and Day, 1986):

1. The firm has the ability to develop strong customer loyalty based upon perceived product quality and retain this loyalty as the market evolves.
2. The firm has the ability to develop a broad product line to help discourage entries and combat nichers.

TABLE 3.10
PERILS OF HIGH-GROWTH MARKETS

Major Premises Underlying Argument That Firms Should Invest in High-Growth Markets	Limitations of Premises
1. It is easier to gain share in growth markets since: a. New users will not have entrenched brand/firm loyalties that have to be overcome; b. Competitors are less likely to react aggressively to market share erosion as long as their sales are growing at a satisfactory rate.	The pioneer has to make sizeable investments to attract users to an unfamiliar product by informing them of the advantages, persuading them that the benefits are greater than the risks, and educating them in using the product; the later entrants have a relatively easier and less expensive task in this regard and also the benefit of learning from the pioneer's mistakes. More realistically, competitors' reactions are likely to be influenced by their performance expectations, and also depend on their financial and managerial resource capabilities.
2. Share gains are worth more in growth markets since the profit stream associated with each share point will accrue over a longer period of time (the growth and maturity periods).	This depends on the ability of the firm to hold onto its share in the face of likely scenarios such as changing key success factors, intense competition, and market fragmentation.

TABLE 3.10 (*continued*)

Major Premises Underlying Argument That Firms Should Invest in High-Growth Markets	Limitations of Premises
3. The firm can get a head start on the experience curve and thus gain a sustainable competitive cost advantage and discourage potential competitors.	If one or more competitors choose to follow an experience curve based pricing strategy, this would precipitate a price war.
	Cost declines owing to experience do not happen automatically; management must make it happen, have the resources to make it happen, and insure that it remains proprietary.
	It may be feasible for late entrants to neutralize the experience-based cost advantage of the early entrant by using more modern technology.
	Some competitors may have cost advantages that are independent of experience.
4. There is less price pressure in high-growth markets with demand often exceeding supply. The excess demand may support premium prices.	Attractive margins generally attract more competitors.
	Guided by the experience curve logic, some competitors may choose to price low (even below cost, in anticipation of eventual cost declines).
5. Early participation provides technological expertise; experience with first generation technology can lead to superior and more timely second-generation technology.	An early commitment to a technology may turn out to be a disadvantage as alternate technologies emerge.
	Rather than trying to gain a foothold in the second-generation technology, firms often attempt to counter the threat of a new technology by investing research funds in improving current technology.
6. Early aggressive entry will deter later entrants; by sending the right market signals and erecting entry barriers by establishing a strong brand image, preempting distribution channels, etc., a firm can make the market look less appealing to potential entrants in spite of the high rate of market growth.	The ability of a firm to deter later entrants will depend on the nature and size of barriers it is capable of erecting.

Source: Based on text of pages 410 to 415 of Aaker, D. A. and G. S. Day (1986), "The Perils of High-Growth Markets," *Strategic Management Journal,* 7 (September–October), 409–421.

3. The firm has the ability to discourage prospective competitors from entering the market and make existing competitors accept market share erosion.

4. The required investments are not substantial.

5. Technological change is not likely to be so rapid and abrupt as to create obsolescence problems.

6. The experience curve phenomenon is pronounced in the industry; an early entrant can benefit from the experience curve phenomenon and the experience curve based competitive advantages of the early entrant cannot easily be overcome by later entrants.

7. Absolute cost advantages can be achieved by early commitment to raw materials, component manufacture, distribution channels, and so forth.

8. The initial price structure is likely to be high in view of the product's ability to offer superior value over that of the products it will displace.

Caveat: Explore All Feasible Strategic Options for Turning Around Poor Performers

The portfolio matrix approaches employ an analytic framework for identifying SBUs that a firm should retain in its portfolio and those it should delete. Analytic rigor, however, should not make a firm oblivious to the role that managerial initiative, imagination, and creativity can play in improving the performance of poorly performing SBUs. It is imperative for top management to carefully explore the feasibility of turning around poor performers by evaluating a multiplicity of options before making an often irreversible decision to delete them from the portfolio. Sheth (1985), for example, lists nine strategic options that managers should evaluate before deciding that a product or service should be dropped. As indicated in Table 3.11, these options differ with respect to market and use focus.

LIMITATIONS OF PORTFOLIO MATRIX APPROACHES

Portfolio matrix models have been critiqued for their shortcomings in a number of areas. A brief discussion of the major shortcomings follows.

Pitfalls in Assumptions The general validity of some of the assumptions underlying the BCG growth-share matrix approach have been questioned. For instance, the experience curve phenomena (discussed in chapter 4) used to justify the desirability of pursuing a strategy of high market share in high-growth markets is not generalizable across product-markets. Technological innovation, inflation, market redefinition, inter-product experience transfer, and limits to experience are some of the pos-

TABLE 3.11
STRATEGIC OPTIONS FOR TURNING AROUND POOR PERFORMERS

Market Focus	Use Focus	Strategic Alternatives
A. Present Markets	Present Uses	1. Entrenching—increasing market share by taking business away from the competition.
		2. Switching from end users to intermediaries—selling the product or service to someone who can resell it more effectively.
		3. Creating mandatory consumption—manipulating forces outside the marketing mix to force consumption of the product.
B. New Markets	Present Uses	4. Going international—marketing the product or service in a foreign country through one of four substrategies.
		i. Global marketing—no change in product or market.
		ii. Product differentiation—altering product, price, and packaging.
		iii. Market differentiation—altering promotion and distribution.
		iv. Unique marketing—adjusting all elements of the marketing mix.
		5. Broadening the product horizon—redefining the business to position the product against a new set of competitors.
C. Present Markets	New Uses	6. Finding new applications—searching for new or additional functional needs to satisfy.
		7. Finding new situations—seeking out new or additional nonfunctional needs to satisfy in new times, new places, and new positionings.
D. New Markets	New Uses	8. Repositioning—redefining the image to position the product into new usage situations in new markets.
		9. Redefining markets—shifting customers and competitive arenas; position the product in a completely different market.

Source: Adapted from text of Sheth, Jagdish N. (1985), *Winning Back Your Market,* New York: John Wiley & Sons.

sible factors that can mitigate or negate the experience effect. Furthermore, prescriptions advocating the universal advisability of pursuing a strategy oriented toward achieving high market share regardless of the environmental and organizational context have been challenged (e.g., Bloom and Kotler, 1975).

Interdependencies Among SBUs   In conglomerate or unrelated diversified firms, it may be appropriate for top management to make retention/deletion decisions at the *individual* SBU level, *independent* of the other SBUs.[3] However, in related diversified firms, *interdependencies* that exist between SBUs in the firm's portfolio make it inappropriate for top management to make retention/deletion decisions at the *individual* SBU level, *independent* of the other SBUs.

In discussing the concept of strategic field theory, Lewis (1982, 1984) notes that the interdependencies between a firm's businesses should be identified and exploited. The creation and management of linkages across products and markets is viewed as a key to long-run competitive advantage. An illustrative two-dimensional strategic field map that portrays linkages among Procter and Gamble major lines of business and value added steps is presented in Figure 3.4. In this context, the failure to consider the implications of interdependencies among the SBUs (other than their cash generation and usage links) is a major limitation of the matrix approaches to portfolio analysis.

A Static Perspective   For the most part, portfolio matrix analysis focuses on current capabilities rather than the availability of options or ease of effecting strategic changes.

A Deterministic View   The SBU's position in a portfolio matrix is assumed to determine the appropriate strategy.

Resource Allocation Guidelines   Most portfolio models tend to offer generalized strategy recommendations (e.g., invest, divest, harvest) based on a limited number of considerations. Such recommendations might have only limited managerial value and could be very myopic in terms of offering creative alternatives to top management (see, for example, Sheth, 1985).

Resource Constraints   While most discussions of the portfolio approach do not specifically preclude external sources of funds (e.g., the quest for a state of internal cash balance in the BCG approach), there seems to be an implication that the firm cannot raise funds from the capital market. This may not be true if the firm's present product-market portfolio and planned future portfolio are viewed favorably by the capital market (Wensley, 1981).

FIGURE 3.4
THE STRATEGIC FIELD MAP

PROCTER AND GAMBLE STRATEGIC FIELD MARKETS

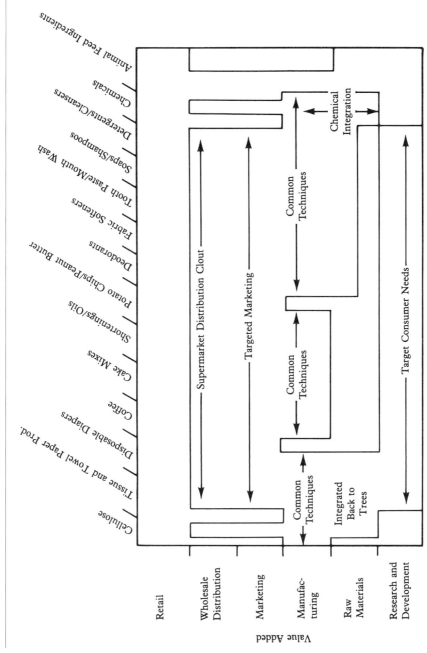

Source: Lewis, W. Walker (1982), "Strategic Marketing Planning," paper presented at the 1982 American Marketing Association Educators' Conference, IL: Chicago.

Operationalization of Dimensions Despite their wide acceptance in industry (Haspeslagh, 1982; Farquhar and Shapiro, 1983; Hamermesh, 1986), a major limitation of portfolio approaches has been the operationalization of the underlying dimensions. Since the classification of SBUs is based on specific definitions of the variables used to operationalize each of the two dimensions (e.g., market share and market growth rate in the BCG approach) and the cut-off points used to categorize these dimensions, the resulting classification may be arbitrary and questionable. For instance, Wind, Mahajan, and Swire (1983) empirically demonstrated that strategic business units can be classified quite differently depending upon the measures used to operationalize dimensions in a particular portfolio model or across various portfolio models. The authors used four different operational measures each of market growth rate and relative market share and assigned a sample of 15 PIMS businesses of a single firm to four growth-share quadrants (low growth-low share; low growth-high share; high growth-low share; and high growth-high share). They found that only three of the 15 businesses were consistently classified into the same quadrant when different measures of market growth rate and relative market share were employed. Furthermore, the use of different rules for dividing the dimensions into high and low categories resulted in contradictory classifications. Finally, as shown in Figure 3.5, the use of different portfolio models (the BCG growth-share matrix, the modified Shell matrix, and the modified life cycle portfolio matrix) also resulted in the assignment of several SBUs to different growth-share quadrants.

Overall, the findings of their research led Wind, Mahajan and Swire to conclude that when using standardized portfolio models the classification of any business into a specific portfolio position depends on four factors:

1. the operational definition of the dimensions used,
2. the rule used to divide a dimension into low and high categories,
3. the weighting of the variables constituting the composite dimensions, if composite dimensions are used, and
4. the specific portfolio model used.

The spectre of arriving at conflicting inferences as a result of using different operational measures and/or portfolio matrices raises serious concerns about how well the intended purpose underlying this exercise is served (i.e., the assignment of different missions to the various SBUs in the firm's portfolio and optimal allocation of resources among the SBUs on the basis of objective considerations). Additionally, the confidence that can be placed in cash flow projections for future years on the basis of which resource allocation are to be made to maintain a state of cash balance during the current and future years is also likely to diminish.

There might, however, be certain unintended benefits if the use of different operational measures and/or portfolio approaches leads to conflicting

FIGURE 3.5
A COMPARISON OF THE RESULTS OF THREE STANDARDIZED PORTFOLIO
MODELS

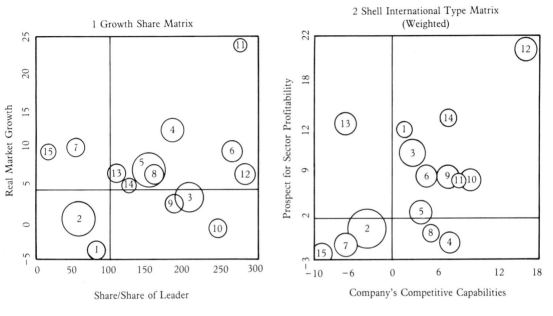

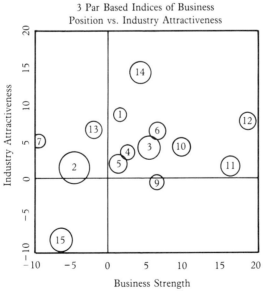

Source: Wind, Yoram, Vijay Mahajan and Donald J. Swire (1983), "An Empirical Comparison of Standardized Portfolio Models," *Journal of Marketing*, 47 (Spring), 89–99.

results. The resource allocation process and assignment of missions to the SBUs would no longer be largely based on formulas and mechanistic rules and guidelines, but would also be based on deliberation and informed reasoning by the executives involved in the strategic market planning process. For example, a SBU classified as a cash cow using one set of operational measures and as a dog using a different set of operational measures is likely to lead to productive dialogue among concerned executives on how best to manage a particular SBU rather than resort to a mechanistic decision in favor of milking the cash cow or divesting the dog.

COMPETITIVE STRATEGY MODELS

As the preceding discussion indicates, the primary focuses of the portfolio matrix approaches to strategic market planning are what SBUs a firm should retain in its portfolio, which ones should be deleted, how resources should be allocated among SBUs retained in the firm's portfolio, and what mission or objectives should be assigned to these SBUs. However, portfolio matrix approaches provide little insight into related issues, such as how a firm should compete in a given business environment, whether it should compete across all market segments or in select market segments, and how can it achieve a sustainable competitive advantage. The remainder of this chapter examines the concept of competitive advantage and provides an overview of competitive strategy matrices that address these questions.

Sustainable Competitive Advantage[4]

Competitive strategy is generally defined as an integrated set of actions taken by the firm that produce a sustainable advantage over competitors. A competitive advantage is meaningful only when three distinct conditions are met:

1. Customers perceive a consistent difference in important attributes between the firm's product or service and those of its competitors.
2. That difference is the direct consequence of a capability gap between the firm and its competitors.
3. Both the difference in important attributes and the capability gap can be expected to endure over time.

Differentiation In Important Attributes   For a firm to enjoy a competitive advantage in a product-market segment, the difference or differences between the firm and its competitors must be felt in the marketplace. That is, the differences must be reflected in some product/delivery attribute that is a key buying criterion for the market. In addition the product must be differentiated enough to win the loyalty of a significant set of buyers.

Product/Delivery Attributes   These include not only such familiar elements as price, quality, aesthetics, and functionality, but also broader attributes such as availability, consumer awareness, visibility, and after-sales service. Anything that affects customers' perceptions of the product or service, its usefulness to them, and their access to it is a product/delivery attribute. Anything that does not affect these perceptions is not.

Key Buying Criterion   To be strategically significant, an advantage must be based on the positive differentiation of an attribute that is a key buying criterion for a particular market segment and that is not offset by a negative differentiation in any other key buying criterion. In the end, competitive advantage is the result of all net differences in important product/delivery attributes, not just one factor, such as price or quality. Differences in other, less important attributes may be helpful at the margin, but they are not strategically significant. In any one product-market segment, however, only a very few criteria are likely to be important enough to serve as the basis for a meaningful competitive advantage.

Footprint In The Market   To contribute to a sustainable competitive advantage, the differences in product/delivery attributes must command the attention and loyalty of a substantial customer base. In other words, they must produce a "footprint in the market" of significant breadth and depth. *Breadth* refers to how many customers are attracted to the product above all others by the difference in product attributes? What volume do these customers purchase? *Depth* pertains to how strong a preference this difference has generated. Would minor changes in the balance of attributes cause the customers to switch?

Capability Gap   Positive differentiation in key product/delivery attributes is essential to competitive advantage. However, a differentiation that can be readily erased does not by itself confer a meaningful advantage. An advantage is durable only if competitors cannot readily imitate the firm's superior product/delivery attributes. In other words, a gap in the capability underlying the differentiation must separate the firm from its competitors; otherwise, no meaningful competitive advantage can exist. A capability gap exists when the function responsible for the differentiated product/delivery attribute is one that only the firm in question can perform, or one that competitors (given their particular limitations) could do only with maximum effort.

Capability gaps fall into four categories:

1. **Business Systems Gaps:** These result from the ability of the firm to perform individual functions more effectively than competitors and from the inability of competitors to easily follow suit.

2. **Position Gaps:** These result from prior decisions, actions, and circumstances. Reputation, consumer awareness and trust, and order backlogs, which can represent important capability gaps, are often the legacy of an earlier management generation.
3. **Regulatory/Legal Gaps:** These result from government's limiting the competitors who can perform certain activities, or the degree to which they can perform those activities.
4. **Organization or Managerial Quality Gaps:** These result from an organization's consistent ability to innovate and adapt more quickly and effectively than its competitors.

Note that only the first category, business system gaps, covers actions that are currently under the control of the firm. It should also be realized that in some instances, competitors who could close the capability gap may refrain from doing so for a variety of reasons. These include:

1. **Inadequate Potential:** A simple calculation may show competitors that the costs of closing the gap would exceed the benefits, even if the possessor of the advantage did not retaliate. For example, the danger of cannibalizing existing products may preclude an effective response.
2. **Corresponding Disadvantage:** Competitors may believe that acting to close the capability gap will open gaps elsewhere (in this or other market segments) that will more than offset the value of closing this one.
3. **Fear of Reprisal:** Even though it initially would appear worth doing so, competitors may refrain from filling the capability gap for fear of retaliatory action by the firm. "Fear of reprisal" is probably among the most common strategic situations in business, but it must be considered unstable over time, as competitors' situations and managements shift.

The Sustainability of a Competitive Advantage   There is not much value in an advantage in product/delivery attributes that do not retain their importance over time. The sustainability of competitive advantage is also a function of the durability of the capability gap that created the attractive attribute.

Pursuing the Wrong Sustainable Competitive Advantage   Although the attainment of sustainable competitive advantage is the goal of competitive strategy, it is not an end in itself, but a means to an end. A corporation is not in business just to achieve a sustainable advantage over its competitors, but to create wealth for its shareholders. Thus, actions that contribute to sustainable competitive advantage but detract from creating shareholder wealth may be good strategy in the competitive sense, but bad strategy for the corporation. Examples of pursuing the wrong sustainable competitive advantage are:

1. Low-cost capacity additions in the absence of increased industry demand.
2. Aggressive learning-curve pricing strategies that sacrifice too much current profit.

The Competitive Advantage Matrix

As shown in Figure 3.6, the size of the competitive advantage that can be achieved (small or large) and the number of ways of achieving competitive advantage (few or many) in a given industry setting constitute the key dimensions underlying the competitive advantage matrix. Differences across industries along these dimensions form the basis for distinguishing between four industry/competitive settings:

1. volume industries
2. stalemate industries
3. fragmented industries
4. specialized industries

Concerns about the validity of some of the assumptions underlying the BCG growth-share matrix prompted BCG to propose a new matrix that supposedly reflects the realities of the changed business environment. In describing the changing business environment, Lochridge noted:

"In the 1970s, high inflation coupled with low growth, increased competition in the traditional fields, added regulation, and dramatic growth in international trade again changed the rules of the game. Strategies in pursuit of market share and low-cost position alone met unexpected

FIGURE 3.6
THE COMPETITIVE ADVANTAGE MATRIX

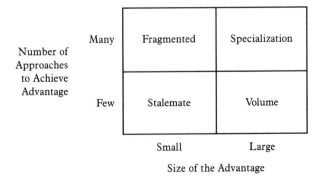

Source: Lochridge, R. K. (1981), "Strategy in the 1980s," *BCG Perspectives,* Number 241. Reprinted with permission of Boston Consulting Group, Cambridge, Massachusetts.

difficulties as segments specialists arose and multiple competitors reached economies of scale. The most successful companies achieved their success by anticipating market evolution and creating unique and defensible advantages over their competitors in the new environment" (Boston Consulting Group 1981; p. 12).

While the BCG growth-share matrix views the pursuit of high market share favorably in all industry contexts, the new BCG's competitive advantage matrix views a strategy of market share leadership as desirable in only certain industry contexts. The following hypothesized interrelationship between market share, profitability, and firm size in various industry settings (Figure 3.7) clarifies this point (Hax and Majluf, 1984).

FIGURE 3.7
UNDERLYING RELATIONSHIPS BETWEEN ROI AND MARKET
SHARE IN THE COMPETITIVE ADVANTAGE MATRIX

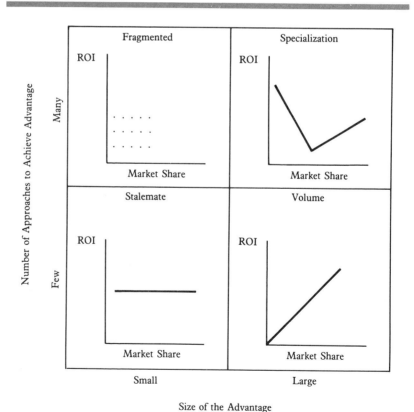

Source: Reproduced with permission from: Hax, A. C., and N. S. Majluf (1984), *Strategic Management: An Integrated Perspective*, Englewood Cliffs, N.J.: Prentice-Hall, p. 152.

Volume businesses A strategy of market share leadership and cost reduction would be meaningful in view of the close association between market share and profitability.

Stalemate businesses Profitability is not related to the size of the firm. The difference between the most profitable and least profitable firms will be relatively small.

Fragmented businesses Market share and profitability are uncorrelated. Firm profitability is independent of size.

Specialized businesses Small firms that distinguish themselves from their competitors by pursuing a focused strategy are likely to be the most profitable.

The Strategic Gameboard[6]

Buaron (1981) notes that a firm's decisions pertaining to the *scope* of competition, *mode* of competition, and the *timing* of the overall action and its individual phases should be based on a continuous analysis of the firm's strengths, vulnerabilities, and resources in relation to those of its competitors. The strategic gameboard summarized in Figure 3.8 describes the options open to a firm regarding the "scope" and "mode" components of strategy. The vertical axis represents a continuum of where-to-compete options ranging from a sharp focus on a narrow market niche to competing across an entire market. The horizontal axis represents a continuum of how-to-compete options ranging from playing entirely by the accepted rules of the industry to disregarding the rules and inventing new ones.

Buaron (1981) notes that the thinking behind same-game strategies is basically *deductive* and *analytical*. These same-game strategies treat the business and the environmental forces as givens, and a firm gains a competitive advantage by identifying the needs of a particular market or market segment and developing an approach to meet them. On the other hand, the thinking behind new-game strategies is *intuitive* and *opportunistic*. The new-game strategist explores ways to influence the environment, redefine market boundaries, or reshape market behavior to fit the company's strengths. He further notes that although most competitive battles are still being fought on one of the same-game quadrants of the strategic gameboard, truly decisive contests are being waged by a handful of companies that have chosen to try their fortunes on the new-game side.

A competitive advantage achieved through the pursuit of a new-game strategy is likely to be more enduring than those achieved through same-game strategies. Furthermore, even in the absence of an immediate competitive threat and added costs and risks, under certain conditions it may be desirable for a firm to switch from a same-game to a new-game strategy if such a move could lead to a substantial and enduring competitive advantage.

FIGURE 3.8
THE STRATEGIC GAMEBOARD

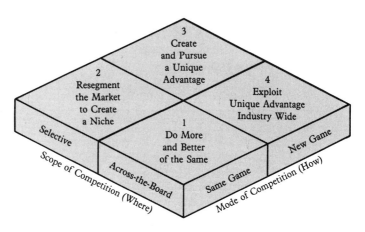

Strategy	Approach	Results
1 Across-the-board same game *Do more and better of the same* 	No attempt to change industry structure (technology, manufacturing, distribution) Similar customer segmentation	**Same key success factors** Little or no product differentiation Fierce competition, often based on price Low short-term risk, low commitment
2 Selective same game *Resegment the market to create a niche* 	No attempt to change existing industry structure No radically new way of doing business Market resegmented to exploit company strengths	**Same key success factors** Limited competition in individual niche Opportunity to focus limited resources Moderate risk and commitment
3 Selective new game *Create and pursue a unique advantage* 	Focus on small and or latent market segment Fundamental changes to business/industry structure Creation of new and/or different customers Market redefinition to suit company strengths	**New key success factors** Conventional wisdom refuted Higher profits and longer-term advantage Moderate risk; sustained commitment
4 Across-the-board new game *Exploit unique advantage industry wide* 	Focus on entire market Fundamental changes to business/industry structure Focus on competition vs. market/customers Market redefinition to suit company strengths	**New key success factors** Conventional wisdom made irrelevant Higher profits and longer-term advantage High risk; sustained major commitment

Source: Buaron, Roberto (1981), "New-Game Strategies," *McKinsey Quarterly* (Spring), 27.

Analysis of the Business System and Environment   The search for opportunities to gain a competitive advantage not only calls for in-depth analysis of competitors and customers, but also requires thoughtful analysis of the business system and the business environment. The business system comprises the sequence of steps by which companies in a given business produce and distribute goods or services. Each stage of the system presents several options to the firm, as well as a series of questions such as:

How are we doing this now?
How are our competitors doing it?
What is better about their way? About ours?
How else might it be done?
How would these options affect our competitive position?
If we changed what we are doing at this stage, how would the other stages be affected?

The *business system framework* can be used to analyze the activities of the firm and its competitors as well as to identify opportunities to gain a competitive advantage. It can be used to uncover the sources of greatest economic leverage in a business—that is, those points at which the company could erect formidable cost or investment barriers against its competitors. It is also a tool for analyzing competitors' costs and understanding the sources of a competitor's current advantage in providing lower costs or economic value to the customer. Table 3.12 provides additional insights into the stages of the business system and examples of leverage points at each stage. This tool is discussed in greater depth in chapter 7's assessment of industry competition and competitors.

Changes in the business environment, and in some cases, the absence of change, often signal new-game opportunities. A number of situations indicative of opportunities for new game strategies are summarized below (Buaron, 1981: 36–37):

1. Emergence of new manufacturing process technology in the same or a closely related industry that could potentially revolutionize cost structures.
2. A head-on battle between major competitors employing the same business system.
3. Shifts in the economic, social, or regulatory environment that could have very different effects on competitors with different business systems.
4. The emergence of substitute products or technologies that could fundamentally change the economics of important customers.
5. Major changes in raw materials or in their sources that may offer an opportunity either to gain control of the sources or seize a competitive cost advantage.

TABLE 3.12
THE BUSINESS SYSTEM AND SOURCES OF ECONOMIC LEVERAGE IN THE SYSTEM

Stages in the Business System	Technology	Product Design	Manufacturing	Marketing	Distribution	Service
	• Source • Sophistication • Patents • Product/process choices	• Function • Physical characteristics • Aesthetics • Quality	• Integration • Raw materials • Capacity • Location • Procurement • Parts production • Assembly	• Prices • Advertising/promotion • Sales force • Package • Brand	• Channels • Integration • Inventory • Warehousing • Transportation	• Warranty • Speed • Captive/independent • Prices
Leverage Points	• Lower-cost processes	• Parts standardization	• Higher-yield/lower-cost raw materials • Parts interchangeability • Extensive automation	• Volume base	• Regional market share	• Installed units base

Source: Adapted from: Exhibits II and III of Buaron, Roberto (1981), "New-Game Strategies," *McKinsey Quarterly* (Spring), 34–35.

6. Over-commitment by the market leader to a particular business system, greatly reducing his flexibility in responding to unconventional forms of competitive attack.

7. A trend towards forward and/or backward integration in the industry, which may augur a shakeout or suggest new ways to structure the business system.

8. A state of flux in industry technology, with most major participants still undecided about which way to jump.

9. New trade regulations, economic problems, or a competitive shakeout with major impacts on suppliers or customers.

10. A long-term, static, competitive equilibrium in the industry, with all participants using the same business system and similar strategies.

The Generic Strategies Matrix

The Strategic Planning Associates' generic strategies matrix (Lewis, 1982) summarized in Figure 3.9 provides an alternative perspective for competitive strategy. Here, the question of "how to compete" is viewed as contingent upon two factors—customer price sensitivity and product mystique. Product mystique pertains to real or perceived differences among competitive product offerings.

The strategic behavior patterns viewed as conducive to superior performance for businesses in these quadrants are as follows:

FIGURE 3.9
THE GENERIC STRATEGIES MATRIX

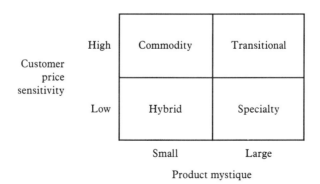

Source: Lewis, W. Walker (1982), "Strategic Marketing Planning," paper presented at the 1982 American Marketing Association Educators' Conference, IL: Chicago.

Hybrid: avoid price wars at all cost; talk quality but don't spend much on it.

Commodity: focus on volume/market share and cost reduction.

Specialty: focus on adding special value that would set the firm's product apart.

Transitional: talk price, talk quality; build financial reserves in anticipation of competitive product improvements that would make customers less sensitive to price.

TOWARDS A CONTINGENCY PERSPECTIVE OF PRODUCT-MARKET STRATEGY

Product portfolio and competitive strategy matrices reflect the shift in thinking among strategy researchers from *situation specific and universal law perspectives* to a *contingency perspective.*

Abell (1978) describes the interrelationship between four sets of variables relevant to strategy formulation—strategic variables, situational variables, company specific variables, and performance variables—very succinctly:

"*Strategies* of Type A,
in *markets/situations* of Type B,
pursued by *companies* of Type C,
will lead to *performance* of Type D" (Abell, 1978; p. 2, emphasis added).

The contingency approach in strategy literature views the appropriateness of different objectives and strategies as contingent upon the competitive setting of the business (Zeithaml, Varadarajan and Zeithaml, 1988)[7]. The competitive setting is generally defined in terms of environmental and/or organizational contingencies as shown by the following research thrusts.

1. The appropriateness of pursuing alternative strategies under various environmental contingencies. [For example, strategies for: competing in stagnant industries (Hamermesh and Silk, 1979), in declining industries (Harrigan, 1980), in hostile environments (Hall, 1980), in fragmented, mature, and declining industries (Porter, 1980), and different stages of the product life cycle (Kotler, 1988).]

2. The appropriateness of pursuing alternative strategies under various organizational contingencies. [For example, strategies for: high-market-share businesses (Bloom and Kotler, 1975), low-market-share businesses (Hamermesh, Anderson, and Harris, 1978), effective low-market-share businesses (Woo and Cooper, 1981, 1982; Woo, 1984), market leaders, challengers, followers, and nichers (Kotler, 1988).]

3. The appropriateness of pursuing alternative strategies under various environmental and organization contingencies [For example: strategies for leaders and followers in low and high-growth markets (Day, 1986; 175–178)].

A CONCLUDING NOTE

Because of their diversity, multiproduct/multibusiness organizations have certain advantages over single business firms. However, diversity often leads to a knowledge gap between the corporate level and the business level in an organization (Haspeslagh, 1982). This gap generally results because, while the corporate level has the power to commit resources, it often possesses only a superficial knowledge of each business. On the other hand, the business level managers tend to be highly knowledgeable about their respective businesses, but lack the total corporate picture that is required to make sound resource allocation decisions. The portfolio approaches to strategic market planning constitute alternative frameworks for bridging the gap that exists between the corporate and business levels in the organization. However, the potential to use portfolio approaches is not restricted to the corporate level.

The portfolio matrix approaches to strategic market planning have remained in the forefront of management practice for almost two decades. A survey of a sample of *Fortune* 1000 firms revealed that about half of those companies used portfolio matrix approaches as part of their formal planning process (Haspeslagh, 1982). Portfolio analysis aids organizations in their planning efforts in three major respects. It facilitates the allocation of resources, improves the quality of strategic thinking at the business unit level, and increases corporate management's understanding of the business units and of the overall corporate portfolio (Hamermesh, 1986).

The many facets of the portfolio approach to strategic market planning have been subjected to extensive scrutiny and their limitations brought to light. The limitations not withstanding, when used under appropriate organizational contexts (in multidivisional diversified organizations) as a diagnostic aid and *not* as a prescriptive strategy aid, they constitute valuable strategic market planning tools.

NOTES

1. Portions of this section are adapted from Hax and Majluf (1984).
2. Although not shown in Table 3.3, *nonviable* is incorporated as a sixth level along the competitive position dimension in certain matrix conceptualizations of the life-cycle portfolio matrix. Since this implies the

firm's realization that the business is nonviable, exiting through liquidation or divestiture is the only viable strategic response. The stage of industry maturity is not a relevant issue here.

3. The distinction between related diversified and unrelated diversified firms is discussed in the chapter on intensive, integrative and diversification growth strategies.

4. The discussion of competitive advantage is adapted with permission from: Coyne (1986).

5. Some writers refer to Figure 3.6 as the new BCG matrix in order to differentiate it from the BCG growth-share matrix.

6. This section is adapted with permission from Buaron (1981).

7. See Zeithaml, Varadarajan and Zeithaml (1988) for an extensive review of literature on contingency approaches in: (i) strategic management and strategic market planning; (ii) organizational theory and marketing organization design; and (iii) organizational behavior and marketing behavior.

REFERENCES

Aaker, David A. and George S. Day (1986), "The Perils of High-Growth Markets," *Strategic Management Journal*, 7 (September–October), 409–421.

Abell, Derek (1978), "Alternative Strategies for Strategy Research in Marketing," Report No. 78–100, Cambridge, MA: Marketing Science Institute.

———— and John S. Hammond (1979), *Strategic Market Planning: Problems and Analytical Approaches*, Englewood, NJ: Prentice-Hall.

Arthur D. Little, Inc. (1980), *A Management System for the 1980s*, San Francisco, CA: Arthur D. Little.

Bloom, Paul N. and Philip Kotler (1975), "Strategies for High Market Share Firms," *Harvard Business Review*, 53 (November–December), 63–72.

Boston Consulting Group (1981) *Annual Perspective*, Boston: The Boston Consulting Group.

Buaron, Roberto (1981), "New-Game Strategies," *The McKinsey Quarterly* (Spring), 24–40.

Capon, Noel and Rashi Glazer (1987), "Marketing and Technology: A Strategic Coalignment," *Journal of Marketing*, 51 (July), 1–14.

Clifford, D. K., Jr. and R. E. Cavanagh (1985), *The Winning Performance: How America's High Growth Midsize Companies Succeed*, New York: Bantam Books.

Coyne, Kevin P. (1986), "Sustainable Competitive Advantage—What It Is, What It Isn't," *Business Horizons*, 29 (January–February), 54–61.

Day, George S. (1986), *Analysis for Strategic Market Decisions*, St. Paul, MN: West.

Farquhar, Carolyn R. and Stanley J. Shapiro (1983), *Strategic Business Planning in Canada: The Use of Analytical Portfolio Models*, Ottawa: The Conference Board of Canada.

Foster, Richard N. (1981), "Linking R&D to Strategy," *The McKinsey Quarterly* (Winter), 35–52.

Hall, W. K. (1980), "Survival Strategies in a Hostile Environment," *Harvard Business Review*, 58 (September–October), 75–85.

Hamermesh, Richard G. (1986), "Making Planning Strategic," *Harvard Business Review*, 64 (July–August), 115–119.

Hamermesh, Richard G., M. J. Anderson, Jr., and J. E. Harris (1978), "Strategies for Low Market Share Businesses," *Harvard Business Review*, 56 (May–June), 95–108.

Hamermesh, R. G. and Steven B. Silk (1979), "How to Compete in Stagnant Industries," *Harvard Business Review*, 57 (September–October), 161–168.

Harrigan, K. R. (1980), *Strategies for Declining Businesses*, Lexington, MA: Heath.

Harris, John M., Robert W. Shaw, Jr., and William P. Sommers (1981), "The Strategic Management of Technology," *Outlook*, 5 (Fall/Winter), 20–26.

Haspeslagh, Philip (1982), "Portfolio Planning: Uses and Limits," *Harvard Business Review*, 60 (January–February), 58–72.

Hax, A. C. and N. S. Majluf (1984), *Strategic Management: An Integrated Perspective*, Englewood Cliffs, NJ: Prentice Hall.

Hofer, Charles W. and Dan Schendel (1978), *Strategy Formulation: Analytical Concepts*. St. Paul, Minnesota: West.

Hughes, Malcolm (1981), "Portfolio Analysis," *Long Range Planning*, 14 (February), 101–103.

Hussey, David E. (1978), "Portfolio Analysis: Practical Experience with the Directional Policy Matrix," *Long Range Planning*, 11 (August), 2–8.

Kotler, Philip (1988), *Marketing Management: Analysis, Planning, and Control*, 6th ed. Englewood Cliffs, NJ: Prentice-Hall.

Levitt, Theodore (1983), *The Marketing Imagination*, New York: The Free Press.

Lewis, W. Walker (1982), "Strategic Marketing Planning," paper presented at the American Marketing Educators' Conference, Chicago, Illinois (August).

———. (1984), "The CEO and Corporate Strategy in the Eighties: Back to Basics," *Interfaces* (January–February), 3–9.

Nemec, Jr., Joseph (1981), "Technology Commercialization: An Overview," *Outlook*, 5 (Fall/Winter), 28.

Patel, Peter and Michael Younger (1978), "A Frame of Reference for Strategy Development," *Long Range Planning*, 11 (April), 6–12.

Porter, Michael (1980), *Competitive Strategy*, New York: The Free Press.

Robinson, S. J. Q., R. E. Hichens, and D. P. Wade (1978), "The Directional Policy Matrix: Tool for Strategic Planning," *Long Range Planning*, 11 (June) 8–15.

Sheth, Jagdish N. (1985), *Winning Back Your Market*, New York: John Wiley and Sons.

Wensley, Robin (1981), "Strategic Marketing: Betas, Boxes, or Basics," *Journal of Marketing*, 45 (Summer), 173–182.

Wind, Yoram, Vijay Mahajan and Donald S. Swire (1983), "An Emperical Comparison of Standardized Portfolio Models," *Journal of Marketing*, 47 (Spring), 89–99.

Woo, Carolyn Y. (1984), "Market-share Leadership—Not Always So Good," *Harvard Business Review*, 62 (January–February), 50–54.

——— and Arnold Cooper (1981), "Strategies of Effective Low Share Businesses," *Strategic Management Journal*, 2 (July–September), 301–318.

_____ (1982), "The Surprising Case for Low Market Share," *Harvard Business Review,* 60 (November–December), 106–113.

Zeithaml, Valarie A., P. Rajan Varadarajan and Carl P. Zeithaml (1988), "The Contingency Approach: Its Foundations and Relevance to Theory Building and Research in Marketing," *European Journal of Marketing,* 22(7), 37–64.

CHAPTER 4

BUSINESS STRATEGY AND THE

EXPERIENCE CURVE

Introduction

The Experience Curve Phenomenon
The Nature of Experience Effects
Sources of Cost Reduction—Exogenous
Progress, Scale Effects and
Experience Effects
Measurement and Prediction of
Experience Effects

Strategic Implications
Achieving Competitive Cost Advantage
Anticipating Future Developments
Experience Curve Strategies and Product
Life Cycle
Pursuing an Experience-Curve-Based
Strategy: Additional Considerations
Analysis of Experience Effects of Different
Cost Components
Analysis of Shared Experiences
Technology Life Cycles: Implications For
Experience-Curve-Based Strategies
Neutralizing or Circumventing the
Experience Advantage

Caveats and Limitations
Appropriateness of Pursuing
Experience-Curve-Based-Strategies
Validity of Assumptions

A Concluding Note

References

INTRODUCTION

It has been observed in many industries and for many products that the average total cost per unit, measured in constant currency, declines by a constant percentage with every doubling of cumulative experience. Experience here refers to the total number of units of a particular product produced by the firm up to a particular point in time (i.e., the accumulated volume of production/output), and not the number of years or months since the company began making that product. Cost declines ranging from 10 to 30 percent for every doubling of cumulative experience have been observed in a variety of industries. The most striking and sustained cost declines with experience have been found in industries characterized by high labor content (ship building), complex assembly operations (aircraft), or high unit volumes of standardized products (semiconductors).

This chapter provides an overview of the experience curve phenomenon and its implications for strategic market planning. In addition, limitations of the experience curve concept and the risks inherent in pursuing an experience curve-based share building strategy are discussed.

THE EXPERIENCE CURVE PHENOMENON

The Nature of Experience Effects

The experience curve constitutes an extension of the learning curve, its historical predecessor. While the learning curve focuses on the relationship between direct labor hours or the labor component of total cost and cumulative experience, the experience curve focuses on the relationship between all value-added costs and cumulative experience.[1] Strictly speaking, the experience curve phenomenon is applicable only to value-added costs, such as manufacturing, marketing, distribution, and administration, over which the firm has control. However, by extension and approximation, the experience curve phenomenon is applicable to total costs, when:

1. the value added to the product accounts for a large percentage of the total cost of a product; and/or,
2. the costs of purchased items fall as suppliers reduce their prices with a decline in their costs due to experience.

Experience curves are usually plotted with the horizontal axis representing the cumulative units produced and the vertical axis representing the cost per unit (expressed in constant currency adjusted for inflation). Graphic representations of the relationship between cumulative experience and unit costs are shown in Figures 4.1 and 4.2. Figure 4.2 is a logarithmic

FIGURE 4.1
THE EXPERIENCE CURVE REPRESENTED ON A LINEAR SCALE

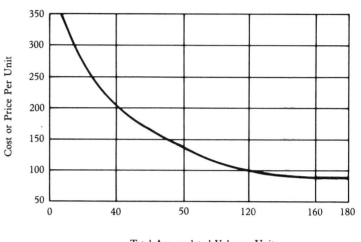

Total Accumulated Volume, Units

Source: Perspectives on Experience, p. 13, © The Boston Consulting Group, Inc. Boston, 1968.

FIGURE 4.2
THE EXPERIENCE CURVE REPRESENTED ON A LOG-LOG SCALE

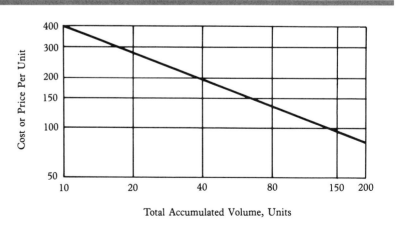

Total Accumulated Volume, Units

Source: Perspectives on Experience, p. 13, © The Boston Consulting Group, Inc. Boston, 1968.

plot of Figure 4.1. In Figure 4.2, the logarithm of cumulative experience is plotted against logarithm of the cost per unit. When unit costs decline by a constant percentage with cumulative experience, a log-log plot of cumulative experience versus cost per unit takes the form of a straight line.

Cost declines caused by experience effects may not be readily discernible if cost data are expressed in current dollars unadjusted for inflation. Hence, as indicated in Figures 4.1 and 4.2, any experience analyses must be performed in constant dollars. Implicit price deflators for a nation's gross national product published by the government are commonly used to adjust cost data for inflationary effects.[2]

The experience curve phenomenon has been examined in various contexts and at variable levels of aggregation. The following examples illustrate the types of experience curves that have been studied:

1. *Firm* level experience curves examining the behavior of *costs* and *prices* as a function of cumulative experience (Figure 4.3, A and B).
2. Experience curves examining the behavior of *costs* and *prices* as a function of experience at the *competitor* level and *industry* level (Figure 4.3, C and D).
3. Experience curves examining the behavior of *costs* with cumulative experience at the *product* level (a plot of total unit costs) versus the *components* level (plots of elements of total costs) (Figure 4.3, E).
4. Experience *cost* curves and *price* curves at the *product class* level [e.g., steam turbine generators; random access memory (RAM) chips] versus specific *product categories* (e.g., 400-MW steam turbine generators; 256K RAM chips) within the broad product class (Figure 4.3, F).

The primary focus of experience curves is the relationship between cost and experience. However, because of the nonavailability of information about competitors' costs or industry average costs, most industry level experience curves tend to be plots of average price for the industry as a whole versus experience. As shown in Figure 4.3, the measures of cumulative experience employed tend to vary across industries. The total number of units produced may not always be the most appropriate basis for measuring cumulative experience. For instance, the experience curve phenomenon may not be readily discernible if a firm manufacturing refrigerators in various sizes ranging from 2 cubic feet to 26 cubic feet of storage space were to employ the number of units produced as a measure of cumulative experience. Cumulative experience expressed in terms of cubic feet of refrigeration space may be a more appropriate measure when the experience curve phenomenon is being examined at the aggregate product level. The following examples on p. 119 of alternative bases employed for measuring cumulative experience further clarify this point.

FIGURE 4.3
SAMPLE EXPERIENCE CURVES

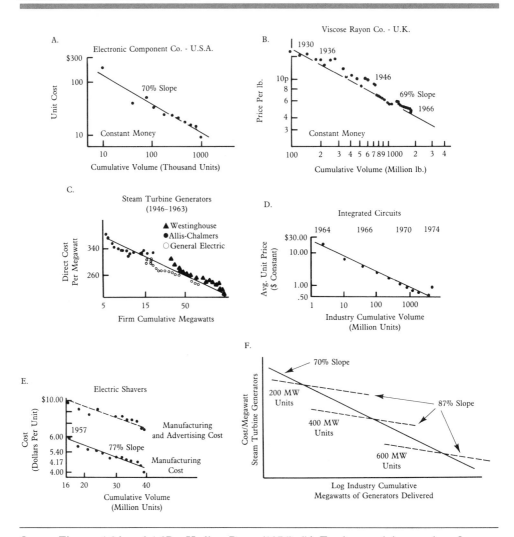

Source: Figures 4.3A and 4.3B—Hedley, Barry (1976), "A Fundamental Approach to Strategy Development," *Long Range Planning,* 9 (December), 2–11.

Figures 4.3C, 4.3D, and 4.3E—Boston Consulting Group, *Perspectives on Experience,* Boston, Massachusetts.

Figure 4.3F—Day, George S. and David B. Montgomery (1983), "Diagnosing The Experience Curve," *Journal of Marketing,* 47 (Spring), 44–58.

Product/Service	Measure of Cumulative Experience
Integrated circuits	Units
Steam turbine generators	Megawatts
Broiler chickens	Live weight pounds
Viscose rayon	Pounds
Primary magnesium	Short tons
Long-distance telephone service	Long-distance conversations
Life insurance	Billion policy years
Rail transportation	Billion traffic units

Studies encompassing products in the chemicals, petrochemicals, paper, steel, electronics, knit products, mechanical goods, and other industries document cost and price experience curves. These studies also suggest that the cost experience curve concept is fairly robust with respect to variations in factor input conditions.[3]

Sources of Cost Reduction: Exogenous Progress, Scale Effects and Experience Effects[4]

Experience curve strategies are particularly appropriate when the demand for a product is sensitive to price. If price is the basis for competition, a key question to be addressed is whether a firm can achieve major cost reductions and establish a competitive cost advantage by riding down the experience curve (Amit, 1986). In most industries, exogenous progress, economies of scale, and basic improvements arising from cumulated output (experience effects) constitute the three major sources of cost reduction.

Exogenous progress refers to cost reductions that are the result of: (1) advances in general technical knowledge; (2) inputs from suppliers and customers; and (3) feedback from customers. In most instances, all industry participants are likely to benefit from these sources of cost reduction. The ability of a firm to achieve a competitive cost advantage along this dimension depends on its bargaining power with suppliers and buyers (Ghemawat, 1985). For instance, a firm's ability to integrate backwards improves its bargaining power vis-a-vis its suppliers. Chapter 7 provides a more detailed discussion of how competitive forces such as the bargaining power of suppliers and customers influence a firm's competitive strategy.

The *scale effect* refers to the potential of large businesses to operate at a lower unit cost than their smaller counterparts can. Economies of scale are generally reflected in a number of cost elements, such as capital costs, operating costs, purchased raw material costs, transportation and storage costs, marketing expenditures, and R&D. However, the most substantial effects of scale are generally reflected in the capital cost per unit of installed capacity, and the operating cost per unit of output (Abell and Hammond, 1979). Successfully achieving a competitive cost advantage through investments in scale economies often depends on the extent to which competitors are unwilling to invest in comparable, large, efficient facilities. Otherwise, overcapacity at the industry level could lead to a competitive gridlock (Ghemawat, 1985).

Experience effects or cost reductions achieved by the firm as a result of *learning from accumulated output* represents the third major source of cost reduction. Since most cost reductions achieved in this area remain proprietary to the firm, they tend to be the most enduring source of competitive cost advantages. However, such cost reductions do not occur naturally. They result from substantial and concerted efforts by firms to lower costs by exploiting various potential sources of cost reduction. These sources include:

1. *Labor Efficiency*   As workers repeat a particular production task, they become more dexterous and learn improvements and shortcuts that increase their collective efficiency. The greater the number of worker-based operations, the greater the amount of learning that can accrue from experience. This learning effect goes beyond the labor directly involved in manufacturing. Maintenance personnel, supervisors, and persons in other line and staff manufacturing positions also increase their productivity, as do people in marketing, sales, administration, and other functions. For instance, a survey of 13,000 new products launched by 700 companies found that the cost of introduction of new products declined along a 71 percent experience curve slope (Booz, Allen, and Hamilton, 1982).

2. *Work Specialization and Methods Improvements*   Specialization increases worker proficiency at a given task. For instance, when two workers who formerly did both parts of a two-stage operation each specialize in a single stage, they tend to become more efficient in performing the more specialized task. Redesigning work operation methods can also result in greater efficiency.

3. *New Production Processes*   Process innovations and improvements can be an important source of cost reductions, especially in capital-intensive industries. The low-labor-content semiconductor industry, for instance, achieves experience curves of 70 to 80 percent from improved production technology by devoting a large percentage of its research and development to process improvements. Similar process improvements have been observed in refineries, nuclear power plants, and steel mills.

4. *Getting Better Performance from Production Equipment*   When first designed, a piece of production equipment may have a conservatively rated output. Experience may reveal innovative ways of increasing its output.

5. *Changes in the Resource Mix*   As experience accumulates, a producer can often incorporate different or less expensive resources in the

operation. For instance, less skilled (lower cost) workers can replace skilled (higher cost) workers or automation can replace labor.

6. *Product Standardization* Standardization allows the replication of tasks necessary for worker learning. A case in point was the pursuit of a strategy of deliberate standardization in the production of the Ford Model T. As a result, from 1909 to 1923, the model's price was repeatedly reduced following an 85 percent experience curve (Abernathy and Wayne, 1974). Even when flexibility and/or a wider product line are important marketing considerations, standardization can be achieved by modularization. For example, by making just a few types of engines, transmissions, chassis, seats, and body styles, an auto manufacturer can achieve experience effects arising from specialization in each part. These parts in turn can be assembled into a wide variety of models. This point is further elaborated on in a later section focusing on shared experience.

7. *Product Redesign* As experience is gained with a product, both the manufacturer and customers gain a clearer understanding of its performance requirements. This understanding allows the product to be redesigned to conserve material, greater efficiency to be incorporated in its manufacture, and less costly materials and resources to be substituted for more costly ones, while at the same time improving performance. The new designs and substitution of plastic, synthetic fiber, and rubber for leather in ski boots are examples of this.

Measurement and Prediction of Experience Effects

The strategic value of the experience curve concept arises because historic cost declines resulting from experience effects are *measurable* and future cost reductions achievable for specific amounts of cumulative experience are *predictable*. The projected cost of a future unit of output resulting from the experience curve effect can be estimated using a simple negative exponential relationship.[5]

Let,

E_B denote base experience or cumulative output to date,

C_B denote the base cost or cost of unit E_B in constant currency (i.e., adjusted for inflation), and

E_P denote projected experience or projected cumulative output at a future point in time.

Given the above, the *projected cost* C_P (in constant currency) of unit E_P can be estimated by using the experience curve formula

$$\frac{\text{Projected}}{\text{Cost}} = \text{Base cost} \left(\frac{\text{Projected experience}}{\text{Base experience}}\right)^{-b} \qquad (1)$$

where,

b denotes the elasticity coefficient of the experience function $(0 < b < 1)$ and reflects the elasticity of unit costs with respect to cumulative output.

In symbolic notation,

$$C_P = C_B \left(\frac{E_P}{E_B}\right)^{-b} \tag{2}$$

If, in the above equation, E_P/E_B is 2, and b is 0.235, then C_P will be equal to $[C_B (0.85)]$. That is, the projected cost of the future unit of output C_P, (when cumulative experience is doubled) will be equal to 85 percent of the cost of unit C_B.

To estimate the cost of a future unit of output using the above equation, the firm has to first examine historical cost data and analyze the past patterns of cost decline with cumulative experience. Based on such analysis, the percentage decline in costs with the accumulation of experience and the elasticity coefficient of the experience function b can be computed. By substituting the value of the elasticity coefficient in Equation 1, the projected cost of a future unit of output can be estimated. Tables of correspondence summarizing the interrelationship between the percentage decline in cost realized with every doubling of cumulative experience, the implied slope of the experience curve, and the elasticity coefficient of experience function b are published in a number of sources (Boston Consulting Group, 1972; Sallenave, 1976). Table 4.1 is illustrative of the information on this topic that is readily available.

TABLE 4.1
VALUE OF EXPERIENCE CURVE EXPONENT FOR
VARIOUS RATES OF COST DECLINE

Observed cost decline in percent with doubling of cumulative experience (C)	0	5	10	15	20	25	30
Slope of experience curve (M)	1.00	0.95	0.90	0.85	0.80	0.75	0.70
Elasticity coefficient of the experience function (b)	0	0.074	0.152	0.234	0.322	0.450	0.515

Source: Adapted from Sallanave, J. P. (1976; p. 18), *Experience Analysis for Industrial Planning*, Lexington, Mass.: Lexington Books.

STRATEGIC IMPLICATIONS

The strategic implications of the slope of the experience curve and rate of accumulation of experience can be summarized as follows:

Slope of Experience Curve   All things being equal, a firm that fails to reduce costs along an experience curve *slope* that is at least equivalent to that achieved by its competitors will eventually find itself in a position of competitive cost disadvantage.

Rate of Experience Accumulation   All things being equal, a firm that fails to accumulate experience at least as rapidly as its competitors will find itself in a position of competitive cost disadvantage.

Firms unable to achieve a position of competitive cost advantage by riding down the experience curve should explore other sources of competitive advantage (Hedley, 1976).

Achieving Competitive Cost Advantage

If the selling price is assumed to be exogenous (i.e., all competitors sell at a uniform, market-determined price), then the firm with the greatest cumulative experience will have the lowest unit costs and the highest profit margin (see Figure 4.4). All things being equal, for a firm competing to achieve a cost advantage over its competitors (i.e., become the lowest cost producer), it must accumulate experience faster than its industry competitors. The key to accumulating experience faster than competitors is pursuing an aggressive market-share-building strategy.[6]

FIGURE 4.4
PROFIT MARGIN IMPLICATIONS OF
CUMULATIVE EXPERIENCE DIFFERENTIALS

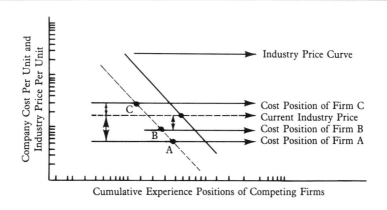

Source: Adapted from "The Experience Curve Reviewed: I The Concept" (1973), *Perspectives*, No. 124, Boston: The Boston Consulting Group.

In an evolving industry where experience effects are pronounced and price is a major determinant of industry demand, by pursuing an aggressive market share building strategy and promoting its product at a price lower than its current costs as well as below its competitors' prices, a firm may place itself in a position to accumulate experience faster than its competitors. Even though a firm's prices may initially be lower than its costs, with the accumulation of experience, costs will fall below price. Texas Instruments (TI) reportedly used this approach to achieve a dominant position in the markets for electronic pocket calculators and semiconductors. This strategy led TI to register major share gains in both markets and achieve a substantial reduction in unit costs to levels below those of its prices. At a unit price of several hundred dollars, the size of the market for electronic pocket calculators was relatively small. However, at a price below $100, a mass consumer market emerged for the product, supplanting the relatively small industrial and institutional market that existed before.

A number of other companies have been equally successful in pursuing experience-curve-based strategies. For instance, in the soft contact lens industry, Bausch & Lomb successfully capitalized on the experience curve concept by investing in automation, computerized lens design, and capacity expansion. The firm was not only in a position to realize substantially higher gross margins relative to its competitors, but also increase its market share from 55 to 65 percent (Ghemawat, 1985). Other firms that are reported to have been particularly successful in exploiting the experience curve concept include Black & Decker (power tools), Briggs & Stratton (small engines), Emerson Electric (electric motors), and DuPont (chemicals).

There are also case histories of failed experience-curve-based strategies. For instance, Douglas Aircraft Co. fixed prices for the DC-9 on the basis of an 85% experience curve. When the hoped-for cost reductions failed to materialize, its losses forced Douglas' acquisition by the McDonnell Company (Mecklin, 1966). In the titanium dioxide industry, DuPont, hoping to capitalize on the experience curve, decided to preempt competitors by investing $410 million over a seven-year period. Unfortunately, industry capacity utilization fell from 88 to 64 percent and DuPont's return on sales dropped from 7.5 percent to less than 4.0 percent (Ghemawat, 1985).

Anticipating Future Developments[7]

Timely strategic actions are made possible when experience curves are used as an early warning system. This point is evident in Figure 4.5, which shows the cost and price experience curves of a polyester fiber manufacturer. Based on the fact that industry prices were declining on a 75 percent curve while the firm's costs were declining on an 86 percent curve, the plant's management should have recognized well ahead of time that the cost and price experience curves were converging rapidly. Only in 1980, when the plant failed to make any profit, did the management embark on a cost reduction program. Unfortunately, around this time, there was a slowdown in the demand for the product and the plant could neither operate at full capacity nor achieve any reduction in unit costs. The plant was ultimately closed in 1983.

As pointed out by Sallenave (1985), the effective use of experience curve analysis could have helped the firm anticipate future developments and evaluate the merits of alternative courses of action such as:

1. investing in plant capacity expansion to accumulate experience faster and drive the unit cost down,
2. retooling and/or improving the production process to operate on a 75 percent cost slope (i.e., operating on a cost curve paralleling the price curve),
3. exiting from the commodity type regular polyester fiber market and focusing on special-purpose polyester fibers that command a higher price,
4. selling the plant to another firm while still profitable, and
5. converting the plant to the manufacture of a different product.

FIGURE 4.5
USING EXPERIENCE CURVES AS AN EARLY WARNING SYSTEM

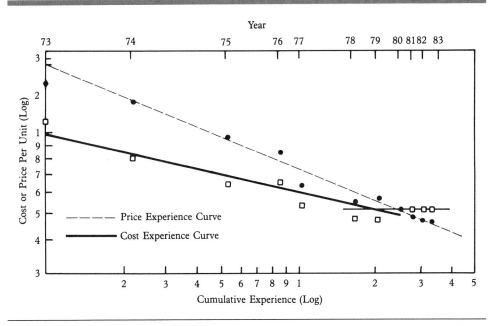

Source: Sallenave, J. P. (1985), "The Use and Abuse of Experience Curves," *Long Range Planning*, 18 (January–February), 64–72.

Experience Curve Strategies and Product Life Cycle

Experience curve strategies offer a greater prospect for achieving a competitive cost advantage if pursued during the earlier stages of the product life cycle, as opposed to during later stages. By the time a product reaches the mature stage, nearly all predictable, experience-related cost reductions should have been achieved. Moreover, in high-growth markets, accumulated experience doubles far more rapidly than it does in mature markets. As a result, costs decline substantially for all producers during periods with a high market growth rate, but decline even more rapidly for competitors who are rapidly gaining market share. This logic suggests that early investments in building market share in high-growth markets may be desirable.[8] Table 4.2 provides additional insights into the importance of accumulating experience faster than competitors in industries with pronounced experience effects. The table shows the time frame within which various doublings will occur for different growth rates in production. Note that with a zero growth rate in production, it would take 16 months for the fourth doubling of cumulative experience to occur. The comparable

TABLE 4.2
TIME REQUIRED TO ACCUMULATE VARYING LEVELS OF EXPERIENCE FOR DIFFERENT GROWTH RATES

Month	Monthly Output for 0% Growth Rate in Production	Cumulative Experience	Months Required for Various Doublings of Cumulative Experience	Monthly Output for 0% Growth Rate in Production	Cumulative Experience
1	1000	1000		1000	1000
2	1000	2000	1st doubling: 2 months	1100	2100
3	1000	3000		1210	3310
4	1000	4000	2nd doubling: 4 months	1331	4641
5	1000	5000		1464	6105
6	1000	6000		1611	7716
7	1000	7000		1772	9488
8	1000	8000	3rd doubling: 8 months	1949	11437
9	1000	9000		2144	13581
10	1000	10000		2358	15939
11	1000	11000			
12	1000	12000			
13	1000	13000			
14	1000	14000			
15	1000	15000			
16	1000	16000	4th doubling: 16 months		

*First month's volume is treated as base point.

number for production growth rates of 10 percent and 20 percent are 10.04 months and 7.85 months, respectively.

The behavior of costs and prices over the major stages of the product life cycle for products demonstrating pronounced experience effects is illustrated in Figure 4.6. During the early *introductory stage,* prices are typically held below current costs in anticipation of lower future costs that should result from demand stimulation. Experience-based cost declines will eventually lead to positive profit margins during the latter part of the introductory stage. The *growth stage* is generally characterized by the market leader holding a price umbrella over high-cost producers entering the market and building share. In effect, the market leader is trading future market share for current profits. The *industry shake-out stage* is characterized by an observable sharp break in the price trend. When one of the competitors believes its interest will best be served by lowering the price faster than industry costs are declining and acts accordingly, an industry shake-out results, leading to the exit of marginal competitors. Although the industry shake-out stage is characterized by a sharp break in the price trend, prices cannot decline faster than costs indefinitely. The *maturity*

Months Required for Various Doublings of Cumulative Experience	Monthly Output for 20% Growth Rate in Production	Cumulative Experience	Months Required for Various Doublings of Cumulative Experience
	1000	1000	
1st doubling: 1.92 months	1200	2200	1st doubling: 1.89 months
	1440	3640	2nd doubling: 3.22 months
2nd doubling: 3.54 months	1728	5368	
	2074	7442	3rd doubling: 5.23 months
3rd doubling: 6.20 months	2488	9930	
	2986	12916	
	3583	16499	4th doubling: 7.85 months
4th doubling: 10.04 months			

FIGURE 4.6
PRODUCT LIFE CYCLE STAGES AND THE
INDUSTRY PRICE EXPERIENCE CURVE

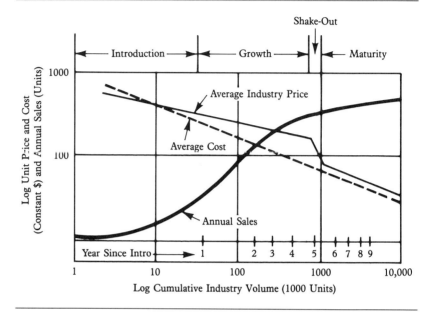

Source: Day, George S. and David B. Montgomery (1983), "Diagnosing the Experience Curve," *Journal of Marketing*, 47 (Spring), p. 51.

stage is characterized by the return of profit margins to normal levels and prices that parallel the industry cost experience curve all along (Boston Consulting Group, 1972; Abell and Hammond, 1979; Day and Montgomery, 1983).

Pursuing an Experience Curve-Based Strategy: Additional Considerations

The long-term viability of pursuing a share-building strategy based on the experience curve concept, as well as forecasting future costs, calls for a number of additional considerations. Some of the more important analytical considerations involve: (1) analyzing the experience curves for different cost components; (2) searching for, analyzing, and exploiting opportunities for shared experience; and (3) understanding the implications of technology life cycles for experience-curve-based strategies.

Analysis of Experience Effects for Different Cost Components

The cost of an individual product declines because of the existence of the experience effect for the cost components (e.g., metal stamping, molding parts, assembly, packaging, servicing, etc.) that combine to make the product (Abell and Hammond, 1979). In effect, the experience curve of the finished product is the additive result of the experience curves of the major cost components. However, at any point in time, differences might exist across cost components with respect to the cumulative experience acquired by the firm. Furthermore, there might be differences in the experience curve slopes of the major cost components. Under these circumstances, the experience curve at the product level would be the result of the complex interactions of the experience curves of its cost components. These complex interactions may not be readily discernible from an analysis of a log-log plot of the overall experience at the product level.

The percentage of total costs accounted for by various cost components vary based on various amounts of cumulative experience at the product level. This may not be evident from an examination of the aggregate product level experience curve, but could have far-reaching implications for the sustainability of a firm's competitive cost advantage. For example, as shown in Table 4.3, in the beginning stages, cost components A, B, and C account for 70 percent, 20 percent, and 10 percent, respectively, of the total unit cost of $100. When the firm's experience with the product reaches 10,000 units, components A, B, and C account for 28 percent, 44 percent, and 27 percent, respectively, of the total unit cost of $36.34. Finally, when the firm's experience with the product reaches 1,000,000 units, components A, B, and C account for 11 percent, 34 percent, and 53 percent, respectively, of the total unit cost of $13.00. Note that while component A accounts for the largest percentage of total unit cost during the initial stages, component C accounts for the largest percentage of total unit cost during later stages. This implies that the firm that is likely to enjoy a long-term competitive cost advantage will be the one with the greatest cumulative experience for cost component C. A firm is likely to fall into an experience trap if its share-building strategy for the product is based on its competitive cost advantage with respect of cost component A.

Analysis of Shared Experiences

Table 4.3 further shows that when the firm's experience with the product is 100 units, its experience with cost components A, B, and C is 100 units, 10,100 units, and 1,000,200 units, respectively. The differences in experience suggest that component A is unique to the product in question, component B is common to some of the products made by the firm, and component C is common to a number of products made by the firm. This illustration is one of the most common manifestations of shared experience, in which certain components are common to two or more products made by the firm.

Shared experience has implications for the addition of new products to the firm's product-mix, the deletion of products from its present product-mix, and proposed market share strategies (build, maintain, or harvest). New products can benefit from shared experiences to the extent that they share cost components with the present products in the firm's product-

TABLE 4.3
ABSOLUTE AND PERCENT OF TOTAL COST ACCOUNTED FOR BY COST
COMPONENTS FOR VARIOUS LEVELS OF CUMULATIVE EXPERIENCE

| | *Cost Component* | | | | |
| | *A(75 Percent Curve; 1 Item Per Unit)* | | | *B(80 Percent Curve;* | |
Experience With The Product	Component Experience	Cost Per Unit	Percent of Total Unit Cost	Component Experience	Cost Per Unit
100 Units	100	$70.00	70.0%	10,100	$20.00
10,000 Units	10,000	10.35	28.4%	20,000	16.05
1,000,000 Units	1,000,000	1.53	11.7%	1,010,000	4.53

Source: Adapted from Abell, D. F., and J. B. Hammond (1979), *Strategic Market Planning: Problems and Analytical Approaches*, Englewood Cliffs, NJ: Prentice-Hall, p. 126.

mix. Some cost advantages enjoyed by products retained in the firm's product-mix would be lost if products that were deleted shared certain cost components with products in the former group. The case histories that follow provide additional insights into the importance of searching for, analyzing, and/or exploiting shared costs from the standpoint of product additions and deletions.

1. Consider a company that makes three products—an electric pencil sharpener, a fan, and a drill.[9] The pencil sharpener holds the leading share of its market, the fan has the third-largest share in its market, and the drill ranks a distant fourth in a very large market. Each of the three products has as its principal component an electrical motor representing about 30% of the manufactured cost. For this firm, exiting from the electric drill market in view of its low market share would imply cutting back on the total production of electric motors, thereby slowing the progress of sharpeners and fans down their respective experience curves, and possibly imperiling their market shares (Kiechel, 1981). On the other hand, adding a fourth electrical product to the firm's portfolio that would also use the electric motor as its principal component could speed the progress of the sharpeners, fans, and drills down their respective experience curves.

2. An examination of Chrysler Corporation's product line (as of 1987) provides further insight into the importance of exploiting opportunities for cost reduction through shared experience.[10] Since 1980, all new car models introduced by the company were variations on a single theme: the K car first marketed under the names Dodge Aries and Plymouth Reliant. Working with one basic engine, transmission, and underbody structure, the company introduced a variety of new models distinguished by their external appearance and market positioning. These cars ranged in size from the compact Dodge Shadow/

1 Item Per Unit)	C(80 Percent Curve; 1 Item Per Unit)			
Percent of Total Unit Cost	Component Experience	Cost Per Unit	Percent of Total Unit Cost	Total Unit Cost
20.0%	1,000,200	$10.00	10.0%	$100.00
44.2%	1,020,000	9.94	27.4%	36.34
34.6%	3,000,000	7.02	53.7%	13.08

Plymouth Sundance to the full-size Chrysler New Yorker Turbo/ Dodge Dynasty. The K–car basic chassis was also the foundation for its Dodge Daytona, Dodge 600, Chrysler LeBaron, and Chrysler LeBaron GTS cars, Dodge Caravan/Plymouth Voyager minivans, Dodge Grand Caravan/Plymouth Grand Voyager stretch minivans, Chrysler Imperial luxury limo car, and Chrysler TC by Maserati, a sporty convertible. Although some of these models contained modifications such as a shortened basic chassis to accommodate compacts, and a lengthened chassis for bigger cars, the incremental costs of such modifications were much less than the cost of developing an altogether new chassis for new car models.

However, it should be noted that if this shared components strategy is extended beyond realistic limits, the company might face the risk that customers will perceive the models as lacking in distinctiveness. For instance, in the face of technologically superior competitive offerings, Chrysler's LeBaron Coupe (a K car variant) has been unable to make inroads into the high-price, high-image, high-margin market segment despite its sleek styling. During the early eighties, Chrysler's precarious financial situation led it to stick with the K car and develop variants of the K car distinguished by body styling and market positioning. Critics contend that even after the firm became profitable it failed to invest in developing distinctively new cars, but chose instead, to spend its earnings on stock buybacks and acquisitions. After four years of sales increases, Chrysler's car sales fell 22.8 percent in 1987.

Technology Life Cycles: Implications for Experience-Curve-Based Strategies[11]

The emerging literature on technology life cycles has led to refinements in experience curve logic (Foster, 1982; Kiechel, 1981). Technology life cycle graphs chart the product and process performance histories of successive technologies as a function of the R&D effort in terms of R&D man-hours invested or dollars spent. The life cycles of successive technologies are predicted to reveal a pattern similar to that depicted in slanted S-shaped curves (Figure 4.7). The focus here is not on the life cycle of a particular technology, but the life cycles of a family of successive technologies. The lower left hand end of the S-curves implies that, after the onset of an R&D effort designed to develop a particular technology, a substantial amount of effort produces only modest gains in performance. The vertical portion of the curve represents a phase characterized by major breakthroughs and substantial advances in product and process performance as a result of the R&D effort. The right hand end of the curve indicates that the limits of a particular technology may have been reached. The positioning of the lower left hand portions of the curves representing technologies A and B in Figure 4.7 implies that the initial product and process performance of the newer technology is at a higher level than that of its predecessor. For a period of time, the competing technologies might co-exist. However, major product and process performance breakthroughs resulting from the R&D effort invested in the newer technology might ultimately shift the balance in favor of the new technology.

The implications of technological change for an experience curve-based strategy is clear. If a firm with the largest cumulative experience and market share were to show a single-minded commitment to a particular technology, it would face the risk of losing its competitive cost advantage owing to the sharp drop in costs that may be achieved by competitors employing a new technology. To guard against such a scenario, it is imperative for the market leader to gain a foothold in the new technology, invest in its development, and shift to the new technology at an appropriate time. A case in point is tire cords, which were made first from cotton, followed by rayon, nylon, and polyester, respectively. Each succeeding technology eventually outperformed its predecessor and firms that championed the earlier technologies lost market leadership to the newcomers. Oblivious to the limits of varying technologies, by trying to champion its own technology rather than moving into a more promising alternative, each successive leader is reported to have made it easier for challengers to enter the tire cord businesses (Foster, 1982).

Neutralizing or Circumventing the Experience Advantage

Firms at a cost disadvantage in relation to the industry leader (the firm with the largest cumulative experience and market share) need not be content with lower profit margins. Rather than riding the same experience curve as the rest of the industry including the leader, a firm may be in a position to create a new, steeper experience curve and ultimately neutralize the cost advantage of the industry leader through technological innovation.

FIGURE 4.7
TECHNOLOGY LIFE CYCLES

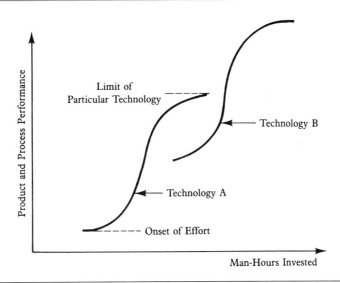

Source: Richard N. Foster. (1982), "A Call for Vision in Managing Technology," *McKinsey Quarterly* (Summer) 26–36.

Differentiation is another alternative available to a firm at a cost disadvantage. Rather than attempting to compete on a price basis with the industry leader, or being content with lower profit margins than what the industry leader enjoys, a firm could explore the feasibility of incorporating distinctive features into its products for which a segment of the market is prepared to pay a higher price. The following comparison of the strategic profiles of Texas Instruments and Hewlett Packard in the electronics industry illustrates the viability of both cost leadership and differentiation strategies (Kotler, 1988).

Texas Instruments (Cost Leadership)	Hewlett-Packard (Differentiation)
Competitive advantage in large standard markets based on long-run cost position	Competitive advantage in selected small markets based on unique, high-value products
High volume/low price	High value/high price
Rapid growth	Controlled growth
Experience curve cost driven	Delivery and quality oriented
High vertical integration	Limited vertical integration

The relative merits of pursuing a cost leadership strategy versus a differentiation strategy are further elaborated in Box 4.1.

BOX **4.1**

THE EXPERIENCE CURVE LOGIC VERSUS THE
PIMS* LOGIC

A central tenet of the experience curve approach is the use
of low prices (initially even below cost) as a key to building market share.
In effect, accumulating experience through the pursuit of a share-building
strategy is viewed as a key to lowering costs, achieving a position of
sustainable competitive cost advantage, and enjoying long-term profitability.
However, Peters and Austin (1985) caution that if the firm's offering were
to lack an acceptable level of service and quality, it might be vulnerable to
attack from a competitor's offering of superior quality. In the face of such an
attack, the firm's competitive advantage might not be sustainable.

In contrast, based on an analysis of businesses in the PIMS data base,
the Strategic Planning Institute advocates the pursuit of a quality oriented
approach to building market share and achieving sustainable competitive
advantage (Buzzell and Gale, 1987). The logic underlying the PIMS position
is that, by achieving a relative perceived product quality advantage over that
of its competitors, a business can gain market share. In turn, gains in
market share are expected to lead to a lowering of costs owing to experience
effects and economies of scale. Superior quality will also provide a business
with the leverage to price its offering at a level higher than the industry
average. The relatively higher prices and relatively lower costs are viewed
as the key to achieving relatively higher profit margins over the long-term.

In their critique of experience curve based strategies, Peters and Austin
(1985) note that experience curve logic and PIMS logic are diametrically
opposed from a cause-and-effect standpoint. They characterize the
experience curve approach as "buying your way in via heavy discounting"
and the PIMS approach as "earning your way in via quality and service."
Despite such criticism of experience curve logic, both cost leadership and
differentiation are viable strategies in a number of industries.

*PIMS—Profit Impact of Market Strategy. Chapter 5 presents a detailed
discussion on the findings of PIMS data based research.
Source: Buzzell, Robert D. and Bradley T. Gale (1987), *The PIMS Principles:
Linking Strategy to Performance*, New York: Free Press.
Peters, Tom and Nancy Austin (1985), *A Passion for Excellence*, New York:
Random House.

CAVEATS AND LIMITATIONS

The Appropriateness of Pursuing
Experience-Curve-Based Strategies

Misuse or misapplication of the experience curve concept has often been the root cause of disillusionment with experience-curve-based strategies (Aaker, 1988; Henderson, 1984; Sallenave, 1985). For instance, in reference to the BCG competitive advantage matrix (see Figure 3.7), an experience-curve-based competitive cost advantage may not be relevant in *fragmented industries* (e.g., restaurants) or *specialization industries* (e.g., magazines), since price is less often a dominant consideration in purchasing decisions in these industries. This could also be true of *stalemate industries* (c.g., steel) in which price is a dominant purchase criterion, but there is little prospect of an experience-curve-based cost advantage. The experience curve phenomenon is most directly applicable to firms competing in commodity-based, *volume-sensitive industries* in which low cost is one of the few potential sources of sustainable competitive advantage (Aaker, 1988). If price is not the basis for competition in a particular market, then investing in cost leadership to become a price leader may not be as important as alternative investments in such areas as R&D to achieve technological leadership (Amit, 1986).

What, then, are useful guidelines for embarking on an experience-curve-based strategy? Ghemawat (1985) cautions that embarking on an experience-curve-based strategy should be based on answers to the following questions, rather than simple prescriptions.

1. Does the industry exhibit a significant experience curve effect?
2. Is demand price sensitive?
3. Do the returns from an experience-curve-based strategy justify the risks of technological obsolescence?
4. Is there a significant antitrust risk?
5. How much strategic leverage does an experience-curve-based strategy offer?
6. How do the financial resources of the firm compare with those of competitors who are either currently following an experience-curve-based strategy or contemplating the pursuit of such a strategy?
7. What are the potential sources of cost reduction on which an experience-curve-based strategy can be built? Would these reductions be proprietary to the company?

Validity of Assumptions

It is often implicitly assumed in experience curve analysis that: (1) all competitors have the same overhead structures; (2) all firms ride the same experience curves; and (3) a firm's position on the industry experience curve is determined by its market share position. Hence, market share dominance is viewed as an indicator of the firm's relative cost position and as a proxy for relative profit performance. This line of reasoning suffers from several shortcomings:

1. It tends to overlook the possibility that competing firms may be in a position to ride a steeper experience curve (i.e., achieve greater cost reductions) through technological innovations.
2. Likewise, the possibility that competing firms may be in a position to shift to a lower (but parallel) experience curve by shifting production to low labor cost countries tends to be ignored (Day, 1977).
3. When cost reductions can be achieved primarily from economies of scale by investing in more efficient, automated facilities and through vertical integration, cumulative experience may not be the key to achieving a position of competitive cost advantage. In these situations, a new entrant to the market may be more efficient than more experienced producers (Day and Montgomery, 1983).

The globalization of competition has also increased the importance of other factors relative to cumulative experience as determinants of relative costs. These factors include:

1. the firm's relative effectiveness in statistical process control,
2. its relative productivity,
3. its international comparative advantage (the relative costs of wages, materials, energy, and capital), and
4. the inventory and logistics costs associated with the proliferation of models and options (Buzzell and Gale, 1987).

A CONCLUDING NOTE

The use of the experience curve phenomenon as an element in a firm's strategy is based on the following logic. Average costs decline with cumulative experience. Therefore, a firm may be in a position to establish a competitive cost advantage by accumulating experience faster than its competitors can. If the realized unit cost reductions are followed by a corresponding cut in prices, the firm may be able to rapidly penetrate the market and thus gain market share. To the extent that a firm is successful in increasing its market share by pursuing an experience-curve-based strategy, its profits will rise (Amit, 1986).

An experience-curve-based strategy might not, however, be the appropriate course to pursue if factors other than low price are of greater importance to buyers. While certain product categories are characterized by a high level of price competition (e.g., microprocessor chips), this is not the case in other product categories (e.g., watches, cosmetics). For example, an experience-curve-based strategy that benefited Texas Instruments in the case of electronic pocket calculators failed badly in the case of digital watches. Perhaps most consumers had a utilitarian outlook in their purchase of calculators, but with digital watches, functional as well as aesthetic attributes played an important role.

Sometimes firms, owing to their single-minded focus on reducing costs, may be sowing the seeds for their own failure. Overzealousness in building market share and accumulating experience faster than competitors might make a firm oblivious to the limitations of experience-curve-based market share strategies. An obsession with reaping the benefits of experience curve cost economies can result in a strategic posture in the marketplace that presents a severe disadvantage when significant shifts in market response occur (Wensley, 1981). The limits of experience-curve-based strategies (i.e., strategies based on achieving a competitive cost advantage) are often reached not because a firm has exhausted all possible means for reducing costs, but rather, are determined by the market's demand for product change, the rate of technological innovation in the industry, and competitors' abilities to use product performance as the basis for competition (Abernathy and Wayne, 1974).

NOTES

1. The concept of the learning curve and its relevance and limitations have been extensively reviewed in a number of sources (Abernathy and Wayne, 1974; Yelle 1979).
2. See Sallenave (1976, pp. 65–71) for an exposition of the steps involved in restating current currency cost data in constant currency utilizing the price deflator tables developed for the U.S. Gross National Product.
3. See Day and Montgomery (1983) for a review of empirical studies on cost and price experience curves.
4. Portions of this section are adapted from Abell and Hammond (1979) and Ghemawat (1985).
5. See Montgomery and Day (1984) and Varadarajan (1989) for a discussion on more complex functional specifications of the experience curve.
6. Alberts (1989), however, argues that the key to generating a cost advantage is innovation and not building market share. He further makes a case that in most market circumstances, building rate of return and not building share, is the most profitable way for a unit to exploit an innovation-caused cost advantage.
7. This illustration is adapted from Sallenave (1985).
8. It is, however, important to be aware of the perils of high-growth markets discussed in Chapter 3.
9. This illustration is adapted from Kiechel (1981).
10. This illustration is adapted from Taylor (1987, 1988).
11. This section is adapted from Foster (1982).

REFERENCES

Aaker, David A. (1988), *Strategic Market Management*, 2nd ed., New York: John Wiley and Sons.

Abell, D. F. and J. S. Hammond (1979), *Strategic Market Planning: Problems and Analytical Approaches*, Englewood Cliffs, NJ: Prentice-Hall, 1979.

Abernathy, William J. and Kenneth Wayne (1974), "Limits of the Learning Curve," *Harvard Business Review*, 52 (September–October), 109–119.

Alberts, William W. (1989), "The Experience Curve Doctrine Reconsidered," *Journal of Marketing*, 53 (July), 36–49.

Amit, Raphael (1986), "Cost Leadership Strategy and Experience Curves," *Strategic Management Journal*, 7 (May–June), 281–292.

Bloom, P. E. and P. Kotler (1975), "Strategies for High Market Share Companies," *Harvard Business Review*, 53 (November–December), 63–72.

Booz, Allen, and Hamilton (1982), *New Product Management for the 1980s*, New York.

Boston Consulting Group (1972), *Perspectives on Experience*, Boston, MA.

Buzzell, Robert D. and Bradley T. Gale (1987), *The PIMS Principles: Linking Strategy to Performance*, New York: Free Press.

Day, G. (1977), "Diagnosing the Product Portfolio," *Journal of Marketing*, 41 (April), 29–38.

———, and David B. Montgomery (1983), "Diagnosing the Experience Curve," *Journal of Marketing*, 47 (Spring), 44–58.

———, (1986), *Analysis for Strategic Market Decisions*, St. Paul, MN: West.

Foster, Richard N. (1982), "A Call for Vision in Managing Technology," *The McKinsey Quarterly*, (Summer), 26–36.

Ghemawat, P. (1985), "Building Strategy on the Experience Curve," *Harvard Business Review*, 63 (March–April), 143–149.

Hall, G. and S. Howell (1985), "The Experience Curve from the Economist's Perspective," *Strategic Management Journal*, 6 (July–September), 197–212.

Harvard Business School Note (1975), "Experience and Cost: Some Implications for Manufacturing Policy," Note 9-675-228, Boston, MA: Intercollegiate Case Clearing House.

Hax, A. C. and N. S. Majluf (1984), *Strategic Management: An Integrated Perspective*, Englewood Cliffs, NJ: Prentice-Hall.

Hedley, Barry (1976), "A Fundamental Approach to Strategy Development," *Long Range Planning*, 9 (December), 2–11.

Henderson, B. D. (1984), Application and Misapplication of the Experience Curve, *Journal of Business Strategy*, 4 (Summer), 3–9.

Kiechel, Walter (1981), "The Decline of the Experience Curve," *Fortune*, (October 5), 139–146.

Kotler, Philip (1988), *Marketing Management: Analysis, Planning, and Control*, 6th ed., Englewood Cliffs, NJ: Prentice-Hall.

Mecklin, John (1966), "Douglas Aircraft's Stormy Flight Plan," *Fortune*, December, 258.

Montgomery, D. B. and G. S. Day (1984), "Experience Curves: Evidence, Empirical Issues and Applications," in D. Gardner and H. Thomas eds., *Strategic Marketing and Strategic Management*, New York: John Wiley.

Peters, Tom and Nancy Austin (1985), *A Passion For Excellence*, New York: Random House.

Sallenave, J. P. (1976), *Experience Analysis for Industrial Planning*, Lexington, MA: Lexington Books.

——— (1985), The Uses and Abuse of Experience Curves, *Long Range Planning*, 18 (January–February), 64–72.

Taylor III, Alex (1987), "Lee Iacocca's Production Whiz," *Fortune* (June 22), 36–44.

———(1988), "Iacocca's Time of Trouble," *Fortune* (March 14), 79–88.

Varadarajan, P. Rajan (1989), "Market Share Objectives and the Maximum Sustainable Growth of a Multi-dimension Firm: A Portfolio Strategy Perspective; Working paper, Texas A&M University, College Station, TX.

Wensley, Robin (1981), "Strategic Marketing: Betas, Boxes or Basics," *Journal of Marketing*, 45 (Summer), 173–182.

Yelle, Louis E. (1979), "The Learning Curve: Historical Review and Comprehensive Survey," *Decision Sciences*, 10 (April), 302–328.

CHAPTER 5

ANALYSIS OF POOLED BUSINESS

EXPERIENCE: THE PIMS PROGRAM

Introduction

An Overview
Unit of Analysis
Research Objectives
The PIMS Competitive Strategy Paradigm
The PIMS Data Base
Key Variables

Major Research Findings
Market Position and Profitability
Product/Service Quality and Profitability
Product Value, Market Share, and
Profitability
Market Share and Order of Market Entry
Investment Intensity and Profitability
Market/Industry Factors and Profitability
PIMS Regression Models
PIMS Findings on Start-Up Businesses and
Portfolios of Businesses
Using PIMS Findings for Strategic Decision
Making

PIMS Management Reports
The "Par" Report
The Strategy Analysis Report
The Optimum Strategy Report
The Report on "Look-Alikes"

Limitations of PIMS Research Studies:
Critique and Comments
PIMS Philosophy
Level of Analysis
Pooling of Cross-Sectional Data
Time Frame of Data
High Correlations Between Independent
Variables
Format of Results Reported
Measurement and Scaling

Operational Definition of Constructs
Strategic Value of Findings

Major PIMS Findings: A Closer Examination
The Relationship Between Market Share and
Profitability
The Relationship Between Investment
Intensity and Profitability

A Concluding Note

References

Appendix
PIMS Data Forms

INTRODUCTION

The Profit Impact of Market Strategy (PIMS) data base is by far the most extensive strategic information data base developed to date. This extraordinary data base of approximately 450 companies and 3,000 strategic business units (SBUs) covers a wide variety of industries, products/services and markets.[1] The data base is a pool of information reflecting the experiences of SBUs of participating companies. The PIMS Program was initiated to provide inputs to the SBU level planning efforts of participant companies. Through the analysis of the pooled business experience of member companies, PIMS attempts to answer questions such as "What *strategy*, pursued under what *conditions* produces what *results*?" The PIMS Program is an on-going, multicompany research activity administered by the Strategic Planning Institute (SPI), a non-profit, member-governed organization. It originated as an internal project of the General Electric Company, where it was used for over a decade as a tool for corporate and division-level planning.

The PIMS data base has been utilized to address a broad range of research questions in the areas of: (1) market structure, market share and competitive strategy; (2) marketing costs; (3) vertical integration; (4) productivity and unionization; (5) product and service quality; (6) planning systems and applications; (7) product innovation, research, and development; (8) new ventures; (9) capital investments; and (10) acquisitions.[2] The data base has been extensively used by researchers in the areas of business policy and strategy (Hambrick and MacMillan, 1984; Woo and Cooper, 1982; Zeithaml and Fry, 1984), economics (Caves and Porter, 1976, 1978), finance (Branch, 1980), and marketing (Buzzell, 1981; Varadarajan, 1985a, 1985b; Wind, Mahajan, and Swire, 1983). A number of articles that provide detailed reviews of PIMS data based research, as well as the limitations of the PIMS stream of research, have been published to date (Anderson and Paine, 1978; Lubatkin and Pitts, 1983, 1985; Naylor, 1978; Ramanujam and Venkatraman, 1984; Wensley, 1981, 1982). Issues pertaining to the measurement, operationalization, validity, and reliability of PIMS variables have been addressed in a few articles (Phillips, Chang, and Buzzell, 1983; Parasuraman and Varadarajan, 1988; Wind, Mahajan and Swire, 1983).

The chapter begins with an overview of the PIMS program. The unit of analysis, research objectives, nature, and composition of the PIMS data base, and key strategy and performance variables examined in PIMS studies are discussed in this section. This discussion is followed by a detailed review of PIMS findings pertaining to the major determinants of SBU performance. Major limitations of PIMS research are then reviewed. The chapter concludes with a brief discussion of the role of portfolio analysis techniques and PIMS in the strategic market planning process.

AN OVERVIEW

Unit of Analysis

The unit of observation in PIMS is a strategic business unit (SBU). The SBU can either be a division, product line, or other profit center within its parent company that sells a distinct set of products and/or services to an identifiable group of customers, in competition with a well-defined set of competitors, and for which meaningful separation can be made of revenues, operating costs, investments, and strategic plans. The member companies contribute business-experience data with respect to one or more of their businesses to help create the pooled data base.

Research Objectives

A primary objective of the PIMS project is to uncover the "laws of the marketplace" relating to (1) profit level, (2) other outcomes of strategic actions, and (3) outcomes of changes in the business environment. Based on an analysis of the experiences of businesses operating under *similar* conditions, PIMS attempts to answer questions such as:

1. What profit rate is *"normal"* for a given business, considering its particular market, competitive position, technology, cost structure, and so forth?
2. If the business continues on its *current track*, what will its future operating results be?
3. What *strategic changes* in the business have promise for improving these results?
4. Given a *specific* contemplated future strategy for the business, how will profitability or cash flow change, in the short-term and long-term? (Strategic Planning Institute, 1976).

The PIMS Competitive Strategy Paradigm

The PIMS competitive strategy paradigm views an SBU's performance as a function of three sets of variables. These variables characterize:

1. the structure of the market in which the SBU competes,
2. the competitive position of the SBU in that market, and
3. the strategy pursued by the SBU.

These variables are posited to have a direct effect on performance as well as an interactive effect (Buzzell and Gale, 1987). Figure 5.1 provides a simplified representation of the PIMS competitive strategy paradigm.

The PIMS Data Base

The foundation for all of SPI's research is the PIMS data base, consisting of market, strategic, and financial information for about 3,000 SBUs contributed by approximately 450 member companies. The data cover periods ranging from 2 to 10 years for each strategic business unit. The types of businesses represented in the data base include consumer durables, consumer nondurables, capital goods, raw materials, industrial components, industrial supplies, services, and distribution. About two-thirds of these businesses market their offerings nationally in the United States and/or Canada, and 16 percent serve regional markets in North America. European firms are also represented, with about two hundred each from the United Kingdom and other Western European countries.

Key Variables

The PIMS data base contains information on over 100 items for each SBU. These items include characteristics of the (1) *market environment*, (2) *competitive position* of the SBU, (3) *strategy* pursued by the SBU, and (4) *operating results* obtained. Table 5.1 provides an overview of the type of information on each SBU available in the PIMS data base.

The data base is created by inputting data collected from the participating companies using standardized forms developed and supplied by SPI. The forms are designed to break down the required data items into simple elements that can readily be assembled from financial or marketing records, or that can be established by someone familiar with the specific business. A sample of questions from these forms is reproduced in the Appendix to the chapter.

SPI maintains stringent conditions of security and confidentiality for all contributed data. The procedures in effect include the following:

1. All dollar data are rescaled by the company contributing them (by multiplying the information by an arbitrary "disguise factor" known only to that company) before entry into the data base.
2. The business is not identified as to the name of the product or market represented. The sole identification of the business is a code number.

FIGURE 5.1
THE PIMS COMPETITIVE STRATEGY PARADIGM

Major Influences on Business Performance

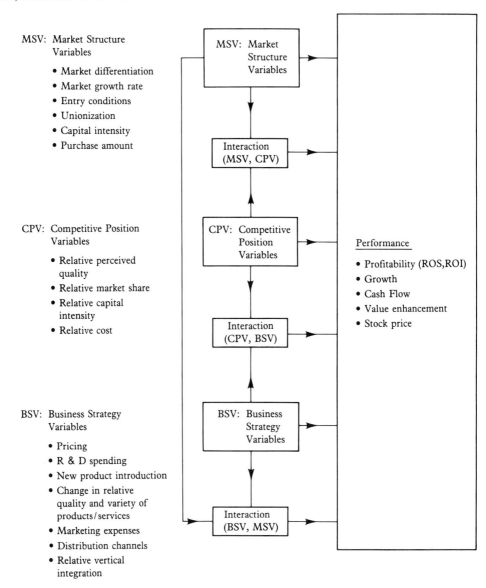

MSV: Market Structure
Variables

• Market differentiation
• Market growth rate
• Entry conditions
• Unionization
• Capital intensity
• Purchase amount

CPV: Competitive Position
Variables

• Relative perceived
quality
• Relative market share
• Relative capital
intensity
• Relative cost

BSV: Business Strategy
Variables

• Pricing
• R & D spending
• New product introduction
• Change in relative
quality and variety of
products / services
• Marketing expenses
• Distribution channels
• Relative vertical
integration

MSV: Market
Structure
Variables

Interaction
(MSV, CPV)

CPV: Competitive
Position
Variables

Interaction
(CPV, BSV)

BSV: Business
Strategy
Variables

Interaction
(BSV, MSV)

Performance

• Profitability (ROS,ROI)
• Growth
• Cash Flow
• Value enhancement
• Stock price

Source: Adapted from Buzzell, R. D., and B. T. Gale (1987), *The PIMS Principles: Linking Strategy to Performance*, New York: Free Press, p. 28.

TABLE 5.1
SELECTED PIMS MEASURES OF MARKET ENVIRONMENT,
COMPETITIVE POSITION, BUSINESS UNIT STRATEGY AND
PERFORMANCE

A. Characteristics of the Market Environment

- Long-run growth rate of the market
- Short-run growth rate of the market
- Rate of inflation of selling price levels
- Number and size of customers
- Purchase frequency and magnitude

B. Competitive Position and Strategy of the Business Unit

- Share of the served market
- Share relative to largest competitors
- Product quality relative to competitors
- Prices relative to competitors
- Pay scales relative to competitors
- Marketing efforts relative to competitors
- Pattern of market segmentation
- Rate of new product introductions

C. Structure of the Production Process

- Capital intensity
- Degree of vertical integration
- Capacity utilization
- Productivity of capital equipment
- Productivity of people
- Inventory levels

D. Discretionary Budget Allocations

- R&D budgets
- Advertising and promotion budgets
- Sales force expenditures

E. Strategic Moves

- Patterns of change in the controllable elements above

F. Operating Results

- Profitability results
- Cash flow results
- Growth results

3. The identity of the company owning the business is also coded.
4. Access to the data base is limited to the participating companies, PIMS researchers, and other researchers working on approved projects, and is based on the extent that they need to know.

The data base, however, provides broad descriptions of the participating businesses in terms such as type of business (consumer durable business, consumer nondurable business, capital goods business, etc.), and standard industrial classification group at the four-digit level.

MAJOR RESEARCH FINDINGS

The major PIMS findings on the determinants of business unit performance, measured in terms of profitability and net cash flow, are summarized in Table 5.2. The remainder of this section focuses on PIMS research findings pertaining to: (1) market position and profitability; (2) product/service quality and profitability; (3) product/service value, market share and profitability; (4) market share and order of market entry; (5) investment intensity and profitability; and (6) market/industry factors and profitability.

Market Position and Profitability

PIMS studies focus on three interrelated measures of market position: market share rank, market share, and relative market share. The operational definition of relative market share (RMS) employed in PIMS studies differs from the BCG definition of relative market share discussed in Chapter 2. RMS is defined in PIMS research as the ratio of the market share of the SBU to that of the combined market share of the SBU's three leading competitors.[3] That is

$$RMS = \frac{\text{Market share of SBU "i"}}{\text{Combined market share of SBU i's three leading competitors}}$$

Several PIMS studies suggest that market position (relative market share) has a positive effect on business profitability (Figure 5.2). However, PIMS data also reveal that there are both highly profitable, low-market-share businesses and relatively less profitable, high-market-share businesses. Among PIMS businesses with market shares of 10 percent or less, about one in four have an ROI of 20 percent or more; and among PIMS businesses with market shares of 40 percent or more, about one in four have a return on investment (ROI) of less than 20 percent. PIMS studies also suggest that SBUs with a high relative market share may be less aggressive than their smaller share rivals in pursuing share building strategies (Kijewski, 1978).

TABLE 5.2
MAJOR STRATEGIC INFLUENCES ON THE PROFITABILITY AND
NET CASH FLOW OF A BUSINESS

1. ***Investment intensity*** This variable has a *negative* effect on percentage measures of profitability and cash flow.
2. ***Productivity*** Businesses producing a high added value per employee are *more* profitable than those with a low added value per employee.
3. ***Market position*** The absolute and relative market share of a business have a *positive* impact on its profit and cash flow.
4. ***Served market growth rate*** This factor has a *positive* effect on dollar measures of profit, *no* effect on percent measures of profit, and a *negative* effect on all measures of net cash flow.
5. ***Product and/or service quality*** Quality in relation to competitors' offerings (as viewed by the customer) has a *favorable* effect on all measures of financial performance.
6. ***Innovation/differentiation*** A business' extensive actions in the areas of new product introduction, R&D, marketing effort, etc. have a *positive* effect on its performance only if the business is in a strong market position to begin with.
7. ***Vertical integration*** For businesses competing in mature and stable markets, vertical integration (making rather than buying) impacts *favorably* on performance. In rapidly changing markets, the opposite is true.
8. ***Cost push*** The impact of wage and salary increases, increase in raw material prices, and the presence of a labor union are quite *complex*. Their impact on profit and cash flow depend on the ability of the firm to pass along the cost increase to its customers, and/or its ability to absorb the high costs internally.
9. ***Current strategic effort*** The current direction of change with respect to the above profit and cash flow factors is frequently *opposite* to that of the factor itself. For instance, while high market share has a *positive* effect on cash flow, efforts to increase share have a *negative* effect on cash flow.

Source: Adapted from Schoeffler, S. (1977), "Nine Basic Findings on Business Strategy," *The PIMSLETTER on Business Strategy,* Cambridge, Mass: The Strategic Planning Institute.

Since a market-share-building strategy could be costly in certain situations, it is desirable to pursue such a strategy only after taking into consideration anticipated costs and expected benefits. For instance, PIMS research reveals that the effectiveness of pursuing a strategy of increasing market share is greater under the following conditions:

FIGURE 5.2
MARKET POSITION BOOSTS RATES OF RETURN

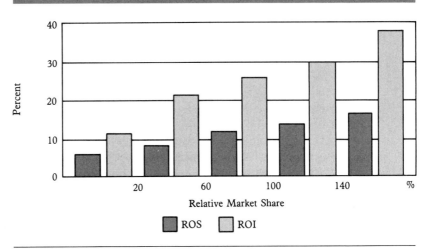

Source: Strategic Planning Institute (1986), *Major Principles of Business Unit Strategy*, Cambridge, Mass: The Strategic Planning Institute.

- a rapidly growing market,
- a relatively young industry,
- technological factors that mandate a high degree of vertical integration,
- minimal unionization of employees,
- the absence of major product or process patents shielding the business, and
- market entry situations that require a high rate of marketing expense.

Hence, while a business facing many of the above conditions may find it worthwhile to aggressively expand its market share, it may be less profitable to do so when only a few of these factors are present (Schoeffler, 1977b).

The positive relationship between market share and profitability is attributable to a number of factors. For instance, having lower costs relative to competitors is a key factor underlying the higher profitability of high-share businesses. Their lower costs stem from learning and scale economies, bargaining power with suppliers, and backward integration. One of the primary sources of profitability of high-market-share businesses (lower costs rather than higher prices) is further elaborated in Box 5.1.

Product/Service Quality and Profitability

The product/service quality of an SBU relative to those of its leading competitors is expressed in PIMS studies as an index that can range from

FIGURE 5.3
RELATIVE QUALITY BOOSTS RATES OF RETURN

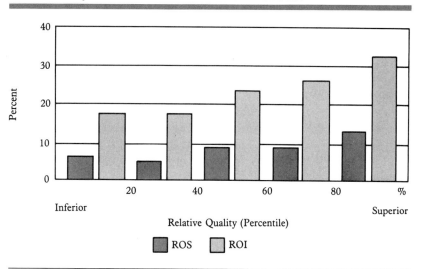

Source: Strategic Planning Institute (1986), *Major Principles of Business Unit Strategy,* Cambridge, Mass.: The Strategic Planning Institute.

−100 to +100. PIMS employs an elaborate approach to measure product/ service quality. Participating SBUs are first asked to identify all key non-price product and service attributes that count in the consumers' purchase decision making process. They are then asked to assign importance weights to the product and service attributes by allocating a total of one hundred points among the attributes. Next, the respondents are asked to rate their performance and the performance of their leading competitors on a scale of one to ten with respect to each product and service attribute. By multiplying the importance weight of each attribute by the corresponding performance rating and adding across attributes, an overall quality rating score for the SBU and its leading competitors is computed (Buzzell and Gale, 1987; also see the Appendix to this chapter).

In the long run, according to PIMS studies, the most important single factor affecting SBU performance is the quality of its products and services relative to those of its competitors (Figure 5.3). The positive effect of relative product/service quality on business profitability is attributable to factors such as stronger customer loyalty, higher repeat purchases, and/or lower vulnerability of superior quality offerings to price wars.

With the exception of commodity-type products, most products generally compete in terms of both price and quality. PIMS research suggests that a significant relationship exists between product quality and profits under almost all business conditions. The quality of products and/or serv-

BOX **5.1**

THE SOURCE OF PROFITABILITY OF HIGH-SHARE BUSINESSES*

Many studies have reported the existence of a close link between market share and profitability. A pertinent question in this context is whether the high profitability is the result of efficiency-related effects, or the result of market manipulations by participants in highly concentrated markets.

FIGURE 5.1.1
BUSINESSES WITH DIFFERENTIATED PRODUCTS

	Market Share (%)		
Relative Direct Cost	Low (14)	(29)	High
Low	103.5	102.4	100.5
Product Quality (8)			
(36)	103.0	102.2	99.7
High	105.2	103.3	100.9

ices offered by industry pioneers or those who entered a market during its early stages generally tends to be superior than that of competitors' offerings. Nevertheless, relative newcomers can also pursue an active quality improvement strategy. Although this strategy may cause a short-term profit decline, the associated market share gains enhance the prospects of increases in long-term profits (Buzzell, 1978). PIMS research also reveals that heavy marketing is not a substitute for inferior quality. A high level of marketing effort (as seen in marketing expenditure as a percent of sales) does not help enhance the ROI of inferior quality offerings (Figure 5.4).

Analysis of PIMS businesses reveals that often businesses that have succeeded in improving the quality of their products choose to increase product price as well. However, since customers are sensitive to both price

PIMS research reveals that firms having high market shares do not derive their profitability from charging consumers higher prices for their products. Rather, the higher profits earned by high market share businesses result from lower costs (see Figure 5.1.1), not higher prices (see Figure 5.1.2). These cost reductions are the result of experience curve effects, economies of scale, or merely consumer's preferences for the products of well-known companies.

FIGURE 5.1.2
BUSINESSES WITH DIFFERENTIATED PRODUCTS

Relative Price (%)	Market Share (%)		
Product Quality	Low (14)	(29)	High
Low	100.5	101.0	102.1
(8)	105.1	105.0	101.1
(36)	109.1	107.2	108.9
High			

(100 = Price *equal* to those charged by competitors)

*Gale, Bradley T. and Ben Branch (1979), "The Dispute About High-Share Businesses," *The PIMSLETTER on Business Strategy*, Number 19.

and quality in their purchasing decisions, by charging a premium price a company may not realize all of the potential for increasing its market share. Furthermore, in many instances it has been found that the ROI is actually higher for firms that have kept their prices at a moderate level or below that of their major competitors while improving product quality (Chussil and Schoeffler, 1978).

Examining the combined effect of product quality and relative market share on business profitability provides further insights into the importance of these two variables (Figure 5.5). While SBUs offering superior product quality and having high relative market share have the highest ROI, those offering inferior product quality and having low relative market share have the lowest ROI.

FIGURE 5.4
HEAVY MARKETING IS NO SUBSTITUTE FOR INFERIOR QUALITY

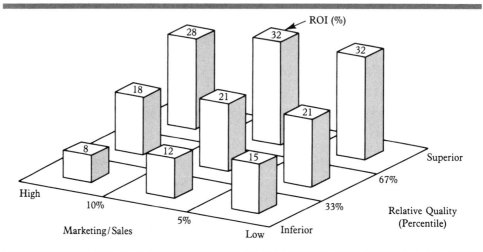

Source: Strategic Planning Institute (1986), *Major Principles of Business Unit Strategy,* Cambridge, Mass: The Strategic Planning Institute.

FIGURE 5.5
QUALITY AND SHARE BOTH DRIVE PROFITABILITY

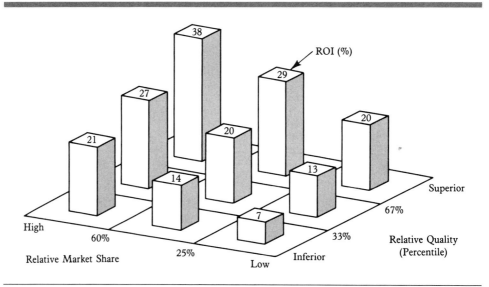

Source: Bradley T. Gale and Ben Branch, "Beating the Cost of Capital," PIMSLETTER No. 32, 1984.

Product Value, Market Share, and Profitability

In general, it is possible to distinguish between nine value positions an SBU may adopt (Table 5.3). Here, value denotes the ratio of relative quality to relative price. PIMS research reveals that product value bears a strong relationship to market share and profitability. As shown in Table 5.4, improving product value enhances an SBU's prospects for gaining share. PIMS research also reveals that firms having a low current market share or those in low-growth industries can benefit the most from enhancing product value. Similarly, late entrants can compensate for their lack of experience in the marketplace by offering higher value products to consumers (Chussil and Downs, 1979). The relative effectiveness of enhancing value by improving product/service quality versus lowering prices is elaborated in greater detail in Box 5.2.

Market Share and Order of Market Entry

A number of PIMS studies have uncovered a systematic relationship between market share and the order of market entry (market pioneer, early follower or late entrant) for consumer and industrial goods businesses. The three entrant categories have been found to have significantly different strategic profiles, with market pioneers tending, on the average, to outperform late entrants (Lambkin 1988). A study of PIMS businesses competing in mature consumer goods industries found market pioneers to have an average market share of 29% versus 13% for late entrants. A similar

TABLE 5.3
PRODUCT QUALITY, PRICE, AND VALUE POSITIONS

	Relative Quality		
Relative Price	Low	Average	High
High	**Inferior value:** Substandard quality at a premium price.	**Poor value:** Average quality at a premium price.	**Average value:** Superior quality at a premium price.
Average	**Poor value:** Substandard quality at an average price.	**Average value:** Average quality at an average price.	**Better value:** Superior quality at an average price.
Low	**Average value:** Substandard quality at a discount price.	**Better value:** Average quality at a discount price.	**Superior value:** Superior quality at a discount price.

BOX **5.2**

FORMULATING A QUALITY IMPROVEMENT
STRATEGY*

PIMS research reveals that the price and customer-perceived quality of a product are important determinants of market share. As shown in Figure 5.2.1, these two competitive dimensions can be plotted to form a price-performance curve. The price performance curve shows the value consumers derive from purchasing a particular product. Products which fall above the 45 degree line (Figure 5.2.2) provide less value and those below the line offer higher value. The price-performance curve implies that firms can gain a competitive advantage in terms of value by either lowering prices or by improving the quality of their products.

PIMS research shows that a quality improvement strategy is often the more effective alternative because price reductions are easily matched by competitors, especially if the products are uniform throughout the industry. This results in overall smaller profit margins combined with a high likelihood that the ultimate gain in market share will be limited by competitors matching the firm's price reductions. Product quality improvements, on the other hand, usually have a longer effect since they may be difficult to imitate. The expenses involved in redesigning a production process to improve quality may also help the firm stay ahead of its competitors.

PIMS research shows that improving value is a significantly more potent form of improving market share than lowering prices alone. Firms can build more value into their products using a variety of approaches. For many companies, technological innovations have served as the primary vehicle for augmenting the value of the products they offer. Other companies have developed highly effective quality control systems that have led to high levels of customer satisfaction. However, unless management realizes the inherent worth of value, a value improvement strategy is likely to fail and not result in market share gains. To be effective, the value concept must pervade all levels of management.

*Gale, Bradley T. and Richard Klavans (1984), "Formulating a Quality Improvement Strategy," *The PIMSLETTER on Business Strategy*, Number 31.

FIGURE 5.2.1
CUSTOMERS PAY MORE FOR BETTER PRODUCTS

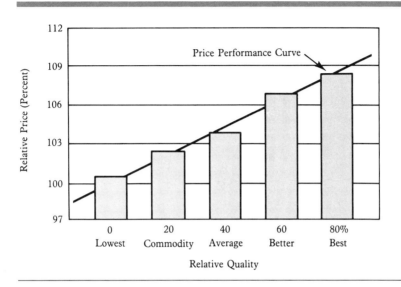

FIGURE 5.2.2
RELATIVE PRICE AND RELATIVE QUALITY DETERMINE VALUE
AND PRODUCT POSITION

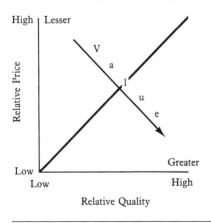

TABLE 5.4
HIGH AND RISING VALUE INCREASE
ODDS OF GAINING SHARE
(Percentage of Businesses Gaining Share)

| | Beginning Value | | |
	Low		High
Rising	60	58	62
Change in			
Value	43	55	57
Falling	40	40	57

Source: Bradley T. Gale and Richard Klavans,
"Formulating a Quality Improvement Strategy,"
PIMSLETTER No. 31, 1984.

pattern was found to persist in mature industrial goods industries as well. PIMS businesses that were market pioneers were found to have an average market share of 29% versus 15% for late entrants (Robinson and Fornell 1985; Robinson 1988). This pattern of relationship is attributed to the competitive advantages that can result from being the first in the market. For instance, being the first mover in the market, the pioneer can benefit from proprietary experience and by participating in the definition of industry standards (Robinson and Fornell 1986). A recent review of theoretical and empirical literature traces first-mover advantages to three primary sources: (1) technological leadership, (2) preemption of assets, and (3) buyer switching costs (Lieberman and Montgomery 1988).

1. **Technological leadership.**
   A. **Experience effects.** Where technological advantage is a function of cumulative experience, the first-mover may be in a position to achieve a sustainable cost advantage, provided it can insure that organizational learning remains proprietary and the firm maintains its market share leadership.
   B. **R&D and patents.** In situations where technological leadership is largely a function of R&D expenditures, pioneers can gain advantage if technology can be patented or maintained as trade secrets.
2. **Preemption of scarce assets.**
   A. **Preemption of input factors.** If the first-mover has superior information, it may be able to purchase assets at market prices below those that will prevail later in the evolution of the market.

   B. Preemption of space. The first mover by resorting to spatial preemption (selecting the most attractive niches in terms of geographic space, shelf space, and product characteristics space) may be in a position to limit the amount of space available for subsequent entrants.
   C. Preemptive investment in plant and equipment. The first-mover can deter entry of other firms through preemptive investment in plant and equipment.
3. **Switching costs and buyer choice under uncertainty.**
   A. Switching costs. Where buyer switching costs exist, late entrants will have to invest extra resources to attract customers away from the first-mover firm. Such costs include the initial transactions costs or investment that the buyer must make in adapting to the late entrant's product and contractual switching costs imposed by the first-mover.
   B. Buyer choice under uncertainty. When buyers have imperfect information regarding product quality, they may be inclined to remain loyal to the first brand they encounter that performs the job satisfactorily. When the first-mover establishes a reputation for superior quality, late entrants may be required to make substantial investments to attract customers to switch from the first-mover firm (see Lieberman and Montgomery 1988).

Investment Intensity and Profitability

A simple measure of capital intensity is the ratio of investment (net or gross book value) to sales. In terms of this measure, it is possible to distinguish between four types of industries:

1. *Fixed capital intensive*—the investment in fixed assets (i.e., plant and equipment) is high relative to the sales revenue generated.
2. *Working capital intensive*—the amount of working capital needed to support a given level of sales is relatively high.
3. *Fixed and working capital intensive*—both types of capital needed to support a given level of sales are relatively high.
4. *Not capital intensive*—both types of capital needed to support a given level of sales are relatively low (Buzzell and Gale, 1987).

Table 5.5 provides additional insights into differences across industries with respect to the above characteristics.

Businesses in the PIMS data base have been found to reveal a systematic pattern of decline in ROI as the investment ratio increases. PIMS analysis of the effects of fixed and working capital intensity reveal that both have an independent, negative relationship to profitability (Figure 5.6). Prominent among the other major PIMS findings pertaining to capital intensity are that:

TABLE 5.5
DIFFERENCES ACROSS INDUSTRIES IN CAPITAL INTENSITY

Ratio of Fixed Capital/Sales	Ratio of Working Capital/Sales	Type of Capital Intensity	Illustrative Industries
High	Low	Fixed Capital Intensive	Commercial Airlines, Telecommunications, Paper Manufacturing
Low	High	Working Capital Intensive	Apparel Book Publishing
High	High	Fixed and Working Capital Intensive	Mining Chemicals
Low	Low	Not Capital Intensive	Retailing

Source: Adapted from Buzzell, R. D., and B. T. Gale (1987), *The PIMS Principles: Linking Strategy to Performance,* New York: Free Press, p. 137.

FIGURE 5.6
FIXED CAPITAL AND WORKING CAPITAL INTENSITY HURT PROFITABILITY

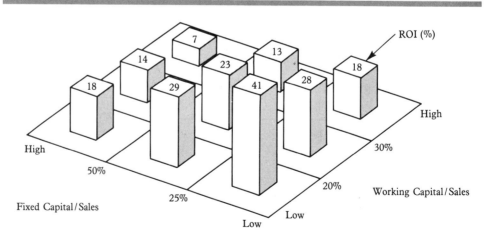

Source: Strategic Planning Institute (1986), *Major Principles of Business Unit Strategy,* Cambridge, Mass: The Strategic Planning Institute.

- high fixed capital intensity (ratio of fixed capital to sales) increases the pressure on a business to maximize capacity utilization,
- a weak market position (low relative market share) and high investment intensity (ratio of investment to value added) has an adverse effect on business profitability, and
- a high level of productivity (value added per employee) helps offset some of the negative effect of high investment intensity on profitability.

The negative relationship between capital intensity and profitability are attributable to a number of factors:

- Capital intensity generally leads to aggressive and often destructive price competition; this is especially true during unfavorable economic conditions and low capacity utilization, since firms may be prepared to sell at any price above variable costs.
- Heavy capital investment often acts as a barrier to exit, thus prolonging the depressed profitability of the businesses.
- A business may be less efficient in using fixed or working capital than its competitors (Buzzell and Gale, 1987).

Market/Industry Factors and Profitability

In addition to the business strategy variables (e.g., product/service quality) and competitive position variables (e.g., market share), PIMS studies reveal that profits are also affected by a series of market and industry factors that are usually outside management's control. For instance:

1. Profits are highest in high-growth markets and lowest in declining markets.
2. Markets in which transactions involve large sums of money tend to be less profitable than ones characterized by small purchase amounts.
3. Products and services that are important to customers (measured as the fraction of the customer's *total* annual purchases of all goods and services represented by the product category) tend to be less profitable than other products and services.
4. Higher levels of employee unionization adversely affect profits.
5. A high level of exports boosts profitability for industry participants; import competition has an adverse effect.

PIMS REGRESSION MODELS

In the previous section, the PIMS findings were presented as simple relationships between a performance variable [return on investment (ROI), return on sales (ROS), or cash flow] and one or two independent variables. However, in most circumstances, the actual performance of an SBU depends on a multiplicity of factors. Accordingly, graphic representations and tabulated values should be interpreted as averages, subject to "all other things being equal."

A large body of findings reported on PIMS businesses are based on the use of multiple linear regression analysis to explain variations in return on investment (ROI), return on sales (ROS), and other business performance measures. Table 5.6 summarizes the observed relationship between ROI and the major dimensions of market structure, competitive position, and business strategy for PIMS businesses. In addition to analyzing relationships between key variables for the total PIMS sample, several PIMS studies have focused on the differences in the strength of the relationship between ROI and various explanatory variables across different types of businesses, market locations, stages of market evolution, and market share rank.[4]

TABLE 5.6
MAJOR INFLUENCES ON BUSINESS PROFITABILITY: AN OVERVIEW
OF PIMS FINDINGS

Profit (ROI) Influences	Direction of Influence on ROI + = Positive; − = Negative	Differences in Strength of Influence on ROI Across Types of Businesses
Competitive Position and Business Strategy Variables		
1. Market Share	+	Has greatest impact on ROI for consumer products.
2. Relative Product/Service Quality	+	Effect is greatest for industrial products and service and distribution businesses.
3. New Products, % of Sales	−	Does not hurt ROI in service and distribution businesses.
4. R&D Expense, % of Sales	−	Does not hurt ROI in service and distribution businesses.
5. Marketing Expense, % of Sales	−	
6. Value Added, % of Sales	+	
7. Fixed Assets, % of Sales (at Capacity)	−	
8. Newness of Plant & Equipment	+	Effect is significant only for consumer products.
9. Labor Productivity	+	
10. Inventories, % of Sales	−	Not a significant factor in service and distribution businesses.
11. Capacity Utilization Rate	+	
12. FIFO Inventory Valuation	+	

TABLE 5.6 (*continued*)

Industry Characteristics/Market Structure Variables		
13. Real Market Growth Rate (Annual %)	+	
14. Stage of Market Evolution		
• Growth Stage	+	
• Decline Stage	−	
15. Rate of Inflation in Selling Prices	+	Not related to ROI for service and distribution businesses.
16. Concentration of Purchases with Few Suppliers	+	
17. Typical Customer Purchase Amount		
• Small	+	Impact on ROI greatest for industrial
• Large	−	product manufacturers.
18. Importance of Product Purchase to Customer		
• Low	+	Impact on ROI greatest for industrial
• High	−	product manufacturers.
19. % of Employees Unionized	−	
20. Industry Exports	+	Effect on ROI significant only for industrial products manufacturers.
21. Industry Imports	−	Effect on ROI significant only for industrial products manufacturers.
22. Standardized Products (vs. Custom-Produced)	+	Customized products not a significant factor for consumer products.

Source: Adapted from Exhibits 3–8, 3–9 and 3–10 of Buzzell, R. D. and B. T. Gale (1987), *The PIMS Principles: Linking Strategy to Performance*, New York: Free Press, pp. 46–48.

Market share, product/service quality, newness of plant and equipment, labor productivity, and vertical integration are among the competitive position and business strategy factors that have a positive influence on ROI. Fixed capital intensity, inventory investment, the rate of new product introduction, and current levels of spending on marketing and R&D are among the factors negatively related to ROI. Focusing next on industry characteristics/market structure variables, the ROI is positively related to market growth rate, supplier concentration, and rate of inflation in selling prices, but inversely related to the extent of employee unionization. A multiple regression equation incorporating the explanatory variables listed in Table 5.6 explains about 39 percent of the variance in ROI, and 31% of the variance in ROS for the entire sample of PIMS businesses.[5]

Table 5.7 lists the 37 independent variables used in another PIMS regression model explaining about 80 percent of the variance in pretax ROI. The variables listed in Table 5.6 are classified into three groups according to the degree to which they may be controlled by management—directly controllable, partially controllable, and largely uncontrollable.

When the factors listed in Tables 5.6 and 5.7 are incorporated into a set of profit-predicting and cash-flow-predicting regression models that assign to each factor its proper weight, they can be used to assess the desirability of alternative strategic moves. The effect of planned *changes* in one or several profit-influencing factors (e.g., change in relative product quality; change in relative price) can be analyzed to determine the profit and cash consequences both *during* the time that the move is to be executed and *after* it has been completed. The models can also provide insights into how the impact of each profit-determining factor is influenced by other factors. For example, PIMS research reveals that high levels of plant and equipment per dollar of sales generally reduces the return on investment, but this reduction is small in businesses with a strong market share, and large in businesses with a weak market share. PIMS research also reveals that a high R&D/sales ratio has a positive impact on earnings in highly integrated businesses, but a negative impact in less-integrated businesses (Strategic Planning Institute, 1986).

PIMS Findings on Start-Up Businesses and Portfolios of Businesses

In addition to the PIMS competitive strategy data base comprised of about 3000 SBUs, SPI has developed smaller data bases that focus on specific application topics. The PIMS start-up businesses data base focuses on the strategies of new businesses. Illustrative PIMS findings based on an analysis of the start-up data base are summarized in Box 5.3.

The PIMS portfolio data base focuses on the effects of synergy (see chapter 6 for a discussion on synergy). A study employing this data base found that clusters of businesses competing in similar environments out-perform those competing in dissimilar environments. Portfolios of businesses that have roughly comparable marketing intensity or R&D spending levels or capital intensity outperform portfolios that try to accommodate both high-tech and low-tech, or both marketing-intensive and nonmarketing intensive, or both capital-intensive and noncapital-intensive businesses (Wells, 1984).

Using PIMS Findings for Strategic Decision Making

As we had pointed out in Chapters 2 and 3, portfolio approaches are intended for use as diagnostic aids, not as strategy prescriptive tools. Likewise, the PIMS findings pertaining to the relationship between business unit strategy, competitive position and performance, and the PIMS

TABLE 5.7

DETERMINANTS OF BUSINESS PROFITABILITY: PIMS VARIABLES CLASSIFIED
BY DEGREE OF MANAGERIAL CONTROLLABILITY*

Directly Controllable by Management (Goals/Strategies)	Partially Controllable by Management	Largely Uncontrollable by Management (Environmental)
Market Position	Instability of Market Share	Industry Long-Run Growth
Price Relative to Competition	Relative Pay Scale[a]	Short-Run Market Growth
Product Quality	Capacity Utilization[b]	Industry Exports
New Product Sales	Corporate Size	Sales Direct to End User
Manufacturing Cost/Sales	Change in Market Share	Share of Four Largest Firms
Receivables/Sales	Change in Selling Price Index	Buyer Fragmentation Index
Vertical Integration	Change in Vertical Integration	Investment Intensity[c]
		Fixed Capital Intensity[c]
Inventory/Purchase	Market Position Impact	Competitive Market Activity
Sales/Employees		Change in Capital Intensity
Mktg. Less Sales Force Expense/ Sales		Investment Intensity Impact
R&D Expenses/Sales		
Corporate Payout		
Degree of Diversification		
Growth of Sales		
Change in Product Quality		
Change in Advances and Promotions/Sales		
Change in Sales Force Expansion/ Sales		
Change in Return on Sales		

*The PIMS independent variables are categorized according to the degree to which they may be controlled by management.
[a]Only controllable by increasing.
[b]Only controllable in the short run.
[c]Only controllable at the entry level.

Source: Anderson, C. R. and Paine, F. T. (1978), "PIMS: A Reexamination," *Academy of Management Review*, 3 (July), p. 607.

BOX **5.3**

KEYS TO SUCCESS FOR ADOLESCENT
BUSINESSES*

Recent PIMS research has identified three key factors that contribute to the success of the new business ventures that corporations engage in. They are:

- the characteristics of the market in which the business operates,
- the corporate environment, and
- the nature of the competitive strategies pursued.

The market characteristics found to be most favorable to new business performance are:

- high market growth
- proprietary technology, and
- barriers to entry.

A corporate environment that encourages SBU independence has been found to generate the highest ROIs among adolescent businesses. This may be the result of the different management approach required to run a new business as opposed to a mature business.

Although the corporate and market environments play important roles in the success of a new business, they generally cannot be controlled by business-unit managers to any significant extent. What can be controlled are the strategies that the managers of the SBU choose to follow. The most important of these are:

- relative market share,
- breadth of the product line,
- product quality, and
- degree of vertical integration.

PIMS research indicates that the larger the market share and the broader the product lines, the higher the potential performance of the new SBU. Offering high-quality products was also found to improve business performance, but this effect was magnified when coupled with maintaining prices at moderate levels. Finally, downstream integration has a positive relationship to profits, although this did not hold for upstream integration.

*Miller, Alex, John Guiniven and Bill Camp (1985), "Keys to Success for Adolescent Businesses," *The PIMSLETTER on Business Strategy*, Number 35.

regression models are not intended to serve as strategy prescriptions and formulas for resolving specific business issues. Rather, PIMS-data-based analyses are intended to provide additional inputs to the situation-specific analysis that is always needed to arrive at sound decisions (Buzzell and Gale, 1987).

PIMS MANAGEMENT REPORTS

In addition to reporting general findings such as those summarized in the previous sections, SPI makes available to its member companies special reports based on specific analyses of individual businesses. Table 5.8 provides an overview of the focus of PIMS special reports. A brief discussion of each follows.[6]

The "Par" Report

The "Par" Report specifies the return on investment that is normal (or "par") for a business, given the characteristics of its market, competition, position, technology, and cost structure. Judging by the experiences of

TABLE 5.8
PIMS MANAGEMENT REPORTS: AN OVERVIEW

PAR REPORTS

What ROI (or cash flow) is *normal* for this combination of strategic circumstances?
What are the business's strengths and weaknesses?

STRATEGY ANALYSIS REPORT

What would happen to

- **profit**
- **cash**
- **value of business**
- etc.

if the business makes certain strategic changes?

OPTIMUM STRATEGY REPORT

What combination of strategic moves would *optimize* a given measure of profit, cash, or value of the business?

REPORT ON STRATEGIC "LOOK-ALIKES"

What combination of *tactical moves* would maximize the probability of successfully executing the selected strategy?

Source: Strategic Planning Institute, Cambridge, Massachusetts (1983).

other businesses with *similar* characteristics, the par report speculates whether this business is the kind that normally earns a three- or thirty-percent return on investment. Also, it identifies the major strengths and weaknesses of the business that account for its performance above or below "par." A more detailed discussion on the PIMS concept of "par" profitability is presented in Box 5.4.

The Strategy Analysis Report

The Strategy Analysis Report is a computational pretest of several possible *strategic moves* that a business can pursue. Judging by the experience of other businesses making a similar move from a similar starting point in a similar business environment, this report provides insights into the short- and long-term consequences of each such move. It specifies the profit (or loss) likely to result from projected changes, along with the associated investment and cash flow. This report is useful to top management because it shows the potential effects of broad moves in market share, margin, capital intensity, and integration. Middle management benefits from this report since the potential effects of specific action programs are explored; e.g., the effects of improving relative product quality, increasing the ratio of marketing expense to sales, achieving improvements in capacity utilization or employee productivity, and effecting changes in R&D outlays.

The Optimum Strategy Report

The Optimum Strategy Report identifies the *combination* of several strategic moves that is likely to lead to optimal results for the business as judged by the experiences of other businesses operating under similar circumstances. The optimal combination of strategic moves can be identified from the standpoint of different measures of profit performance, including discounted cash flow, return on investment, and short-term earnings.

Report on "Look-Alikes" (ROLA)

The Report on "Look-Alikes" provides managers with a way to uncover effective tactics for accomplishing their strategic objectives (for example, increasing profitability or cash flow, gaining market share, or improving productivity or product quality). By comparing businesses that are strategically similar to the business of interest (its "look-alikes") and analyzing them, ROLA identifies strategic and operating characteristics that helped successful businesses attain specified objectives. For example, if the objective is to increase net cash flow, data on those look-alike businesses that succeeded in increasing their cash flow and on those that did not succeed are compared. The analysis entails examining over one hundred tactical data elements to uncover what the successful businesses did differently from the unsuccessful businesses. The observed differences in behavior are then tested to identify the most reliable actions to improve cash flow.

BOX **5.4**

PIMS defines "par" profitability as the return on investment
that is normal for a business, given the characteristics of its market,
competition, position, technology, and cost structure. It is judged relative to
the experiences of other businesses with similar characteristics. Businesses
have been found to experience deviations from par owing to three sets of
factors.

1. strategic factors,
2. operating effectiveness factors, and
3. transitory factors.

Strategic factors have the most stable and enduring effect on profitability
and hence define par. Although improvements in operating effectiveness
factors do not generally cause profitability to remain permanently above par,
their effects do not erode very quickly. Transitory factors cause only
temporary deviations in profitability from par. Illustrative of the three sets of
factors are the following:

Examples of Strategic Factors:

- Relative Product Quality
- Relative Market Share
- Investment Intensity
- Growth of Served Market
- Vertical Integration

Elements of Operating Effectiveness:

- Effectiveness of Labor Utilization
- Effectiveness of Market Strategy
- Effectiveness of Working Capital Usage

Examples of Transitory Factors:

- Business Cycle
- Weather Conditions
- Problems of Union Relations
- Technological Problems or Breakthroughs

*Branch, Ben (1981), "Above-Par or Below-Par Profitability," *The PIMSLETTER
on Business Strategy*, Number 26.

FIGURE 5.7
LOOK-ALIKE ANALYSIS

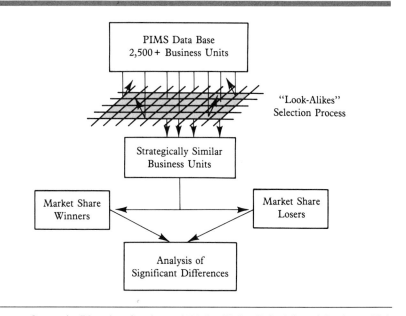

Source: Strategic Planning Institute (1986), *Major Principles of Business Unit Strategy,* Cambridge, Mass: The Strategic Planning Institute.

Figure 5.7 provides an overview of the procedure underlying look-alike analysis.

LIMITATIONS OF PIMS RESEARCH STUDIES: CRITIQUE AND COMMENTS

A number of articles critical of the PIMS philosophy, models, methodology, and results have been published (Anderson and Paine, 1978; Lubatkin and Pitts, 1983, 1985; Scherer, 1980; Wensley, 1981, 1982). A concerted attempt to overcome the limitations pointed out by critiques of prior research studies is often evident in subsequently published PIMS studies. Some of the major limitations of the PIMS approach pointed out by critiques and brief comments summarizing subsequent developments are detailed in this section.

PIMS Philosophy

Critique   The PIMS Program is not a total strategy concept. It is useful primarily as an analysis and diagnostic appraisal device. It assumes a single objective (maximization of ROI) in much of its analysis. This criterion may be overly conservative and shortsighted. Since ROI is usually measured in the short term, it may (1) inhibit investment in plant and equipment, (2) discourage new investments that may not produce a significant return for several years, (3) result in possible elimination of marginal products or product groups, (4) lead to upward price adjustment for low return items, and the lowering of inventories to improve returns. Problems resulting from these decisions may include long-term unemployment, capacity shortage, and diminished sales growth.

Comment The importance of creating shareholder wealth through enhancing the market value at the *company level* is widely accepted. Although conceptualizing, defining, and measuring market value at the *business unit level* (the unit of analysis in PIMS studies) is a somewhat difficult task, some progress has been made along this front (Branch and Gale, 1983; Buzzell and Chussil, 1985; Buzzell and Gale, 1987).

Value enhancement, the long-term performance measure employed in PIMS studies, is defined as the ratio of the sum of the discounted cash flow and the discounted future market value of a business unit divided by its present market value. The strategic and market differences between SBUs with strong initial competitive positions and *excellent* long-term performance versus SBUs with a strong initial competitive position but *poor* long term performance have been examined in a PIMS study (Buzzell and Gale, 1987). As compared to poor long-term performers, excellent long-term performers were found to have spent more on R&D and marketing in the base period and have consistently higher relative product quality levels. PIMS studies focusing on the determinants of long-term performance employ SBUs in the data base for which relevant data is available for at least seven years.

Level of Analysis

Critique All of the PIMS analyses are conducted at the SBU level. However, these analyses do not take into consideration the synergistic effects of SBUs for the entire organization. It is conceivable that the interrelationships among the SBUs may have substantial positive or negative effects on the performance of individual SBUs, as well as on overall organizational performance.

Comment It is widely acknowledged that a major shortcoming of a number of studies in strategic market planning is the inability to identify, much less evaluate, the "synergistic" relationships among business units in a corporation. For instance, with reference to studies investigating the relationship between the diversification strategy of a firm and its overall corporate performance, Abell (1980, pp. 20–21) points out that these studies fail to address the question of how product-market strategies of *individ-*

ual businesses within the corporation relate to overall performance. The PIMS portfolio data base comprised of information about portfolios of businesses has been used to address questions such as, "How is the overall performance of the portfolio affected by linkages among the SBUs and by similarities or differences in the SBUs?" (Wells, 1984).

Pooling of Cross-Sectional Data

Critique   The PIMS approach is based on data from many firms, which are combined and treated as being from the same population. Without pooling of time-series and cross-sectional data, it would be impossible to obtain sufficient statistical degrees of freedom, but pooling risks combining firms that are dissimilar in their strategies. Although heterogeneity in the data is desirable to reflect the competitive or differential advantage that businesses possess in the marketplace, the results can be misleading if substantial heterogeneity exists.

Comment   A number of PIMS research studies have focused on the determinants of ROI for subsamples of businesses, classified by: (1) type of business; (2) market location; (3) stage of market evolution; (4) market share rank; (5) generic strategy groupings; (6) business unit age; and (7) production technology employed.[7] It should, however, be noted that, while analysis of subgroups of PIMS businesses may reduce the severity of pooling-related problems, it does not totally eliminate them.[8] For instance, it is conceivable that even a subsample of PIMS businesses such as the consumer nondurables subsample pools information from such seemingly different businesses as frozen foods, breakfast cereals, beverages and cosmetics. Unfortunately, because of client confidentiality, no test for the appropriateness of pooling is possible (Varadarajan and Dillon, 1981, 1982).

Time Frame of Data

Critique   PIMS research studies are based on data for a single time period, or at best, a few time periods. Hence, variations owing to the environmental factors may not have been picked up by the model.

Comment   Most of the early PIMS research findings reported were based on single-time-period data and the use of cross-sectional statistical methods. Until recently, the possibilities of longitudinal analyses were limited because the data available for each SBU covered relatively short time spans (four to five years). Now, however, sufficient data are available for longer time periods (ten years or more) for a number of PIMS businesses. This allows much greater use of time series methods.

One area identified by SPI for fruitful use of time series techniques is strategic change. Questions such as, "What are the effects of improving product quality? What other strategic changes typically accompany quality improvement? How big must a change be to have significant impact? Does the rate at which change occurs make a difference? and Is the effect of a gradual change the same as that of an abrupt one?" have been identified as worthy of future research.

The time series data currently available for a longer period of time are also likely to facilitate better estimation of the structure of the lagged effect. Since *changes in strategy* usually require several years to implement and the effects of these changes tend to be spread over several subsequent years, the need to develop models to estimate lagged effects of strategic change is being recognized.

High Correlations Between Independent Variables

Critique   One half of the variables included in one of the PIMS models are at least partially beyond the direct control of management (see Table 5.7). Furthermore, there may be high correlations or causal relationships among many of these variables, resulting in erroneous results.

Comment   A large body of PIMS data-based research addressing questions such as "What *strategy*, pursued under what *conditions*, produces what *results*?" does take into consideration the distinction between firm-controllable strategy variables and uncontrollable situational variables (Hambrick, MacMillan, and Day, 1982; Hambrick and MacMillan 1984). Furthermore, the PIMS competitive strategy paradigm (see Figure 5.1) clearly distinguishes between three sets of variables related to SBU performance, namely: market structure variables, competitive position variables, and business strategy variables. While, for the most part, market structure variables may be beyond the control of individual firms, the blurring of distinction between firm controllable marketing mix variables and environmental variables have been highlighted in recent literature (Kotler, 1986).

An examination of the correlations between the twenty-two major profit influences (variables listed in Table 5.6) that are employed as explanatory variables in PIMS regression models reveals that the multicollinearity problem is far less severe than imagined. Only eight of two hundred thirty-one correlation coefficients between all pairs of explanatory variables are greater than 0.30 in the correlation matrix (Buzzell and Gale, 1987; p. 276). The largest correlation coefficient is 0.35. It is, however, conceivable that the multicollinearity problem could be more severe in the thirty-seven-variable PIMS regression model that explains about 80 percent of the variance in pretax ROI.

Format of Results Reported

Critique   The results reported by PIMS in the form of cross-tabulations are prone to misinterpretation since they ignore the effects of other variables. Also, the PIMS results do not report the standard errors of regression estimates of the coefficients. If these standard errors are high, the accuracy of the predictions would be questionable.

Comment There is always a need to exercise caution in interpreting results reported in the form of cross-tabulations. These tables generally show the relationship between a performance variable and one or two independent variables at a time. However, in most circumstances, actual performance depends on a multiplicity of factors. Hence, tabulated values should be interpreted as averages, subject to "all other things being equal." Likewise, there is a need to exercise caution in interpreting regression results that do not report the standard errors of regression coefficient estimates.

Measurement and Scaling

Critique To assure the anonymity of respondents and simplify the cross-tabulations of the data, most of the questions involving a continuous variable are precoded into categories which, although monotonically increasing, are not equidistant. These data are treated in the regression analyses as interval scaled data, and the unequal distances between the various categories are ignored. Furthermore, the approach employed to measure some of the PIMS variables is subjective in nature.

Comment The measurement of intrinsically metric competitive strategy variables using ordinal scales is not merely a matter of researcher convenience. Often, it is a *necessity* because of the difficulty in generating reliable interval or ratio data on competitive dimensions that are theoretically continuous. For instance, a firm's *relative* sales force expenditure level (i.e., the ratio of its expenditures over total industry expenditures) is a continuous measure ranging from zero to one. However, owing to the lack of accurate competitive data, a firm may find it impossible to ascertain its exact position on the zero to one continuous scale (Parasuraman and Varadarajan, 1988). Regarding this limitation, businesses contributing to the PIMS data base have expressed their inability to provide accurate estimates of their shares of total competitive activity (Buzzell and Wiersema, 1981).

From its inception, the PIMS Program has attempted to focus on as many dimensions of strategy as possible. The criteria employed for the inclusion of variables were: (1) their general relevance across industries; and (2) the ability to measure the variable in reasonably clear terms. Some of the PIMS measures, such as relative product quality, are judgmental. However, a subjective measure of relative product quality is viewed as preferable to an omission of the variable from the scope of analysis for want of a more objective measure (Buzzell and Gale, 1987).[9]

Operational Definitions of Constructs

Critique Some variables included in the PIMS regression model may have an impact on profitability owing to the way they are constructed rather than their "true" relationship. Examples include investment intensity and various expense items. For instance, since ROI is defined as the ratio of sales less certain expenses to investment, investment intensity can be expected to show an inverse relationship to ROI and in fact does so. Similarly, expenses tend to depress ROI as their level increases.

Comment This issue is explored in greater length in the section titled "The Relationship Between Investment Intensity and Profitability: A Closer Examination."

Strategic Value of Findings

Critique The strategic value of PIMS results pertaining to the positive relationship between market share and ROI might be limited since it ignores factors such as adequacy of financial resources, viability of position if the effort to increase market share fails, and the influence of environmental factors in allowing the company to pursue the chosen strategy.

Comment A number of PIMS studies point out that since a share-building strategy could be costly in certain situations, it should be pursued only after considering anticipated costs and expected benefits (Schoeffler, 1977b). A more detailed exploration of this issue is presented in the next section.

MAJOR PIMS FINDINGS: A CLOSER EXAMINATION

An examination of strategic market planning literature reveals that the greatest controversy and sustained research interest has centered on the PIMS findings relating to: (1) the relationship between market share and profitability; and (2) the relationship between investment intensity and profitability. A brief discussion of the ongoing debate surrounding these findings follows.

The Relationship Between Market Share and Profitability

The earliest and most widely publicized PIMS finding is that high market share businesses are more profitable than low market share businesses (Buzzell, Gale, and Sultan, 1975). A sequel to this study reexamined the relationship between market share and profitability using a substantially larger sample of PIMS businesses for three distinct time periods (1970–75, 1976–79, and 1980–85) and found the relationship to be quite stable across time periods. The *gross* impact on ROI per 10 points of market share were found to be 4.8, 4.5, and 5.2 points, respectively, for the above time periods. Furthermore, after adjusting for the effect of other key profit influences, the *net* impact of a 10-point difference in market share on ROI was found to be about 3.5 points (Buzzell and Gale, 1986).

Among the questions that have been repeatedly raised are: Is this relationship universal? Should high market share be the guiding principle in managing strategic business units? Studies focusing on these issues have proposed numerous qualifications. These qualifications can be traced to the following key issues: (1) the moderating effects of industry, environmental, and organizational variables; (2) the incidence of highly profitable, low-market-share businesses; (3) the pooling of cross-sectional data; (4) the operational definition of market share; and (5) causal versus spurious relationships.

Moderating Effects Porter (1980) speculates that the relationship between market share and profitability could be industry specific. That is, in some industries the relationship could be positive, in others, it could be inverse, and in still others, it could be U-shaped. A U-shaped relationship implies that both low- and high-market-share businesses would be more profitable than businesses with a market share in the mid-range. As detailed in chapter 3, the form of the relationship between market share and profitability may be moderated by two factors: (1) the size of the competitive advantage and (2) the number of ways to achieve competitive advantage. A close association between market share and profitability is posited to exist only in volume businesses (those industries in which there are few ways of achieving competitive advantage and the size of the advantage is large), but not in fragmented, specialized, or stalemated businesses (Hax and Majluf, 1984, pp. 153–154.)

Incidence of Highly Profitable Low Market Businesses A number of PIMS studies have focused on the business strategies of highly profitable, low-market-share businesses and relatively less profitable, high-market-share businesses (Woo and Cooper, 1981, 1982; Woo, 1984). Effective low market share PIMS businesses are concentrated in product-market environments characterized by very low real market growth and infrequent product changes. Their competitive strategies are strongly characterized by a selective focus on specific strengths, such as intense marketing, high product value, and careful cost control (Woo and Cooper, 1981, 1982). A pertinent question in this context is, "How pervasive is the incidence of highly profitable, low-market-share SBUs and relatively less profitable, high-market-share SBUs?" A study of a PIMS sample of the

FIGURE 5.8
RELATIONSHIP BETWEEN RETURN ON EQUITY AND MARKET
SHARE AT THE INDUSTRY AND FIRM-GROUP LEVELS

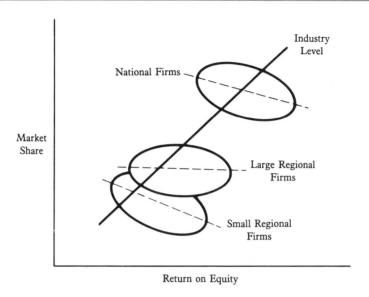

Source: D Schendel and G. R. Patton, (1978), "A Simultaneous Equation Model of Corporate Strategy," *Management Science*, 24 (November), p. 1617.

641 businesses with shares of 10 percent or less revealed that only about one in four had an ROI of 20 percent or more. In contrast, three-fourths of the PIMS businesses with shares of 40 percent or more were found to have an ROI of 20 percent or more (Buzzell and Gale, 1986).

Pooling Issues Upon analyzing the corporate strategy of firms in the brewing industry over the period from 1952 to 1971, Schendel and Patton (1976) found that market share showed a positive relationship with profitability (return on equity) at the industry level. However, this relationship was negative for three different groups of firms that were homogenous with respect to firm size and geographic scope. Schendel and Patton attribute this conflicting result to the heterogeneity problem generated by the pooling of firms. As shown in Figure 5.8, the three homogeneous groups— small regional firms, large regional firms, and national firms—depict a negative relationship between market share and profitability. However, when the parameters are estimated for the heterogenous industry-level sample, a positive relationship emerges. The implication of their study is that, because of the pooling of all types of businesses and industries, the results of PIMS models may be misleading.

FIGURE 5.9
RELATIONSHIP BETWEEN MARKET SHARE AND ROI

Return on Investment (Percent) — Absolute Market Share: 10 20 30 40 50 60 (%)

Return on Investment (Percent) — Market Share Rank: 5 or Worse, 4, 3, 2, 1

Return on Investment (Percent) — Share Relative to Largest Competitor: 1/8 1/4 1/2 1 2 4 8

Return on Investment (Percent) — Share Relative to 3 Largest Competitors: 10 20 30 100 200 (%)

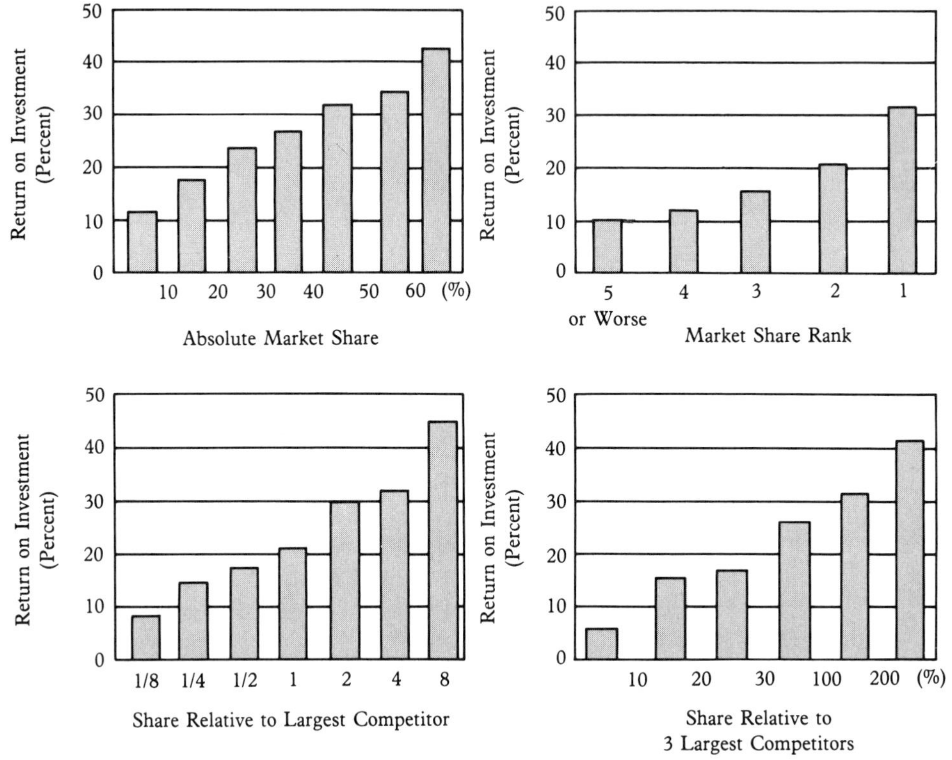

Source: Buzzell, R. D., and B. T. Gale (1987), *The PIMS Principles: Linking Strategy to Performance,* New York: Free Press, p. 94.

Market Share Definition Differences in the conceptualization and operational definition of market share employed in PIMS versus other studies may be part of the reason behind differences in the observed findings. As noted in chapter 2, the definition of market share depends upon the choice of unit of measurement, product definition, time, definition of market, and the nature of the denominator. Consequently, different measures can yield different market share values and different conclusions concerning the relationship between market share and profitability. Although it is conceivable that the strength of the relationship between market share and profitability might be influenced by how market share is defined and computed, one would expect the direction of the relationship to persist regardless of the measure employed. PIMS studies reveal a consistent pattern of relationship between market share and ROI, regardless of the measure of market share employed. Figure 5.9 summarizes the relationship between ROI and four different measures of market share: (1) absolute market share; (2) market share rank; (3) share relating to largest competitor—the BCG measure of relative market share; and (4) share relative to the three largest competitors—the PIMS measure of relative market share.

Causal or Spurious Relationship While acknowledging the existence of a positive relationship between market share and profitability, a number of studies have raised the question of whether the relationship might be spurious (Jacobson and Aaker, 1985; Prescott, Kohli, and Venkatraman, 1986). This would be the case if both market share and high profitability are the result of a third factor such as management skill. Prescott, Kohli, and Venkatraman (1986) analyzed the relationship between market share and business profitability in eight homogenous, competitive environments. They observed a positive, significant association between market share and profitability in seven of the eight competitive environments examined; however, the relationship was direct in three environments and predominantly spurious in four other environments. Even in environments with a strong direct effect, a sizeable spurious relationship was found to exist. This study suggests that the pursuit of market share as a goal must be cautiously undertaken.

Buzzell and Gale (1986) characterize the debate on "spurious" versus "causal" relationships between market share and profitability as a red herring. They note that market share *in itself* doesn't "cause" anything, but reflects two kinds of forces that *do* cause high or low profits: (1) the relative cost positions of competing businesses owing to scale effects and/or experience effects; and (2) the ability of the firm to successfully develop and market a product or service that meets the distinctive needs of its target market. Buzzell and Gale's conceptualization of the key causal factors underlying the relationship between market share and profitability is illustrated in Figure 5.10 and summarized below.

1. Through careful selection of served markets and skillful conception and design of a product/service, an SBU can offer a product/service that is perceived as superior in quality *relative* to its competitor's offerings.
2. Superior quality will enable an SBU to gain market share as well as charge higher than average prices. PIMS studies indicate that on average, the product/service quality of high-market-share businesses is greater than that of low-market-share businesses. Furthermore, on average, the price of superior-quality product/service offerings is higher than that of inferior-quality product/service offerings.
3. A position of high market share achieved by offering a superior product/service will enable the SBU to lower its costs by capitalizing on scale effects and experience effects. PIMS studies indicate that, on

FIGURE 5.10
PRIMARY LINKAGES BETWEEN MARKET SHARE AND PROFITABILITY

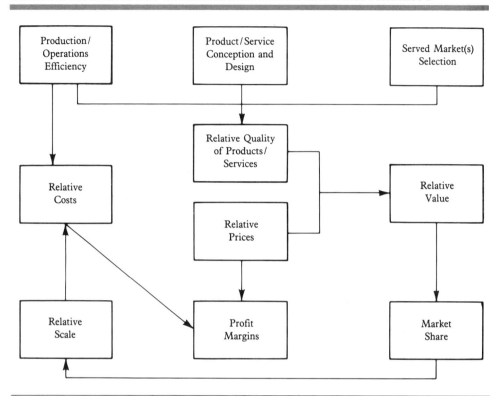

Source: Buzzell, Robert D. and Bradley T. Gale (1986), "Does Market Share Still Matter?," Strategic Planning Institute, Cambridge, Mass.

average, the *relative* costs are lower for high market share businesses than they are for low market share businesses.

4. The ability of an SBU offering a superior product/service to charge higher than average prices coupled with lower costs relative to competitors will lead to higher profit margins. Hence, the observed relationship between market share and profitability.

The Relationship Between Investment Intensity and Profitability

A second major PIMS finding that has been extensively researched and debated concerns the relationship between investment intensity and profitability. The PIMS findings suggest that investment intensity has a strong negative effect on the SBU's return on investment (Figure 5.6). A study focusing on the relationship between profitability and capital intensity in subsamples of PIMS businesses (e.g., growing vs. mature businesses, market leaders vs. followers, high market share vs. low market share business) found the negative relationship to persist across subsamples (Hambrick and MacMillan, 1984). PIMS analyses of profit margins and capital intensity are corroborated by findings based on the analysis of the FTC lines of business data base and the Compustat data base. For example, the analysis of the Compustat data base companies showed that capital intensive companies earned relatively lower rates of return and were more leveraged (Buzzell and Gale, 1987; p. 137). A brief discussion on the issues at the center of the controversy follows.

A Mathematical Artifact   Although the nature of the relationship uncovered by the PIMS Program is correlational in nature, the causal implications are striking. Is a capital intensive business prone to be less profitable than a less capital intensive business? Consider, for example, the following mathematical manipulation:

$$\text{ROI} = \frac{\text{Revenue} - \text{Cost}}{\text{Investment}} = \frac{\text{Net Profit}}{\text{Investment}}$$

$$= \frac{\text{Sales}}{\text{Investment}} \times \frac{\text{Net Profit}}{\text{Sales}}$$

$$= \text{Capital Turnover} \times \text{Profit Margin}$$

$$= \frac{1}{\text{Capital Intensity}} \times \text{Profit Margin}$$

This manipulation clearly indicates that profitability is indirectly related to capital intensity. Consequently, there is some concern that the PIMS finding may be a mathematical artifact. The relationship does, however, suggest that to increase profitability, an SBU should increase capital turnover (decrease capital intensity), and/or increase profit margin. In addition to the definitional effect, the observed nature of the relationship between ROI and capital intensity can be expected if in a capital intensive industry:

1. the demand weakens and competing firms enter into a price or marketing war to attempt to generate sales to help cover their high fixed costs,
2. the demand declines and the firms cannot easily escape the fray (unless they resort to big write-offs), and
3. the major customers and suppliers are aware that the firm faces huge fixed costs, thus making it more vulnerable to business negotiations (Hambrick and MacMillan, 1984).

Benefiting From Investments in Capital Intensity   The term capital intensity is sometimes used to connote large absolute investment outlays in dollar amounts. However, when capital intensity is defined as a ratio of investment to sales, as is the case in PIMS research, a high level of capital intensity does not necessarily imply a large absolute investment. In the latter context, businesses become capital intensive for a variety of reasons. For instance, it may become capital intensive as a result of:

- a business investing in establishing preemptive capacity,
- industry over-capacity resulting from simultaneous capacity expansion by a number of competitors,
- offering better credit terms, leading to an increase in a business' receivables relative to sales,
- striving for better product availability, leading to an increase in a business' finished goods inventory relative to sales,
- maintaining high levels of work-in-process inventory relative to sales to guard against shortages of supplies,
- increasing the amount of investment in a business by integrating backwards, but failing to realize a more-than-commensurate reduction in costs and/or increase in sales, and
- investing in the substitution of capital for labor, but failing to realize a more-than-commensurate increase in output per employee (Buzzell and Gale, 1987).

A question that merits deliberation in this context is, "Under what conditions are additional investments in the above areas that would increase an SBU's capital intensity justifiable?" The mathematical relationship outlined earlier suggests that if an SBU's profit margin is greater than its capital intensity, a firm can increase ROI even with an increase in capital intensity. Hambrick and MacMillan (1984) suggest that strategists should address the following issues before making additional investments:

1. Will the asset itself be quickly obsolete?
2. Is the market about to become segmented, thereby requiring shorter, more flexible production runs?
3. How available and stable will the work force be?
4. How available will raw materials be?
5. Can market share be maintained?
6. Will competitors fight or flee?
7. Are there alternative uses for the assets?
8. Does the firm have the strategic experience and aptitude to exploit the asset?

Increasing Capital Intensity—An Emerging Trend   Ohmae (1985) notes that a growing number of industries are undergoing a steady transformation from labor intensive to capital intensive industries. While investments in automation have vastly increased productivity, this has also resulted in an irreversible shift from labor intensity to capital intensity. As a case in point, Ohmae cites the auto and semiconductor industries. He further notes that the conventional practice of locating operations in countries with low labor costs to bring down variable costs is proving to be less effective in many industries for a number of reasons. For example, in industries where product life cycles are short, constant changes in molds, jigs, tools and components make production locations remote from the core engineering group very inconvenient. Also, inexperienced, low-cost labor in developing countries must first be trained, but once trained and experienced, labor does not stay cheap very long.

In Ohmae's view, the following are some of the strategic implications of this shift from labor-to-capital intensive production:

1. Deep and immediate penetration of all major markets is critical to achieving the economies of scale needed to defray the heavy initial investment and the outlays for continuing production process innovation.
2. Being close to the customer is more important than ever to keep product lines attuned to the demands of the market and responsive to competitive challenges.

A CONCLUDING NOTE

The PIMS Program constitutes one of the most comprehensive and penetrating treatments of how strategic choices and market conditions affect business performance. The analysis of business experience exemplified by the PIMS Program complements the portfolio approach to strategic market planning. Both approaches share a common starting point. SBU objectives and strategies are viewed as dependent on the characteristics of the market place and the SBU's relative competitive position in that market. There are, however, certain major differences.

While the portfolio approaches attempt to explain business performance in terms of a few key factors, the PIMS Program attempts to explain performance differences across businesses by examining a large number of business unit strategy, competitive position, and market structure variables. The linkages between market structure, competitive position, business unit strategy, and performance variables uncovered in the PIMS research studies and the competitive strategy guidelines proposed are based on an empirical analysis of factual data. On the other hand, the strategy guidelines proposed in the portfolio literature are not backed by a comparable degree of empirical evidence.

PIMS-data-based analysis focuses on strategic issues at the strategic business unit level, such as: "How should an SBU compete in its served market? Given the strategy and competitive position of an SBU and its market environment, what is a reasonable expectation for its performance? How are proposed changes in an SBU's strategy likely to affect results?" The portfolio approaches, on the other hand, constitute a valuable analytical input for addressing strategic issues at the corporate level such as: "(1) What product-markets should the firm compete in? (2) What specific objectives should the firm assign to the SBU's in its portfolio? (3) How should resources be optimally allocated among the SBU's commensurate with the objectives assigned to them and the overall objectives of the firm?"

Portfolio analysis techniques provide insights into imbalances in the firm's present portfolio and the strategic imperative for adding new businesses. However, they provide no guidelines for identifying *specific new businesses* that a firm should add to its portfolio. Although PIMS-data-based analysis has been used in certain corporate strategy contexts, such as in evaluating the merits of acquiring a competing business, its contribution to questions pertaining to the addition of specific new businesses to a firm's portfolio is also limited. Analysis based on the PIMS start-up data base and portfolio data base does, however, provide some insights into the desired characteristics of new businesses that a firm may want to add to its portfolio. For instance, it has been reported that:

1. New businesses with marketing linkages to existing businesses in the firm's portfolio outperform those with technology or upstream vertical linkages (Biggadike, 1976).
2. Portfolios of businesses competing in similar environments outperform portfolios competing in dissimilar environments. Portfolios of businesses that have roughly comparable marketing intensity, or R&D spending levels, or capital intensity outperform portfolios that try to accommodate both high-tech and low-tech, or both marketing intensive and nonmarketing intensive, or both capital-intensive and noncapital-intensive businesses (Wells, 1984; Buzzell and Gale, 1987).

Issues relating to the addition of new businesses to a firm's portfolio are the focus of the next chapter on intensive, integrative and diversification growth strategies.

NOTES

1. As we had pointed out in chapter two, the terms product-market unit (PMU), strategic business unit (SBU), strategic business segment and planning/control unit are used interchangeably in strategic market planning literature.

2. For an extensive bibliography of PIMS-data-based journal articles, book chapters, dissertations, case studies, and newsletters, see Buzzell and Gale (1987).
3. See Capon and Spogli (1977) for a discussion of the relative merits and shortcomings of the BCG and PIMS measures of relative market share.
4. Findings based on PIMS analysis of the following subsets of businesses are reported in Buzzell and Gale (1987).
   1. *Type of business:* (i) consumer products; (ii) industrial products; and (iii) services and distribution businesses.
   2. *Market location:* (i) North American; and (ii) other countries.
   3. *Stage of market evolution:* (i) growth and growth maturity; (ii) stable maturity; and (iii) declining maturity and decline.
   4. *Market share rank:* (i) market leaders; and (ii) market followers.
5. The partial regression coefficient estimates for these variables, levels of significance, and other summary statistics have been reported in Buzzell and Gale (1987).
6. Portions of this section are adapted from the Strategic Planning Institute's (1980) publication entitled *The PIMS Program.*
7. See notes 2 and 4.
8. See Bass, Cattin, and Wittink (1978) for a discussion of the conditions under which it may be appropriate to pool cross-sectional data.
9. The PIMS measure of product/service quality currently in use (briefly discussed in the section on product/service quality and profitability; also see chapter appendix) is itself a substantial refinement of a PIMS measure previously employed. A number of other authors have also focused on developing more objective measures of this multidimensional construct. For example, a twenty-six-item instrument for assessing customer perceptions of the quality of a service firm has been proposed by Parasuraman, Zeithaml and Berry (1986).

REFERENCES

Abell, Derek F. and John S. Hammond (1979), *Strategic Market Planning: Problems and Analytical Approaches*, Englewood Cliffs, New Jersey: Prentice-Hall.

Abell, Derek F. (1980), *Defining the Business: The Starting Point of Strategic Planning*, Englewood Cliffs, New Jersey: Prentice-Hall.

Anderson, Carl R. and Frank T. Paine (1978), "PIMS: A Re-Examination," *Academy of Management Review*, 3 (July), 602–611.

Bass, Frank M., Phillippe J. Cattin, and Dick R. Wittink (1978), "Firm Effects and Industry Effects in the Analysis of Market Structure and Profitability," *Journal of Marketing Research*, 15 (February), 3–10.

Biggadike, Ralph E. (1976), "Entry Strategy and Performance," Cambridge, Mass.: Harvard University Press.

Branch, Ben (1980), "The Laws of the Marketplace and ROI Dynamics," *Financial Management* 9 (Summer), 58–65.

Branch, Ben (1981), "Above-Par or Below-Par Profitability," *The PIMSLETTER on Business Strategy*, No. 26.

Branch, Ben and Bradley T. Gale (1984), "Linking Corporate Stock Price Performance to Strategy Formulation," *Journal of Business Strategy*, 4 (Summer), 40–50.

Buzzell, Robert D., Bradley T. Gale, and Ralph G. M. Sultan (1975), "Market Share—A Key to Profitability," *Harvard Business Review*, 53 (January–February), 97–106.

Buzzell, Robert D. (1978), "Product Quality," *The PIMSLETTER on Business Strategy*, No. 4.

Buzzell, Robert D. (1979), "Relatedness," *The PIMSLETTER on Business Strategy*, No. 15.

Buzzell, Robert D. and Frederick D. Wiersema (1981), "Modeling Changes in Market Share: A Cross-Sectional Analysis," *Strategic Management Journal*, 2 (January–March), 27–42.

Buzzell, Robert D. (1981), "Are There Natural Market Structures?" *Journal of Marketing*, 45 (Winter), 42–51.

Buzzell, Robert D. and Mark J. Chussil (1985), "Managing for Tomorrow," *Sloan Management Review*, 26 (Summer), 3–14.

Buzzell, Robert D. and Bradley T. Gale (1986), *Does Market Share Still Matter?*, Cambridge, MA: Strategic Planning Institute.

Buzzell, Robert D. and Bradley T. Gale (1987), *The PIMS Principles: Linking Strategy to Performance*, New York: Free Press.

Capon, Noel and John R. Spogli (1977), "Strategic Marketing Planning: A Comparison and Critical Examination of Two Contemporary Approaches," *Proceedings of the Annual Marketing Educators' Conference*, Chicago: American Marketing Association, 219–223.

Caves, Richard E. and Michael E. Porter (1978), "Market Structure, Oligopoly, and The Stability of Market Shares," *Journal of Industrial Economics*, 26 (June), 289–313.

Caves, Richard E. and Michael E. Porter (1976), "Barriers to Exit," in *Essays In Industrial Organization In Honor of Joe S. Bain*, ed. by Robert T. Masson and P. D. Qualls, Cambridge, MA: Ballinger, 39–69.

Chussil, Mark and Sidney Schoeffler (1978), "Pricing High-Quality Products," *The PIMSLETTER on Business Strategy*, No. 5.

Chussil, Mark and Steve Downs (1979), "When Value Helps," *The PIMSLETTER on Business Strategy*, No. 18.

Chussil, Mark J. (1984), "PIMS: Fact or Folklore—Our Readers Reply," *Journal of Business Strategy*, 4 (Spring), 90–96.

Fruhan, William E. Jr. (1979), *Financial Strategy: Studies in the Creation, Transfer, and Destruction of Shareholder Value.* Homewood, IL: Irwin.

Gale, Bradley T. (1978), "Cross Sectional Analysis—The New Frontier in Planning," *Planning Review*, 6(2), 16–20.

Gale, Bradley T. and Ben Branch (1979), "The Dispute About High-Share Businesses," *The PIMSLETTER on Business Strategy*, No. 19.

Gale, Bradley T. and Ben Branch (1980), "Strategic Determinants of Cash Flow," *The PIMSLETTER on Business Strategy*, No. 25.

Gale, Bradley T. and Richard Klavans (1984), "Formulating a Quality Improvement Strategy," *The PIMSLETTER on Business Strategy*, No. 31.

Gale, Bradley T. and Ben Branch (1984), *"Beating the Cost of Capital,"* The *PIMSLETTER on Business Strategy*, No. 32.

Garvin, David A. (1984), "What Does Product Quality Really Mean," *Sloan Management Review*, 26 (Fall), 25–43.

Hambrick, Donald C., Ian C. MacMillan, and Diana L. Day (1982), "Strategic Attributes and Performance in the BCG Matrix—A PIMS-Based Analysis of Industrial Products Businesses," *Academy of Management Journal*, 25 (September), 510–531.

Hambrick, Donald C. and Ian C. MacMillan (1984), "Asset Parsimony—Managing Assets to Manage Profits," *Sloan Management Review*, 26 (Winter), 67–74.

Hax Arnoldo C. and Nicolas S. Majluf (1984), *Strategic Management: An Integrated Perspective*, Englewood Cliffs, NJ: Prentice Hall.

Jacobson, Robert and David A. Aaker (1985), "Is Market Share All That It's Cracked Up To Be?", *Journal of Marketing*, 49 (Fall), 11–22.

Kijewski, Valarie (1978), "Market Share Strategy: Beliefs vs. Actions," *The PIMSLETTER on Business Strategy*, No. 9.

Lambkin, Mary (1988), "Order of Entry and Performance in New Markets," *Strategic Management Journal*, 9 (Summer: Special Issue on Strategy Content Research), 127–140.

Lieberman, Marvin B. and David B. Montgomery (1988), "First-Mover Advantages," *Strategic Management Journal*, 9 (Summer: Special Issue on Strategy Content Research), 41–58.

Lubatkin, Michael and Michael Pitts (1983), "PIMS: Fact or Folklore?" *Journal of Business Strategy*, 3 (Winter), 38–44.

Lubatkin, Michael and Michael Pitts (1985), "PIMS and the Policy Perspective," *Journal of Business Strategy* 6 (Summer), 88–92.

Miller, Alex., John Guiniven and Bill Camp (1985), "Keys to Success for Adolescent Businesses," *The PIMSLETTER on Business Strategy*, No. 35.

Naylor, Thomas H. (1978), "PIMS: Through A Different Looking Glass," *Planning Review*, Vol. 6, 15–16, 32.

Ohmae, Kenichi (1985), "In Praise of Planning," *Planning Review* (November), 4.

Parasuraman, A., Valarie Ziethaml, and Leonard L. Berry (1986), *SERVQUAL: A Multiple-item Scale for Measuring Customer Perceptions of Service Quality*, Marketing Science Institute, Cambridge, Mass.

Parasuraman, A. and P. Rajan Varadarajan (1988), "Robustness of Ordinal Measures of Competitive Strategy Variables Employed In Business Research: A PIMS Data Based Analysis," *Journal of Business Research*, 17 (August), 101–113.

Phillips, Lynn W., Dae Chang, and Robert D. Buzzell (1983), "Product Quality, Cost Position, and Business Performance: A Test of Some Key Hypotheses," *Journal of Marketing*, 47 (Spring), 26–43.

Porter, Michael E. (1980), *Competitive Strategy: Techniques for Analyzing Industries and Competitors*, New York: The Free Press.

Prescott, John E., Ajay K. Kohli, and N. Venkatraman (1986), "The Market Share-Profitability Relationship: An Empirical Assessment of Major Assertions and Contractions," *Strategic Management Journal*, 7 (July–August), 377–394.

Ramanujam, Vasudevan and N. Venkatraman (1984), "An Inventory and Critique of Strategy Research Using the PIMS Data Base," *Academy of Management Review*, 9 (January), 138–151.

Robinson, William T. (1988), "Sources of Market Pioneer Advantages: The Case of Industrial Goods Industries," *Journal of Marketing Research*, 25 (February), 87–94.

Robinson, William T. and Claes Fornell (1985), "Sources of Market Pioneer Advantages in Consumer Goods Industries," *Journal of Marketing Research*, 22 (August), 305–317.

Robinson, William T. and Claes Fornell (1986), "Market Pioneering and Sustainable Market Share Advantages," *The PIMSLETTER on Business Strategy*, Number 39.

Schendel, Dan, and G. Richard Patton, (1976) "A Simultaneous Equation Model of Corporate Strategy," *Management Science*, 24 (November), 1611–1621.

Scherer, F. (1980), *Industrial Market Structure and Economic Performance*, Chicago, Rand-McNally.

Schoeffler, Sidney, Robert D. Buzzell, and Donald F. Heany (1974), "Impact of Strategic Planning on Profit Performance," *Harvard Business Review*, 52 (March–April), 137–145.

Schoeffler, Sidney (1977a) *Nine Basic Findings on Business Strategy*, Cambridge, Mass: The Strategic Planning Institute.

Schoeffler, Sidney (1977b), "Market Position: Build, Hold or Harvest," *The PIMSLETTER on Business Strategy*, No. 3.

Strategic Planning Institute (1980), *The PIMS Program*, Cambridge, Mass.

Strategic Planning Institute (1986), *Major Principles of Business Unit Strategy*, Cambridge, Mass.

Varadarajan, P., Rajan (1985a), "Product Effort and Promotion Effort Hypotheses: An Empirical Investigation," *Journal of the Academy of Marketing Science*, 13 (Winter), 47–61.

Varadarajan, P. Rajan and William R. Dillon (1981), "Competitive Position Effects and Market Share: An Exploratory Investigation," *Journal of Business Research*, 9 (March), 49–64.

Varadarajan, P. Rajan and William R. Dillon (1982), "Intensive Growth Strategies: A Closer Examination," *Journal of Business Research*, 10 (December), 503–522.

Varadarajan, P. Rajan (1985b), "A Two-factor Classification of Competitive Strategy Variables," *Strategic Management Journal*, 6 (October–December), 357–375.

Wells, John R. (1984), "In Search of Synergy," Doctoral Thesis, Harvard Business School.

Wensley, Robin (1981), "Strategic Marketing: Betas, Boxes or Basics," *Journal of Marketing*, 45 (Summer), 173–182.

Wind, Yoram, Vijay Mahajan, and Donald J. Swire (1983), "An Empirical Comparison of Standardized Portfolio Models," *Journal of Marketing*, 47 (Spring), 89–99.

Woo, Carolyn Y. (1984), "Market-Share Leadership—Not Always So Good," *Harvard Business Review*, 62 (January–February), 50–54.

Woo, Carolyn Y. and Arnold C. Cooper (1982), "The Surprising Case for Low Market Share," *Harvard Business Review*, 60 (November–December), 106–113.

Woo, Carolyn and Arnold C. Cooper (1981), "Strategies of Effective Low Share Businesses," *Strategic Management Journal*, 2 (July–September), 301–318.

Zeithaml, Carl P. and Louis W. Fry (1984), "Contextual and Strategic Differences Among Mature Businesses in Four Dynamic Performance Situations," *Academy of Management Journal*, 27 (December), 841–860.

APPENDIX*

SELECTED QUESTIONS FROM
PIMS DATA FORMS**

Please enter the years for which data is being submitted in **ascending order.** These years should be used consistently throughout the data forms.

19 __ __	19 __ __	19 __ __	19 __ __	19 __ __

301: Size of Market (D)

Indicate the total sales of the market actively served by your business. Your entry should include price inflation (i.e., do not adjust your entry for inflation).

301.0:

302: Number of Competitors

Approximately how many domestic and foreign businesses compete in your served market? "Domestic" means having corporate headquarters in any country within the served market (Line 304, page 8). Include your business. Ignore competitors with less than 1% of served market sales.

Domestic [ ] 302.1

Foreign [ ] 302.2

★Source: Reproduced with permission from: The Strategic Planning Institute, Cambridge, Massachusetts.
**Data Form 1: Business Profile
Data Form 2: Financials
Data Form 3: Assumptions for Strategy Analysis

401: Market Share Rank

Indicate the market share rank (1 = largest, etc.) of your business, in its served market, for each year.

402: Market Shares

Report the annual shares of served market's sales for your business and for each of your three largest competitors. "Share of market" is defined as the sales billed by a business as a percentage of the total sales to your served market.

Define competitors A, B and C on the basis of the most recent year, and use these definitions for all preceding years. If a competitor was not one of the top three in the most recent year of data, its share should not appear on Line 402, even if it was among the top three in prior years.

402.0: Your Business

%	%	%	%	%

402.1: Competitor A (the largest competitor in the *most recent* year)

%	%	%	%	%

402.2: Competitor B (the second largest competitor in the *most recent* year)

Enter "0" in each year your business had only one competitor.

%	%	%	%	%

402.3: Competitor C (the third largest competitor in the *most recent* year)

Enter "0" in each year your business had only one or two competitors.

%	%	%	%	%

403: Three Largest Competitors, Combined
Total (Not Including Your Business)

For each year, enter the **combined** share **in this served market** of the three largest competitors in **that** year. These data will be used to calculate the relative market share of your business, i.e., its share divided by the combined share of your three largest competitors.

| % | | % | | % | | % | | % |

308: Served Market Concentration Ratio

Enter the percentage of sales in your served market currently accounted for by the four largest competing businesses. Include your business if it is one of the four largest.

| % |

303: Geographic Scope of Served Market

Indicate the geographic scope of your served market. Do not respond "More than one country" if 90 percent or more of your served market's sales take place in one country.

Regional within one country ☐ 1

Entire country ☐ 2

More than one country ☐ 3

309: Exports

What percentage (nearest 5%) of finished products or services **produced** within your served market is **consumed** . . . (**Enter a percentage for each line, even if it is zero.**)

in a country **within** your served market but having crossed at least one national boundary? | % |

in all countries **outside** your served market? | % |

310: Imports

What percentage (nearest 5%) of finished products or services **consumed** within your served market is **produced** . . . (**Enter a percentage for each line, even if it is zero.**)

in a country **within** your served market but having crossed at least one national boundary? | % |

in all countries **outside** your served market? | % |

PRODUCT DESCRIPTION

101: Type of Business

Your business is best described as . . .

Consumer Products Manufacturing:

...durable products ☐ 1

...non-durable products ☐ 2

Industrial/Commercial/Professional
Products Manufacturing:

...capital goods ☐ 3

...raw or semi-finished materials ☐ 4

...components for incorporation into finished products ☐ 5

...supplies or other consumable products ☐ 6

...natural resources and agriculture ☐ 7

Services:
...consumer (i.e., more than 50% of end customers are individuals) ☐ 8
...industrial/commercial/professional ☐ 9

Retail and wholesale distribution:
...consumer (i.e., more than 50% of end customers are individuals) ☐ 10
...industrial/commercial/professional ☐ 11

104: Order of Market Entry

At the time your business first entered the served market, it was viewed as . . .

...one of the pioneers ☐ 1

...an early follower ☐ 2

...a later entrant ☐ 3

105: Life-Cycle Stage: Product Technology

Describe the stage of development of the products or services sold by your business.

New: product did not exist five years ago. (If you check this category, please contact your PIMS account manager. The data forms for a Start-Up Business may be more appropriate than these.) ☐ 0

Introductory Stage: primary demand for product just starting to grow; product still unfamiliar to many potential users. ☐ 1

Growth Stage: demand growing at 10% or more annually in real terms; technology or competitive structure still changing. ☐ 2

Maturity Stage: product familiar to a vast majority of prospective users; technology and competitive structure reasonably stable. Real growth ranges between 0% and 10%. ☐ 3

Decline Stage: product viewed as commodity; weaker competitors beginning to exit. Real growth is negative. ☐ 4

106: Life-Cycle Stage: Product Mix

The life-cycle stage of your competitors' current product mix is . . . If unsure, answer "about the same." (**Check one in each column.**)

	Competitor A	Competitor B	Competitor C
...one or more stages newer than your business's	☐ 1	☐ 1	☐ 1
...about the same as your business's	☐ 2	☐ 2	☐ 2
...one or more stages older than your business's	☐ 3	☐ 3	☐ 3

112: Life-Cycle Stage: Operating-Process Technology

Describe the stage of the technological life cycle of your business's operating process.

Introductory Stage: process technology very new and employed by few or no competitors. ☐ 1

Growth Stage: process rapidly gaining acceptance; major changes/advances still common. ☐ 2

Maturity Stage: process has stabilized and has been employed by most or all competitors for some time. ☐ 3

Decline Stage: process being made obsolete by substantially different and more advanced technology. ☐ 4

115–116: Patents and Trade Secrets

Does your business benefit or suffer **to a significant degree** from patents, trade secrets, or other proprietary methods of production or operation? If unsure, answer "Neither." (**Check one in each column.**)

	115:	**116:**
	Products	Processes
Patent disadvantage	☐ 1	☐ 1
Patent advantage	☐ 3	☐ 3
Neither	☐ 2	☐ 2

107: Standardization of Products

The products or services offered by your business and your leading competitors are . . .

...more or less standardized for all customers   ☐ 1

...custom-designed for individual customers   ☐ 2

108: Product-Sales Concentration

What percentage of your sales (nearest 10%) is derived from your largest-selling single product or service?   ☐ %

109: Frequency of Product Changes

Your business and your leading competitors typically change all or part of the product line offered . . . (Include product improvements, product-line extensions, style changes, and new products.)

...seasonally   ☐ 1

...annually   ☐ 2

...periodically (but at intervals longer than one year)   ☐ 3

...sporadically (no regular, periodic pattern of change)   ☐ 4

...not at all   ☐ 0

425: Consequences of Product Failure

If your product or service were to unexpectedly fail during typical use by its **final consumer,** what is the **maximum** damage that the failure might cause under ordinary circumstances? For example, failure of automobile brakes under ordinary circumstances might well cause loss of life; failure of a telephone under ordinary circumstances would probably have relatively minor consequences, even though it is conceivable that such a failure in an emergency might lead to death.

Minor inconvenience
(e.g., newspaper missing a section)

☐ 1

Major inconvenience
(e.g., airline losing luggage)

☐ 2

Temporary physical distress
(e.g., improper dental care causing toothache)

☐ 3

Serious injury or illness

☐ 4

Loss of life

☐ 5

Impossible to estimate

☐ 0

CUSTOMERS

End Customers and Immediate Customers

End customers either consume the products or incorporate them into other products. **Immediate** customers purchase products directly from your business. Immediate customers are **also** end customers when they consume the product or incorporate it into other products.

126: Distribution of Use Among
End-Customer Groups

Approximately what percentage (nearest 10%) of your business's products or services is used by . . . (**Supply an answer on each line, even if the percentage is 0.**)

...households or individual consumers?

[___] %

...manufacturers or service companies, including use of products as components, materials, etc.?

[___] %

...institutional, commercial, or professional customers?
(Include schools, hospitals, etc., in this category.)

[___] %

...government or public utilities?
(Do not include nationalized firms in this category.)

[___] %

...contractors?

[___] %

...natural resource and agricultural businesses?

[___] %

100%

Number of Customers

Approximately how many customers purchase your business's products or services? Enter the average of the last 3 years.

End Customers **127.1:** [ ]   Immediate Customers **128.1:** [ ]

Reliance on Important Immediate Customers

What percentage (nearest 5%) of your business's . . .

129.1: immediate customers account for **50%** of your total sales?   [%]

130.1: total sales is accounted for by your **single largest** immediate customer?   [%]

132: Customers' Purchase Intervals

How often do your business's customers purchase your products or services? Focus on purchase orders, not on delivery schedules. (**Check one in each column.**)

	Largest Immediate Customer	Typical Immediate Customer	Typical End Customer
Weekly or more frequently	□ 1	□ 1	□ 1
Once/week up to once/month	□ 2	□ 2	□ 2
Once/month up to once/6 months	□ 3	□ 3	□ 3
Once/6 months up to once/year	□ 4	□ 4	□ 4
Once/year up to once/5 years	□ 5	□ 5	□ 5
Less frequently than once/5 years	□ 6	□ 6	□ 6
Once	□ 7	□ 7	□ 7
Irregular intervals	□ 0	□ 0	□ 0

134: Percentage of Customers' Annual Purchases

Indicate the percentage of customers' total annual purchases accounted for by purchases of the types of products or services sold by your business. Use after-tax family income for total annual consumer purchases. Use one year's capital expenditures for capital-goods purchases. (**Check one in each column.**)

	Largest Immediate Customer	Typical Immediate Customer	Typical End Customer
Less than 0.25%	☐ 1	☐ 1	☐ 1
From 0.25% up to 1%	☐ 2	☐ 2	☐ 2
From 1% up to 5%	☐ 3	☐ 3	☐ 3
From 5% up to 25%	☐ 4	☐ 4	☐ 4
Over 25%	☐ 5	☐ 5	☐ 5

135: Switching Costs

How costly would it be for the end customer of your type of product or service to switch among products offered by your business and your leading competitors?

Not costly at all	☐ 1
Somewhat costly (some learning costs, no operating costs)	☐ 2
Costly (but requiring no changes in equipment, software, etc.)	☐ 3
Very costly	☐ 4

176–179: Distribution Channels

What percentage (nearest 10%) of your business's sales goes . . .
(Supply an answer on each line even if the percentage is 0.)

	Your Business	Comp. A	Comp. B	Comp. C
176: directly to end customers?	%	%	%	%
177: to end customers via company-owned distribution facilities?	%	%	%	%
178: to wholesalers?	%	%	%	%
179: to retailers?	%	%	%	%
	100%	**100%**	**100%**	**100%**

MARKET DIVERSITY

Compare the breadth of your business's participation in this served market to the breadth of the participation by each of your leading competitors. (**Check one in each column.**)

311: Your competitors serve . . .

	Competitor A	Competitor B	Competitor C
...more end customers than your business	☐ 1	☐ 1	☐ 1
...as many end customers as your business	☐ 2	☐ 2	☐ 2
...fewer end customers than your business	☐ 3	☐ 3	☐ 3

312: Your competitors' ranges of end-customers' annual purchases are . . .

	Competitor A	Competitor B	Competitor C
...broader than that of your business	☐ 1	☐ 1	☐ 1
...similar to that of your business	☐ 2	☐ 2	☐ 2
...narrower than that of your business	☐ 3	☐ 3	☐ 3

313: The geographic areas covered by your competitors' end customers are . . .

	Competitor A	Competitor B	Competitor C
...larger than that of your business	☐ 1	☐ 1	☐ 1
...similar to that of your business	☐ 2	☐ 2	☐ 2
...smaller than that of your business	☐ 3	☐ 3	☐ 3

314: Your competitors serve . . .

	Competitor A	Competitor B	Competitor C
...more types of end customers than your business	☐ 1	☐ 1	☐ 1
...as many types of end customers as your business	☐ 2	☐ 2	☐ 2
...fewer types of end customers than your business	☐ 3	☐ 3	☐ 3

429: Your competitors' ranges of selling prices are . . .

	Competitor A	Competitor B	Competitor C
...broader than that of your business	☐ 1	☐ 1	☐ 1
...about the same as that of your business	☐ 2	☐ 2	☐ 2
...narrower than that of your business	☐ 3	☐ 3	☐ 3

430: Your competitors' product-line breadths are . . .

	Competitor A	Competitor B	Competitor C
...broader than that of your business	☐ 1	☐ 1	☐ 1
...about the same as that of your business	☐ 2	☐ 2	☐ 2
...narrower than that of your business	☐ 3	☐ 3	☐ 3

QUALITY PROFILE

The PIMS quality profiling process is designed to document your quality position, relative to competitors, as perceived by your customers.

416: Specifying Customer

Who specifies whether your business's product or service is chosen? Weight the relative importance of immediate customers, end customers, and advisors in the purchasing decision. If the immediate customer and end customer are the same, enter 0% for end customer.

Immediate Customers   [   ] %

End Customers   [   ] %

Advisor   [   ] %

100%

QUALITY PROFILING SHEET

Complete the quality profiling worksheet for the current year while taking the most important specifying customers' point of view. The worksheet should present a balance of both your customers' and your competitors' customers' views.

1. Identify the key purchase criteria that customers use to define their needs and to choose among suppliers. **Do not include price as a purchase criterion.** There are three categories of criteria: product, service, and image. Examples of typical product-related criteria are efficiency, durability, reliability, and aesthetics. Typical service-related criteria may include delivery, sales-force, and technical assistance. Only provide image-related attributes if brand name per se (e.g., Polo) is a major influence on the purchase decision.

   Identify only as many significant criteria as apply to your product or service. You do not have to fill out every line of the worksheet.

2. Weight (0–100%) the relative importance of each key purchase criterion. The sum of the weights for product, service, and image must equal 100%.

3. Indicate how customers in your served market rate the performance of each competitor on the key purchase criteria. The rating scale is from 0–10, where 10 means you meet the customers' needs perfectly every time, and 0 implies that you fail to meet the needs all the time. The ratings should be your estimate of the perceptions of the specifying customer. If there is any discernible difference in performance, provide a rating differential of at least 1. Rating differentials of 3 or greater represent a wide gap. For this exercise, competitors A, B, and C must be consistent with the largest three competitors previously defined.

4. Estimate the relative importance of quality versus price in the purchase decision of the specifying customer. For example, if this is clearly a quality-driven business, an appropriate answer may be 75% quality, 25% price.

You should consider filling out more than one worksheet if your position has changed significantly in the last five years. It may also be useful to separate different types of specifying customers or different product segments. Please discuss the use of multiple quality worksheets with your account manager.

CURRENT POSITION (19___)

Purchase Criteria (excluding price)	Relative Importance (%)	Performance Ratings (0 Low, 10 High)			
		Your Business	Comp. A	Comp. B	Comp. C
Product Related					
1					
2					
3					
4					
5					
6					
7					
8					
Sub-total	%				

Service Related

1						
2						
3						
4						
5						
6						
7						
8						
Sub-total					%	

Image Related

1			
2			
Sub-total		%	

Total	100%

Quality	
Price	
Total	100%

201

428: Relative Selling Prices

For each year, estimate your competitors' selling prices, relative to the average selling prices of your business.

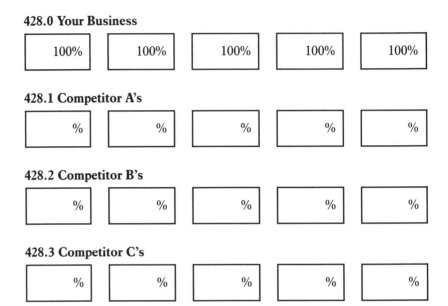

428.0 Your Business

| 100% | 100% | 100% | 100% | 100% |

428.1 Competitor A's

| % | % | % | % | % |

428.2 Competitor B's

| % | % | % | % | % |

428.3 Competitor C's

| % | % | % | % | % |

COMPETITIVE COST PROFILE

Relative Costs

In the following worksheets, enter your competitors' unit-cost structure relative to that of your business. The focus is on the cost per unit of output. In estimating your relative cost position the following should be considered: the type and source of raw materials used, the manufacturing process and manufacturing scale, differences in vertical integration, and the benefits of sharing resources, such as plant or sales force, with other businesses.

Start with the current position. If the relative costs are similar for all the years covered in these data forms, it is sufficient to complete just the form for the current position. If the relative cost positions have changed significantly, please complete an additional form (or forms) for the historical relative cost relationship.

Current Position (19__ __)

	Relative Cost Index			
	Your Business	Comp. A	Comp. B	Comp. C

Relative Cost Per Unit

438: Purchase	100			
439: Manufacturing/Operating	100			
440: Distribution	100			
433: Sales Force	100			
434: Media Advertising	100			
435: Sales Promotion	100			
436: Research and Development	100			
437: Fixed Capital Intensity	100			

Relative Cost Per Employee

431: Hourly Wage Rates	100			
432: Salary	100			

CORPORATE RELATIONSHIPS

141: Corporate Vertical Integration: Backward

Compare the degree of **backward** (toward raw materials) vertical integration of your corporation, in your line of business, with that of the corporations owning each of your leading competitors. If unsure about a competitor, enter "about as much." (**Check one in each column.**)

Your competitors' corporations
are backward integrated . . .

	Competitor A	Competitor B	Competitor C
...more than yours	☐ 1	☐ 1	☐ 1
...about as much as yours	☐ 2	☐ 2	☐ 2
...less than yours	☐ 3	☐ 3	☐ 3

114: Corporate Vertical Integration: Forward

Compare the degree of **forward** (toward end customers) vertical integration of your corporation, in your line of business, with that of the corporations owning each of your leading competitors. If unsure about a competitor, enter "about as much." (**Check one in each column.**)

Your competitors' corporations
are forward integrated . . .

	Competitor A	Competitor B	Competitor C
...more than yours	☐ 1	☐ 1	☐ 1
...about as much as yours	☐ 2	☐ 2	☐ 2
...less than yours	☐ 3	☐ 3	☐ 3

Shared Resources

There are two sides to the sharing issue:
(a) How much of your resources are shared with other businesses?
(b) Where there is sharing, are you a major or minor user of those shared resources?

A: What percent of the following resources of your business are shared with other components of your corporation? (**Check one in each row.**)

	No sharing	Less than 10%	10%-24%	25%-49%	50%-74%	More than 75%
142: Operating facilities	☐ 0	☐ 1	☐ 2	☐ 3	☐ 4	☐ 5
144: Immediate customers	☐ 0	☐ 1	☐ 2	☐ 3	☐ 4	☐ 5
146: Marketing programs	☐ 0	☐ 1	☐ 2	☐ 3	☐ 4	☐ 5

	No sharing	Less than 10%	10%-24%	25%-49%	50%-74%	More than 75%
148: R&D	☐ 0	☐ 1	☐ 2	☐ 3	☐ 4	☐ 5
150: Purchasing	☐ 0	☐ 1	☐ 2	☐ 3	☐ 4	☐ 5

B: What percent of the following shared resources does your business use? (**Check one in each row.**)

	No sharing	Less than 10%	10%-24%	25%-49%	50%-74%	More than 75%
143: Operating facilities	☐ 0	☐ 1	☐ 2	☐ 3	☐ 4	☐ 5
145: Immediate customers	☐ 0	☐ 1	☐ 2	☐ 3	☐ 4	☐ 5
147: Marketing programs	☐ 0	☐ 1	☐ 2	☐ 3	☐ 4	☐ 5
149: R&D	☐ 0	☐ 1	☐ 2	☐ 3	☐ 4	☐ 5
151: Purchasing	☐ 0	☐ 1	☐ 2	☐ 3	☐ 4	☐ 5

PURCHASES AND SALES WITHIN THE CORPORATION

152: Internal Purchases by Your Business

What percentage of your business's purchases (Line 208, Data Form 2, page 5) is obtained from other components of your corporation? Exclude purchases of capital equipment.

0%-10%	11%-20%	21%-30%	31%-40%	41%-50%	Over 50%
☐ 1	☐ 2	☐ 3	☐ 4	☐ 5	☐ 6

153: Internal Sales to Your Business

What percentage of sales of other components of your corporation is represented by their sales to your business? Consider only those components that sell to your business.

0%-10%	11%-20%	21%-30%	31%-40%	41%-50%	Over 50%
☐ 1	☐ 2	☐ 3	☐ 4	☐ 5	☐ 6

156: Internal Suppliers' Transfer Price

Compared to the market price, what is the actual transfer price of items supplied to your business by other components of your corporation?

Transfer price is . . .

...at least 10% below market price ☐ 1

...5% to 10% below market price ☐ 2

...about equal to market price ☐ 3

...5% to 10% above market price ☐ 4

...more than 10% above market price ☐ 5

INTERNAL SALES BY YOUR BUSINESS

158: Internal Sales by Your Business

What percentage (nearest 10%) of your business's sales is made to other components of your corporation?

%	%	%	%	%

159: Your Business's Transfer Price

Compared to the market price, what is the actual transfer price of items supplied by your business to other components of your corporation?

...at least 10% below market price ☐ 1

...5% to 10% below market price ☐ 2

...about equal to market price ☐ 3

...5% to 10% above market price ☐ 4

...more than 10% above market price ☐ 5

160: Arrangements With Internal Customers

The components of your corporation that buy from your business are . . .

...**obliged** to make **all** purchases of your business's types of products from your business.   □ 1

...**obliged** to make **some** purchases of your business's types of products from your business.   □ 2

...**not obliged** to purchase from your business.   □ 3

169: Production Process

What percentages (nearest 10%) of your business's sales were derived from . . .

(Enter a percentage for each line, even if it is zero.)

...products manufactured in small batches (production runs normally under 200)?   ☐ %

...products manufactured in large batches or on an assembly line?   ☐ %

...products manufactured using a continuous process?   ☐ %

...non-manufacturing activities? (Service and distribution businesses should enter "100" in this line and "0" in all others.)   ☐ %

100%

PRODUCTION PROCESS

272: Capacity Utilization

What percentage of the standard (rated) capacity was used, on average, during each year? Include production for inventory. If your business shares operating facilities with other businesses, indicate the overall capacity utilization. (Example: If your business operates with two shifts but would normally use three, its capacity utilization is no more than 67%.)

☐ %   ☐ %   ☐ %   ☐ %   ☐ %

410: Competitors' Capacity Utilization

For each year, estimate the actual capacity utilization (nearest 5%) of each of your leading competitors.

410.1: Competitor A

| % | % | % | % | % |

410.2: Competitor B

| % | % | % | % | % |

410.3: Competitor C

| % | % | % | % | % |

236: Seasonality of Sales, Production, and Purchases

In your business's three consecutive months of heaviest activity in sales, production, and purchases, about how much of total activity takes place? (**Check one in each column.**)

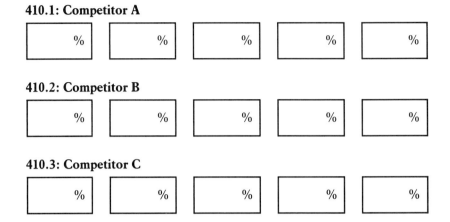

	Sales	Production	Purchases
Not seasonal	☐ 1	☐ 1	☐ 1
1/4 to 1/3	☐ 2	☐ 2	☐ 2
1/3 to 1/2	☐ 3	☐ 3	☐ 3
Over 1/2	☐ 4	☐ 4	☐ 4

NEW PRODUCTS

"New products" may replace existing products or be added to the product line. They may either perform a new (to you) function for your existing market, offer an "old" product to a new market, or be new in both respects. They usually have one or more of the following characteristics: relatively long gestation period, major retooling or other changes to operating facilities, separate promotional budgets, or separate product management. Examples of "new products" are a line of low-calorie soups added to a range of regular soups, and color televisions added to a line of black-and-white televisions. Product improvements, product-line extensions, and style changes are not "new products."

442: New-Product Sales

Estimate the percentage (within 10%) of sales accounted for by new products introduced during that year or the two preceding years, for your business and for each of your competitors. Example: for 1986, enter the percentage of sales generated by new products introduced in 1984, 1985, and 1986.

442.0 Your Business

%	%	%	%	%

442.1 Competitor A

%	%	%	%	%

442.2 Competitor B

%	%	%	%	%

442.3 Competitor C

%	%	%	%	%

441: Development Time for New Products

For your business and for your competitors, what is the typical time-lag between the initial stage of research and development for a new-product concept and the product's first commercial sale?

Less than 1 year ☐ 1

1 year to 2 years ☐ 2

2 years to 5 years ☐ 3

More than 5 years ☐ 4

444: New-Product Patent Protection

Does your business have a significant patent advantage in its . . . (If unsure whether an advantage was significant, answer "No".) (**Check one in each column.**)

...new products?   ...processes for new products?

| No ☐ 1 | | No ☐ 1 |
| Yes ☐ 2 | | Yes ☐ 2 |

444.1   444.2

445: Effect of New Products on Relative Quality

How does the **relative** quality of the new products compare to the **relative** quality of the products already in your product line? If unsure, answer "about the same." (Use the codes shown below.)

☐ ☐ ☐ ☐ ☐

446: Effect of New Products on Relative Price

How does the **relative** price of the new products compare to the **relative** price of the products already in your product line? If unsure, answer "about the same." (Use the codes shown below.)

☐ ☐ ☐ ☐ ☐

Codes: (Use to answer questions 445–446)

> **Relative quality/price of new products is:**
>
> 1. at least 15% lower than existing products'
> 2. 5–15% lower than existing products'
> 3. about the same as existing products'
> 4. 5–15% higher than existing products'
> 5. at least 15% higher than existing products'
> 0. Not applicable; no new products sold this year

448: Response Time

When your business introduced new products, how long did each of your leading competitors take to respond in a manner visible to your immediate customers?

(Check one in each column.)

	Competitor A	Competitor B	Competitor C
Less than one month	☐ 1	☐ 1	☐ 1
One month up to three months	☐ 2	☐ 2	☐ 2
Three months up to six months	☐ 3	☐ 3	☐ 3
Six months up to one year	☐ 4	☐ 4	☐ 4
One year or longer	☐ 5	☐ 5	☐ 5
No visible response	☐ 6	☐ 6	☐ 6
Not applicable: you were responding to this competitor	☐ 7	☐ 7	☐ 7

319: Origin of Latest Entrant

Describe the latest entrant into your served market. Do not include acquisition entrants. (**Check one for each of the three questions.**)

The latest entrant was from . . .

...a foreign corporation
(i.e., headquartered outside your served market) ☐ 1

...a domestic corporation
(i.e., headquartered within your served market) ☐ 2

319.1

The latest entrant was . . .

...a supplier integrating forward ☐ 1

...a customer integrating backward ☐ 2

...a new company formed to serve this market ☐ 3

...other ☐ 4

...geographic expansion ☐ 5

320: Total Market Share of Recent Entrants

Estimate the current combined market shares of all competitors who entered your served market within the last seven years.

☐ %

FINANCIALS

Income Statement

	19_ _	19_ _	19_ _	19_ _	19_ _
201: Sales					
208: Purchases					
209: Value Added					
210: Total Manufacturing Labor					
211: Distribution					
212: Depreciation					
213: Other Manufacturing/Operating					
214: Total Manufacturing/Operating					

215: Sales Force				
216: Media Advertising				
217: Sales Promotion				
218: Other Marketing				
219: Total Marketing				
220: Product Research & Development				
222: Process Research & Development				
224: Total Research & Development				
226: Licensing and Royalty Expenses				
229: General and Administrative				
230: Extraordinary Expenses				
228: Income (before interest & taxes)				

213

BALANCE SHEET

ASSETS

	19__	19___	19___	19___	19___	19___
245: Cash						
246: Accounts Receivable (Net)						
247: Finished-Goods Inventory						
248: Raw Materials and W-I-P						
249: Total Inventory						
251: Other Current Assets						
252: Total Current Assets						
255: Gross Plant & Equipment						
257: Accumulated Depreciation						
258: Net Plant & Equipment						

214

259: Other Non-Current Assets				
Total Assets				

LIABILITIES

260: Short-Term Borrowing				
243: Accounts Payable				
244: Other Current Liabilities				
262: Total Current Liabilities				
264: Investment				
265: Total Liabilities				
263: Working Capital				

Note: Balance sheet data should be entered as averages for each year.

238: Index of Selling Prices

For each year, express your business's average selling prices as a percentage of base year unit selling prices. This index should include inflation and changes in relative price. This index is meant to measure changes in **selling prices only;** do not include the effect of changes in the product mix.

100%	%	%	%	%

239: Index of Basic Materials Costs

For each year, estimate the unit prices your business paid for its basic materials. Express as a percentage of your business's base year unit purchase prices. This index is meant to measure changes in **materials costs only;** do not include the effect of changes in the product mix.

100%	%	%	%	%

241: Index of Average Hourly Wage Rates

For each year, estimate the average hourly wage rate paid by your business. Include the costs of fringe benefits and pension plans. Express as a percentage of your business's base year hourly wage rates.

100%	%	%	%	%

BALANCE SHEET: SUPPLEMENTAL DATA

250: Accounting Method
for Inventory Valuation

Which accounting method does your business use for inventory valuation?

LIFO ☐ 1	LIFO ☐ 1	LIFO ☐ 1	LIFO ☐ 1	LIFO ☐ 1
FIFO ☐ 3	FIFO ☐ 3	FIFO ☐ 3	FIFO ☐ 3	FIFO ☐ 3
Other ☐ 2	Other ☐ 2	Other ☐ 2	Other ☐ 2	Other ☐ 2

273: Special-Purpose Plant and Equipment

Indicate the percentage of P&E in your business (Line 253) dedicated to a special purpose. This is the percentage of P&E that is economically useful only for the product(s) or component(s) it is currently producing.

0% to 10%	☐ 1
11% to 30%	☐ 2
31% to 50%	☐ 3
More than 50%	☐ 4

323: SIC Code

Businesses located in the United States are encouraged (but not required) to supply their SIC category. Businesses located outside the United States are encouraged (but not required) to supply their U.S.-equivalent SIC category.

Show the Standard Industrial Classification group of your business using at least a four-digit category (five or six digits if possible). Please enter "0" for the fifth and/or sixth digits if they are unknown or otherwise unavailable.

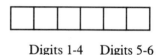

Digits 1-4   Digits 5-6

ASSUMPTIONS FOR STRATEGY ANALYSIS

Served Market

501–502: Assumed Change in
Size of Served Market

Estimate the most likely yearly rate of change in the size of your served market. Your estimate should combine real (unit sales) changes and changes in selling prices.

501:
Short term (years 1 through 4)
+ or −

☐ ☐ %

502:
Long term (Years 5 through 10)
+ or −

☐ ☐ %

503–504: Assumed Change in Selling Prices

Estimate the most likely yearly rate of change in the unit selling prices of products or services within your served market. Your estimate should assume no change in the product mix.

503:
Short term (years 1 through 4)
+ or −

| | % |

504:
Long term (years 5 through 10)
+ or −

| | % |

507–508: Assumed Change in Costs of Purchases

Estimate the most likely yearly rate of change in the unit prices that your business will pay for purchased materials.

507.1:
Short term (years 1 through 4)
+ or −

| | % |

508.1:
Long term (years 5 through 10)
+ or −

| | % |

511–512: Assumed Change in Costs of Plant and Equipment

Estimate the most likely yearly rate of change in the prices your business would have to pay for new plant and equipment.

511:
Short term (years 1 through 4)
+ or −

| | % |

512:
Long term (years 5 through 10)
+ or −

| | % |

ENTRY AND EXIT OF COMPETITORS

522: Probability of Competitor Entry

Estimate the probability that a new competitor will enter your served market within the next three years and gain at least 5% market share.

Unlikely (0% to 10% probability) □ 1

Possible (10% to 50% probability) □ 2

Probable (50% to 90% probability) □ 3

Very likely (90% to 100% probability) □ 4

523: Probability of Competitor Exit

Estimate the probability that a competitor currently holding at least 5% market share in your served market will drop out of your served market within the next three years.

Unlikely (0% to 10% probability)   ☐ 1

Possible (10% to 50% probability)   ☐ 2

Probable (50% to 90% probability)   ☐ 3

Very likely (90% to 100% probability)   ☐ 4

FEASIBLE STRATEGIES

Your answers to these questions will determine the range of possible strategies to be explored. Lines 525 through 530 define the maximum strategic changes that your business could make within the time specified on Line 524.

524: Strategy Implementation Period

Estimate the minimum number of years (between 1 and 8) which, in management's judgment, would be required to undertake and complete a new strategic move. Include not only the time required to implement all desired tactical changes (marketing programs, product-quality improvements, capacity addition, etc.), but also the time which it would take for the market to react to the moves. The end of the implementation period is marked by the achievement of all your business's long-range targets for market share, vertical integration, and/or mechanization. A typical span is four years.

☐ years

525–526: Changes in Market Share

Enter the largest amount by which, in your judgment, your business could raise or lower its market share within the time period specified on Line 524, expressed as a percentage of its current market share (Line 402.0, Data Form 1, page 6). Line 525 is the maximum percentage by which your business could increase market share through the most aggressive growth strategy that **management is willing to contemplate.** Line 526 is the maximum percentage by which your business could decrease market share through the most vigorous feasible harvest strategy that management is willing to contemplate.

525: Maximum increase

$+$ [%   ]

526: Maximum decrease

$-$ [%   ]

527–528: *Changes in Vertical Integration*

Enter the largest amounts by which your business could raise or lower its level of vertical integration, i.e., the ratio of value added (Line 209, Data Form 2, page 5) to sales (Line 201, Data Form 2, page 5), within the time period specified on Line 524, expressed as percentages of its current level of vertical integration. Do not include changes in prices or productivity that could change your business's ratio of value added to sales.

527: Maximum increase

$+$ [%   ]

528: Maximum decrease

$-$ [%   ]

529–530: *Changes in Mechanization*

Changes in mechanization result from changes in your business's production process, such that more (or less) plant and equipment, relative to the current process, is used to produce a given level of output. On Lines 529 and 530, enter the maximum possible percentage increase and the maximum possible percentage decrease in the amount of plant and equipment required to produce each unit of output. Do not include changes in the value of plant and equipment caused by inflation or equipment which could change your business's level of vertical integration.

529: Maximum increase

$+$ [%   ]

530: Maximum decrease

$-$ [%   ]

PERSPECTIVES FROM INDUSTRIAL

ORGANIZATION ECONOMICS

CHAPTER 6

I NTENSIVE, INTEGRATIVE

A ND DIVERSIFICATION

G ROWTH STRATEGIES

Introduction

Assessing Opportunities for Growth
The Product Innovation Spectrum
The Market Structure Profile
The Product-Market Growth Matrix

Intensive Growth Strategies
Market Penetration
Growth Through Market Penetration:
Problems and Challenges
Market Development
Growth Through Market Development:
Problems and Challenges
Product Development
Growth Through Product Development:
Problems and Challenges

Integrative Growth Strategies
Strategic Benefits and Costs of Vertical
Integration
Vertical Integration and Business Unit
Performance
Alternatives to Vertical Integration

Diversification Growth Strategies
Evolution of Diversified Firms
Definition and Conceptualization
Benefits of Diversification
Diversification Motives
Direction of Diversification
Synergy
Mode of Diversification
Diversification Strategy and Firm
Performance: An Overview

A Concluding Note

Appendix
The Measurement of Firm Diversity

References

INTRODUCTION

Alternative growth opportunities open to a firm can be broadly classified as intensive, integrative, and diversification growth opportunities (Kotler, 1988). The strategies employed by firms to take advantage of these classes of opportunities are termed intensive, integrative and diversification growth strategies, respectively. Intensive growth strategies refer to the pattern of resource deployment a firm formulates to take advantage of growth opportunities in its present product-market activity domain. Market penetration, market development, and product development constitute the major growth strategies in this cadre. Market penetration strategies consist of a firm's attempts to grow in its current served markets through more aggressive marketing of its present product offerings. Market development strategies denote a firm's attempts to develop new markets for its present product offerings. Product development strategies represent a firm's efforts to develop new products for its present served markets.

Integrative growth strategies refer to the pattern of resource deployment a firm formulates to take advantage of opportunities for growth in the various stages of the value added chain—raw materials, component production, assembly, distribution, retail, and service. Relative to the firm's present scope of activities in the value chain, backward vertical integration and forward vertical integration denote strategies employed to capitalize on opportunities for growth in the upstream and downstream stages of the value chain, respectively.[1] Diversification growth strategies refer to the pattern of resource deployment a firm develops to capitalize on opportunities for growth outside its present product-market domain. The new directions for growth a firm chooses to pursue might either be related to or unrelated to its present product-market activity scope.

This chapter provides an overview of strategic growth opportunities open to a firm and is organized into four major sections. The first section provides an overview of conceptual frameworks for assessing growth opportunities. The next three sections provide more detailed discussions of intensive, integrative, and diversification growth opportunities and the strategies that can be employed to exploit these growth opportunities.

The product portfolio analysis techniques discussed in chapters two and three provided diverse perspectives and viewpoints on the environmental and competitive conditions under which the pursuit of market share growth, share maintenance, and share harvesting as a strategic objective might be desirable. However, the literature on product portfolios provides only limited insight into how a business can increase its market share or maintain its dominant share in a growth market.[2] The discussion of intensive growth strategies presented in this chapter directly addresses this issue.

The concept of competitive advantage and the value chain were briefly discussed in chapter three. The strategic implications of the experience curve for achieving a competitive cost advantage through the pursuit of an aggressive share-building strategy were discussed in chapter four. Cost reduction is one of the primary motives underlying a firm's vertical integration decisions. Competitive activity comparisons in terms of the scope of value chain activities performed, the way the activities are performed, and their consequences for the cost of each activity as well as total cost can provide a firm with valuable insights into the relative cost position of competing firms (Day and Wensley, 1988). Furthermore, while in certain instances, a strategy of vertical integration may enable a firm to achieve a competitive cost advantage in its present product-markets, in other instances, it could be the basis for a decision to enter new businesses. For instance, Texas Instruments was initially a supplier of components to manufacturers of electronic calculators. Its decision to enter the electronic calculator business can be characterized as a strategy of forward vertical integration as well as diversification into a new product-market.[3] The section on vertical integration focuses on these and other related issues.

It was also pointed out in chapter two that the emergence and widespread use of portfolio models and other analytical approaches to strategic market planning constitute corporate responses to the problems and prospects of managing *diversity* (Haspeslagh, 1982). Some of the pertinent questions in this context are: How do single business firms evolve into diversified, multibusiness firms? What are the motives underlying the decision of firms to diversify into new product-markets? What diversification strategy alternatives are available to firms? These and other issues are addressed in the section on diversification.

ASSESSING OPPORTUNITIES FOR GROWTH[4]

The intensive, integrative, and diversification growth strategies trichotomy constitutes one of the many conceptualizations designed to facilitate systematic identification and effective exploitation of strategic growth opportunities. Numerous other alternative conceptualizations that are characterized by a product focus (Booz, Allen, and Hamilton, 1982; Heany, 1983) a market mix and marketing mix focus (Weber, 1976; Savage and Savage, 1982), a product-market focus (Ansoff, 1957, 1965), and a product-market-technology focus (Abell, 1980) also provide valuable insights in the strategic growth opportunities available to a firm.

The Product Innovation Spectrum

Booz, Allen, and Hamilton, Inc., a leading management consulting firm, conducted a survey of over seven hundred U.S. manufacturers, covering thirteen thousand new product introductions during a five-year period and identified six new product categories that differ in terms of newness to the company and to the marketplace (Booz, Allen, and Hamilton, 1982). Each of these constitutes a potential direction for growth.

- **New-to-the-world-products:** new products that create an entirely new market (for example: personal computers and video cassette recorders).
- **New product lines:** new products that, for the first time, allow a company to enter an established market (for example: Polaroid's introduction of blank recording tapes for video cassette recorders).
- **Additions to existing product lines:** new products that supplement a company's established product line (for example: Kodak's introduction of Disc cameras).
- **Improvements in/revisions to existing products:** new products that provide improved performance of greater perceived value, and replace existing products (for example, Gillette's introduction of Good News disposable razors with pivot head to replace the earlier Good News version without a pivot head).
- **Repositionings:** existing products that are targeted to new markets or market segments (for example, until the early eighties, Timex watches were positioned as purely utilitarian watches that were durable. This image was reinforced by using promotional messages such as "Timex watches can take a licking and keep on ticking", and demonstrated by subjecting the brand to brutal torture tests in television commercials. However, in recent years Timex has been attempting to reposition its brands as more up-scale, slick, and futuristic. This repositioning was undertaken in response to changing watch designs of competitors, and changing consumer tastes).
- **Cost reductions:** new products that provide similar performance at lower costs [for example, replacing integrated circuits (IC) with larger scale integrated circuits (LSI) and very-large-scale integrated circuits (VLSI) in numerous electronic equipments.] (Varadarajan 1986a).

An alternative conceptualization distinguishing between six levels of product innovation (style change, product-line extension, product im-

TABLE 6.1
OPPORTUNITIES FOR GROWTH: THE SPECTRUM OF PRODUCT INOVATION

Is the Market for Product Established?	Is the Business Already Serving Market?	Do Customers Know Functions and Features?	*What is the Design Effort?*		Innovation Type
			Product?	Process?	
Yes	Yes	Yes	Minor	Nil	Style change
Yes	Yes	Yes	Minor	Minor	Product-line extension
Yes	Yes	Yes	Significant	Minor	Product improvement
Yes	Yes	Yes	Major	Major	New product
Yes	No	Yes	Major	Major	Start-up business
No	No	No	Major	Major	Major innovation

Source: Heany, Donald F. (1983), "Degrees of Product Innovation," *Journal of Business Strategy*, 3 (Spring), 4.

provement, new product, start-up business, major innovation) proposed by Heany (1983) is presented in Table 6.1.

The Market Structure Profile

At the *individual product-market level,* the works of Weber (1976) provide a highly operational conceptualization of opportunities for growth. Weber labels the technique employed as market structure profile (MSP) gap analysis. Some of the major types of MSP gaps and sources of gap within each class identified in Weber are:

Type of MSP Gap	Source of Gap
A. Product line gap	Size related
	Options related
	Style, color, flavor, and fragrance related
	Form related
	Quality and price related
	Distributor brand/store brand/private brand related
	Segment related
B. Distribution gap	Geographic coverage related
	Distribution intensity related
	Distribution exposure related
C. Usage gap	Nonusage related
	Less frequent usage related
	Less quantity usage related

Figure 6.1 provides an overview of growth opportunities analysis through market structure profile analysis.

Opportunities for growth at the *individual product-market level* can also be identified by analyzing the values of microsales components (such as number of buyers, usage rate, etc.) underlying a product-market unit's total sales. For example, the total unit sales of a product-market unit in a given period can be alternatively expressed as follows (Varadarajan 1990):

Total unit sales =
  (a) number of buyers (N) $\times$ average frequency of purchase (P) $\times$ average quantity purchased per occasion (Q),

  or

  (b) number of users (N) $\times$ usage rate (U),

  or

  (c) number of heavy users (N_1) $\times$ usage rate (U_1)

  +

  number of moderate users (N_2) $\times$ usage rate (U_2)

  +

  number of light users (N_3) $\times$ usage rate (U_3),

  or

  (d) [number of buyers of product i for end use j (n_{ij}) $\times$ usage rate (U_{ij})] summed over all end uses (e.g., numerous end uses promoted for Arm & Hammer brand baking soda),

  or

  (e) number of trial purchasers (N_1) $\times$ average number of units purchased in a given time frame by trial purchasers (P_1)

  +

  number of repeat purchasers (N_2) $\times$ average number of units purchased in a given time frame by repeat purchasers (P_2).

These expressions indicate that increasing the number of users of the firm's product offerings is one of the many ways that a firm can achieve sales growth at the product-market level. Often, a firm's preoccupation with achieving sales growth by attracting users of competitors' product offerings and users of substitute products, and/or by converting nonusers of the product class might make it oblivious to opportunities for growth presented by other microcomponents underlying a product's total unit sales. The large outlays required to introduce new products and the small percentage of new products that succeed in the marketplace highlight the need to exploit to the fullest extent the growth and profit potential of present products. With reference to the neglect of present products, Savage and Savage (*The Wall Street Journal*, 1982) note with concern that some companies show little interest in their present products and fail to fully exploit their sales and profit potential. Box 6.1 presents a framework for exploiting growth opportunities through the use of market modification and marketing mix modification strategies.

Industry Market Potential (IMP)	Firm's Sales	Market Structure Profile (MSP) Gaps

Product Line Gap
1. Promote new uses†
2. Promote to new users†
3. Introduce new product lines‡
4. Close existing product line gaps
5. Create new product line elements through innovation, positioning, and significant product differentiation

Distribution Gap
6. Broaden geographic distribution coverage — national and international
7. Increase distribution intensity — new outlets and new types of outlets
8. Improve distribution exposure — in present distribution outlets

Usage Gap
9. Encourage nonusers to use the product
10. Stimulate light users to use more
11. Increase the amount used on each use occasion

Competitive Gap*
12. Penetrate the domain of substitutes
13. Penetrate the position of competitors

14. Defend present position

Growth strategies (for increasing the size of the IMP, creating new IMPs, and closing MSP gaps)

229

BOX **6.1**

OPPORTUNITIES FOR GROWTH THROUGH
MARKET MIX AND MARKETING MIX
MODIFICATION

Use focus   Are there other potential uses for the product? It has been reported that a 3M Company scientist trying to develop a super-strong adhesive ended up with one that would not stick very well. The scientist's continued quest to identify a potential use for the adhesive developed led to the ultimate introduction of Post-It Notes, the popular yellow stick-on note pads.

Market focus   Can a broader target market be developed for the product? Johnson & Johnson has been quite successful in its attempts to market its baby oil, baby powder, and baby shampoo to adults.

Is there a market for the unused by-products of the firm? Several lumber companies are also in the kitty litter business.

Is there a social trend that can be exploited? Juice Works, a new line of children's drinks introduced in 1984 by Campbell Soup Company, is made entirely out of natural fruit juices and without added sugar, but yet is sweet tasting. Juice Works is designed to appeal to the growing market of health-conscious and sophisticated consumers.

Promotion focus   Is the product a generic item that can be branded? The success of Butterball brand turkey, Perdue brand chicken, and Sunkist brand oranges attests to the feasibility of this strategy.

Is the product category underadvertised? The chocolate chip cookie business was, prior to the entry of Frito-Lay and Procter & Gamble.

The Product-Market Growth Matrix

The importance of exploiting the growth and profit potential of present products and markets not withstanding, numerous other studies highlight the need for simultaneous efforts directed at developing new products and new markets as well. Ansoff (1957) employed a 2×2 product-market matrix as a frame of reference for distinguishing between the following four basic growth strategies open to a firm:

	PRODUCT FOCUS	MARKET FOCUS	GROWTH STRATEGY
1.	Present products	Present markets	Market penetration
2.	Present products	New markets	Market development
3.	New products	Present markets	Product development
4.	New products	New markets	Diversification

Is there a more compelling way to promote the product? The sales of Procter & Gamble's Pampers brand diapers are reported to have substantially increased after a change in benefit emphasis from convenience to keeping the baby dry and happy.

Can the brand's disadvantages be turned into advantages? Smucker's brand jelly has successfully exploited this approach—"with a name like Smucker's, it has to be good."

Channel focus Is there scope to market the product through new or unconventional channels of distribution? L'eggs was the first brand of pantyhose to be distributed through supermarkets. It should, however, be noted that Hanes Corp. has not been successful in its attempts to pursue a similar strategy in the marketing of cosmetics.

Price focus Can profits and sales volume be increased by lowering rices? Texas Instruments' dominance in the electronic pocket calculators business and Black and Decker's dominance of the hand-held electric tools market is generally attributed to their effective use of experience-curve-based pricing strategies. (It has been observed in a number of industries that costs fall with cumulative experience. In industries where a significant portion of the total cost can be reduced, a firm can gain a cost advantage by pursuing a strategy geared to accumulate experience faster than competitors. This strategy implies that a firm that prices its products to achieve the largest market share will have the largest cumulative experience as well, and hence, the lowest unit cost.)

Source: Varadarajan, P. Rajan (1986a), "Marketing Strategies in Action", *Business,* 36 (January–March), 21.

Concern regarding the ability of a simple dichotomy of the product and market dimensions (present products-new products; and present markets-new markets) to realistically represent various gradations of product and market newness led others to propose extended and/or more detailed versions of Ansoff's 2 × 2 matrix (see Karger and Murdick, 1966; Kollat, Blackwell, and Robeson, 1972; Day, 1975; Abell, 1980; Varadarajan, 1983). For instance, Abell (1980) proposed that in defining the scope of a business, the three relevant dimensions are: the customer functions satisfied, the customer groups served, and the technologies used. As summarized in Table 6.2, the growth opportunities open to a firm can be conceptualized in terms of changes along one or more of these dimensions.

TABLE 6.2
OPPORTUNITIES FOR GROWTH: THE
CUSTOMER FUNCTIONS AND GROUPS
SERVED AND THE TECHNOLOGIES UTILIZED

Growth Opportunity Category	Customer Functions Served	Customer Groups Served	Technology Employed
1	Present	Present	Present
2	Present	Present	New
3	Present	New	Present
4	New	Present	Present
5	Present	New	New
6	New	Present	New
7	New	New	Present
8	New	New	New

INTENSIVE GROWTH STRATEGIES

This section provides a brief overview and real world examples of effective translation and operationalization of market penetration, market development, and product development growth strategies into specific action programs. Table 6.3 summarizes a range of possibilities for the effective exploitation of three broad classes of intensive growth strategies. The figure incorporates several key elements of the product innovation spectrum and market structure profile within the product-market growth matrix framework.

Market Penetration

Market penetration refers to a firm's attempts to increase sales of its present products in present markets. Possible courses of action include:

- increasing the number of users (broadening the customer base) by attracting users of competitors' brands,
- broadening the customer base by converting nonusers into users,
- increasing the frequency of purchase among present users, and
- increasing the average quantity purchased per transaction.

Broadening the customer base and increasing purchase frequency and/or purchase quantity are commonly achieved by:

- more effectively promoting present uses,
- identifying and promoting new uses,
- promoting more varied usage, and
- promoting product usage at different times of the day, different places, and on different occasions.

TABLE 6.3
OPPORTUNITIES FOR GROWTH: THE PRODUCT-MARKET GROWTH MATRIX

	Present Products — Feasible Operational Strategies	Growth Strategy	New Products — Feasible Operational Strategies
Market penetration	1. Increasing number of users by: (a) attracting users of competitors' products; (b) converting nonusers into users. 2. Increasing the frequency of purchase. 3. Increasing the average quantity purchased per transaction.	Growth Strategy — Product development	1. *Product reformulation:* Improving present products with extra ingredients, additives, etc. 2. *Product quality improvement:* Improving the functional performance of present products, e.g., durability, speed, taste, etc. 3. *Product feature additions:* Adding new product features to current product offerings and improving present product features through attempts to modify, substitute, rearrange, or combine existing features, etc. 4. *Product line extensions:* Increasing the breadth of the present product lines by: (i) introducing different quality versions of the product; (ii) introducing additional models and sizes, etc. 5. *Product replacement:* Replacing present product offerings with functionally and/or technologically superior offerings. 6. *New product development:* Introducing new products involving (a) related technology or (b) unrelated technology.
Market Development	Increasing the number of users (attracting new users) by: (a) reaching new market segments within present geographic markets; (b) reaching new market segments through regional, national, or international expansion.	Diversification	

Source: Varadarajan, P. Rajan (1986a), "Marketing Strategies in Action," *Business*, 36 (January–March), 14.

Promoting New Uses   One firm that has achieved considerable success in promoting new uses for its present products is Arm & Hammer. Over the years the company has successfully promoted several new uses for its principal product, Arm & Hammer baking soda. These include promoting use of the product:

- as a refrigerator deodorizer,
- as a bath additive,
- as a swimming pool disinfectant, and
- as a cat litter deodorizer and disinfectant.

It has even sponsored sweepstakes contests encouraging consumers to suggest new uses for the product. The critical importance of promoting new uses for this product are clearly highlighted by two major environmental developments:

1. An increase number of women are joining the workforce, accompanied by a corresponding decline in home baking.
2. The introduction of ready-to-use, packaged food products with baking soda added during the manufacturing process itself (purchased by manufacturers in bulk quantities as a commodity product at a low unit price) and the resultant decline in the purchase of branded baking soda (in small amounts at a high unit price) by households.

The first major new use promoted by Arm & Hammer baking soda was its use as a refrigerator deodorizer. Since practically every household in the United States owns a refrigerator, through effective promotion of this new use, the firm could increase its sales significantly.

Promoting More Frequent Usage and/or Larger Quantity Usage Effective exploitation of use frequency and use-quantity-related growth opportunities is exemplified in a number of successful case histories. For instance, Arm & Hammer, through a series of television commercials and print advertisements, strives to educate consumers that they should place one carton of Arm & Hammer baking soda in the freezer compartment of the refrigerator and another in the refrigerator compartment, and that both should be replaced once very two months.

In contrast to the *brand level focus* (selective demand stimulation) of Arm & Hammer, the Florida State Citrus Commission's successful repositioning of orange juice as an ideal drink for any time of day, not just breakfast, illustrates the effective exploitation of use-frequency-related growth opportunities at the *product class level* (primary demand stimulation).

Promoting Product Usage at New Times   Stemming from the realization that lunch sales accounted for only fifteen to eighteen percent of its total revenue (as compared to the fast food restaurant industry average of thirty-five percent), Pizza Hut chose to focus on increasing its share of the growing, multibillion-dollar, lunch market. Research studies that indicated that customers were favorably inclined towards having pizza for lunch provided they could get it quickly pointed to the existence of a ready market opportunity. Responding to the opportunity, the company undertook to develop equipment for the quick preparation of personal-size pizzas for the lunch market. Following test-market results that were favorable, Pizza Hut undertook a massive redesign of kitchens in Pizza Hut restaurants, and hired and trained personnel for a national launch. Furthermore, to lend credibility to its claim that customers could eat pizza for lunch without having to wait, the company developed a promotional campaign built around the theme "five minutes, guaranteed". Broadcast and print advertisements assured customers that if their order for a personal-size pan pizza was not served within five minutes, they would receive a coupon redeemable for a free personal-size pan pizza (*Marketing News*, 1983).

Growth Through Market Penetration:
Problems and Challenges

Although firms can realize sizeable increases in sales and profits by identifying and promoting new uses, this can in some situations be a time-consuming and frustrating process, as illustrated by the case of Lysol-brand disinfectant spray. Lysol has considerably benefitted over the years from the effective promotion of new uses for it. Since 1966, the manufacturer of Lysol and the Federal Trade Commission (FTC) were involved in an argument over the truthfulness of its new-use promotion that claimed spraying Lysol helps prevent the spread of the common cold. In 1974, Lysol agreed to give up its flu ads, as well as any claims that Lysol might also prevent colds, throat infections, or other upper respiratory diseases. However, it didn't give up on its research. The company funded studies at a leading medical school involving the deliberate infection of college students with the common cold. A sample of students with colds were them asked to handle coffee cups, door knobs, etc. A second sample of students were then asked to handle those very same objects and then rub their eyes and noses. By conducting a variety of such experiments and documenting the results, Lysol presented evidence to the FTC to the effect that spraying Lysol on telephones, doorknobs, bathroom sinks and taps, and other household surfaces helps reduce the spread of the common cold (Abrams, 1983).

Market Development

Market development refers to a firm's attempts to increase the sales of its present products by tapping new markets. As shown in Table 6.3, this is generally accomplished using two broad approaches:

1. reaching new market segments (customer groups) in present geographic markets, and

2. reaching new customer groups through regional, national, or international geographic expansion.

Reaching New Customer Groups in Present Geographic Markets When first introduced in 1979, 3M's Post-It Notes (the yellow stick-on note pads) were primarily targeted at the institutional market (office supplies). In 1984, as part of its market development efforts, 3M introduced Post-It Note Pads in a variety of colors targeted to the consumer market. Commensurate with the market development strategy, the product was distributed through drug, discount, hardware, and grocery stores, and promoted through the mass media (*Business Week*, 1984).

Aggressive pursuit of market-development-related growth opportunities by one firm can sometimes evolve into an industry-wide phenomenon. For instance, M&M/Mars, Hershey Foods Corp., Nestle Co., and other candy marketers target some of their brands specifically towards the adult-market in the eighteen-to-thirty-four year age group. Besides continuously striving to improve their market position in their traditional market segments (composed of children and teenagers), candy marketers in recent years have been targeting a sizeable portion of their effort to cultivate this large group of young adults, who, according to research studies, are more fond of candy than their parents' and grandparents' generations were (*The Wall Street Journal*, 1985).

Reaching New Users Through Geographic Market Expansion The case history of Heineken beer is one among numerous case histories of the successful development of new (international) geographic markets for consumer products. Although, Heineken ranks only fourth worldwide among brewers, it is the most international of brewers and has licensees or distributors in more than one-hundred-fifty countries. With few exceptions, Heineken beer is brewed to look the same and taste the same nearly everywhere and is positioned as a high-class beer that is worth the extra cost. However, the company develops separate advertising campaigns for each country taking into consideration the cultural differences and the diversity of markets served in each. In the United States, its advertising is designed to capitalize on America's fascination with high-quality imports, and Heineken is positioned as a foreign status symbol—the Rolls-Royce of beers. In France, its advertising is designed to entice a nation of wine drinkers to drink more beer. In Italy, since beer is drunk most often with food, the advertising campaign is designed to sell Heineken as a drink for all sorts of occasions that Italians don't normally associate with beer. In Britain, Heineken's marketing strategy is guided by the view that most beer-drinking Britains wouldn't respond favorably to the high-class, exclusive image that Heineken carefully tries to cultivate in other countries. Hence, it makes beer with less alcohol than normal to match competitive local brews and promotes Heineken as a distinctive, yet standard-price beer. Interestingly, unlike in most other parts of the world, where Heineken is promoted as an upscale beer for the upper crust, in view of its widespread usage and popularity in its home country, the Netherlands, the brand is promoted as a standard-price beer for everyone (Hudson, 1984).

Growth Through Market Development: Problems and Challenges

Reaching New Market Segments   Promoting present products to new market segments may at times present seemingly insurmountable barriers, as illustrated by the case of Gerber-brand baby foods. The company is supposedly aware of the fact that a sizeable number of people in the fifteen-to-twenty-two age bracket are closet users of Gerber-brand baby food. Once, the company mailed a free sample of Gerber's Dutch Apple dessert together with a free coupon for a second bottle of Gerber's dessert to thirty thousand readers of teenage magazines. Of all the coupons mailed, about half were redeemed, attesting to the existence of a latent market for the product. Encouraged by the results, the firm pressed ahead with its efforts to penetrate the teenage market with a print advertising campaign in which a youthful model says to her friend, "The secret's out—Gerber isn't just for babies." Despite its best efforts, the company has not been successful in its attempts to promote social acceptance of the consumption of baby food by teenagers in public. An advertising agency executive associated with the task of developing the teenage market for Gerber products is reported to have noted, "the difficult part is to play down the (Gerber) name as much as possible while guaranteeing Gerber quality and yet getting people off the hook for eating baby food" (Bronson, 1981).

Reaching New Geographic Markets   A firm's attempts to grow through geographic market development can be stunted in the face of formidable and entrenched competitors. In 1963, Procter and Gamble (P&G) acquired Folgers, a regional coffee company, and until 1977, Folgers was available only in seventy percent of U.S. markets. When P&G decided to expand its market coverage to include the whole United States, it supported its market development strategy with massive advertising and sales promotion. In response, General Foods, the industry leader, stepped up its efforts to defend its share. Over a four-year period, General Foods increased its expenditures on coffee advertising from $38.4 million in 1977 to $107.3 million in 1980. During the same period, P&G's advertising expenditure on coffee is estimated to have risen from $14 million to $51.4 million. As of 1981, General Foods had forty-two percent of U.S. coffee sales, the same proportion it had in 1977. Although P&G was in a position to increase its share of the U.S. coffee sales from fifteen percent in 1977 to twenty-one percent in 1981, it has been reported that the market share gain achieved was not at the expense of General Foods, but other firms (Smith, 1981).

Campbell Soup Co.'s unsuccessful attempts to penetrate the Brazilian market highlight the social and cultural barriers firms face in the international market development arena. In-depth interviews by company researchers are reported to have revealed that the Brazilian housewife felt that she was not fulfilling her role as a homemaker if she served her family a soup she could not call her own. Research also revealed that Brazilian housewives seemed to prefer dehydrated powdered soup marketed by Campbell's competitors, which they could use as a soup starter, but still add their own flair and ingredients to (*Business Week*, 1981).

Product Development

Product development refers to a firm's attempt to grow by selling new products to its present customers, or improved versions of its present products to its present customers. As detailed in Table 6.3, the following action possibilities constitute the major product development strategies:

- **The product reformulation strategy**—making improvements in present products such as using better ingredients, additives, etc.
- **The product quality improvement strategy**—improving the functional performance of present products, e.g., their durability, reliability, etc.
- **The product feature additions strategy**—building new features into present products.
- **The product line extension strategy**—broadening the product line by introducing additional sizes, forms, models, etc., of present products, and/or different quality versions of present products.
- **The new product development strategy**—introducing new products in present markets that are either related to or unrelated to present products.

A detailed discussion of these product development strategies follows.

The Product Reformulation Strategy   This appears to be the most pervasive strategy, as well as the product strategy of first resort in most industries. For instance, the laundry detergent industry is replete with examples of the introduction of Brand X, followed by the introduction of Improved Brand X, then New, Improved Brand X, and the New Brand X With Additives. A case in point: Bold laundry detergent was reformulated with the addition of a fabric softener and repositioned as Bold 3, a laundry detergent that cleans, softens, and fights static. Cheer-brand laundry detergent underwent a similar product reformulation a couple of years ago and was relaunched as new, all-temperature Cheer.

It has been reported that many of the recent product reformulations of Campbell's Soup Co. have been guided by the principle that all of its products, old and new, must appeal to health-conscious and sophisticated consumers. For example in an attempt to appeal to the more discriminating palates of this target market, Campbell reformulated its Swanson's TV dinners, replacing soggy french fries with more upscale food items (*Fortune*, 1984).

However, not all product reformulations are based on such careful deliberations. Neither are they all viewed favorably by industry observers. Commenting on the introduction of gel versions of Crest- and Colgate-brand toothpastes, a *Wall Street Journal* article noted that "the new introductions won't make teeth whiter nor prevent cavities any better than those manufacturers' current offerings" (Abrams, 1981). Nevertheless, product reformulation and variety extension strategies necessitated by competitive imperatives are quite pervasive in packaged consumer goods industries. For instance, it is conceivable that the introduction of gel versions of Crest- and Colgate-brand toothpastes were **defensive moves** by the firms concerned in response to inroads made by competing gel-type toothpastes such as Aim.

Many frequently purchased, branded consumer-product categories are characterized by marginal and/or diminishing differences between competing brands and infrequent significant technological breakthroughs/ improvements. For instance, fluoride, once the most important feature to toothpaste buyers, is now found in practically every brand of toothpaste. This leaves marketers with little choice but to attempt to gain market share through minor changes in product formulation, appearance, packaging, flavor, etc. The small percentage of new product introductions that succeed in the marketplace is another reason underlying the attempts by firms to breathe new life into their present products through product reformulation.

The Product Quality Improvement Strategy As detailed in chapter five, an extensive body of PIMS research has focused on the relationships between quality, market share, and business profitability. A firm can strive to improve quality along a number of dimensions: performance, features, reliability, conformance, durability, serviceability, aesthetics, and perceived quality (Garvin, 1984). Perceived product quality is a function of intrinsic product quality as well as a number of intangibles such as corporate/brand image and reputation, and the effectiveness of a firm's promotional efforts (advertising, personal selling, sales promotion, and publicity) in communicating superior product quality. A more detailed discussion of the major dimensions of quality is presented in Box 6.2.

BOX **6.2**

DIMENSIONS OF QUALITY

The following eight dimensions can be identified as a framework for thinking about the basic elements of product quality: performance, features, reliability, conformance, durability, serviceability, aesthetics, and perceived quality. Each is self-contained and distinct, for a product can be ranked high on one dimension while being low on another.

1. *Performance*   Performance refers to the primary operating characteristics of a product. For a television set, they would include sound and picture clarity, color, and ability to receive distant stations.

2. *Features*   Features are the "bells and whistles" of products, those secondary characteristics that supplement the product's basic functioning. In many cases, the line separating primary product characteristics (performance) from secondary characteristics (features) is difficult to draw.

3. *Reliability*   Reliability reflects the probability of a product's failing within a specified period of time. Among the most common measures of reliability are the mean time to first failure (MTFF), the mean time between failures (MTBF), and the failure rate per unit time.

4. *Conformance*   Conformance refers to the degree to which a product's design and operating characteristics match preestablished standards. Within the factory, conformance is commonly measured by the incidence of defects: the proportion of all units that fail to meet specifications, and so require

A firm can substantially benefit by pursuing a strategy of quality improvement if:

- quality can be improved,
- the improvement in quality is visible and can be effectively communicated to the consumer, and
- there are a sufficient number of buyers interested in superior quality (Kotler, 1988).

The extent to which a firm can attract competitors' customers and gain market share by pursuing a quality-improvement strategy (or for that matter, any strategy) also depends on the effectiveness of the **countermarketing strategies** and support programs of its competitor(s), as illustrated by the Heinz vs. Hunts ketchup case history. For years, Heinz-brand ket-

rework or repair. In the field, two common measures of conformance are the incidence of service calls for a product and the frequency of repairs under warranty.

5. *Durability*   Durability, a measure of product life, has both economic and technical dimensions. Technically, durability can be defined as the amount of use one gets from a product before it physically deteriorates. Durability becomes more difficult to interpret when repair is possible. Durability and reliability are closely linked. A product that fails frequently is likely to be scrapped earlier than one that is more reliable.

6. *Serviceability*   Consumers are concerned not only about a product breaking down, but also about the elapsed time before service is restored, the timeliness with which service appointments are kept, the nature of their dealings with service personnel, and the frequency with which service calls or repairs fail to resolve outstanding problems. Some of these variables can be measured quite objectively; others reflect differing personal standards of what constitutes acceptable service.

7. *Aesthetics*   Aesthetics—how a product looks, feels, sounds, tastes, or smells—are clearly matters of personal judgment and reflections of individual preferences.

8. *Perceived quality*   Perceptions of quality can be seen as subjective as assessments of aesthetics. Sometimes products are evaluated less on their objective characteristics than on their image, advertising, or brand names.

Source: Excerpted from the text of article by David A. Garvin (1984), "What Does "Product Quality" Really Mean?," *Sloan Management Review,* 26 (Fall), 25–43.

chup, the market leader, was promoted using comparative advertisements to reinforce the message that Heinz was the richest and thickest brand of ketchup on the market. More importantly, the rules of competition in the ketchup business seem to have been set by Heinz which established thickness as the most salient product attribute in the minds of consumers. After successfully developing a ketchup comparable to Heinz in thickness, Hunts, the market challenger, went on the offensive. In advertisements using a celebrity spokesperson, Hunts claimed, "You can't buy a thicker ketchup than Hunts. So why pay more for Heinz?" Around this period, Heinz discontinued using comparative advertisements emphasizing thickness. Besides highlighting the advantages of its packaging innovation— Heinz in squeezable plastic bottles—its advertisements focused on taste, and claimed that in taste tests, consumers preferred Heinz three times more often than they did competitors' brands (Morris, 1984).

The Product Feature Additions Strategy   A strategy of feature improvement aims to add new features that enhance the product's versatility, safety, or convenience. Developments in practically every industry are replete with illustrations of successful product feature improvement strategies. Although feature improvements can easily be imitated by competitors, certain advantages accrue to the firm that is the first to introduce new features:

- It brings the company free publicity.
- It helps generate enthusiasm and build morale among the salesforce, distributors, wholesalers, and retailers.
- It helps the firm build the image of being an innovator, trendsetter, and industry leader.
- It helps attract customer groups that tend to patronize brands that offer the most up-to-date features.
- Features can be added or dropped quickly without incurring considerable expense, or can be made optional (Kotler, 1988).

The Product Line Extension Strategy   Product line or variety extensions are routinely achieved in a number of ways. The introduction of new sizes (super-economy-size toothpaste), forms (deodorant in liquid, powder, spray, and stick forms), compositions (regular Head & Shoulders shampoo and Head & Shoulders shampoo with conditioner), flavors (Jello gelatin, which originally started with six flavors, is now available in more than a dozen), packages (Hi-C fruit flavored drink in glass bottles or paper or metal containers), and varieties (shampoo for dry, normal, and oily hair) are just some of the feasible courses of action.

In most industries, product proliferation (owing to the extensive recourse to product line extension strategies made by firms) has reached the point at which it offers U.S. consumers a range of choice unsurpassed in other parts of the world. For instance, Campbell's canned soup is available in over forty major varieties and numerous subvarieties in each major variety. The firm offers more than a dozen different types of chicken soup alone. Similarly, U.S. smokers, whose number is estimated at fifty million plus, have over two hundred and sixty styles of cigarettes to choose from that differ with respect to flavor, tar, length, package, and positioning. Marlboro, the best selling cigarette in the United States, comes in six styles, Kool comes in ten, and Newport, in eight. The high cost involved in introducing and popularizing a new brand name is reported to be one of the major considerations influencing manufacturers to introduce variations of their present brands. However, product proliferation has not slowed the pace of introduction of new brands significantly. Cigarette manufacturers justify the risk of new brand introductions on the grounds that a one percent share of the market is equivalent to $170 million in revenues, and that a new brand needs only a 0.5 percent share to be considered a success (Loeb, 1983).

In general, dominant firms within the industry tend to view product variety extension as a means of maintaining or increasing market share, and as an indispensable tool in the fierce struggle for supermarket shelf space. On the other hand, low-market-share firms within the industry and potential new entrants tend to view the line extension strategies of dominant firms as a calculated strategy to corner supermarket shelf space, keep out rival brands, and protect their near-monopoly position.

Industry observers of the marketing strategies pursued by most packaged consumer-products manufacturers have been critical of the growing trend towards excessive product proliferation. They have even speculated that the average consumer, who is unlikely to be interested in product variety beyond a point, is being forced to pay the cost of endless product proliferation in numerous packaged consumer-product categories in the form of higher prices of all products manufactured and marketed by the firms concerned. Unfortunately, even in industries in which there appears to be a consensus that product proliferation has gone beyond reasonable limits, in view of the risks involved, firms have not shown great initiative in cutting back on this proliferation by eliminating some of the brands and the sizes, shapes, forms, flavors, scents, colors, etc., within specific brands.

The Product Replacement Strategy   One of the most effective strategies that a firm can use to maintain its leadership position is to introduce new products that are superior replacements for its present product offerings. Often, innovative firms make their own products obsolete by replacing them with technologically, functionally, and/or aesthetically superior products, rather than waiting for their competitors to do so. A strategy of innovative obsolescence is crucial to sales growth and sustained profitability in most industries. Gillette's successful introduction of the Trac II twin-blade razor as a replacement for its conventional, single-blade razor, and its subsequent introduction of the Atra razor with a pivot head as a partial replacement for Trac II razors illustrate the effective implementation of the product replacement strategy.

The New Product Development Strategy   Product innovation is universally recognized as a strategy for building market share in mature as well as expanding markets. P&G's introduction of Pampers-brand disposable diapers in 1961 illustrates the successful marketing of a new product that barely existed yesterday, but that few think they can live without today or tomorrow. Second only to its laundry detergents operations, P&G's disposable diaper business represents approximately twenty percent of its earnings and sales (Rice, 1984). A survey of the corporate executives and product managers of *Fortune* 1000 companies suggested that new products are likely to fuel future industry sales and profit growth to an even greater extent than was the case in the past. The contribution of new products to sales growth is expected to increase by one-third, and the percentage of company profits is expected to increase by one-third, and the percentage of company profits accounted for by new products is expected to increase by forty percent (Booz, Allen, and Hamilton, 1982). Numerous articles and whole texts written on the subject of new product development (Cardozo, 1979; Urban and Hauser, 1980; Wind, Mahajan, and Cardozo, 1981; Booz, Allen, and Hamilton, 1982; Pessemier, 1982; Wind, 1982; Crawford, 1983; Hisrich and Peters, 1984; Urban, Hauser and Dholakia, 1987) provide detailed discussions covering the myriad issues and nuances of new product development strategy.

Growth Through Product Development: Problems and Challenges

Problems and challenges pertaining to specific growth opportunities within the broad domain of product development (product reformulation, product quality improvement, and product line extension) were discussed in earlier sections. The following competitive and environmental developments alluded to in an article (*Business Week*, 1983) focusing on the increasing importance of the marketing function in organizations provide additional insights into some of the problems and challenges pertinent to growth through product development:

- Mass-marketing and brand loyalty have been severely affected by demographic and lifestyle changes.
- The actions of an increasing number of firms are directed towards taking business away from competitors.
- Many markets are breaking into smaller and smaller units, with unique products aimed at defined segments.
- In an attempt to increase sales, companies have been flooding the market with new products and line extensions with marketing support in the form of ads, coupons, giveaways, and sweepstakes.
- The number of entrants in many product categories has increased, resulting in greater market segmentation and shorter product life cycles.
- A seemingly endless flow of me-too parity products and line extensions have made staking unique claims (through differentiation and distinctive positioning) increasingly difficult (*Business Week*, 1983).

INTEGRATIVE GROWTH STRATEGIES

Vertical integration has been defined as the combination of technologically distinct economic processes within the confines of a single firm (Porter, 1980). It describes a variety of make-or-buy arrangements firms use to obtain a ready supply of raw materials and a ready market for their outputs

(Harrigan, 1985), and entails the coordination of vertical relationships between specific business units in a firm's portfolio. Firms often resort to vertical integration when markets cannot allocate resources in a manner that alleviates uncertainty (Williamson, 1975), and it can be a means of avoiding search, negotiation, and regulatory costs (Weik, 1969).[5]

The terms backward or upstream vertical integration and forward or downstream vertical integration describe the relationship between the new business area in which a firm is contemplating investment and the focal business unit. Backward vertical integration entails establishing upstream linkages whereby a new business unit provides raw or semiprocessed materials, components, or services to the business unit in question. Forward vertical integration entails establishing downstream linkages, wherein a new business unit purchases outputs from or acts as a marketing arm for the unit under analysis.

Vertical integration strategies entail decisions relating to which activities a firm should perform in house, how these activities should be related to each other, how much of its needs a firm should satisfy in house, how much ownership equity it should risk in doing so, and when these dimensions should be adjusted to accommodate new competitive conditions (Harrigan, 1985). The options available to firm with regard to (1) the degree of vertical integration, (2) the breadth of integration, (3) the number of stages of integrated activities, and (4) the form of ownership used to control the vertical relationship are summarized in Table 6.4.

Strategic Benefits and Cost of Vertical Integration

There are two primary motives for vertical integration: (1) cost reduction and (2) environmental control. The cost-reduction motive arises when the efficient performance of a function requires the close coordination of several processes. Table 6.5 provides additional insights into the economies of vertical integration. Firms also vertically integrate to gain greater control over the economic environment. Backward integration can insure the supply of scarce raw materials, and forward integration can insure market access through limited distribution channels. A firm may be in a position to realize certain other strategic benefits through vertical integration as well. For instance, it can enhance the firm's ability to tap technologies by promoting close familiarity with the technology of upstream or downstream business. Vertical integration can also improve the ability of the firm to differentiate itself from others by bringing a wider slice of value added under the control of management. Through backward integration, a firm may not only be in a position to internalize the profits earned by suppliers, but also be able to gain insights into the true costs of that input. This could provide the firm with the freedom to adjust the price of its final product to maximize overall profits. Vertical integration also assures the firm that it will receive available supplies in tight periods or that it will

TABLE 6.4
VERTICAL INTEGRATION STRATEGIES AND DEFINING CHARACTERISTICS

A. *Degree of Integration*

    1. *Full integration*   All of a particular input (or output) is transferred in-house to a sister business unit. Often, adjacent, integrated stages are in balance in their through-put volumes.

    2. *Tapered integration*   Some portion (but not all) of firm's requirements for an input are supplied in house or some portion of outputs are sold (consumed) in house.

    3. *Nonintegration*   No internal transfers of inputs (or outputs) to in-house sister units.

B. *Breadth of Integration*

    1. *Broadly integrated*   Many activities (inputs, services, or channels of distribution or consumption) related to the needs of a particular business unit are engaged in. (Broadly integrated strategies need not involve many vertical stages of processing.)

    2. *Narrowly integrated*   Few activities (inputs, services, or channels) are engaged in.

C. *Stages of Integrated Activity*

    1. *Many stages*   The firm is engaged in many vertical related activities—from ultraraw materials to distribution to final consumers—in which buyer-seller relationships could occur.

    2. *Few stages*   The firm is engaged in few vertically related activities in the chain from ultraraw materials to distribution.

D. *Form of Ownership*

    1. *Wholly owned*   Businesses are wholly owned by the firm.

    2. *Quasi-integration*   Less than full ownership and control. Could include joint ventures, franchises, minority equity investments, loan guarantees, or an "understanding" regarding customary relationships.

Source: Adapted from: Kathryn R. Harrigan, (1985), *Strategic Flexibility: A Management Guide for Changing Times.*

have an outlet for its products in periods of low overall demand (Porter, 1980).

Vertical integration not only offers a number of strategic benefits to the firm, but also imposes certain costs. Vertical integration increases the proportion of a firm's costs that are fixed. Since the sales of the upstream business are derived from the sales of the downstream business, factors that cause fluctuations in either business can cause fluctuations in the whole chain (Porter, 1980). Firms must also guard against their vertically integrated posture impeding their strategic flexibility (Harrigan, 1985).

TABLE 6.5
ECONOMIES OF VERTICAL INTEGRATION

1. *Economies of combined operations*   By integrating technologically distinct operations, a firm can achieve efficiencies in manufacturing by reducing the number of steps in the production process and by reducing handling and transportation costs.

2. *Economies of internal control and coordination*   Firms may be in a position to lower the costs of scheduling and coordinating operations by integrating technologically distinct production, distribution, selling, and/or other economic processes within its confines.

3. *Economies of information*   Integrated operations may reduce the need to collect certain types of information about the market.

4. *Economies of avoiding the market*   An integrated firm may be in a position to realize substantial savings on some of the selling, price shopping, negotiating, and transaction costs of market transactions.

5. *Economies of stable relationships*   The stability in buying and selling relationships between the various upstream and downstream stages of an integrated firm may be conducive to the development of more efficient, specialized procedures to enable the firms SBUs to deal with each other.

Source: Adapted from discussion on the economies of integration in Michael E. Porter (1980), *Competitive Strategy: Techniques for Analyzing Industries and Competitors*, New York: Free Press, pp. 303–305.

Vertical Integration and Business Unit Performance

The relationship between vertical integration and business unit performance has been examined in PIMS studies using two different measures of vertical integration—an absolute measure and a relative measure. The absolute measure of vertical integration employed is "value added expressed as a percentage of the sales of a strategic business unit." The relative measures of backward and forward vertical integration (more, about the same, or less vertically integrated) are based on PIMS participant responses that compare their company's degree of vertical integration with those of their competitors. PIMS research findings on vertical integration suggest that: (1) there is no difference in profit margins up to a value added/sales ratio of sixty percent, but from that point onward, returns on sales rise consistently with increasing integration (Figure 6.2,A); (2) while both very low and very high levels of vertical integration are associated with an above-average rate of return-on-investment, profits are lowest for moderate levels of vertical integration (Figure 6.2,B); and (3) since vertical integration entails investment in equipment and facilities, higher degrees

FIGURE 6.2
VERTICAL INTEGRATION, PROFITABILITY AND INVESTMENT INTENSITY

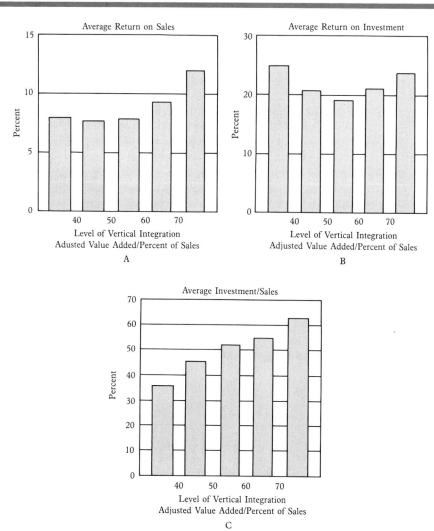

Source: Reprinted with permission from Buzzell, Robert D. and Bradley T. Gale (1987) *The PIMS Principles: Linking Strategy to Performance,* New York: Free Press.

of vertical integration are associated with higher levels of investment intensity (Figure 6.2,C). Additionally, PIMS research suggests that for both consumer and industrial manufacturing businesses, while ROI is usually enhanced by a high degree of backward vertical integration, no systematic relationship is revealed between ROI and different degrees of forward vertical integration (Buzzell and Gale, 1987).

Alternatives to Vertical Integration

A number of recent studies have focused on alternatives to vertical integration that offer the benefits of vertical integration that are important to the context, but that are free of the accompanying costs and disadvantages. Nonintegration strategies, such as maintaining close working relationships with suppliers, long-term contracts, and long-term relationships with suppliers, and quasi-integration strategies, such as minority equity investment, joint ventures, loan guarantees, and prepurchase credits, have been proposed as alternatives to full integration (Harrigan, 1984). Taking note of the prevalence of this phenomenon in the business world, some have pointed out that a growing number of manufacturers are discarding the traditional adversarial relationship with suppliers in favor of one built on cooperation and coordination. For instance, some firms have placed computer terminals in the facilities of their vendors to provide them with up-to-date information on their manufacturing schedules and the dates when specific parts will be needed. Other firms have initiated quality control programs for their suppliers and work closely with them to cut costs and improve product quality and reliability (Adkins and Diller, 1983). In fact, a conceptualization of vertical integration as involving operations that are one hundred-percent owned and physically interconnected to supply one hundred percent of a firm's needs by the firm itself is viewed as outmoded by some scholars (Harrigan, 1985).

DIVERSIFICATION GROWTH STRATEGIES[6]

Diversification has been described as a means of spreading the base of a business to provide improved growth and/or reduce overall risk. This strategy:

- includes all investments except those aimed directly at supporting the competitiveness of existing businesses,
- may take the form of investments that address new products, services, customer segments, or geographic markets, and
- may be accomplished by different methods, including internal development, acquisition, joint ventures, or licensing agreements (Booz, Allen and Hamilton, 1985).

In a study of West European companies jointly sponsored by Booz, Allen, and Hamilton, Inc. and the *Wall Street Journal* (Booz, Allen, and Hamilton, 1985), a sample of over two hundred CEOs were surveyed regarding their attitudes towards diversification, the motives underlying their company's diversification, and their views on factors critical to successful diversification. The highlights of the study are summarized in Table 6.6. Among the major findings of the survey are the following:

1. **Motives**—profitability and growth considerations were listed as the two most important reasons for diversifying.
2. **Direction**—technology-based diversification was rated as the most frequent, as well as the most successful form of diversification.
3. **Mode**—internal development was rated well above mergers, acquisitions, or joint ventures as the preferred and most successful method of diversification.

TABLE 6.6
DIVERSIFICATION: HIGHLIGHTS OF SURVEY OF
EUROPEAN CHIEF EXECUTIVES

1. Degree of success with diversification in recent years (percent of CEOs responding):	
Very successful	12
Quite successful	60
Not very successful	20
Not at all successful	8
2. Relative success of different methods used for diversification (degree of success ranking 0–100):	
Internal development	69
Mergers and acquisitions	58
Join ventures	56
3. Degree of diversification planned over the next five years as compared to present level (percent of CEOs responding):	
Much more	10
Moderately more	51
Unchanged	20
Moderately less	14
Much less	5
4. Planned diversification focus over the next five years (percent of CEOs responding):	
Technology	90
Products/services	74
Geographic markets	62
Customer segments	55
Distribution	45
5. Usefulness of sources of diversification ideas (degree of usefulness ranking 0–100):	
Top management group	75
Line management	66
Planning, R&D, and marketing staffs	57
Business acquaintances	47
Outside directors	37
Mergers and acquisition specialists, bankers	30
The media	18
Government and public authorities	16

TABLE 6.6 *(continued)*

6. Attitudes toward diversification (degree of agreement ranking 0–100):

Successful diversification is one of management's most difficult challenges	96
Diversification is often made without regard to specific corporate objectives	84
Diversification helps balance risks and opportunities	69
Companies often diversify to avoid core business problems	68
Successful companies should not diversify from main business strengths	66
Companies that do not diversify forego key growth opportunities	52

7. Reasons for diversification (degree of importance ranking 0–100):

Increase profitability	77
Increase growth	70
Improve technology base	64
Spread risk	60
Hedge against competition in current business	55
Keep abreast of industry trends	46
Smooth cyclical earning swings	45
Provide management challenges	42
Improve stock evaluation	42
Compensate for unsuccessful new products	38
Bring in new management	35

8. Key factors in successful diversification (degree of importance ranking 0–100):

Management commitment	88
Quality of information	83
Resource overlap	81
Timing of implementation	73
Financial resources	71
Planning	70
Luck	60
Outside advice	42

Source: Table based on results presented in Exhibits 4, 5, 6, 7, 10, 12, 16, and 17 of Booz, Allen & Hamilton, *Diversification: A Survey of European Chief Executives*. New York: Booz, Allen & Hamilton, Inc. 1985.

Among the key issues relating to diversification addressed in this section are the evolution of diversified firms, the motives underlying firms' diversification decisions, the alternative directions and modes of diversification available to firms, and the general nature of the relationship between diversification strategy and performance.

Evolution of Diversified Firms

Industrial organizations that operate simultaneously in multiple product-market domains are said to be diversified. There is general consensus among business historians, industrial organization economists, and strategy researchers that most of the large U.S. industrial organizations are diversified (Chandler, 1962; Gort, 1962; Wrigley, 1970; Wood, 1971; Didrichsen, 1972; Rumelt, 1974; Berry, 1975). This observation applies in particular to the *Fortune* five hundred industrials that are known to account for roughly two-thirds of the output, investment, and employment, and for three-quarters of the profits of U.S. industry (Berg and Pitts, 1979). For instance, Scherer (1980) notes that of the largest two hundred U.S. manufacturing corporations, the proportion operating in more than twenty four-digit SIC industries, rose from nineteen percent in 1950 to thirty-eight percent in 1968; while for the same period, corporations operating in five or fewer four-digit SIC industries became increasingly rare. This seems to suggest that there is a noticeable trend for large, U.S. industrial firms to operate in more four-digit SIC industries. Research investigating the patterns of development of large industrial organizations clearly demonstrates the strategic need for dynamic growth-oriented firms to actively explore opportunities for growth through diversification (Chandler, 1962; Wrigley, 1970; Rumelt, 1974).

Definition and Conceptualization

Diversification has been defined as the extent to which firms classified in one industry produce goods classified in another (Kamien and Schwartz, 1975); as an increase in the number of industries in which firms are active (Berry, 1975); as the extent to which firms operate in several different businesses simultaneously (Pitts and Hopkins, 1982); and as the introduction of new products into new markets (Ansoff, 1957, 1965). Gort (1962) defined diversification in terms of the heterogeneity of output from the point of view of the number of markets served by the output. Two products may be specified as belonging to separate markets if their cross-elasticities of demand are low and if, in the short run, the necessary resources employed in the production and distribution of one cannot be shifted to the other (Gort, 1962). In effect, a company's degree of diversification is viewed to increase as the heterogeneity of the markets served by that company increases.

While economists tend to view an increase in the firm's SIC product count or a decrease in the proportion of total employment that is devoted to a firm's primary business as an indicator of firm diversity, strategy researchers view the essence of diversification as a "reaching out" into new areas requiring the development of new competences or the augmentation of existing ones. Rumelt (1974), for example, conceptualized diversification strategy in terms of:

1. the firm's commitment to diversify per se, together with
2. the strengths, skills, or purposes that span this diversity, demonstrated by the way new activities are related to old ones (Rumelt, 1974, pp. 10–11).

On a similar note, Pitts and Hopkins (1982) have stressed the need to assess the various businesses of a firm in terms of *resource dependence, market discreteness,* and *product difference* to determine the firm's diversity and the degree of diversification implied by the totality of its businesses. From this perspective, a set of activities is considered to be a *discrete business* if the resources involved are separate from those supporting the firm's other activities. Rumelt (1974) defined a discrete business as one that could be managed independently of the firm's other activities. Rumelt identified three types of strategic change that were useful in assessing strategic interdependence:

1. a decision to drop the product-market activity entirely, or, conversely, a decision to greatly increase its relative size;
2. a decision to employ a different product or technology or process, or to use a different type of raw material; and
3. a decision to significantly alter the price, quality, or services associated with the product (Rumelt, 1974; p. 13).

Rumelt suggested that the *separability* or *discreteness* of a particular business can be assessed by evaluating the degree to which its basic nature and scope could be *altered* without materially affecting the operation and strategic direction of other activities (Rumelt, 1974; p. 12; emphases added). Pitts (1974) notes that two businesses should be viewed as different if it appears as though they would be most effectively operated independently of one another in terms of the production and marketing functions—i.e., if different production facilities and separate distribution channels were likely to be needed to properly run the two businesses.

Benefits of Diversification

Diversified multibusiness organizations enjoy certain advantages relative to their predecessor, the single business functionally organized firm. Besides the advantage of lower risk, diversified corporations benefit to a greater extent from the increased utilization of their *technical, managerial,* and *financial* resources. For instance, these firms have wider opportunities to more broadly commercialize the benefits of technological developments. They are in a better position to improve significantly the utilization of managerial resources in light of the large number and wide variety of managerial positions that exist in such organizations. And finally, their diversified operations allow the transfer of funds from mature, low-growth businesses to newer, high-growth businesses without relying excessively on outside sources to finance growth.

Diversification Motives

The expansion of a firm's scope of product-market activities is often an expression of management's drive toward the effective utilization of the firm's financial, human, and material resources. Salter and Weinhold (1978) list a number of reasons that impel firms to diversify. These include:

- to mitigate the effects of a decline in the sales and earnings growth rate of its businesses in the mature stage of the product life cycle,
- to capitalize on new products developed through internal R&D efforts,
- to capitalize on new products that can be channeled through present distribution systems,
- to smooth fluctuations and cyclical income streams and build a balanced portfolio of businesses,
- to expend excess cash reserves and lower the risk of being taken over,
- to effectively utilize the general management skills of top management personnel,
- to attract and retain talented managers, and to promote self-development and nurture general management skills through the assignment of a wide range of tasks and responsibilities,
- to overcome the constraints on growth in present product-market areas imposed by regulatory and legal barriers, and
- to respond to competitive pressures.

Marketing-related motives are often an important consideration in a firm's diversification decisions. For instance, based on a review of an FTC (1980) sponsored study, Kerin and Varaiya (1985) note that chief among the marketing related motives underlying a firm's merger and acquisition decisions are:

- to expand sales and asset growth, market share, or market position more rapidly than could be done by internal expansion while avoiding the risks of internal start-ups,
- to add new products and services to reduce dependence on an existing product mix, and
- to offset seasonal or cyclical fluctuations evident in present products and businesses.

Direction of Diversification

The diversification literature is replete with numerous conceptualizations of alternative directions for growth through diversification that firms can pursue or have pursued. Table 6.7 constitutes a partial list of alternative conceptualizations of general patterns of diversification. For the most part,

TABLE 6.7
TYPOLOGIES OF DIVERSIFICATION STRATEGIES

Author	Broad Diversification Categories	Finer Sub-categories
1. Ansoff (1957, 1965)	Horizontal diversification Concentric diversification Conglomerate diversification	
2. Wrigley (1970)	Single product firm Dominant product firm Related product firm Unrelated product firm	
3. Wood (1971)	Horizontal expansion Vertical integration Narrow Spectrum diversification Broad Spectrum diversification	
4. Didrichsen (1972)	Defensive supplemental diversification Offensive supplemental diversification	
5. Rumelt (1974, 1982)	Single business Dominant business	Dominant vertical Dominant unrelated Dominant constrained Dominant linked
	Related business	Related constrained Related linked
	Unrelated business	Unrelated passive Acquisitive conglomerate
6. Pitts (1976)	Internal diversification Acquisitive diversification Mixed mode diversification	
7. Dominique (1976)	Vertical integration Technology diversification Market diversification Conglomerate diversification	
8. Salter & Weinhold (1978)	Unrelated diversification Related diversification	 Vertical integration Related complimentary diversification Related supplementary diversification Horizontal integration

(continued)

TABLE 6.7 (*continued*)

Author	Broad Diversification Categories	Finer Sub-categories
9. Booz, Allen & Hamilton, Inc. (1985)	Scope of diversification	Technology Products/services Geographic markets Customer segments Distribution channels
	Direction of diversification	Core Core extensions Related activities Unrelated activities
10. Roberts & Berry (1985)	Market diversification	Market: Same New familiar New unfamiliar
	Technology diversification	Technology: Same New familiar New unfamiliar
	Mode of diversification	Internal development Acquisition Licensing Internal venture Joint venture or alliance Venture capital and nurturing Educational acquisition

the motives, direction, and/or mode of diversification form the basis underlying these conceptualizations.

In general, each new activity a firm embraces can be built upon a central core skill, or an observable link to one of the many core skills the firm possesses. It may also be totally unrelated to existing skills, or may call for skills new to the firm. *Related diversification* refers to adding new activities that are tangibly related to the collective skills or strengths of the company (Rumelt, 1974). *Unrelated diversification* refers to pursuing growth in product-market domains in which the key success factors are unrelated to each other (Didrichsen, 1972).

Finer classifications of related diversification and unrelated diversification are discussed in a number of sources. For example, Salter and Weinhold (1978) distinguish between supplementary and complementary related diversification, and Didrichsen (1972) distinguishes between offensive supplemental (unrelated) diversification and defensive supplemental (unrelated) diversification.

Supplementary Related Diversification   This denotes entry into new product-markets where a company can use its existing functional *skills* or *resources*. Such diversifications are typically most valuable to companies with a strong competitive position and a desire to extend their corporate competence to new areas of opportunity. The base on which this form of diversification is built can either be a proprietary functional skill or a more general corporate capability (Salter and Weinhold, 1978).

Complementary Related Diversification   This involves adding functional *skills* or *resources* to the company's existing distinctive competence while leaving its product-market commitment relatively unchanged. This type of diversification is most valuable to companies in attractive industries whose competitive or strategic position could be strengthened by changing (or adding to) their value-added position in the commercial chain. Such a strategy often leads to a form of vertical integration as these new functional skills and/or resources are more closely linked to the diversifying company's core businesses (Salter and Weinhold, 1978).

Defensive Supplemental Diversification   This describes the behavior of firms currently doing a substantial business in a relatively homogeneous area that diversify defensively into unrelated areas when faced with declining prospects in their original business. Such firms find it necessary to supplement their earnings by diversifying into unrelated and more profitable areas to survive (Didrichsen, 1972).

Offensive Supplemental Diversification   This describes how firms already doing a substantial business in a homogeneous area and operating very successfully may diversify into unrelated areas to invest *excess capital* (Didrichsen, 1972).

Narrow vs. Broad Spectrum Diversification   An alternative conceptualization of feasible directions of diversification discussed in the field of industrial organization economics (see Berry 1971; Jacquemin and Berry, 1979; Wood, 1971) is the distinction drawn between narrow spectrum diversification (NSD) and broad spectrum diversification (BSD). The proposed distinction between NSD and BSD is based upon the highly detailed product classification system developed by the U.S. Federal Government—the Standard Industrial Classification (SIC) system. Further details about the SIC system are presented in the Appendix to this chapter. Narrow spectrum diversification (NSD) denotes diversification into a new, four-digit SIC industry category, but within the firm's present scope of activities at the two-digit SIC industry category level. Broad spectrum diversification (BSD) denotes diversification into a new, four-digit SIC industry category outside the firm's present scope of activities at the two-digit SIC industry category level.

Narrow spectrum diversification is generally viewed as diversification into areas closely related to a firm's primary activities and areas of technical expertise. Broad spectrum diversification, on the other hand, is viewed as diversification into areas either unrelated to or less closely related to a firm's primary activities and areas of technical expertise (Jacquemin and Berry, 1979; Palepu, 1985; Varadarajan, 1986b; Varadarajan and Ramanujam, 1987).

However, it should be noted that the question of whether a new market (new technology) is related or unrelated to a firm's present market (present technological capabilities) is relative rather than absolute. Table 6.8 lists questions that are relevant in assessing the degree of relatedness between: (1) a firm's base market(s) and the new market it contemplates entering; and (2) a firm's present technological capabilities and the technological capability requirements for successful introduction of the new product.

Synergy

Synergy is generally viewed as a key component of any strategy (see Ansoff, 1965; Hofer and Schendel, 1978), and constitutes a major factor in a firm's decision relating to the direction of diversification. Synergy refers to the combined impact of two businesses being greater than the sum of each functioning independently. Competing in two or more product-markets is said to result in synergy if:

- the combined costs are less than the sum of their parts,
- the combined required investment is less than the sum of its parts, and/or
- the combined sales are greater than the sum of their parts.

Potential sources of marketing synergy in a diversified organization include:

- using common channels of distribution,
- using a common sales organization,
- using common warehousing facilities,
- making combined purchases of space or time in the advertising media,
- capitalizing on opportunities for joint advertising, sales promotion, and/or personal selling,
- capitalizing on opportunities for the transfer of marketing expertise and skills from one product-market arena to another, and
- cross selling products/services across markets.

The concept of synergy suggests that, all other things being equal, related diversification would lead to better performance than unrelated diversification would. For instance, Porter (1987) notes that a diversification strategy based on a transfer of skills or shared activities is more conducive to superior performance than one not so based. To the extent that a

TABLE 6.8
INDICATORS OF MARKET AND TECHNOLOGY RELATEDNESS

Indicators of Market Relatedness		Indicators of Technology Relatedness	
High Market Relatedness	1. Do the main features of the new market relate to or overlap with existing markets, e.g., are both base and new markets consumer markets?	High Technology Relatedness	1. Is the technological capability used within the corporation without being embodied in products, e.g., required for component manufacture (incorporated in processes rather than products)?
	2. Does the company presently participate in the market as a buyer (relevant to backward integration strategies)?		2. Do the main features of the technology relate to or overlap with existing corporate technological skills or knowledge?
	3. Has the market been monitored systematically from within the corporation with a view to future entry?		3. Do technological skills or knowledge exist within the corporation without being embodied in products or processes, e.g., at a central R&D facility?
	4. Does knowledge of the market exist within the corporation without direct participation in the market e.g., as a result of previous experience of credible staff?		4. Has the technology been systematically monitored from within the corporation in anticipation of future utilization, e.g., by a technology assessment group?
Low Market Relatedness	5. Is relevant and reliable advice available from external consultants?	Low Technology Relatedness	5. Is relevant and reliable advice available from external consultants?

Source: Adapted from Roberts, E. B., and C. A. Berry (1985), "Entering New Businesses: Selecting Strategies for Success," *Sloan Management Review,* 27 (Spring), 3–17.

firm's businesses complement or supplement each other or use similar resources, the potential for synergism exists (Reed, 1979). Related diversification offers greater potential for a firm to exploit the commonalties of the involved businesses to obtain economies of scale or synergies based on the exchange of skills or resources (Aaker, 1988). While marketing and technological synergies are more critical in related diversification, the financial dimension of managerial synergy is more critical in unrelated diversification since this involves the management of an investment portfolio rather than of a product-market portfolio.

While it is generally viewed as desirable for a firm to attempt to generate and exploit synergy across business units, exploiting the synergy potential calls for conscious managerial effort—i.e., effective management of the interbusiness unit relationship. Firms pursuing closely related diversification strategies can be expected to enjoy higher profits only if they effectively exploit their core skills to gain the advantages of synergies (Backaitis, Balakrishnan, and Harrigan, 1984). Furthermore, as pointed out by Porter (1987), imagined synergy is much more common than real synergy. He notes:

> GM's purchase of Hughes Aircraft simply because cars were going electronic and Hughes was an electronic concern demonstrates the folly of paper synergy. Such corporate relatedness is an ex post facto rationalization of a diversification undertaken for other reasons (p. 54).

Finally, even in instances in which a strategy of related diversification is characterized by synergistic relationships, the chances of success are limited if the basic elements and premises of the strategy are not understood and accepted by (1) the managers responsible for implementation of the strategy, and/or (2) the investment community. The latter point is elaborated in Box 6.3.

Noting that diversified companies do not compete, only their business units do, Porter (1987) contends that for diversification to create shareholder value, either the corporation must bring some significant competitive advantage to the new business unit, or the new business unit must offer the potential for significant competitive advantage to the corporation.

He points out that a firm's diversification moves are likely to create shareholder value only when the following tests are passed:

1. **The Attractiveness Test** The industries chosen for diversification must be structurally attractive or capable of being made attractive.
2. **The Cost-of-entry Test** The cost of entry must not capitalize all the future profits.
3. **The Better-off Test** Either the new unit must gain competitive advantage from its link with the corporation, or vice versa.

Mode of Diversification

Internal development and acquisition are commonly viewed as the primary modes of diversification available to a firm. However, it should be noted that other alternative modes of diversification, such as joint ventures (strategic partnerships), licensing, providing venture capital and nurturing, educational acquisition, etc., have been growing in importance in recent years (Roberts and Berry, 1985; Varadarajan and Rajaratnam, 1986).[7] Table 6.9 provides additional insights into alternative modes of diversification and their advantages and limitations.

Diversification Strategy and Firm Performance: An Overview

One test of the effectiveness or ineffectiveness of alternative diversification strategies pursued by firms is the performance outcomes of such diversification endeavors. As an area of research, diversification has a rich tradition and has been examined by business historians (e.g., Chandler, 1962; Didrichsen, 1972), economists (e.g., Gort, 1962; Berry, 1975), and researchers in the areas of business policy and strategy (e.g., Rumelt, 1974; Montgomery, 1982), finance (e.g., Reid 1968; Weston and Mansinghka, 1971), marketing (e.g., Levitt, 1975; Dubofsky and Varadarajan, 1987; Varadarajan, 1986b), and public policy (e.g., Davidson, 1985; 1986; 1987). This section provides an overview of the empirical findings reported to date on the relationship between diversification strategy and firm performance. A brief discussion of a related issue, the measurement of diversification, is presented in the Appendix to this chapter.

Salter and Weinhold (1979) note that the general conclusion emerging from the works of several economists (Conn, 1973; Holzman, Copeland, and Hayya, 1975; Melicher and Rush, 1973; Reid, 1968; Weston and Mansinghka, 1971) is that "unrelated diversification does not lead to higher corporate returns" (p. 22). For instance, Weston and Mansinghka (1971) found that when performance is measured by the ratio of net income to net worth, it is somewhat higher for conglomerate firms, but the difference is not statistically significant. They noted, however, that *defensive diversification* (diversification out of industries with low profitability) often enabled firms to increase their profitability from inferior to average levels.

The study by Salter and Weinhold (1979) indicates that conglomerates are poor performers relative to the industry averages, particularly with regard to capital productivity measures. Over the period from 1967 to 1978, the average return on total assets for thirty-six diversified firms studied by Salter and Weinhold was found to be twenty percent lower than it was for the *Fortune* five hundred firms. Based on a study of two hundred and six American corporations, Nathanson and Cassano (1982) concluded that diversity can hurt profits, but that appropriate organizational structures and strategies can help mitigate the damage. They note that different

BOX **6.3**

THE INFLUENCE OF THE INVESTMENT
COMMUNITY ON THE DIVERSIFICATION
STRATEGIES OF A FIRM: THE UNITED
AIRLINES SAGA

Over a period of time, United Airlines acquired a number of companies in related areas, including Westin Hotels, Hertz Car Rental, and Hilton International Hotels. The CEO of the company responsible for its acquisition of Hertz and Hilton envisioned creating a company that would satisfy all the major travel related service needs of its customers—air travel, car rental, and hotel accommodation. In 1987, the company even changed its name from United Airlines Inc. to Allegis Corp.

The investment community, however, was skeptical about the CEO's grand vision and felt that the company should concentrate its efforts on competing in the air travel business, rather than spreading its resources thinly across a number of areas.

The following edicts seem to best summarize the contrasting viewpoints of the company and the investment community, respectively:

1. The whole is worth more than the sum of the parts.
2. The sum of the parts is worth more than the whole.

The Whole is Worth More Than the Sum of the Parts   The CEO envisioned that by putting together and managing effectively (i.e., exploiting the synergies) the operations of United Airlines, Hertz Car Rental, Westin Hotels, and Hilton International Hotels, the firm could create more wealth for its shareholders.

The Sum of the Parts is Worth More Than the Whole   The investment community, on the other hand, believed that by splitting the company into parts and selling some of the parts (the car rental and hotel businesses) to the highest bidders, the company could create more wealth for its shareholders.

Finally, it was the investment community's viewpoint that prevailed. Over the period from February to June, 1987, the company's stock price rose from the mid-fifties to the high eighties on impending rumors of takeover, offers by the unions representing United Airlines to acquire the company, and other developments. The chronology of developments summarized below culminated in the resignation of Allegis' CEO on June 9, 1987 and the board of directors' decision to sell off the company's car rental and hotel divisions and change the name of the company back to United Airlines.

1970: Western International Hotel, Westin's Predecessor Merges With United Airlines.

June 1985: UAL agrees to acquire RCA Corp.'s Hertz unit.

October 1985: UAL acquires Pan American World Airway's Pacific operations for $750 million.

August 1986: Labor strife wrecks United's plan to acquire Frontier Airlines.

December 1986: UAL agrees to buy Transworld Corp.'s Hilton International Co. unit in a transaction valued at $980 million.

April 1987: The union representing United pilots launches a $4.5 billion takeover bid for the airline; Allegis management rejects the offer as "grossly inadequate" and grants golden parachutes to the CEO and seven other top officials.

May 12, 1987: Boeing Co. enters an unusual antitakeover aircraft-financing arrangement with Allegis.

May 26, 1987: Coniston Partners, a New York investment firm that holds a thirteen percent Allegis stake, announces it will seek to gain control of the Allegis board.

May 28, 1987: Allegis directors propose a plan to distribute $60 a share to stockholders and keep the company intact in a last-ditch effort to forestall a takeover.

June 4, 1987: United pilots propose a restructuring plan that would break up the company and pay holders $70 a share. Allegis stock soars as a result, heightening pressure on management to sweeten its offer.

June 9, 1987: The CEO, under pressure from directors, employees, and shareholders, resigns his post.

June 1987 to December 1987: Over the course of the next few months, United Airlines entered into agreements to sell its Hertz Car Rental, Westin Hotels, and Hilton International Hotels to other companies.

For additional insights see: *Wall Street Journal* (1987), "Allegis Shakeup Came as Shareholder Ire Put Board Tenure in Doubt," June 11, 1 and 12; *Fortune* (1987), "How Dick Ferris Blew It," July 6, 42–46.

TABLE 6.9
ALTERNATIVE MODES OF DIVERSIFICATION:
MAJOR ADVANTAGES AND DISADVANTAGES

New-Business Development Mechanisms	Major Advantages	Major Disadvantages
Internal developments	Use existing resources.	Time lag to break even tends to be long (on average eight years). Unfamiliarity with new markets may lead to errors.
Acquisitions	Rapid market entry.	New business area may be unfamiliar to parent.
Licensing	Rapid access to proven technology. Reduced financial exposure.	Not a substitute for internal technical competence. Not proprietary technology. Dependent upon licensor.
Internal ventures	Use existing resources. May enable a company to hold a talented entrepreneur.	Mixed record of success. Corporation's internal climate often unsuitable.
Joint ventures or alliances	Technological/ marketing unions can exploit small/ large company synergies. Distribute risk.	Potential for conflict between partners.
Venture capital and nurturing	Can provide window on new technology or market.	Unlikely alone to be a major stimulus of corporate growth.
Educational acquisitions	Provide window and initial staff.	Higher initial financial commitment than venture capital. Risk of departure of entrepreneurs.

Source: Roberts, E. B., and C. A. Berry (1985), "Entering New Businesses: Selecting Strategies for Success," *Sloan Management Review,* 27 (Spring), 3–17. Reprinted with permission.

diversification strategies require different degrees of centralization, delegation, levels of divisional autonomy, and sizes of staff at the corporate and group levels. Nathanson and Cassano found a consistent decline in return on capital employed as product diversity increases for corporations of all sizes. Based on their analysis, the authors noted that firms can diversify into new markets with fewer ill effects on the bottom line than diversifying into new products would create.

In a landmark study, Rumelt (1974) proposed a system for classifying, analyzing, and evaluating the performance of large, industrialized corporations. Rumelt classified firms into four broad diversification categories and nine finer subcategories based on three ratio measures. (A more detailed discussion on categorical and continuous measures of firm diversity is presented in the Appendix to the chapter.)

1. **The specialization ratio** (SR), defined as "the proportion of a firm's revenues that can be attributed to its largest single business" (Rumelt 1974; p. 14),
2. **The related ratio** (RR), defined as "the proportion of a firm's revenues attributable to its largest group of related businesses" (Rumelt 1974; p. 16), and
3. **The vertical ratio** (VR), defined as "the proportion of the firm's revenues that arise from all by-products, intermediate products, and end products of a vertically integrated sequence of processing activities." (Rumelt 1974; p. 23).

Table 6.10 summarizes Rumelt's strategic classification of businesses on the basis of their specialization ratio, related ratio and vertical ratio.

Based on an analysis of the diversification patterns of a sample of *Fortune* five hundred firms from 1949 to 1969, Rumelt reported that unrelated businesses had significantly higher corporate growth rates, but the lowest rates of capital productivity. Related-constrained firms (firms that diversify into related areas on the basis of one single core-skill) were found to outperform related-linked firms (firms that diversify into related areas on the basis of any one of a number of core-skills, with single linkages), who in turn were found to outperform unrelated diversifiers or the conglomerates (firms that diversity into businesses that cannot capitalize on any of their primary core-skills and have to develop or acquire new skills). Salter and Weinhold (1979) summarized the significance of Rumelt's work (1974, 1977) quite succinctly:

> Rumelt's two studies neatly summarize the dilemma many companies face. Sticking close to traditional businesses can condemn a company to mediocre performance. However, wide ranging diversification places the productivity of capital at significant risk. (pp. 24–25).

However, follow-up studies focusing on Rumelt's original sample or subsets of the total sample have arrived at somewhat divergent conclusions (Bettis and Hall, 1982; Christensen and Montgomery, 1981; Montgomery, 1979; Rumelt, 1982). Christensen and Montgomery (1981) noted that differences in performance between firms pursuing different diversification strategies go beyond skeletal patterns of product linkages and include

TABLE 6.10
STRATEGIC CLASSIFICATION OF BUSINESS BASED ON
SPECIALIZATION, RELATED AND VERTICAL RATIOS

Ratio Range	Major Classification	Ratio Range	Subclassification Within Major Diversification Categories	Remarks
1. SR ≥ .95	Single Business	—	(i) Single business	
2. .70 ≤ SR < .95	Dominant Business	VR ≥ .70	(ii) Dominant-vertical	
		VR < .70 & RR < 1/2 (SR + 1)	(iii) Dominant-unrelated	
		VR < .70 RR ≥ 1/2 (SR + 1)	(iv) Dominant-constrained or (v) Dominant-linked	Classification of business as (iv) or (v); (vi), or (vii); and (viii), or (ix) based on qualitative considerations
3. SR < .70	Related Business		(vi) Related-constrained or	
		RR ≥ .70	(vii) Related-linked	
4. SR < .70	Unrelated Business		(viii) Unrelated-passive or	
		RR < .70	(xi) Acquisitive conglomerate	

Source: Adapted from: Rumelt, Richard P. (1974). *Strategy, Structure and Economic Performance.* Boston: Division of Research, Graduate School of Business Administration, Harvard University.

the characteristics of the markets in which the firms participate. Related-constrained firms, for example, were found to operate in more profitable, faster growing, and more highly concentrated markets than other firms do. Likewise, the unrelated portfolio firms were found to have lower market shares and to be positioned in less profitable, less concentrated, and smaller markets in the sample. The authors found no statistically significant differences across diversification-strategy categories.

Bettis and Hall (1982) examined Rumelt's subsamples for related-linked, related-constrained, and unrelated firms. Based on the results of their study, the authors noted that the performance differences Rumelt (1974) found between related and unrelated diversified firms are due largely to the presence of a number of pharmaceutical firms in the related-constrained diversified category, rather than to differences in diversification strategy per se. The researchers also found no significant performance differences between firms pursuing related-constrained and related-linked diversification strategies.

Rumelt's (1982) subsequent analyses controlling for industry effects corroborated Christensen and Montgomery's (1981) findings about the importance of market structure variables in explaining performance. Rumelt found that, of the variance in return on capital explained by the strategic categories, about twenty-one percent can be attributed to industry effects. Nevertheless, a pattern of declining profitability premiums with increasing diversity was found to persist even after adjusting for industry participation. The dominant vertical and unrelated business categories showed levels of profitability significantly below those of the other categories. As in the earlier study (Rumelt, 1974), the related-constrained group was the most profitable. Rumelt (1982) also outlined a number of theoretical arguments in support of the posited relationship between diversification strategy and performance, even after controlling for industry effects.

Bettis and Mahajan (1985) examined the risk/return performance of related and unrelated diversified firms for a sample of eighty firms, and reported that, on the average, related diversified firms outperformed unrelated diversified firms. However, in light of the presence of a number of poorly performing related-diversified firms in the sample, the authors cautioned that related diversification offers no guarantee of a favorable risk/return performance, and, hence should be viewed as a necessary but not a sufficient condition for achieving superior performance. Furthermore, the authors noted that although different diversification strategies result in similar risk/return profiles, a favorable risk/return performance may be extremely hard to achieve with unrelated diversification.

Based on an analysis of the return on sales of a sample of twelve predominantly related diversified firms and twelve predominantly unrelated diversified firms in the food industry, Palepu (1985) found the former group to be marginally more profitable than the latter. However, the difference was not statistically significant. Based on an analysis of a sample of over two hundred large U.S. firms, Varadarajan (1986b) found that firms pursuing a predominantly related diversification strategy outperform firms pursuing a predominantly unrelated diversification strategy.

PIMS research studies suggest that, on average, portfolios of businesses that have roughly comparable marketing intensities or R&D spending levels or capital intensities outperform portfolios that are a mix of both high-technology and low-technology, or both marketing-intensive and nonmarketing-intensive, or both capital-intensive and noncapital-intensive businesses (Wells, 1984; Buzzell and Gale, 1987).

Porter (1987) examined the acquisition and divestiture activities of thirty-three large U.S. companies from 1950 to 1986. He used the percentage of acquired units retained by the company as an indicator of the relative success of a firm's diversification activities and its contribution to corporate performance. Porter's analysis revealed that on average, more acquisitions were divested than retained. The divestiture rate was greater than fifty percent for acquisitions in new industries, and over sixty percent for acquisitions in entirely new fields. The divestiture rate for unrelated acquisitions in entirely new fields was found to be greater than seventy percent.

In summary, viewed in the aggregate, empirical studies reported to date on the relationship between diversification and capital productivity suggest that related diversification is more conducive to superior performance. However, it should be noted that results to the contrary have been reported in some studies. A more detailed discussion of the conditions under which it might be desirable for a firm to pursue a strategy of unrelated diversification is presented in chapter ten.

A CONCLUDING NOTE

Growth and profitability are among the pantheons of corporate virtue. Critical to a firm's realization of its growth and profit aspirations are analyses of opportunities for growth in (1) its present product-market domains, and (2) new product-market domains that are either related to or unrelated to its present portfolio of businesses. A systematic analysis of alternative growth opportunities provides a firm with guideposts for deciding which products and markets it should emphasize in its quest for growth and profitability. Techniques for assessing the structural attractiveness of the industries in which a firm is presently competing and new industries into which it is contemplating entry are discussed in the next chapter.

NOTES

1. Horizontal integration (acquisition of one or more competitors) is listed as a third integrative growth strategy in some sources (e.g., Kotler, 1988). Strictly speaking, however, horizontal integration constitutes an *entry strategy* (i.e., acquisition) or a *way* to take advantage of market penetration, market development, and product development growth opportunities.

2. The extensive body of literature on experience curves, which is closely tied to the growth-share matrix, primarily focuses on the desirability of pursuing an aggressive pricing strategy that would enable a firm to attain market share leadership, accumulate the largest cumulative experience, and achieve a competitive cost advantage.

3. Some authors view vertical integration and diversification as distinct phenomenon, while others view vertical integration as a form of diversification. For instance, Harrigan (1985) notes: ". . . vertical integration is one of the first diversification strategies firms consider as they progress from being single business companies, . . . (p. 67)"

4. This section and the next section entitled "Intensive Growth Strategies" and are adapted from Varadarajan (1986a).

5. In marketing, make-or-buy (vertically integrate or contract out) decisions arise in the formulation of advertising, salesforce management, and distribution strategies. Although this topic is outside the scope of this book, a brief note is in order. If markets for advertising, distribution, and personal selling services were perfectly competitive, outsiders would be pressured to keep costs and prices down. Hence, there would be no need to vertically integrate to assure low-cost supply. The most efficient method for performing these marketing functions under conditions of market imperfections have been examined in marketing literature from a transaction cost perspective (Anderson and Coughlan, 1987; Anderson and Gatignon, 1986; Anderson and Weitz, 1986; Dwyer and Oh, 1988; Ruekert, Walker, and Roering, 1985). Transaction cost analysis (see Williamson, 1975) blends institutional economics, organizational theory, and contract law to examine the conditions under which transactions are performed more efficiently within an organization under hierarchical control (through vertical integration), as opposed to between independent entities under market control (through contracting in the marketplace).

6. For an extensive review of research on diversification, see Ramanujam and Varadarajan (1989).

7. See Varadarajan and Rajaratnam (1986; Figure 2; p. 10) for a more complete list of alternative entry strategies or modes of diversification and an extensive discussion on strategic marketing alliances.

APPENDIX

MEASUREMENT OF FIRM DIVERSITY

The degree of diversification, or the extent of a business firm's departure from its primary product-market domains, is hard to measure. In general, the overall concept of firm diversity comprises *product diversity, market diversity, technological diversity,* and *structural diversity.* As Didrichsen (1972) notes:

> The description of diversity is found in a clarification of the products produced and the markets served, the corporate strategy which has led to this product-market posture, the underlying technology, the organizational structure the firm employs to manage its diversity, the particular competence it draws on, and the managerial style and personality of the people who have brought it all about. (Didrichsen, 1972, p. 208)

Understandably, the complex and multidimensional nature of a firm's diversity defies quantification in simple terms. The various approaches to measuring a firm's diversity that have been proposed to date can be broadly classified into two groups:

1. continuous measures based on either a simple product count or more sophisticated weighted average measures; and
2. categorical measures based on a quantitative evaluation of the firm's product-market scope and diversification rationale [see Pitts and Hopkins (1982) and Shaikh and Varadarajan (1984) for extensive reviews].

The Business Count Approach and Its Variants

One of the most widely used methods of measuring a firm's diversity has been to count the number of products constituting the firm's total portfolio. The product count measure of firm diversity is based upon the highly detailed product classification system established by the U.S. Federal government—the Standard Industrial Classification (SIC) system. The SIC system is a numerical system developed by the Federal government to classify all types of economic activity within the U.S. economy. The system is based on establishment classifications in which each of a firm's establishments (e.g., plants) is classified according to its primary activity. However, in its classification decisions, the Office of Management and Budget does not follow any single principle, such as the use of the products, the market structure, the nature of raw materials, etc. (Standard Industrial Classification Manual, 1972, p. 645).

Researchers have been able to determine the total number of two-, three-, or four- digit SIC categories in which a firm operates concurrently by analyzing data published by a number of business information service firms, such as:

- Dun and Bradstreet's Market Identifier, Million Dollar and Billion Dollar Directories, and Directory of Corporate Ownership,
- The Economic Information System (EIS) Data File,
- The Fortune Plant and Production Directory (discontinued since 1966), and
- The 10-K statements and annual reports of firms.

Meising (1976) and Carter (1977), among others, have employed the product count measure of firm diversity in their studies.

Unfortunately, the simple product count system fails to recognize differences in the size and distribution of businesses. Scherer (1980) reports that merely counting product lines exaggerates in some respects the overall significance of diversification, since the product volume distributions of most firms are highly skewed, with a few product lines accounting for the bulk of sales or employment, and numerous others being relatively small. Despite such limitations, research based on simple product count data does provide certain valuable insights.

More sophisticated product count measures that used weighted average measures to take into account the relative importance of each SIC involvement to the particular firm have been proposed and/or employed by Berry (1975), Carter (1977), Montgomery (1979, 1982), Gort (1962), Hirschman (1964), Jacquemin and Berry (1979), and Gorecki (1980), among others. Most weighted measures are variants of the general equation:

$$D = \sum_{i=1}^{N} P_i W_i \qquad (1)$$

where

D = extent of diversification,
P_i = the share of the ith business relative to the firm as a whole at the two-digit, three-digit, or four-digit SIC level,
W_i = an assigned weight, and
N = the number of businesses constituting the firm's portfolio.

For instance, the Herfindahl index measure of firm diversity is a special case of this general formulation, where the assigned weight W_i equals $(1 - P_i)$. That is:

$$D = \sum_{i=1}^{N} P_i (1 - P_i) = 1 - \sum_{i-1}^{N} P_i^2 \qquad (2)$$

Montgomery (1979) further refined the general formula for assessing a firm's degree of diversification at the two-digit, three-digit, and four-digit SIC levels by adding a denominator:

$$D = 1 - \frac{\Sigma P_{ij}^2}{(\Sigma P_{ij})^2} \qquad (3)$$

where P_{ij} = the percentage of a firm's i's total sales that are in market j. The denominator was added as an adjustment to the original measure to accommodate the use of firm sales data *not* summing to one. Using the Economic Information Systems (EIS) Data File, as Montgomery did, this would be the case whenever part of a firm's sales were in foreign markets.

The entropy measure of firm diversity proposed by Jacquemin and Berry (1979) weights each P_i by the logarithm of $1/P_i$. That is:

$$D = \sum_{i=1}^{N} P_i \ln (1/P_i) \qquad (4)$$

A desirable feature of the entropy measure is the ability to decompose the firm's total diversity into additive elements: (1) an "unrelated" component that measures the extent to which a firm's output is distributed in products *across* unrelated industry groups and (2) a related component that measures the distribution of the output among related products *within* the industry groups. The entropy measure, however, still retains the computational simplicity of the other index measures (see Jacquemin and Berry, 1979; Palepu 1985). That is, the total entropy measure can be expressed as the sum of two terms:

$$E_T = \sum_{s=1}^{S} P_s (E_W) + E_A \qquad (5)$$

where
E_T is the entropy measure of total diversification at the four-digit level,
S is the number to two-digit industry groups in which the firm competes ($\leq N$, the number of four-digit industries in which the firm competes),
P_s is the proportion of the firm's sales accounted for by its two-digit industry group s,
E_W is the four-digit entropy measure of diversification within a two-digit industry group,
E_A is the two-digit level entropy measure of diversification across two-digit industry groups.

The first term in this measure is a weighted average of the firm's four-digit diversification within each two-digit industry group, and the second is the entropy measure of diversification of the firm across two-digit industry groups.

Economists have often used yet another method to measure diversity. Instead of the product count, the firm's specialization ratio is computed as the ratio of **employment** in the firm's primary business to the firm's total employment. For instance, using employment data, Berry (1975) computed the Herfindahl Index to assess a firm's diversity by calculating such a specialization ratio at the four-, three-, and two-digit SIC levels for the 1967 *Fortune* five hundred firms. He concluded that diversity tends to increase as a firm's specialization ratio decreases.

Scherer (1980) reports that the Census Bureau's tabulation of specialization ratios for companies whose primary line of activity was in a manufacturing industry category showed that the specialization ratio declined from eighty-one percent in 1958 to seventy-seven percent in 1963, to seventy-one percent in 1967, and to sixty-seven percent in 1972.

Using a specialization ratio to quantify the degree of diversity, however, raises a problem in interpretation. Since labor productivity differs across industries and with various members of the labor force, a higher or a lower specialization ratio does not necessarily indicate higher or lower revenue generation for the firm. However, a reduction in the specialization ratio does indicate a trend towards moving outward from a firm's primary business, and to that extent, is a qualified proxy for the degree of diversification (Scherer, 1980).

An Approach Based on Strategies

As an alternative to the continuous measures of firm diversity traditionally used by industrial organization economists, Wrigley (1970) proposed a *categorical* measure of firm diversity. Wrigley conceived of the idea of developing a specialization ratio not in terms of employment as the economists did, but in terms of a major product's importance to the firm. Wrigley defined the "specialization ratio" (SR) as the proportion of a firm's annual revenues attributable to the largest, discrete, product-market activity and proposed the following diversification categories:

1. Single product firm: $SR \geq 0.95$
2. Dominant product firm: $0.70 \leq SR < 0.95$
3. Related product firm: $SR < 0.70$ **and**
   a firm that diversifies by adding new activities that are tangibly related to its collective skills and strengths.
4. Unrelated product firm: $SR < 0.70$ **and**
   a firm that diversifies into areas that are not related to its original skills and strengths, other than financial.

Rumelt (1974) built upon Wrigley's conceptualization and developed a more sophisticated system for analyzing, categorizing, and evaluating the performance of large industrialized corporations. Towards this end, he developed two other ratios—the related ratio and the vertical ratio—in addition to the specialization ratio. Noting that Wrigley (1970) employed a broader concept of product than is usually meant by the term, Rumelt proposed a revised set of four major diversification categories—single business, dominant business, related business, and unrelated business. These categories represent the underlying logic behind diversification moves, as well as the relationship between existing businesses and new businesses (Rumelt, 1974). (Rumelt's proposed strategic classification of businesses on the basis of their specialization, related, and vertical ratios is summarized in Table 6.10). As a further refinement, Rumelt (1982) proposed a seven-group, multivariate measure of firm diversity based on four ratios—specialization ratio (SR), vertical ratio (VR), related core ratio (RC), and related ratio (RR).

Whereas the product count measure of firm diversity is more objective, the categorical system proposed by Wrigley (1970) and Rumelt (1974, 1982) involves subjective, qualitative evaluations of the firm's product-market scope and the rationale underlying the firm's diversification strategy. In this context, a frequently voiced opinion has been that the categorical classification system may not be reliable in view of its excessive dependence on qualitative judgments. However, Montgomery (1982) notes that the reproducibility of Rumelt's diversification category assignments may not be as severe a problem as it was feared to be. Montgomery updated six of Rumelt's categories up to 1977 and used both the product count diversification measure and Rumelt's categorical measure to test whether the strategic grouping so involved would differ. She found that SIC-based measures of diversification increase consistently with Rumelt's strategy categories (p. 304). Of the one hundred and twenty-eight businesses she classified for the year 1974, one hundred and twenty-five were in agreement with Rumelt's original assessment.

NOTES

1. This section is adapted from Varadarajan (1986b) and Shaikh and Varadarajan (1984).

REFERENCES

Aaker, David A. (1988), *Strategic Market Management*, Second Edition. New York: Wiley.

Abell, Derek F. (1980), *Defining the Business: The Starting Point of Strategic Planning*. Englewood Cliffs, NJ: Prentice-Hall, Inc.

Abrams, Bill (1981), "Warring Toothpaste Makers Spend Millions Luring Buyers to Slightly Altered Products," *The Wall Street Journal*, September 21, 33.

Abrams, Bill (1983), "Lysol's Maker Keeps Fighting FTC Over Advertising Claims," *The Wall Street Journal*, February 24, 29.

Adkins, Lynn and Wendy Diller (1983), "Industry's Quiet Revolution," *Dun's Business Month*, (June), 72–75.

Anderson, Erin and Anne T. Coughlan (1987), "International Market Entry and Expansion via Independent or Integrated Channels of Distribution," *Journal of Marketing*, 51(January), 71–82.

Anderson, Erin and Hubert Gatigon (1986), "Models of Foreign Entry: A Transaction Cost Analysis and Propositions," *Journal of International Business Studies*, (Fall), 1–26.

Anderson, Erin and Barton A. Weitz (1986), "Make-or-Buy Decisions: Vertical Integration and Marketing Productivity," *Sloan Management Review*, 28(Spring), 3–19.

Ansoff, H. Igor (1957), "Strategies for Diversification," *Harvard Business Review*, 30(September–October), 113–124.

Ansoff, H. Igor (1965), *Corporate Strategy*, New York: McGraw-Hill.

Backaitis, Nida T., Ramamurthy Balakrishnan, and Kathryn R. Harrigan (1984), "Market Share, Diversification, and Profitability: The Continuing Debate," paper presented at the Fourth Annual Strategic Management Society Conference (October 10–18), Philadelphia.

Berg, Norman and Richard A. Pitts (1979), "Strategic Management: The Multibusiness Corporation," in *Strategic Management: A New View of Business Policy and Planning*, D. E. Schendel and C. W. Hofer, eds., Boston, MA: Little, Brown, and Company.

Berry, Charles H. (1971), "Corporate Growth and Industrial Diversification," *Journal of Law and Economics*, 14(October), 371–383.

Berry, Charles H. (1975), *Corporate Growth and Diversification*, Princeton, NJ: Princeton University Press.

Bettis, Richard A. and William K. Hall (1982), "Diversification Strategy, Accounting Determined Risk, and Accounting Determined Return," *Academy of Management Journal*, 25(June), 254–264.

Booz, Allen, and Hamilton, Inc. (1982) *New Products Management for the 1980s*, New York: Booz, Allen, and Hamilton, Inc.

Booz, Allen, and Hamilton, Inc. (1985), *Diversification: A Survey of European Chief Executives*, New York: Booz, Allen, and Hamilton, Inc.

Bronson, Gail (1981), "Baby Food It Is, But Gerber Wants Teenagers to Think of It As a Dessert," *The Wall Street Journal*, July 17, 29.

Business Week (1981), "Campbell Soup Fails to Make It to the Table," October 12, 66.

Business Week (1983), "Marketing: The New Priority," November 21, 96–106.

Business Week (1984), "3M's Aggressive New Consumer Drive," July 16, 114–122.

Business Week (1984), "How Chesebrough-Ponds Put Nail Polish in a Pen," October 8, 196–200.

Buzzell, Robert D. and Robert T. Gale (1987), *The PIMS Principles: Linking Strategy to Performance*, New York: The Free Press.

Cardozo, Richard N. (1979), *Product Policy*, Reading, MA: Addison-Wesley.

Carter, John R. (1977), "The Search for Synergy: A Structure-Performance Test," *Review of Economics and Statistics*, 59(August), 279–289.

Chandler, Alfred D. Jr. (1962), *Strategy and Structure*, Cambridge, MA: MIT Press.

Christensen, H. Kurt and Cynthia A. Montgomery (1981), "Corporate Economic Performance: Diversification Strategy versus Market Structure," *Strategic Management Journal*, 2(October–December), 327–343.

Coase, Ronald H. (1937), "The Nature of the Firm," *Economics*, 4 (November), 386–405.

Conn, Robert G. (1973), "Performance of Conglomerate Firms: Comment," *Journal of Finance*, 2(May), 381–388.

Crawford, C. Merle (1983), *New Products Management*, Homewood, IL: Irwin.

Davidson, Kenneth M. (1985), *Megamergers: Corporate America's Billion-Dollar Takeovers*, Cambridge, MA: Ballinger.

Davidson, Kenneth M. (1986), "Megamergers: A Scorecard of Winners and Losers," *Wall Street Journal* (January 20), 14.

Davidson, Kenneth M. (1987), "Do Megamergers Make Sense?," *Journal of Business Strategy*, 7(Winter), 40–48.

Day, George S. (1975), "A Strategic Perspective of Product Planning," *Journal of Contemporary Business* (Spring), 1–34.

Day, George S. and Robin Wensley (1988), "Assessing Advantage: A Framework for Diagnosing Competitive Superiority," *Journal of Marketing*, 52(April), 1–20.

Didrichsen, Jon (1972), "The Development of Diversified and Conglomerate Firms in the United States, 1920–1970," *Business History Review*, 46 (Summer), 202–219.

Dubofsky, Paulette and P. Rajan Varadarajan (1987), "Diversification and Measures of Performance: Additional Empirical Evidence," *Academy of Management Journal*, 30(September), 597–607.

Dwyer, Robert F. and Sejo Oh (1988), "A Transaction Cost Perspective of Vertical Contractual Structure and Interchannel Competitive Strategies," *Journal of Marketing*, 52(Fall), 21–34.

Federal Trade Commission (1980), *The Process of Conglomerate Mergers*, Washington, D.C.: Government Printing Office.

Fortune (1984), "Eight Big Masters of Innovation," October 15, 76.

Fortune (1987), "How Dick Ferris Blew It," July 6, 42–46.

Garvin, David A. (1984), "What Does 'Product Quality' Really Mean?," *Sloan Management Review*, 26 (Fall), 25–43.

Gorecki, P. K. (1980), "A Problem of Measurement from Plants to Enterprise in the Analysis of Diversification: A Note," *The Journal of Industrial Economics*, 28(June), 327–334.

Gort, Michael (1962), *Diversification and Integration in American Industry*, Princeton, NJ: Princeton University Press.

Gruenwald, George (1985), *New Product Development*, Chicago, IL: Crain Books.

Harrigan, Kathryn R. (1984), "Formulating Vertical Integration Strategies," *Academy of Management Review*, 9 (October), 638–652.

Harrigan, Kathryn R. (1985), *Strategic Flexibility: A Management Guide for Changing Times*, Lexington, Mass: Lexington Books.

Haspeslagh, Philippe (1982), "Portfolio Planning: Uses and Limits," *Harvard Business Review*, 60 (January–February), 59–73.

Heany, Donald F. (1983), "Degrees of Product Innovation", *Journal of Business Strategy*, 3(Spring), 3–14.

Hirschman, A. O. (1964), "The Paternity of an Index," *American Economic Review*, 54(No. 1), 761–762.

Hisrich, Robert D. and Michael P. Peters (1984), *Marketing Decision for New and Mature Products*, Columbus, OH: Charles E. Merrill Publishing.

Hofer, Charles W. and Dan Schendel (1978), *Strategy Formulation: Analytical Concepts*, St. Paul, MN: West Publishing.

Holzman, Oscar J., Ronald M. Copeland, and Jack Hayya (1975), "Income Measures of Conglomerate Performance," *Quarterly Review of Economics and Business*, 15(Summer), 67–78.

Hudson, Richard L. (1984), "Competition Gets Scrappy in Heineken's Beer Markets," *Wall Street Journal*, August 24, 24.

Jacquemin, Alexis P. and Charles H. Berry (1979), "Entropy Measures of Diversification and Corporate Growth," *The Journal of Industrial Economics*, 27(June), 359–369.

Kamien, M. I. and N. L. Schwartz (1975), "Market Structure and Innovation: A Survey," *Journal of Economic Literature*, 13(March), 1–37.

Karger, D. W. and R. G. Murdick (1966), "Product Design, Marketing and Manufacturing Innovation," *California Management Review*, 28(Winter), 33–42.

Kerin, Roger A. and Nikhil Varaiya (1985), "Merger and Acquisitions in

Retailing: A Review in Critical Analysis," *Journal of Retailing*, (Spring), 9–34.

Kollat, David T., Roger D. Blackwell, and James F. Robeson (1972), *Strategic Marketing*, New York: Holt, Rinehart, and Winston.

Kotler, Philip (1988), *Marketing Management*, 6th ed., Englewood Cliffs, NJ: Prentice-Hall.

Levitt, T. (1975), "Dinosaurs Among the Bears and Bulls," *Harvard Business Review*, 53(January–February), 41–53.

Loeb, Margaret (1983), "Giving Smokers Added Value is Tobacco Firms' Latest Idea," *Wall Street Journal*, August 30, 27.

Marketing News, "Pizza Hut Asserts Presence in Lunch Market," April 29, 1983, p. 4.

Melicher, Ronald W. and David F. Rush (1973), "The Performance of Conglomerate Firms: Recent Risk and Return Experience," *Journal of Finance*, 28(May), 381–388.

Miesing, Paul (1976), "Diversification by Already Established Firms as a Means of Overcoming Barriers to Entry," *Proceedings*, American Institute for Decision Sciences, 262–264.

Montgomery, C. A. (1979), "Diversification, Market Structure, and Firm Performance: An Extension of Rumelt's Model," Ph.D. dissertation, Purdue University.

Montgomery, C. A. (1982), "The Measurement of Firm Diversification: Some New Empirical Evidence," *Academy of Management Journal*, 25(June), 299–307.

Morris, Betsy (1984), "Thwack! Smack! Sounds Thrill Makers of Hunt's Ketchup," *The Wall Street Journal*, April 27, 1, 17.

Nathanson, Daniel A. and James S. Cassano (1982), "Organization, Diversity, and Performance," *The Wharton Magazine*, 6(Summer), 19–26.

Palepu, Krishna (1985), "Diversification Strategy, Profit Performance, and the Entropy Measure," *Strategic Management Journal*, 6(July–September), 239–255.

Pessemier, Edgar A. (1982), *Product Management: Strategy and Organization*, New York: NY: Wiley.

Pitts, Robert A. (1974), "Incentive Compensation and Organization Design," *Personnel Journal*, 338–348.

Pitts, Robert A. (1976), "Diversification Strategies and Organizational Policies of Large Diversified Firms," *Journal of Economics and Business*, 28, (Spring-Summer) 181–188.

Pitts, Robert A. (1977), "Strategies and Structure for Diversification," *Academy of Management Journal*, 20(March), 197–208.

Pitts, Robert A. and Donald H. Hopkins (1982), "Firm Diversity: Conceptualization and Measurement," *Academy of Management Review*, 7(October), 620–629.

Porter, Michael E. (1980), *Competitive Strategy: Techniques for Analysing Industries and Competitors*, New York: The Free Press.

Porter, Michael E. (1985), *Competitive Advantage: Creating and Sustaining Superior Performance*, New York: The Free Press.

Porter, Michael E. (1987), "From Competitive Advantage to Corporate Strategy," *Harvard Business Review*, 65(May–June), 43–59.

Ramanujam, Vasudevan and P. Rajan Varadarajan (1989), "Research on Corporate Diversification: A Review and Synthesis," *Strategic Management Journal*.

Reed, S. F. (1979), "Corporate Growth by Strategic Planning, Part II: Developing a Plan," *Mergers and Acquisitions*, 12(No. 3), 4–27.

Reid, Samuel (1968), *Merger, Managers, and Economy*, New York: Mc Graw-Hill.

Rice, Faye (1984), "Trouble at Procter & Gamble," *Fortune*, March 5, 70.

Roberts, Edward B. and Charles A. Berry (1985), "Entering New Businesses: Selecting Strategies for Success," *Sloan Management Review*, 27(Spring), 3–17.

Ruekert, Robert W., Orvill C. Walker, Jr., and Kenneth J. Roering (1985), "The Organization of Marketing Activities: A Contingency Theory of Structure and Performance," *Journal of Marketing*, 49(Winter), 13–25.

Rumelt, Richard P. (1974), *Strategy, Structure, and Economic Performance*, Boston, MA: Division of Research, Graduate School of Business Administration, Harvard University.

Rumelt, R. P. (1977), "Diversity and Profitability," Working Paper MBL-51, Graduate School of Management, University of California at Los Angeles.

Rumelt, Richard P. (1982), "Diversification Strategy and Profitability," *Strategic Management Journal*, 3(October–December), 359–369.

Salter, Malcolm S. and Wolf S. Weinhold (1978), "Diversification via Acquisition: Creating Value," *Harvard Business Review*, 56(July–August), 166–176.

Salter, Malcolm S. and Wolf S. Weinhold (1979), *Diversification Through Acquisition*, New York: The Free Press.

Salter, Malcolm S. and Wolf S. Weinhold (1981), "Choosing Compatible Acquisitions," *Harvard Business Review*, 59(January–February), 117–127.

Scherer, Frederick M. (1980), *Industrial Market Structure and Economic Performance*, Boston, MA: Houghton Mifflin.

Shaikh, Abdul Karim and P. Rajan Varadarajan (1984), "Measuring Firm Diversity: A Review and Synthesis," in R. W. Belk et al., (eds.) 1984 AMA Educators' Conference *Proceedings* (Chicago: American Marketing Association), August, 185–189.

Smith, Anne Mackay (1981), "Both General Foods and P&G Look Like Coffee War Victors," *The Wall Street Journal*, October 29, 25.

Standard Industrial Classification Manual (1972), Washington, D.C. U.S. Office of Management and Budget

Staudt, Thomas A. (1954), "Program for Product Diversification," *Harvard Business Review*, 32(November–December), 121–131.

Urban, Glen L. and John R. Hauser (1980), *Design and Marketing of New Products*, Englewood Cliffs, NJ: Prentice-Hall.

———and Nikilesh Dholakia (1984), *Essentials of New Product Management*, Englewood Cliffs, NJ: Prentice-Hall.

Varadarajan, P. Rajan (1983), "Intensive Growth Strategies: An Extended Classification," *California Management Review*, 25(Spring), 118–132.

Varadarajan, P. Rajan and Daniel Rajaratnam (1986), "Symbiotic Marketing Revisited," *Journal of Marketing*, 50(January), 7–17.

Varadarajan, P. Rajan (1986a), "Marketing Strategies in Action," *Business*, 36 (January–March), 11–23.

Varadarajan, P. Rajan (1986b), "Product Diversity and Firm Performance: An Empirical Investigation," *Journal of Marketing*, 50(July), 43–57.

Varadarajan, P. Rajan and Vasudevan Ramanujam, (1987), "Diversification and Performance: A Reexamination Using a New Two-Dimensional Conceptualization of Diversity in Firms," *Academy of Management Journal*, 30(June), 380–397.

Varadarajan, P. Rajan (1990), "Product Portfolio Analysis and Market Share Objectives: An Exposition of Certain Underlying Relationships," *Journal of the Academy of Marketing Science*, 18 (Winter).

Wall Street Journal (1982), "Ten Ways to Restore Vitality to Old, Worn-out Products," (February 18), 23.

Wall Street Journal (1985), "Candy Makers Step Up Fight Over America's Sweet Tooth," June 13, 29.

Wall Street Journal (1987), "Allegis Shakeup Came as Shareholder Ire Put Board Tenure in Doubt," June 11, 1, 12.

Weber, John A. (1976), *Growth Opportunity Analysis*, Reston, VA: Reston Publishing Company.

Weik, J. L. (1969), "An Analysis of the Relation of Vertical Integration and Selected Attitudes and Behavioral Relationships in Competing Channel Systems," Ph.D. dissertation, Michigan State University.

Wells, John R. (1984), "In Search of Synergy," Doctoral Thesis, Harvard Business School.

Weston, J. Fred and Surenda K. Mansinghka (1971), "Tests of the Efficiency Performance of Conglomerate Firms," *Journal of Finance*, 26(September), 919–936.

Williamson, Oliver E. (1975), *Markets and Hierarchies: Analysis and Antitrust Implications*, New York: The Free Press.

Wind, Yoram J., Vijay Mahajan, and Richard N. Cardozo (1981), *New Product Forecasting*, Lexington, MA: Lexington Books.

Wind, Yoram J. (1982), *Product Policy: Concepts, Methods, and Strategy*, Reading, MA: Addison Wesley.

Wood, Adrian (1971), "Diversification Merger and Research Expenditures: A Review of Empirical Studies," in *The Corporate Economy: Growth Competition, and Innovative Potential*, R. Morris and A. Wood, eds., Boston, MA: Harvard University Press.

Wrigley, Leonard (1970), "Divisional Autonomy and Diversification," DBA dissertation, Harvard University.

ASSESSMENT OF INDUSTRY

COMPETITION AND COMPETITORS

Introduction

**Industry Competition and
Profit Potential**
   Existing Firms in the Industry
   Potential Entrants to the Industry
   Suppliers to the Industry
   Buyers of the Industry Product
   Product Substitutes
   Implications of Industry Competition for
      Strategic Market Planning

Strategic Groups
   Formation of Strategic Groups
   Implications of Strategic Groups for Strategic
      Market Planning

Generic Strategies
   Porter's Generic Strategy Framework
   Abell and Hall Generic Strategy Frameworks
   Implications of Generic Strategies for
      Strategic Market Planning

The Value Chain
   Implications of the Value Chain for Strategic
      Market Planning

Emerging Trends in Industry Competition
   Information Technology and Industry
      Competition
   The Emergence of Global Markets and
      Global Competitors

A Concluding Note

References

INTRODUCTION

Assessing industry competition and competitor behavior is central to the study and practice of strategic market planning. Although portfolio matrix approaches and the PIMS empirical results offer useful guidelines for strategic market planning, neither explicitly considers competitors. For example, in the strategic analysis of product-markets, four important questions are frequently posed:

1. Are there certain unique forces that drive competition in a product-market?
2. How is competition defined and how are relevant competitors identified in a product-market?
3. Do competitors in a product-market adopt specific competitive strategies?
4. How can the activities performed by a firm and its competitors in the design, production, marketing, distribution, and support of its product be used to establish a competitive advantage in the marketplace?

Insights into these questions can be found in paradigms from industrial organization economics (Scherer, 1980; Shapiro, 1989). Porter (1980, 1981, 1985) has expanded on these paradigms and proposed (1) a framework to delineate forces of competition in an industry, (2) the concept of strategic groups to define relevant competitors, (3) a set of generic strategies pursued by competitors, and (4) the value chain concept. These paradigms provide a frame of reference for addressing these questions.

This chapter has two objectives. First, it summarizes the key concepts developed in industrial organization economics that are applicable to understanding industry competition and competitors. Second, insights from these concepts deemed useful to strategic market planning are assessed.

INDUSTRY COMPETITION AND PROFIT POTENTIAL

Both external and internal forces drive competition in an industry. Forces outside the industry affect all firms in that industry in varying degrees. Internal forces or structural factors within an industry determine the competitive dynamics within an industry. External and internal forces combine to determine the profit potential of an industry, which in turn distinguishes one industry from another in terms of its attractiveness to present and potential industry participants.

Porter (1985, p. 4–5) adopts the position that long-term profitability in an industry is measured by the average difference between the rate of return on investment and the cost of capital for firms in that industry. This perspective on profitability echos the views of Fruhan (1979, p. 42) who observed: "Managers who are successful in taking advantage of the competitive environment so as to earn returns in excess of their capital costs create enormous wealth for their shareholders." Marakon Associates (1986) has taken this thinking a step further by examining the relationship between industry profitability and the market-to-book-ratio for firms in an industry. They measure profitability based on the difference between return on equity and the cost of equity capital, and shareholder wealth based on the market value of shareholder equity divided by the book value of shareholder equity. Marakon Associates point out that economic forces both external and internal to the industry produce wide variations in industry profitability. The profitability of individual firms or business units is in turn determined by the economic forces affecting supply and demand in its product-markets, its competitive position, and its strategy (Marakon Associates, 1986, p. 2). The results of these forces are depicted in Figure 7.1 for fourteen U.S. industries and the profitability of one specific industry—paper and forest products.[1]

Five structural forces affect industry profitability by shaping competition (Scherer, 1980; Porter, 1980):

1. existing firms in the industry,
2. potential entrants to the industry,
3. suppliers to the industry,
4. buyers of the industry product, and
5. product substitutes for the industry product.

Each of these forces can have either a positive or a negative effect on industry profitability. What follows is a synthesis of Porter's (1980) views on these forces. In addition, the hypothesized effects of these forces on an industry are suggested.

Existing Firms in the Industry

Existing firms in an industry influence industry profitability by using tactics that either reduce the revenue potential for the industry product (e.g., through price competition) or increase the cost of delivering the product to industry buyers (e.g., through higher advertising budgets, or increased customer service or warranties). For example, rivalry among airlines to improve their competitive position through fare competition and frequent flier programs has influenced the profit potential of this industry through much of the 1980s.

The intensity of rivalry, however, is moderated by a number of structural factors. These factors include the number and diversity of competitors, industry growth, fixed or storage costs, product differentiation, and exit

FIGURE 7.1
PROFITABILITY OF 14 U.S. INDUSTRIES AND THE PAPER
AND THE FOREST PRODUCTS INDUSTRY

Profitability of 14 U.S. Industries—Spring 1986

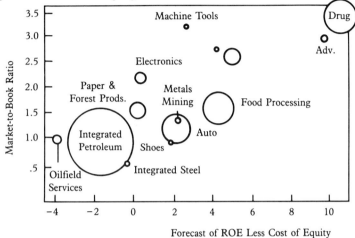

Profitability of Paper and Forest Products Companies—Spring 1986

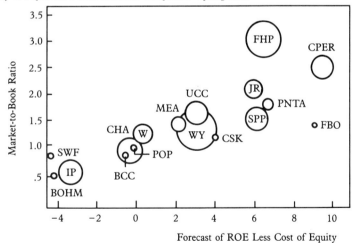

BOHM	Bohemia	FHP	Fort Howard Paper	SPP	Scott Paper
BCC	Boise Cascade	IP	International Paper	SWF	Southwest Forest
CHA	Champion International	JR	James River	UCC	Union Camp
CSK	Chesapeake	MEA	Mead	W	Westvaco
CPER	Consolidated Paper	PNTA	Pentair	WY	Weyerhaeuser
FBO	Federal Paper Board	POP	Pope & Talbot		

Source: Marakon Associates (1986), "The Ultimate Poison Pill: Closing the Value Gap," *Commentary* (San Francisco: Marakon Associates).

TABLE 7.1
FACTORS MODERATING RIVALRY AMONG EXISTING FIRMS

Factor	Hypothesized Impact on Industry Profits
Number and Diversity of Competitors	High concentration (industry domination by few firms) generates higher industry profits since the industry leader or leaders play a coordinative role through mechanisms such as price leadership.
	Diversity among competitors (in terms of size, ownership, strategies, origins, etc.) depresses industry profits because of their different circumstances and goals.
Industry Growth	Slow industry growth depresses industry profits by increasing market share expansion rivalry among firms and by demanding more financial and managerial resources.
Fixed or Storage Costs	High fixed or storage costs tend to depress industry profits since firms often resort to price cutting to increase capacity utilization.
Product Differentiation	Low perceived differentiation (i.e., commodity or near commodity products) reduces prices (since choice by the buyer is based on price) and depresses industry profits.
Exit Barriers	High exit barriers (such as specialized assets, fixed costs including labor agreements and resettlement costs, emotional barriers, government and social restrictions, and sharing of facilities, markets, etc. by business units) depress industry profits since marginal firms do not leave the industry.

barriers. The likely impact of these factors on industry profits is summarized in Table 7.1.

High concentration or domination by a few firms tends to generate higher profits for an industry. This tendency exists because the industry leader or leaders can play a coordinative role through mechanisms such as price leadership.

On the other hand, diversity among competitors, slow industry growth, high fixed or storage costs, low perceived product differentiation, and high exit barriers tend to depress industry profitability. Diversity among competitors (in terms of size, ownership, strategies, and origins) presents a case in which competitors may have objectives other than profitability (e.g., an outlet for excess capacity or dumping) for staying in the industry. Slow industry growth tends to increase market share expansion objectives among industry participants. These objectives impose more demands on the financial and managerial resources of firms and, hence, depress industry profits. For high-fixed-cost industries, firms often resort to price cutting to increase capacity utilization, thus depressing industry profits. Lack of product differentiation leads buyers to base their choices largely on price and service and to contribute to decreasing industry profits. Finally, high exit barriers (such as specialized assets or labor agreements) make it difficult for marginal firms to leave the industry, which in turn depresses industry profitability.

Potential Entrants to the Industry

New entrants represent a second possible threat to existing firms in an industry. In their efforts to establish themselves in the industry, new entrants may use tactics that adversely affect industry profit potential. These tactics may include setting a lower price for the industry product or ensuring a lower product cost if these entrants bring new technology or capacity to the industry. For example, Wal-Mart's ability to acquire goods directly from manufacturers at large discounts, to store them at its own distribution centers, and to deliver to stores within a day's drive has threatened the existence of community retail stores.

Threat of entry, however, is moderated by industry barriers to entry and possible retaliation from existing firms. High barriers to entry and retaliation deter potential entrants from entering an industry and minimize the threat of potential entrants to industry profitability.

Barriers to entry arise from six major sources: economies of scale, product differentiation, capital requirements, buyer switching costs, distribution channels, and absolute cost advantage. The likely impact of these sources in deterring new entrants and industry profit is summarized in Table 7.2.

Economies of scale, whether present in manufacturing, purchasing, or other business functions, tend to decrease product unit cost. Scale economies affect potential entrants, since they require potential entrants to either (1) enter the industry on a large scale and face reactions from competitors or (2) enter on a small scale at a cost disadvantage. Both options are unprofitable. High product differentiation tends to generate customer loyalty, making it difficult for potential entrants to establish a customer base. The large capital requirements for entering the industry, the absolute cost advantage (because of proprietary technology, government subsidies, etc.) held by existing firms in the industry, and the lack of access to distribution channels tend to deter potential entrants. Finally, if the cost of switching from an existing firm's product to the product offered by a potential entrant is high, buyers tend to refrain from purchasing the potential entrant's product.

Suppliers to the Industry

Suppliers to an industry affect industry profitability through the price they charge for supplied goods or services. The intensity of their impact on

TABLE 7.2
FACTORS CREATING BARRIERS TO ENTRY

Factors	Hypothesized Impact on Industry Profits
Economies of Scale	Scale economies (whether present in manufacturing, purchasing, research and development, marketing, service network, sales force utilization, or distribution) deter potential entrants because of cost advantage. This minimizes the impact of potential entrants on industry profits.
Product Differentiation	Product differentiation deters entry since existing firms may have brand identification and customer loyalty. This has a positive impact on industry profits.
Capital Requirements	The large capital requirements deter potential entrants and have a positive impact on industry profits.
Switching Costs	The high switching cost to the buyers (one-time cost of switching from one supplier's product to the other supplier's product) deters new entrants and has a positive impact on industry profits.
Distribution Channels	The lack of access to distribution channels deters potential entrants and has a positive impact on industry profits.
Absolute Cost Advantage	Cost advantages (whether because of proprietary technology, favorable access to location or new materials, government subsidies, etc.) deter potential entrants and have a positive impact on industry profits.

profitability depends on their bargaining power over industry participants. Bargaining power, however, is moderated by several structural factors including the number of suppliers, the competition to the suppliers produced by substitute products sold to the industry, the volume sold, the differentiation among the suppliers' products, and the threat of forward integration into the industry from suppliers. Table 7.3 summarizes the likely impact of these factors on the bargaining power of the suppliers and industry profitability.

Supplier bargaining power is at its zenith when: (1) the buyer group is more fragmented than the supplier group, (2) there are no substitutes for the product offered by the supplier group to the buyer group, (3) the buyer group is not a major customer of the supplier group, (4) the product offered by the supplier group is an important input into the product offered by the buyer group, (5) the supplier group's products are differentiated so that the buyer group cannot play one supplier group against another, and (6) the supplier group can integrate forward into the buyer group.

TABLE 7.3
FACTORS MODERATING SUPPLIERS' BARGAINING POWER

Factor	Hypothesized Impact on Industry Profits
Number of Suppliers	A supplier group depresses industry profits if it is more concentrated (dominated by few companies) than the industry it sells to, since it can influence the prices, quality, and terms it offers to the industry.
Substitute Products	A supplier group depresses industry profits if the product it sells to the industry does not compete with substitutes or is an important input to the industry.
Volume Sold	A supplier group depresses industry profits if the industry is not an important customer of the supplier group.
Product Differentiation	A supplier group depresses industry profits if the group's products are differentiated since the industry cannot play one supplier against another.
Forward Integration	A supplier group depresses industry profits if it poses a credible threat of forward integration into the industry.

Buyers of the Industry Product

Buyers of an industry product can influence industry profitability by demanding lower prices (by playing one firm against another), higher quality, and more and better services. Buyer's influence, however, depends upon their bargaining power, which is tempered by six factors. These factors include (1) the number of buyers and the volume purchased by them from the industry, (2) the product differentiation offered by the industry to buyers, (3) the profitability potential of buyers, (4) the threat of backward integration into the industry from buyers, (5) the importance of the industry product to buyers and, (6) the influence of buyers (e.g., retailers) on the ultimate consumers who buy the industry product from buyers. Buyer power is evident in the U.S. defense industry, in which the federal government is the dominant purchaser. The likely effect of these factors on industry profitability is summarized in Table 7.4.

The bargaining power of a buyer group is magnified when (1) the seller group is more fragmented than the buyer group (there are more sellers than buyers), (2) the buyer group purchases a significant volume of the product sold by the seller group, (3) the product sold by the seller group is standard or undifferentiated, (4) the buyer group operates at a lower profit margin and attempts to improve its profitability by lowering the purchasing cost of the product it buys from the seller group, (5) the product sold by the seller group is not an important input into the product

TABLE 7.4
FACTORS MODERATING BUYERS' BARGAINING POWER

Factor	Hypothesized Impact on Industry Profits
Number of Buyers and Volume Purchased	A buyer group depresses industry profits if it is concentrated (few buyers) or purchases a large volume of the total industry sales.
Product Differentiation	A buyer group depresses industry profits if the product it purchases from the industry is standard or undifferentiated.
Profits	A buyer group depresses industry profits if it is not highly profitable and attempts to improve its profitability by lowering the purchasing cost of the product it buys from the industry.
Backward Integration	A buyer group depresses industry profits if it can integrate backward.
Products/Services Offered by Buyers	A buyer group depresses industry profits if the industry's products is unimportant to the quality of the buyer group's products or services.
Influence on Consumers' Purchasing Decisions	A buyer group (e.g., retailers) depresses industry profits if it can influence consumers' purchasing decisions.

offered by the buyer group, and (6) the buyer group can influence the end users of the seller group's product.

Product Substitutes

Industries producing substitute products can influence industry profitability by limiting the prices industry participants can command for their product. The intensity of influence, however, is moderated by the functional similarity between the industry product and the substitutes, price/performance trade-offs offered by the substitutes, and profit margins provided by substitute products. Substitute products that (1) are similar to the product offered in an industry, (2) offer better price/performance to their buyers and (3) offer higher profit margins to their manufacturers tend to depress industry profits. However, if no product substitutes exist, industry profitability is improved. The likely effects of these factors on industry profitability are summarized in Table 7.5.

Implications of Industry Competition for Strategic Market Planning

Decisions regarding what product-markets to retain, delete from, and add to a firm's product-market portfolio should be assessed after analyzing the specific forces of competition present in a product-market. Consider, for example, the decision to enter a specific product-market. This decision

TABLE 7.5
FACTORS MODERATING THE IMPACT OF SUBSTITUTE PRODUCTS

Factor	Hypothesized Impact on Industry Profits
Functional Similarity	High functional similarity (products that can perform the same function as the product of the industry) depresses industry profits.
Price-Performance Trade Off	Substitute products that provide better price-performance than the industry product depress industry profits.
Profitability of Substitute Products	Substitute products produced by industries earning higher profits depress industry profits.

most certainly will be guided by entry barriers. If barriers are high and/or a sharp retaliation from the competitors currently serving the product-market is expected, the decision to enter that product-market should be reassessed. As illustrated below, product-markets will usually be dominated by one or more of six entry barriers.

INDUSTRY	DOMINATING ENTRY BARRIER
Soft Drinks	Product differentiation (brand identification) and bottling network
Cosmetics	Product differentiation (brand identification)
Mainframe Computers	Economies of scale and capital requirements
Investment Banking	Product differentiation
Wine	Economies of scale and access to distribution channels

Emerging product-markets, however, present a unique challenge for a firm. An emerging product-market is characterized by a product that is so innovative that it initiates a whole new market or industry. Examples include disposable diapers (Pampers), introduced by Proctor and Gamble, and personal computers, introduced by Apple.

Emerging product-markets exhibit an absence of competitive ground rules and an initial industry structure that is likely to be different from the ultimate structure (Porter 1980, pp. 232–233). Firms contemplating entry into emerging product-markets therefore need to consider the timing of their entry. For example, should the firm enter the market first and hope to convert a pioneering advantage into higher market share and profits? Or should the firm wait for the product-market to evolve and follow the pioneer with a similar or an improved product? The choices made by a firm can have important implications. According to one study, second entrants obtain on the average only about three-quarters of the market

TABLE 7.6
CONSUMER MARKETS WHERE PIONEERS MAINTAINED A DOMINANT POSITION

Market	Pioneers	Early Entrants	Later Entrants	Outcome
Low-calorie beer	Rheingold's Gablingers (1960s) Meister Brau Lite (1960s) Miller Lite (1975)	Schlitz Light (1976)	Anheuser-Busch's Natural Light (1977) Michelob Light (1978) Bud Light (1981)	Miller Lite holds sixty percent of the market, due primarily to massive advertising support.
Disposable diapers	P&G's Pampers (1961–66) Borden's White Lamb (1965) Scott Paper Baby Scotts (1966)	K-C's Kimbies (1971) Scott's Raggedy Ann & Andy (1971) Curity (1971)	P&G's Luvs (1976) Scott's Tots (1976) K-C's Huggies (1977) J&J (1978)	Pampers holds the largest share, but it is losing share to Luvs and Huggies as the market moves upscale.
Personal stereos	Sony Walkman (1979)	Panasonic Toshiba Sanyo (1980–82)	Aiwa (1982)	Sony still holds about fifty percent of the market.
Microwave ovens	Raytheon's Amana Radarange (early 1960s) Litton (1964)	Sharp (1973) Sanyo (1973)	Sunbeam (1979) Samsung Lucky-Goldstar (1980s) —K Mart —Penney's —Magic Chef	Amana and Litton split more than half of the market, but imports are gaining share in the growing lower end.

Smoke detectors	GE (1972) GE Home Sentry (1975) Emhart 911 (1975) Pyrotronic (1974)	Pittway's First Alert Norelco's Smokey Gillette's Capt. Kelly Teledyne (all 1976)	GE held the dominant position until the late 1970s, when its growth ebbed and First Alert moved into first place.
Bottled waters	Perrier (1977)	Previous market leaders were Arrowhead and Sparkletts	Perrier pioneered snob appeal rather than the pollution solution. Market growth is now shifting back to still water.
Running shoes	Nike	Previous market leaders were Adidas and Puma Brooks Etonic New Balance	Nike quickly surpassed Adidas and Puma as the market grew. Early entrants could not surpass Nike. The battle has now shifted to apparel and overseas markets, where Adidas still dominates.

Source: Schnaars, S. P. (1986), "When Entering Growth Markets, Are Pioneers Better Than Poachers?," *Business Horizons*, March–April, 29.

share of the pioneer, and later entrants are able to garner progressively smaller shares (Urban, Carter, Gaskin, and Mucha, 1986).

However, the timing of an entry strategy is not always so clear cut. An analysis of timing strategies by Schnaars (1986) shows mixed results. Table 7.6 summarizes seven case studies in which pioneers maintained a dominant market position; Table 7.7 describes five case histories in which late entrants gained a dominant market position. These twelve cases indicate that no one entry strategy is best in all situations. The order of entry *per se* does not seem to determine market position, but, rather, the nature of entry barriers (e.g., costs of production, cost of advertising, brand loyalty, product positioning, product quality) that the pioneer builds (Robinson and Fornell, 1985; Liberman and Montgomery, 1988; Fershtman, Mahajan, and Muller, 1990).

Decisions to retain or delete a product-market also require an understanding of the dominant forces of competition, as illustrated by the following examples:

INDUSTRY	DOMINANT FORCE OF COMPETITION
Vacuum tubes	Substitute products
Ocean-going tankers	Buyers (oil companies)
U.S. steel industry	Substitute products (and foreign competition)
Bottling companies	Suppliers (soft drink concentrate producers)

It is noteworthy that little empirical work exists that documents the specific effect of the five forces of competition on organizational performance. What research that does exist provides only tentative support for their effect on decision making (Lusch, Lazniak, and Harris, 1986). More promise appears to exist in the study of strategic groups within an industry.

STRATEGIC GROUPS

The five competitive forces provide a contextual framework for all the firms in an industry. Although these forces collectively determine industry profitability, the profit performance of individual firms depends upon the nature and execution of competitive strategies in the industry. According to Porter (1980, p. 4), "The goal of competitive strategy for a business unit in an industry is to find a position in the industry where the company can best defend itself against these competitive forces or can influence them in its favor."

Formation of Strategic Groups

A firm's competitive strategy can be defined using several dimensions that differentiate it from other firms in the industry, which in turn should contribute to its relative performance in the industry. At a minimum, these

CONSUMER MARKETS WHERE LATER ENTRANTS GAINED DOMINANT POSITION

Market	Pioneers	Early Entrants	Later Entrants	Outcome
Video-cassette recorders	CBS/Motorola (1968–71) AVCO's Cartridge TV (1972) Sony's Betamax (1975) —Zenith —Sanyo	Matsushita VHS (1977) —Panasonic —Quasar —JVC —RCA —GE —Magnavox —Sylvania —Sharp		Sony gained dominant share through its extensive marketing expenditures but then lost it to the superior design and lower cost of Matsushita.
Diet soft drinks	Cott (1950s) Kirsch's No-Cal (1950s) Royal Crown Diet Rite Cola (1962)	Coke's Tab (1963) Pepsi's Patio Cola (1963) Diet Pepsi (1964)		Tab and Diet Pepsi quickly dominated the market with massive advertising expenditures.
Personal computers	Apple (1977) Tandy TRS-80 (1977)		IBM-PC (1981) Osborne (1981)	IBM quickly dominated the business market, using marketing clout and product innovation.
Hand-held calculators	Bowmar Brain (1971) Canon Pocketronic (1970)	Texas Instruments (1972)	Foreign producers	TI moved into first place in 1973 with a strategy based on low-cost production.
Digital watches	Hamilton Watch Co.'s Pulsar (1971–77) Intel's Microma (1972–77)	National Semi-Conductor (1974) Texas Instruments Litronix Fairchild (all 1975)	Timex (1977) Very low-cost Japanese producers	Pulsar lost out to low-cost producer TI, who lost out to still lower-cost foreign manufacturers.

Source: Schnaars, S. P. (1986), "When Entering Growth Markets, Are Pioneers Better Than Poachers?," *Business Horizons,* March–April, 30.

dimensions consist of two sets of activities: (1) business *scope* commitments and (2) business *resource* commitments (Cool and Schendel, 1987). Business scope commitments include: (1) the target market segments of the business, (2) the types of products and services offered in the target markets, and (3) the geographic reach of the product-market strategy. Resource commitments include the allocation of resources to those functional areas considered central to achieving and retaining a competitive advantage in targeted product-markets. When a set of firms compete within an industry on the basis of similar combinations of scope and resource commitments, they are considered participants in a *strategic group*. It is noteworthy that this perspective on strategic group formation is also related to the identification of generic strategies discussed later in this chapter.

Originally coined by Hunt (1972), strategic groups have been identified in a variety of industries using a variety of dimensions. Table 7.8 shows the many dimensions used to formulate strategic groups.

The number of strategic groups in an industry can vary from one (all firms compete based on the same dimensions) to the total number of firms in the industry (each firm competes based on a unique set of dimensions). However, the number of groups in an industry and group membership depend on a number of factors. Most importantly, strategic groups are sensitive to the particular dimensions used and the number of dimensions employed. Different dimensions can produce different strategic groups and result in a situation in which group membership changes. Furthermore, even if the same dimensions are used, different groups and group membership can emerge over time.

Consider the U.S. pharmaceutical industry. Suppose two dimensions were used to identify strategic groups for fourteen of the largest pharmaceutical firms. One dimension was a scope commitment reflected in the percentage of business sales volume accounted for by prescription sales. The other dimension was a resource commitment—research and development expenditures as a percentage of sales. This two dimensional view of the U.S. pharmaceutical industry produces a "map" like the one shown in Figure 7.2. Four strategic groups emerge, with group membership indicated.

A two-dimensional analysis of an industry provides only an initial look at its structure. Other dimensions might produce a very different map. For example, advertising expenditures as a percentage of sales could be used as a resource commitment dimension. The percentage of business volume sales sold through a specific distribution channel could be a dimension of the scope commitment. Alternative or multiple dimensions could produce very different strategic group formations. A reanalysis of the U.S. pharmaceutical industry is a case in point. In their study of this industry, Cool and Schendel (1987) examined seven scope-related dimensions and eight resource-related dimensions simultaneously, including the two di-

TABLE 7.8
EMPIRICAL STUDIES ON STRATEGIC GROUPS

Study	Industry	Basis for Strategic Group Formation
Hunt (1972)	"White goods"	Product line basis • degree of product diversification • differences in product differentiation • extent of vertical integration
Newman (1973, 1978)	34 four-digit "producer goods" industries: chemical processes	Degree of vertical integration
Porter (1973)	38 three-digit "consumer goods" industries	Relative size of firm • leader/follower classification
Hatten (1974), Hatten and Schendel (1977)	Brewing industry	Manufacturing variables • number, age, capital intensity of plants Marketing variables • number of brands, price and receivables/sales Structural variables • eight-firm concentration ratio • firm size
Hatten, Schendel, and Cooper (1978)	Brewing industry	Manufacturing, marketing, and financial variables (leverage, merger/acquisition behavior)
Harrigan (1980)	Declining industries: receiving tubes synthetic soda ash baby foods acetylene percolators cigars leather tanners rayon	Dimensions of firms' strategic posture; strategic mapping used to identify groups
Caves and Pugel (1980)	U.S. manufacturing industry—sample	Relative size of firm
Oster (1982)	Nineteen consumer goods industries from Compustat	Product strategy • Advertising/sales ratio
Ramsler (1982)	Banking industry— 100 largest non-U.S. banks	Product market differentiation, size, geographic scope

(continued)

TABLE 7.8 (*continued*)

Study	Industry	Basis for Strategic Group Formation
Ryans and Wittink (1985)	Airline industry	Financial strategy clustering of residuals from capital asset pricing model (security returns)
Baird and Sudharsan (1983)	Office equipment/ electron computing	Financial Strategy variables—Leverage, current ratio, return on assets, dividend payment ratio, times interest earned, size
Primeaux (1985)	Textiles Petroleum	Size Investment behavior
Howell and Frazier (1983)	Medical supply and equipment	Customer groups served Customer needs served (due to Abell, 1980)
Hayes, Spence, and Marks (1983)	Investment banking	Logit analysis involving match between characteristics of investment bank and characteristics of individual customers; four main groupings identified
Hergert (1983)	2,450 SBUs representing fifty industries; broad sample of US manufacturing industry	Mix of variables 1. Advertising/sales 2. R & D/sales 3. Assets/sales 4. Business unit sales/parent sales 5. Market share
Dess and Davis (1984)	Paints and allied products	A range of twenty-one marketing variables
Hawes and Crittenden (1984)	Supermarkets	Marking strategy variables 1. Target market 2. Product 3. Promotion 4. Price 5. Buying 6. Display
Lahti (1983)	Finnish knitwear industry, 1969–1981	Size: small, medium, large Nature of the product group
Hatten and Hatten (1985)	Brewing	Marking strategy variables 1. Price 2. Advertising 3. Number of brands 4. National relative market share

Source: McGee, J. and H. Thomas (1986), "Strategic Groups: Theory, Research and Taxonomy," *Strategic Management Journal*, 7 (March–April), 141–160.

FIGURE 7.2
TWO DIMENSIONAL VIEW OF STRATEGIC GROUPS IN THE U.S.
PHARMACEUTICAL INDUSTRY (EARLY 1980s)

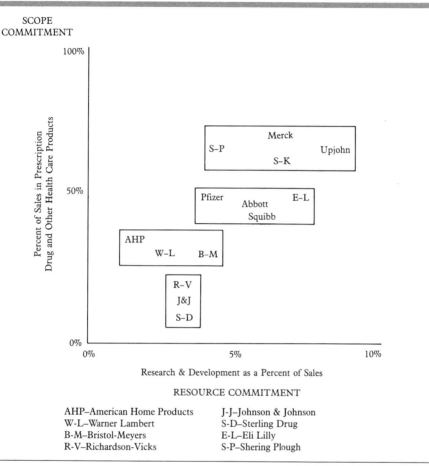

RESOURCE COMMITMENT

AHP–American Home Products	J-J–Johnson & Johnson
W-L–Warner Lambert	S-D–Sterling Drug
B-M–Bristol-Meyers	E-L–Eli Lilly
R-V–Richardson-Vicks	S-P–Shering Plough

Source: Company Annual Reports

mensions described in Figure 7.2. This analysis, which examined twenty-
two large and small firms, produced as many as six strategic groups in the
industry. Their longitudinal analysis over a twenty-year period also illustrated the dynamic nature of strategic group formation—the number of
groups and their membership change over time (see Table 7.9).

Implications of Strategic Groups for Strategic Market Planning

Strategic groups do provide a practical mechanism for assigning industry
participants to groups on the basis of strategic dimensions. However, issues
related to identifying appropriate dimensions upon which to develop

TABLE 7.9
STRATEGIC GROUP FORMATION IN THE U.S. PHARMACEUTICAL INDUSTRY: 1963–1982

Time Period	Strategic Group					
	I	II	III	IV	V	VI
1963–1969	Abbott	American Home	Johnson & Johnson	Searle	Carter-Wallace	Marion
	Lederle	Bristol-Myers	Morton-Norwich	Warner-Lambert	Robins	
	Lily	SmithKline	Pfizer		Rorer	
	Merck	Sterling Drug	Richardson-Vicks			
	Squibb		Schering-Plough			
	Upjohn		Syntex			
1970–1974	Abbott	Bristol-Myers	Merck	Robins	Marion	
	American Home	Carter-Wallace	Pfizer	Rorer		
	Lederle	Johnson & Johnson	Schering-Plough			
	Lily	Morton-Norwich	Searle			
	Squibb	Richardson-Vicks	Sterling Drug			
	Warner-Lambert	SmithKline	Upjohn			

300

Period	Group 1	Group 2	Group 3	Group 4	Group 5	Group 6
1975–1979	Abbott American Home Bristol-Myers Lederle Warner-Lambert	Syntex Lily Merck Pfizer Schering-Plough Squibb Sterling Drug Upjohn	Johnson & Johnson Morton-Norwich Richardson-Vicks Robins Searle SmithKline Syntex	Carter-Wallace Marion Rorer		Lederle
1980–1982	Abbott American Home Bristol-Myers Pfizer SmithKline Warner-Lambert	Lily Merck Upjohn	Johnson & Johnson Schering-Plough Squibb Sterling Drug	Searle Syntex	Carter-Wallace Marion Morton-Norwich Richardson-Vicks Robins Rorer	

Source: Redrawn from Karel O. Cool and Dan Schendel (1987), "Strategic Group Formation and Performance: The Case of the U.S. Pharmaceutical Industry, 1963–1982," *Management Science* (September), 1102–1124.

groups, their number, and the dynamic versus static analysis of strategic group formation remain problematic.

Decisions concerning which product-markets to retain, delete, or add to a firm's portfolio need to be further assessed in terms of the particular strategic group the product-market belongs to. Consider, for example, the decision to enter a new product-market. The nature and intensity of entry barriers and the scope of retaliation from current competitors will differ for different strategic groups. In this situation, strategic group analysis should provide a means of assessing: (1) the strategic group the firm should consider entering, (2) the type and level of entry barriers the firm will face when penetrating the chosen strategic group, (3) the number and type of competitors the firm will encounter, (4) the strategic dimensions that will make the firm similar to its strategic group members and different from members of other strategic groups, and (5) the relative effect of the five forces of competition on its relative profitability.

Since strategic groups define "subindustries" within an industry, the decision to enter a new product-market may also involve moving from one strategic group to another within the same industry (as was apparent in the longitudinal analysis of the U.S. pharmaceutical industry). In such a situation, a firm will face "mobility" barriers (as compared to entry barriers), which will affect its move from one group to another group in the same industry. Table 7.10 lists three types of mobility barriers to be considered when evaluating such entries: (1) market-related strategies, (2) industry supply characteristics, and (3) the characteristics of the firm.

TABLE 7.10
SOURCES OF MOBILITY BARRIERS

Market-Related Strategies	Industry Supply Characteristics	Characteristics of Firms
Product line	Economies of scale:	Ownership
User technologies	production	Organization structure
Market segmentation	marketing	Control systems
Distribution channels	administration	Management skills
Brand names	Manufacturing	Boundaries of:
Geographic coverage	processes	firms
Selling systems	R&D capability	diversification
	Marketing and distribution systems	vertical integration
		Firm size
		Relationships with influence groups

Source: McGee, J. and H. Thomas (1986), "Strategic Groups: Theory, Research and Taxonomy," *Strategic Management Journal,* 7 (March–April), 141–160.

GENERIC STRATEGIES

Assuming that broad forces of competition drive total industry profitability, how then do individual firms create defendable positions within an industry to deal with those forces, to out-perform competitors, and to produce superior rates of return relative to other industry participants? The answer to this question lies in the pursuit and execution of generic strategies. Numerous types of generic strategies have been proposed, several of which were described in chapters three and four, dealing with portfolio models. Others have been identified and are shown in Table 7.11.

Three perspectives on generic strategies are considered in this chapter. Furthermore, an attempt is made to integrate them and illustrate some important implications for and limitations to strategic market planning.

Porter's Generic Strategy Framework

Porter (1980) has suggested three internally consistent generic strategies for creating a defendable position and superior profitability within an industry: (1) cost leadership, (2) differentiation, and (3) focus. The advantages, disadvantages, execution requirements, and risks associated with each are summarized in Table 7.12.

Cost Leadership   A cost leadership strategy involves producing a standardized product at very low per-unit cost for many price-sensitive buyers (e.g., black-and-white television manufacturers). The competitive advantage achieved by this strategy is in *per-unit-cost* and the competitive product-market scope is *industry-wide*. Having a low-cost position yields high margins and above-average returns relative to other industry participants.

The attainment of a low-cost position, however, requires the firm to be a market share leader in its industry and to make a continued commitment to capital investment in plant and equipment and other technological improvements. The pursuit of a cost leadership strategy also requires the firm to have the skills, resources, and organizational mechanisms to effectively control expenses.

Differentiation   A differentiation strategy emphasizes producing a product that is unique industry-wide and appeals to many price-insensitive buyers. Product uniqueness is based on nonprice attributes such as product design or technology, distribution networks, and customer service. Competitive advantage in this strategy arises from *product differentiation* and the competitive product-market scope is *industry-wide* (e.g., soft drink producers).

The product differentiation strategy generates brand or customer loyalty. Even though this strategy may preclude the firm from becoming an industry-wide market share leader (owing to product uniqueness), it may produce high margins and an above-average return relative to that of other

TABLE 7.11
TYPOLOGIES OF GENERIC STRATEGIES

Author and Strategy Label	Characteristics of Strategy Type
Buzzell et al. (1975)	
1. Building	High investment to increase market share position
2. Holding	Investment at market norms to maintain market share
3. Harvesting	Low investment allowing market share to decrease; cost controls to generate cash flow and profitability
Utterback and Abernathy (1975)	
1. Performance maximizing	Emphasis on product and/or service performance; technology, and product R & D emphasized
2. Sales maximizing	Marketing emphasis to increase total sales and market share of firm
3. Cost minimizing	Emphasis placed on process technology/R & D to decrease total cost of production
Hofer and Schendel (1978)	
1. Share increasing	High investment to increase share of market
2. Growth	Maintain position in expanding markets, investment at industry norms
3. Profit	Investment at industry norms, cost controls to "throw off cash"
4. Market concentration and asset reduction	Realignment of resources to focused, smaller segments
5. Turnaround	Improve strategic posture, may require investment
6. Liquidation	Generate cash while withdrawing from market
Vesper (1979)	
1. Multiplication	Expansion of market share by multiplying present market structures
2. Monopolizing	Eliminate competition, establish barriers to entry, and control resources
3. Specialization	Specialize in products and/or production process
4. Liquidation	Give up business and market position

Wissema et al. (1980)

1. Explosion — Improve competitive position in short term
2. Expansion — Improve competitive position in long term
3. Continuous growth — Maintain growth in expanding markets, normal investment
4. Slip — Give up market share to generate cash in growing market
5. Consolidation — Give up market share to generate cash in stable market
6. Contraction — Liquidate assets and terminate market position

Miles (1982)

1. Domain defense — Preservation of traditional product-market
2. Domain offense — Attacking strategies based on
   1. Product innovation
   2. Market segmentation

Kotler and Achrol (1981)
Marketing Warfare
(A) Attack strategies
   1. Frontal attack — Attack the competitor's strengths rather than its weaknesses
   2. Flanking attack — Attack the competitor's weaknesses
   3. Encirclement attack — Attack the competitor's weaknesses as well as strengths
   4. Bypass attack — Avoid a direct attack on the competitor
   5. Guerrilla attack — Make small and periodic attacks to harass and demoralize the competitor, hoping to establish permanent footholds

(B) Defense strategies
   6. Position defense — Use all your resources to fortify or consolidate your position
   7. Flanking defense — Strengthen your weaknesses
   8. Preemptive defense — Attack competitors before they strike you
   9. Counteroffensive defense — Attack competitors when they attack you
   10. Mobile defense — Give up the weaker positions and consolidate resources at pivotal positions

Source: Adapted from: Galbraith, C. and D. Schendel (1983), "An Empirical Analysis of Strategy Types", *Strategic Management Journal*, 4 (April–June), 153–173.

TABLE 7.12
PORTER'S GENERIC COMPETITIVE STRATEGIES

Generic Strategy	Advantages	Disadvantages	Implementational Requirements		Threats of Risks to Generic Strategy
			Skills and Resources	Organizational	
Overall cost leadership	• Protects the firm from the five competitive forces (rivalry from competitors, powerful buyers, powerful suppliers, substitute products, and new entrants) by providing a higher profit margin than its competitors • Yields the firm above average returns in its industry	• Often requires a high relative market share or other advantages such as favorable access to raw materials • Imposes severe pressure on the firm to keep up its position by reinvesting in plant and equipment, scrapping obsolete assets, avoiding product line proliferation, and being alert to technological improvements	• Sustained capital investment and access to capital • Process engineering skills • Intense supervision of labor • Products designed for ease of manufacture	• Tight cost control • Frequent, detailed control reports • Structured organization and responsibilities • Incentives based on meeting strict quantitative targets	• Technological change that nullifies past investments or learning • Low-cost learning by industry newcomers or followers, through imitation or through their ability to invest in state-of-the-art facilities • Inability to see required product or marketing change because of the attention placed on cost • Inflation in costs that narrow the firm's ability to maintain enough of a price differential to offset competitors' brand images or other approaches to differentiation

Differentiation	• Protects the firm from the five competitive forces by providing brand or customer loyalty and higher margins than its competitors • Viable strategy for earning above-average returns in the industry	• May preclude gaining a high market share • May require charging high prices and trading-off the cost position if activities (R&D, product design, etc.) are costly	• Strong marketing abilities • Product engineering • Creative flair • Strong capability in basic research • Corporate reputation for quality or technological leadership • Long tradition in the industry or unique combination of skills drawn from other businesses • Strong cooperation from channels	• Strong coordination among functions in R&D, product development, and marketing • Subjective measurement and incentives instead of quantitative measures • Amenities to attract highly skilled labor, scientists, or creative people	• The cost differential between low-cost competitors and the differentiated firm becomes too great for differentiation to hold brand loyalty. Buyers thus sacrifice some of the features, services, or image possessed by the differentiated firm for large cost savings • Buyers' need for the differentiating factor falls. This can occur as buyers become more sophisticated • Imitation narrows perceived differentiation, a common occurrence as industries mature

(*continued*)

TABLE 7.12 (continued)

Generic Strategy	Advantages	Disadvantages	Implementational Requirements		Threats of Risks to Generic Strategy
			Skills and Resources	Organizational	
Focus	• Firm can achieve either differentiation from better meeting the needs of the particular target market or lower costs in serving this target market • Firm can serve its narrow strategic market more efficiently or effectively than competitors who are competing more broadly • May potentially yield above-average returns in the industry	• Does not achieve low cost or differentiation from the perspective of the market as a whole • Puts limitations on the overall market share achievable	• Combination of the above policies directed at the particular strategic target	• Combination of the above policies directed at the particular strategic target	• The cost differential between broad-range competitors and the focused firm widens to eliminate the cost advantages of serving a narrow target or to offset the differentiation achieved by focus • The differences in desired products or services between the strategic target and the market as a whole narrow • Competitors find submarkets *within* the strategic target and outfocus the focuser

Source: Adapted from Porter, M. E. (1980), *Competitive Strategy*, New York: The Free Press, Chapter 2, 34-46.

industry participants. Strong marketing and product development skills are prerequisites for this strategy.

Focus   A focused strategy involves the production of a product that fulfills the needs of particular buyers in an industry. That is, the firm markets its products to a particular market segment in the industry that may not be attractive to firms whose focus is industry-wide. The needs of this market segment may be so unique that the industry-wide differentiated product may not appeal to this segment and *therefore be of no interest to a firm following a differentiation strategy.* At the same time, the cost of delivering a product to this segment may actually go up and therefore be unattractive to a firm pursuing a cost leadership strategy. The competitive advantage of a focus strategy resides in either *low cost or product differentiation* and the competitive product-market scope is a narrow *target segment.*

The focus strategy precludes a firm from becoming a market share leader and low-cost producer industry-wide. However, it may yield high margins and above-average returns relative to the industry as a whole.

The Abell and Hall Generic Strategy Frameworks

Two additional generic frameworks used to distinguish competitive strategies have been suggested by Abell (1980) and Hall (1980). Abell (1980) has argued that defining a business just in terms of products offered and markets served may not be adequate because of the ambiguity surrounding the meaning of these terms. For instance, he pointed out that the term *product* could either refer to the *function* it performs or the *technology* on which it is based. Similarly, the term *market* could either refer to the *buyers* of a product or the *functions* the product performs for the customer. Abell suggested that the product should be considered as a physical *manifestation* of the application of a particular technology designed to satisfy a particular function for a particular customer group (Abell, 1980, p. 170). Following this line of reasoning, he proposed that a business be defined in terms of:

1. scope,
2. the differentiation of the company's offerings from one another, across segments, and
3. the differentiation of the company's offerings from those of competitors.

Furthermore, the scope and the differentiation should be viewed in terms of the following three factors:

1. Customer groups served,
2. Customer functions served,
3. Technologies utilized.

Based on the dimensions of scope and differentiation, Abell (1980) identified three generic strategies: (1) focused, (2) undifferentiated, and (3) differentiated. These strategies are detailed in Table 7.13.

To discern generic strategies, Hall (1980) classified firms using two possible sources of competitive advantage—relative delivered cost (low, average, high) and degree of product/service differentiation (high, average, low)—as the underlying dimensions. However, Hall's analysis of firms in eight basic U.S. industries indicated that very few firms (only three of the sixteen top performing firms in eight basic industries) possessed both sources of competitive advantage—the lowest delivered cost *and* high product/service differentiation. Most firms exhibited a single-minded determination to achieve one of two competitive positions within their respective industries:

1. the lowest delivered cost position relative to competition, coupled with both an *acceptable* delivered quality and a pricing policy designed to gain profitable volume and market share growth;
2. the *highest* product/service/quality differentiation position relative to the competition's, coupled with both an *acceptable* delivered cost structure and a pricing policy designed to gain margins sufficient to fund reinvestment in product/service differentiation. (Hall 1980, pp. 78–79).

A composite picture of generic strategies emerges from the view of Porter, Abell, and Hall. Figure 7.3 provides a three-dimensional conceptual scheme for exploring the viability of alternative generic strategies, performing industry analysis, and grouping firms into strategic subgroups.

Implications of Generic Strategies for Strategic Market Planning

Key decisions in strategic market planning can be influenced by the generic strategies followed by competitors as well as the firm itself. Consider, for example, the airline industry (Wright, 1987).

Laker Airways, and later People Express, became very successful based on their pursuit of a cost focus strategy. Both airlines focused on a consumer segment that desired a low price and was willing to accept a lower level of service. Recognizing growth in this consumer segment, many major airlines responded by offering their own discount services. This trend in air travel made a cost focus strategy increasingly inappropriate for many airlines and was replaced by cost leadership as the preferred competitive strategy. From a strategic market planning viewpoint, the choice for many airlines was reduced to one of the following options: (1) find markets (i.e., less traveled routes) where the cost focus strategy could still be maintained, (2) change the company's orientation from cost focus to cost leadership and compete at an industry-wide level with a different set of competitors (the strategy followed by the five major airlines—American,

TABLE 7.13
BUSINESS DEFINITION AND ALTERNATIVE GENERIC STRATEGIES

Business Definition: Strategic Alternatives	Scope and Differentiation	Factors to Consider in Choice of Business Definition
Focused strategy:		
Emphasizes effectiveness as opposed to efficiency	Narrow scope with respect to customer group, customer function, or technology dimension	**A. Customer buying behavior variables:**
Seeks the potential benefits of specialization	Highly differentiated from competitors' offerings	1. Customer sensitivity to price
		2. Customer sensitivity to nonprice
		3. Customer desire to purchase "full line" of products, or "systems," as opposed to individual components
		4. Similarity/differences in customer needs across customer groups, customer functions, and technology segments
Undifferentiated Strategy:		
Emphasizes efficiency as opposed to effectiveness	Broad scope across any or all of the three dimensions	**B. Resource variables:**
Seeks the potential benefits of scale economies and/or experience effects associated with higher volumes of standardized products	Low differentiation across customer groups, customer functions, or technology segments	1. Similarities/differences in resources required (marketing, manufacturing, R&D, etc.) to serve multiple customer groups, and/or functions utilizing alternative technologies
Differentiated Strategy:		
Emphasizes both efficiency and effectiveness	Broad scope across any or all of the three dimensions	**C. Cost behavior variables:**
The more differentiated the approach is across segments, the more effectiveness will be achieved at the expense of efficiency	High differention across customer group, function, and/or technology dimensions	1. Economies of broad participation across customer groups, customer functions, and/or technology segments
The less differentiated the approach is across segments, the more efficiency will be achieved at the expense of effectiveness		2. Cost/volume relationships—scale and/or experience effects
		D. Company skills related variables:
		Range of skills (marketing, manufacturing, R&D, etc.) possessed by firm

Source: Adapted from text: D. F. Abell (1980), *Defining the Business: The Starting Point of Strategic Planning*, Englewood Cliffs, NJ: Prentice-Hall, 178–181.

FIGURE 7.3
DIMENSIONS UNDERLYING GENERIC STRATEGIES

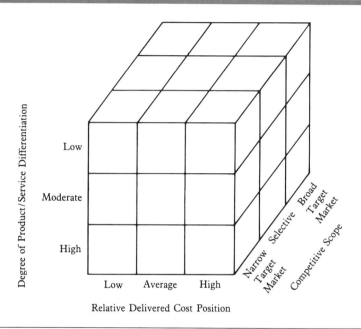

Delta, Northwest, United, and Texas Air) and (3) find markets where a competitive strategy could be based on nonprice attributes, akin to a differentiation focus strategy (the strategy adopted by MGM Grand Airlines to appeal to affluent travelers).

The case of the airline industry indicates the interactive relationship between generic strategies (i.e., how a firm can approach certain product-markets) and choice of product-markets in a firm's portfolio (i.e., which product-markets to add, delete, or retain).

While conceptually appealing, generic strategies are characterized by practical limitations. For example, the success of a differentiation strategy is based on how effectively differentiation can be created and sustained in the marketplace. In fact, the competitive advantage offered by the differentiation strategy is meaningful only when the following conditions are met (Coyne, 1986):

1. Customers perceive a consistent difference in important attributes between the firm's product or service offerings and its competitor's offerings.
2. The differences between the firm and its competitors with respect to important attributes are due to the capability gap between the firm and its competitors.

3. Both the difference with respect to important attributes, as well as the capability gap, can be expected to endure over time.

Furthermore, although the three generic strategies can be adopted singly or in combination, their adoption by a firm will be influenced by the firm's resources and the nature and life cycle of the industry. Wright (1987) has outlined the following clarifications on the adoption of generic strategies:

- Because of greater access to resources, only larger firms in an industry may compete by using the cost leadership or differentiation strategy. Smaller firms can only viably compete with the focus strategy.
- Larger firms will not compete by using a focus strategy as their only strategy option, since it would not be attractive for them. Furthermore, because of the different functional emphases required in the implementation of generic strategies (i.e., cost control in cost leadership and product development and marketing in differentiation), a focus strategy may only be logically pursued in conjunction with the differentiation general strategy. Larger firms that compete by using cost leadership would do so instead of other strategies;
- Because of the nature and/or life cycle of the industry itself, certain generic strategy options may not be available to a firm in an industry (e.g., differentiation or focus strategies in commodity industries and cost leadership in an industry where competitors have already accumulated greater cumulative volume or better access to low-cost inputs);
- Although firms that compete with a cost leadership generic strategy will have higher returns with a large market share, a differentiation strategy can also provide a firm higher returns with larger market share. That is, a differentiation generic strategy should not preclude a firm from becoming a profitable market share leader.

In short, generic strategy determination, like strategic group formation and analysis, is marked by considerable shadings. Both concepts' principal contribution is a frame of reference with which to think strategically.

THE VALUE CHAIN

According to Porter (1985, p. 36), a firm is "a collection of activities that are performed to design, produce, market, deliver, and support its product." Therefore, to gain competitive advantage over its rivals in the marketplace, a firm must either perform these activities at a lower cost or perform them in a manner that produces differentiation.

To further understand the competitive advantage provided by these activities, Porter has suggested the concept of a "value chain," which was originally proposed by McKinsey and Company (Buaron, 1981). A value chain is a set of interrelated activities performed by a firm to create, sup-

FIGURE 7.4
THE GENERIC VALUE CHAIN

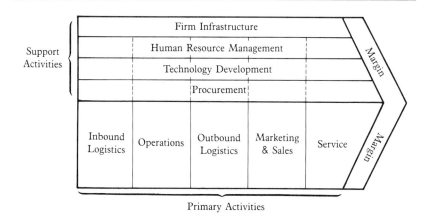

Source: Porter, M. E. (1985), *Competitive Advantage*, New York: The Free Press, 37.

port, and deliver its product. As depicted in Figure 7.4, this concept suggests that the activities performed by a firm can be divided into two major groups consisting of five generic types of primary activities and four generic types of support activities, respectively, which are called "value activities." The value a firm creates is measured by the amount buyers are willing to pay for its product. A firm will be profitable as long as the value it creates is more than the cost of performing value activities.

As detailed in Table 7.14, primary activities are performed in the physical creation, distribution, marketing, and after-sale-service of the product. On the other hand, as summarized in Table 7.15, support activities provide the infrastructure and the human, technology, and other types of inputs that allow the primary activities to take place. Therefore, a firm's value chain is a system of interdependent primary and support activities. Furthermore, in a particular industry, this system may be a part of a larger "value system" in which the firm's activities are linked with the value chains of suppliers, channels, and customers.

Implications of the Value Chain for Strategic Market Planning

How can the value chain assist a firm in evaluating its decisions regarding what product-markets to retain, delete from, or add to its product-market portfolio? The value chain is a tool that provides an assessment of the activities that a firm performs to design, produce, market, deliver, and support its product in the marketplace. Such an assessment of activities, for instance, is a logical framework for exploring how new product-markets

TABLE 7.14
GENERIC CATEGORIES OF PRIMARY VALUE ACTIVITIES

Generic Category of Primary Value Activities	Inbound Logistics	Operations	Outbound Logistics	Marketing and Sales	Service
Objective of the Value Activity	To receive, store, and disseminate inputs to products	To transform inputs into the final form	To collect, store, and physically distribute the product	To provide means by which buyers can buy the product and to induce them to buy it	To provide service to enhance or maintain the value of the product
Value Activities Performed	Material handling, warehousing, inventory control, vehicle scheduling, returns to suppliers	Machining, packaging assembly, equipment maintenance, testing, printing, facility operations	Finished goods, warehousing, material handling, delivery operation, order processing, scheduling	Advertising, promotion, sales force, pricing, channel selection, channel relations	Installation, repair, training, parts supply, product adjustment

Source: Adapted from Porter, M. E. (1985), *Competitive Advantage*, New York: The Free Press, 39–40.

TABLE 7.15
GENERIC CATEGORIES OF SUPPORT VALUE ACTIVITIES

Generic Category of Support Primary Activity	Firm Infrastructure	Human Resource Management	Technology Development	Procurement
Objective of the Value Activity	To support the entire chain at the business unit or the corporate level	To support the human resource needs of the other primary and support activities and the entire value chain	To improve the product and the process	To purchase inputs used in the entire value chain
Value Activities Performed	General management, planning, finance, accounting, legal, government affairs, and quality management	Recruiting, hiring, training, development, and compensation of all types of personnel	Component design, feature design, field testing, process engineering, and technology selection	Qualifying new suppliers, procurement of different groups of purchased inputs, and ongoing monitoring of suppliers' performance

Source: Porter, M. E. (1985), *Competitive Advantage*, New York: The Free Press, 40–45.

can be created by enhancing or changing the way the product is currently produced and offered in the marketplace either by the firm or its competitors. Consider the following examples in which the various firms create opportunities by changing or enhancing value-creating activities:

- Domino's Pizza established its presence in the marketplace by being the only national chain that delivered. They promised delivery to customers within 30 minutes. The firm had a natural appeal for customers who were located close to colleges and military bases (*Business Week*, 1983).
- Since 1853, potato chip making has been a fragmented market. Because they are fragile, potato chips cannot be shipped more than two hundred miles, and even at that distance, a quarter of the chips get broken. Furthermore, potato chips spoil quickly and can't remain on the shelf for more than two months. By developing a process similar to papermaking, Proctor and Gamble introduced Pringle potato chips that were easy to manufacture, could be stacked on top of each other in a sealed container, have a shelf life of at least a year, and could be transported and distributed nationally (Vanderwicken, 1974).
- California Cooler, a mixer of carbonated wine and fruit juice, was developed into a national product using packaging and distribution channels not traditionally used by the wine manufacturers. By positioning the product as a genuine alternative to wine, beer, and liquor, the product was inventoried and sold by beer distributors rather than wine distributors because the former had more contacts with liquor stores, restaurants, and bars. In order to make beer distributors more comfortable with the product, it was sold in twelve-ounce bottles, in packages of four and six, and in twenty-four bottle cases to match the usual packaging of beer products. The product was priced to allow beer distributors to achieve margins close to thirty-three percent, higher than the typical margins of twenty percent on beer products (*Business Week*, 1984).

EMERGING TRENDS IN INDUSTRY COMPETITION

Given the nature of forces that drive competition in an industry and the strategic options that are available to a firm in an industry to develop competitive advantage, what trends can be expected to further influence industry competition and, hence, the conduct and practice of strategic market planning? This question is the focus of this section. More specifically, this section highlights two emerging trends: information technology, and the emergence of global markets.

Information Technology and Industry Competition

Information technology (IT) refers to the collective means of assembling and electronically storing, transmitting, processing, and retrieving words, numbers, images, and sounds (Gerstein, 1987, p. 5).

Information technologies are expected to influence business operations and the quality of our work life as well as our home life (Booz, Allen, and Hamilton, 1983). In a survey of *Fortune* one thousand companies, the responding senior corporate executives believed that evolving technologies related to advanced computer capabilities were likely to have the greatest potential impact on businesses in the 1980s (Booz, Allen, and Hamilton, 1981). Developments in microelectronics, computer-aided manufacturing, computer-aided design, and software engineering were expected to play prominent roles in business operations.

More than fifty percent of the U.S labor force is involved in the "information" sector today, and this sector of the economy is outgrowing every other sector, including the service sector (Brand, 1987). Information technologies are making it possible to develop expert systems that analyze and make decisions normally made by experts (Kupfer, 1987; Leonard-Barton and Sviokla, 1988) and anticipate products of the future that will influence the competitive balance of industries (Brand, 1987).

Articulating the impact of information technologies on the design of organizations, Peter Drucker (1988) has professed that the typical business in the 1990s will be information- or knowledge-based. The organization of the future will be composed largely of specialists who will direct and discipline their own performance through organized feedback from colleagues, customers, and headquarters. According to Drucker, information is data endowed with relevance and purpose. Converting data into information thus requires knowledge, and knowledge, by definition, is specialized. Hence, large and successful information-based organizations will be comprised of specialists. They will have no middle management and will resemble a hospital or a symphony rather than a typical manufacturing company.

How are information technologies likely to impact the conduct and practice of strategic market planning? How are the decisions regarding which product-markets to retain, add to, and delete from a firm's portfolio likely to be affected by information technologies?

Parsons (1983), Porter and Millar (1985), Wiseman (1985), Keen (1986), and Gerstein (1987) have proposed that in existing product-markets, information technologies are likely to (1) create a competitive advantage and (2) change the balance between the forces undermining industry competition. Information technologies are also expected to assist a firm in spawning businesses in completely new industries and creating new businesses within existing businesses.

Creating Competitive Advantage   Efforts to understand how information technology will alter competitive advantage are recent in origin. One framework for analyzing the impact of information technologies on the development of competitive advantage has been suggested by Gerstein and Reisman (1982). They point out that two factors or dimensions merit attention. As shown in Table 7.16, one dimension distinguishes between information technology applications that are "operationally critical" and those that are not. An operationally critical application is one upon which the day-to-day activities of an organization depended and without which it cannot function. For example, the daily operation of an airline depends on its reservation system.

A second dimension represents the degree to which the information technology application provides a competitive advantage to the organization. An information technology application capable of creating a competitive advantage assists the organization in satisfying a marketplace need more effectively or efficiently than its competitors. It affects the value activities in the firm's value chain and allows the firm to either differentiate itself from other firms or to be the low-cost producer of the product. Examples of competitive advantage include the 1979 introduction of the automatic tellers (ATMs) distribution network in New York City by Citibank. Although other banks have since introduced this service, Citibank did differentiate itself from its competitors by introducing it.

TABLE 7.16
INFORMATION TECHNOLOGY—STRATEGIC MARKET PLANNING LINKAGE

		Degree of Operational Dependence on Information Technology	
		Low	*High*
Degree of Competitive Advantage Provided by Information Technology	*Low*	I • Traditional financial reporting and routine accounting systems	II • Reservations systems used by hotel chains • Automatic teller machines (today)
	High	III • Electronic home banking • Expert system	IV • Citibank automatic teller machines (ATM) network (in 1979) • Reservations systems developed by airlines (e.g., Apollo by United Airlines in 1976)

Source: Adapted from Gerstein and Reisman (1982), "Creating Competitive Advantage with Computer Technology," *Journal of Business Strategy,* 3 (Summer) 57–58.

The four cells in Table 7.16 exhibit the strategic role played by information technologies in creating a competitive advantage for a firm. For example, IT applications in cell I tend to be reporting systems that are neither strategically important nor an absolute necessity for an organization. Many stand-alone personal computer uses, for example, can be included in this cell. Cell III, on the other hand, includes IT applications that are "auxiliary services" or services that are nice to have, but upon which the firm does not yet depend (e.g., electronic home banking, expert systems).

Cells II and IV represent IT applications that are essential for the day-to-day operations of a firm. However, only the IT applications in cell IV offer a competitive advantage. For example, IT applications in cell II include businesses that rely on automated transaction processing, such as financial services, automobile rental firms, and airlines. The applications in cell IV clearly represent IT applications that can provide a competitive advantage for a firm. However, this advantage may not be sustainable. The transient nature of competitive advantage developed by Citibank through its ATM network represents an example of a unsustainable advantage.

Table 7.17 highlights IT applications of some of the value chain activities that can assist a firm in creating competitive advantage either by lowering cost or differentiating a product. Illustrative applications in Table 7.18 show how information technologies have been used by firms like Hertz to augment and differentiate its service from its competitors and by casinos in Atlantic City to reduce their cost of providing complimentary services to their customers.

Changing the Balance Between the Forces of Industry Competition   As discussed earlier, five competitive forces drive industry profitability: the power of buyers, the power of suppliers, the threat of new entrants, the threat of substitute products, and the rivalry among existing competitors. Information technologies can change the balance between the five competitive forces and, hence, industry profitability.

Consider, for example, the reservation information systems developed in the airline industry and their impact on the rivalry among competitors.[2]

Before the airline industry was deregulated in 1978, there were 330,000 fares available to airline customers. At present, there are more than seven million individual fares available to customers in the United States. Furthermore, unlike before deregulation, when a typical airline perhaps did not change its schedule more than four or five times a year, airlines today change their schedules daily, adding new destinations, products, and prices. Given the fare challenge, more than eighty-eight percent of all travel agencies use computers for their day-to-day business.

TABLE 7.17
INFORMATION TECHNOLOGY APPLICATIONS PROVIDING COMPETITIVE
ADVANTAGE IN THE VALUE CHAIN

| | Nature of Competitive Advantage | |
	Low Cost	Product Differentiation
Product Design & Development	Product Engineering Systems	R&D Data Bases
	Project Control Systems	Professional Work Stations
		Electronic Mail
		CAD (Computer Assisted Design)
		Custom Engineering Systems
		Integrated Systems for Manufacturing
Operations	Process Engineering Systems	CAM
	Process Control Systems	Quality Assurance Systems
	Labor Control Systems	Systems for Suppliers
	Inventory Management Systems	Quality Monitoring Systems
	Procurement Systems	
	Quality Monitoring Systems	
Marketing	Streamlined Distribution Systems	Sophisticated Marketing Systems
	Centralized Control Systems	Market Data Bases
	Econometric Modeling Systems	Graphic Display Systems
		Telemarketing Systems
		Competition Analysis Systems
		Modeling Systems
		Service-oriented Distribution Systems
Sales	Sales Control Systems	Differential Pricing Systems
	Advertising Monitoring Systems	Office/Field Communications
	Systems to Consolidate Sales Function	Customer/Sales Support Systems
	Strict Incentive/Monitoring Systems	Dealer Support Systems
		Customer Order Entry Systems
Administration	Cost Control Systems	Office Automation to Integrate Functions
	Quantitative Planning & Budgeting Systems	Environment Scanning & Non-quantitative Planning Systems
	Office Automation for Staff Reduction	Teleconferencing Systems

Source: Adapted from Parsons, G. L. (1983), "Information Technology: A New Competitive Weapon," *Sloan Management Review,* Fall 1983, 12.

TABLE 7.18
ILLUSTRATIVE INFORMATION TECHNOLOGY APPLICATIONS OF
CREATING COMPETITIVE ADVANTAGE

Competitive Advantage	IT Application
Product Differentiation	Hertz, the car rental agency, uses information technology systems to augment and differentiate its service from its competitors' by offering its customers reports that specifically meet their needs. Available in various languages (including English, French, German, Italian, and Spanish), the Hertz customized printout provides directions for hotels, office buildings, convention sites, and sports arenas in major U.S. cities. Once the traveler specifies the desired destination, the printout specifies expressways, exits, turns and time duration of the trip. In some cities, the printout outlays a grid structure on the map to present the information graphically.
Cost Differentiation	Gambling casinos such as Caesar's Palace, Bally's, and Harrah's in Atlantic City spend a sizeable amount on complimentary services including food, accommodation, and transportation via private jet for high rollers. The casinos wish to maximize the spread between the high rollers' losses and the amount they spent on providing complimentaries to them. To reduce the cost of complimentary service and improve the odds of maximizing this spread in their favor, casinos employ information systems that provide analyses on customers including their game preferences, betting patterns, and food preferences. The information systems are used to identify the "best" prospects and to design an appropriate package of complimentary services for them.

Also fueling the fare rivalry among airlines are the reservation information systems Sabre and Apollo developed by American Airlines and United, respectively. Apollo service is used by almost 8000 travel agency locations in the United States, Canada, Europe, the Orient, and the South Pacific. The system contains schedules and airfares for more than six hundred and forty airlines worldwide. It keeps track of fourteen thousand hotels and condominiums and provides links to seventeen car rental companies. It assists in booking vacation packages, and Broadway plays, renting limousines, and determining currency exchange rates.

Reservations systems have revolutionized the travel agency business. For example, since the 1976 debut of Sabre (developed at a cost of $350 million), travel agents have more than doubled their share of total bookings, boosting American Airlines' market share as well. In fact, since airlines pay American a fixed fee for each leg of a trip booked through the Sabre system, American earns a higher return on investment by booking tickets than it does by flying airlines.

In recent years, reservation systems have been challenged for creating rivalry among airlines. Sabre, for example, has been alleged to favor American flights. Allegations by Braniff Airlines in 1982 that American had used its Sabre system to drive Braniff out of business by cancelling Braniff reservations and switching passengers to American flights led to wide-ranging federal investigations of Sabre and Apollo. In 1984, convinced that reservation systems give American and United unfair advantage, eleven airlines filed an antitrust suit against them.

This example is but one of several which illustrate the use of information technology to influence forces of industry competition. Table 7.19 includes other IT applications in which information technology has been used to shift the competitive forces in favor of buyers or to create substitute products.

Creation of New Product-Markets Information technologies assist firms in creating new businesses in new industries and increasing new product-markets for and from existing businesses.

The Cash Management Account (CMA) introduced by Merrill Lynch in 1977 is an example of a new business made possible by information technologies. The CMA provided three types of services to its clients under one umbrella: credit through a standard margin account, cash withdrawal by check or a Visa debit card issued by Banc One in Columbus, Ohio, and automated investment of funds in a money market account managed by Merrill Lynch. The new product created its own industry and brought in several thousand new accounts that had not been with Merrill Lynch previously. In the early 1980s, banks and other financial service organizations entered the market with similar products, eroding the pioneering position held by Merrill Lynch (Wiseman, 1985).

Information technologies also make it possible for firms to create new product-markets for their existing businesses. Communication satellites have made it possible for newspapers such as *The Wall Street Journal*, the *New York Times*, and *USA Today* to transmit their pages to scattered printing plants in the United States to produce a product for the national audience. Information Systems made available to their agents by insurance

TABLE 7.19
ILLUSTRATIVE INFORMATION TECHNOLOGY APPLICATIONS
OF CHANGING THE BALANCE OF THE COMPETITIVE FORCES IN
AN INDUSTRY

Competitive Force	IT Application
Buyer Power	The on-line inventory control and purchasing system developed by Equitable Life Assurance allows its purchasing agents at the various warehouses that supply the essential office supplies to its field and regional offices to purchase the supplies from Equitable headquarters or go outside. The system enabled Equitable to reduce the bargaining power of its office-item suppliers since during negotiations with the vendors, purchasing agents can access the system's data base to learn the terms of recent deals for items they would like to purchase.
Substitution	Electronic telephone directories, such as the French Minitel system, are substituting for the traditional telephone directories. The French Minitel is a small TV-like screen that attaches to a phone, and connects the user to more than 100,000 pages of telephone directory listings (including all the telephone numbers in France). Users can quickly search for any listing and save shelf space required to store phone books.

companies such as State Farm Insurance assist agents in identifying prospects for the cross-selling of company products. Information technologies have also made it possible to develop new businesses from within existing businesses. Some such illustrative applications are included in Table 7.20.

The above discussion clearly emphasizes the role information technology can play in the conduct and practice of strategic market planning. However, as exhibited in Table 7.16, the competitive advantage offered by a information technology either in an existing product-market or in creating a new product-market may not be everlasting. We need to understand how information technology can be used by a firm not only to create competitive advantage, but also to sustain it. In that respect, it is important to understand how the value created by information technology can be evaluated and measured.

The literature dealing with IT applications has been biased toward innovation. As argued by Rogers (1986), for example, the consumer accept-

TABLE 7.20
ILLUSTRATIVE INFORMATION TECHNOLOGY APPLICATIONS
OF NEW PRODUCT-MARKET CREATIONS FROM
EXISTING BUSINESSES

Industry	IT Application
Retailing	
Sears	Using its excess telecommunications and computer capacity, Sears sells its credit-authorization and transaction-processing services to Phillips Petroleum Company and retail remittance-processing services to Mellon Bank.
Airline	
Japan Airlines (JAL)	To generate fee-generating applications for its underutilized worldwide computer-based reservation system, JAL uses it to book tickets around the world for sports events, concerts, and plays.
Banking	
Liberty National Bank & Trust Company, Oklahoma	Utilizing its experience in operating a network of automated teller machines, Liberty National Bank in Oklahoma joined with an independent retailer to found a chain of automated gasoline stations. Fuel pumps in these stations are directly linked to the bank's computers. At these stations, Liberty customers can use their bank card, which deducts the transacted amount directly from the customer's account.

Source: Wiseman, C. (1985), *Strategy and Computers*, Homewood, IL: Dow-Jones.

ance and social implications of information technologies are not yet well understood. For example, a growing number of banks are now using ATMs, but with varying degrees of success. This information technology is still resisted by some consumers, either because it replaces the human contact tellers provide or because of safety concerns. Antitrust cases, such as the one filed against American Airlines and United in the airline industry, indicate that information technology may be perceived to provide an unfair competitive advantage to some firms, therefore hurting other firms as well as customers.

In spite of the above concerns, we can expect information technology to play a significant role in shaping industry competition and the conduct and practice of strategic market planning in the 1990s.

The Emergence of Global Markets
and Global Competitors

Kenichi Ohmae, managing director of the Tokyo office of McKinsey and Company, Inc., has observed that in advanced industrial countries, such as Japan, the United States, and the Western European countries, consumers' lifestyles are becoming more alike, the marketplace demands of these countries are becoming similar, and the national economies are becoming dependent on each other (1987). People in these countries find the same things interesting or attractive and demand and use the same products to satisfy their needs.

The emergence of such trends has been even articulated to exist among people worldwide (Levitt, 1983). Coke, McDonald's, and Kodak are often cited as examples of global brands that appeal to consumers worldwide (Simon-Miller, 1986, Moskowitz, 1987). In recent years, an increasing number of key industries, such as the automobile, motorcycle, agricultural equipment, aerospace, military hardware, telecommunications, electronics, and luxury product industries, have become global industries since firms in these industries originate, produce, compete, and market their products worldwide. Johnson and Johnson, for example, manufactures its health care products in forty-seven countries and markets these products in one hundred and fifty-two countries. In 1986, sales from overseas markets constituted forty-three percent of its total revenues (Johnson and Johnson, 1986). In 1987, fifty-four percent of IBM's total revenues came from overseas operations (Kirkland, 1988). There are now about one hundred and seventy-five auto makers worldwide that produce more than forty-five million cars, trucks, and buses a year to satisfy the worldwide demand of $384 billion, or two and one-tenths percent of the world's GNP (Taylor, 1987). As pointed out by Lee Iacocca (1987, p. 5) "The car industry used to be the 'Big Three'; now it's becoming the 'Big Thirty.' "

Almost every market in the free world has now been penetrated with products made by foreign competitors. For example, thirty-nine percent of Japan's total exports, thirty-six percent of Korea's total exports, eighty-one percent of Canada's total exports, and eighty-seven percent of Mexico's total exports come to the United States (Iacocca, 1987). Similarly, major U.S. companies in the various industries, such as aerospace, computer equipment, oil field machinery, medical equipment, and chemicals industries, export a significant percentage of their products overseas (*Business Week*, 1988). At least eighty-nine international retailers from Europe, Canada, Australia, and Japan have opened stores in the United States selling everything from fashion-forward clothing and ready-to-assemble furniture to mod socks and raincoats. Similarly, U.S.-based retailers such as Toys "R" Us, The Gap Inc., and Esprit are opening outlets around the world (Smith, 1988). In addition, some popular brand names in the United States are controlled by foreign companies. For example, Baskin-Robbins ice cream is sold by Allied-Lyons, a British firm, and Lean Cuisine frozen dinners are supplied by Stouffer, a Nestlé unit (Moskiwitz, 1987).

To transform global challenges into new opportunities, a multiproduct, multimarket firm cannot be myopic in its scope and coverage. The question, however, is what strategic product-market alternatives are available to a diversified firm in a global industry? Consider the four-cell matrix depicted in Table 7.21. The horizontal dimension represents the market focus of a firm, whereas the vertical dimension represents the type of competitors it faces in the industry. Except for Cell I, representing a situation in which the firm markets a product only in its own country and also faces competitors from only its own country, the cells represent the various facets of a global industry.

Cell II, for example, represents a situation in which a firm marketing a product in its own country also competes with competitors who are from other countries. Even though this firm is not marketing its product in other countries, it is still involved in a global industry and hence cannot ignore global competitors in its own territory. Examples include British retailers such as Laura Ashley in the U.S. retailing market. The company markets finely manufactured clothing and home fashions in the United States, with annual sales of $280 million in 1986. It plans to open a store in every U.S. city with a population of more than one million and hence cannot be ignored by major U.S. retailers (Smith, 1988).

TABLE 7.21
GLOBAL MARKETS AND COMPETITION IN AN INDUSTRY

Type of Competitors	Market Focus of a Firm			
		Country-Centered		Global
Domestic (from the same country)	I	A firm marketing a product in its own country only competes with other firms from its own country	III	A firm marketing a product in a foreign country (or countries) competes with local competitors as well as competitors from its own country
Domestic and Foreign	II	A firm marketing a product in its own country only competes with firms from its own country as well as from other countries	IV	A firm marketing a product in a foreign country (or countries) competes with local competitors as well as competitors from its own country and other countries

Cell III, on the other hand, involves a situation in which a firm from a foreign country also competes with firms from its own country in a foreign market or markets. That is, although the competitors are from the same country, they are operating in a global industry. In the automobile industry, for example, BMW and Daimler-Benz from West Germany compete with each other for the luxury car market in the United States and hence operate in a global market.

Finally, Cell IV represents a situation in which firms from different countries compete with competitors from their own countries as well as from other countries in marketing their products in a foreign market or markets. This situation is currently represented in several consumer product industries, such as the electronics and automobile industries. In the automobile industry, for example, multiple competitors from the same country (e.g., Toyota, Nissan, Honda, Mazda, Mitsubishi, Suzuki, Daihatsu, and Isuzu from Japan) compete with multiple competitors from other countries (e.g., General Motors, Ford, and Chrysler from the United States) in multiple countries.

In exploring global markets, a pertinent question is: Can a firm in Country A market its product in Country B without changing the product (and other marketing-mix elements such as promotion, price, or distribution) and earn a desirable return?

Answers to this question have not been without controversy (Kotler, 1986; Porter, 1986; Sheth, 1986; Wind, 1986). Citing examples of companies like Coca-Cola, Marlborough and Levi-Strauss, Levitt (1983), for example, has suggested that the key to the worldwide success of a firm is the development of global standardized products that will appeal to markets worldwide. This will enable the firm to take advantage of scale economies and obtain a better return on its investment. Management consultants like Ohmae (1987) have even suggested that, given shorter life cycles for new products and global competition for worldwide markets, a multiproduct, multimarket firm should follow a "sprinkler" model (i.e., introduce a new product simultaneously in all the worldwide markets) rather than a "waterfall" model (i.e., introduce a new product sequentially in the various world markets) in penetrating global markets.

The development of global standardized products, however, assumes that consumer needs in the various countries are the same. This assumption, however, certainly may be valid for some products (e.g., consumer electronics) and for some world markets (e.g., Japan, North America, and Western European). The development of a global product, however, is only one of several options that are available to a firm in developing its strategic global market plans. Consider, for example, the four-cell matrix shown in Table 7.22. The horizontal dimension represents the similarity or the difference between market needs across countries. The vertical dimension represents the nature of the product configuration. As depicted in this table, leaving aside the option of the global product, there are three other

TABLE 7.22
ASSESSMENT OF GLOBAL PRODUCT-MARKET OPPORTUNITIES

Product Configuration		*Market Needs*		
		Same		Different
Same	I	Universal or Global Product	III	Market Segmentation
Different	II	Product Segmentation (modified product)	IV	Specialty Segmentation (country-tailored product)

Source: Adapted from Sheth, J. (1986), "Global Markets or Global Competition," *Journal of Consumer Marketing*, 3 (Spring), 10.

options that need to be considered by a firm. The first option, depicted in Cell II, represents a situation in which market needs across countries may be the same, but the product needs to be modified from country to country to fit the local market. Examples include appliances, automobiles, and other housing products for which affordability and size become major differentiation factors across countries. It should be noted that although there may be certain products that can be marketed as standardized products in some countries, the same standardized products may fail in other countries. For example, the Barbie doll made by Mattel was sold without modification in sixty countries. Its penetration in the Japanese market was not achieved until its features were changed in accordance with the local preferences (Kotler, 1986).

The second option, Cell III in Table 7.22, represents the situation in which the product is targeted to different market segments in different countries. Examples here include cameras and magazines. The Canon AE1 camera, for example, was targeted with fundamentally different positioning for different buyers in Europe, Japan, and the United States (Porter, 1986). Similarly, *Playboy* magazine is read by relatively young people in the United States, but it is targeted to mature business professionals in France and Germany (Sheth, 1986).

Finally, the third option, Cell IV in Table 7.22, represents the situation in which a firm needs to develop tailor-made products for each country. Examples here include consumer packaged goods and personal care products such as cosmetics. Consumers' needs for these products vary from country to country.

The above discussion suggests that the emergence of global markets and competitors is likely to impact the conduct and practice of strategic market planning. Decisions regarding which product-markets to add to, delete from, or retain in a firm's portfolio are likely to be impacted by an understanding of global markets and competitors. New product-market entry decisions overseas by U.S. companies have been reported to constitute the largest segment of international business blunders (Ricks, 1983). The development and understanding of concepts, paradigms, and analytical approaches, therefore, will be essential for the conduct and practice of strategic market planning in the emerging global village. This will require an understanding of the product-market conditions, global competitive forces, and organizational and governmental arrangements that make it feasible for a firm to be a global competitor (Ferguson, 1988).

A CONCLUDING NOTE

The assessment of competition and competitors is the foundation of strategic market planning. As summarized in Figure 7.5, industrial organization economics has provided several key constructs for understanding

FIGURE 7.5
THE INDUSTRIAL ORGANIZATION ECONOMICS
FRAMEWORK FOR ASSESSMENT OF COMPETITION
AND COMPETITORS

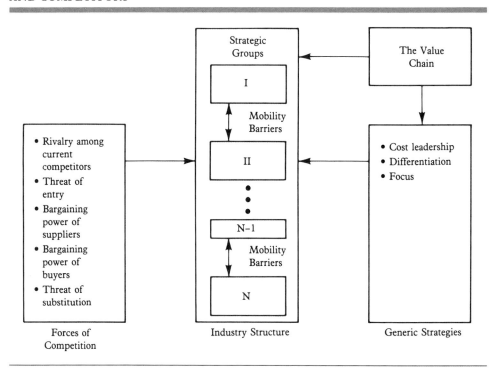

competition and competitors. For a firm, the identification and understanding of its strategic group and value chain, the assessment of the competitive forces and mobility barriers of its strategic group, and the evaluation of available generic strategies are key elements in making the decisions necessary to implement strategic market planning.

The application of these constructs, however, needs to be practiced with caution. In any product-market, a firm competes with other firms in its pursuit of sales based on the opportunities offered by the relevant market environment. It does so by offering better "value" to its customers at a relatively lower delivered cost than its competitors (Ohmae, 1982). Therefore, a lopsided, exclusive focus on competitors that ignores customer needs can degenerate its competitive advantage in the marketplace. Constructs such as strategic groups, generic strategies, and the value chain, although conceptually appealing, may be difficult to implement. As discussed in this chapter, strategic group formation is sensitive to the dimensions used to group firms. Consequently, based on the particular dimensions used to group firms, a firm can be classified as competing with different sets of competitors. Furthermore, this classification can even vary over time.

Similarly, the implementation of generic strategies requires an understanding of market factors that differentiate a firm's product from its competitors, the constraints imposed by the firm's resources, and the nature and life-cycle of the industry. For example, as discussed in this chapter, smaller firms in an industry can only viably compete by using the focus strategy. Similarly, a cost leadership strategy may not be available to a firm in an industry in which competitors have already accumulated greater cumulative volume or better access to low-cost inputs. The value chain tends to perhaps oversimplify the infinite number of activities performed by a firm.

In spite of these shortcomings, the concepts and tools presented in this chapter do provide a systematic approach toward understanding competition and competitors. The importance of this approach to those making product-market portfolio decisions is further underscored by the observation that in any given product-market, it is usually the reaction or initiative of a few key competitors that determines the stability of the competitive situation. In fact, Henderson (1979, p. 90) has argued that a stable competitive market never has more than three or four significant competitors, the largest of which has no more than four times the market share of the smallest. Based on PIMS market share data for the four largest competing businesses in a particular product market, Buzzell (1981) has reported that in the PIMS data base, the average leading competitor's market share is thirty-two and seven-tenths percent, while the average shares for the second, third, and fourth largest competitors are eighteen and eight-tenths percent, eleven and six-tenths percent, and six and nine-tenths percent, respectively. That is, collectively, the top four competitors in a product-market accounted for about seventy percent of the market share.

The above observations suggest that the long-term viability of any product-market in a firm's product-market portfolio is inextricably linked to the firm's understanding of its competition and competitors. The competition and competitors determine the group membership of an industry. Recent developments in information technologies and the emergence of global competition further underscore the need to understand the dynamics of forces of industry competition.

NOTES

1. Chapter 9 expands on the notion of profitability as measured by the difference between rate of return and cost of capital. Aspects of shareholder wealth creation are also examined in this chapter.
2. This description is based on data provided in Zeeman (1986) and Petre (1985).

REFERENCES

Abell, D. F. (1980), *Defining the Business: The Starting Point of Strategic Planning.* Englewood Cliffs, NJ: Prentice Hall.

Baird, I. S. and D. Sudharsan (1983), "Strategic Groups: A Three Mode Factor Analysis of Some Measures of Financial Risk," Working Paper 931, Bureau of Economic and Business Research, University of Illinois at Urbana-Champaign.

Bettis, R. A. and D. Welks (1987), "Financial Returns and Strategic Interaction: The Case of Instant Photography," *Strategic Management Journal*, 6 (November–December), 549–564.

Booz, Allen, and Hamilton, Inc. (1981). *Technology Management: Survey Results.* New York: Technology Management Group, Booz, Allen, and Hamilton, Inc.

Booz, Allen, and Hamilton, Inc. (1983). *The Strategic Management of Information Technology.* New York: Booz, Allen, and Hamilton, Inc.

Boston Consulting Group (1972). *Perspective on Experience.* Boston, Mass: Boston Consulting Group.

Brand, S. (1987). *The Media Lab.* New York: Viking Penguin, Inc.

Broadcasting (1982), "Moving Those Movies," March 19, 133.

Buaron, R. (1981), "How to Win the Market-share Game? Try Changing the Rules," *Management Review*, 70 (January), 8–16.

Business Week (1983), "Domino's Pizza: How It Became the Number Two Chain," August 15, 114.

Business Week (1984), "The Concoction That's Raising the Spirits in the Wine Industry," October 8, 182–186.

Business Week (1987), "Disney's Magic: A Turnaround Proves Wishes Can Come True," March 19, 65.

Business Week (1988), "The Long Arm of Small Business," February 29, 63–6.

Buzzell, R. D. (1981), "Are There 'Natural' Market Structures," *Journal of Marketing*, 45 (Winter), 42–51.

Buzzell, R. D., B. T. Gale and R. G. M. Sultan (1975), "Market Share: A Key to Profitability," *Harvard Business Review*, 53, January–February, 97–106.

Caves, R. E. and Thomas Pugel (1980), *Intra-Industry Differences in Conduct and Performance: Viable Strategies in U.S. Manufacturing Industries.* New York University Monograph.

Cool, K. O. and D. Schendel (1987), "Strategic Group Formation and Performance: The Case of the U.S. Pharmaceutical Industry, 1963–1982," *Management Science*, 33 (September), 1102–1124.

Coyne, N. P. (1986), "Sustainable Competitive Advantages—What It is, What It Isn't," *Business Horizons*, 29 (January–February), 54–61.

Dess, G. G. and P. S. Davis (1984), "Porter's (1980) Generic Strategies as

Determinants of Strategic Group Membership and Organizational Performance," *Academy of Management Journal,* 27, 467–488.

Drucker, P. F. (1988), "The Coming of New Organizations," *Harvard Business Review,* 66 (January–February), 45–53.

Ferguson, C. H. (1988), "From the People Who Brought You Voodoo Economics," *Harvard Business Review,* 66 (May–June), 55–62.

Fershtman, C., V. Mahajan, and E. Muller (1990), "Market Share Pioneering Advertising: A Theoretical Approach," *Management Science,* (forthcoming).

Fortune (1987), "Putting Magic Back into Kingdom," January 5, 165.

Fruhan, William (1979). *Financial Strategy: Studies in the Creation, Transfer and Destruction of Shareholder Value.* Homewood, IL: Richard D. Irwin.

Gerstein, M. S. (1987). *The Technology Connection.* Reading, MA: Addison-Wesley.

Gerstein, M. S. and H. Reisman (1982), "Creating Competitive Advantage with Computer Technology," *Journal of Business Strategy,* 3 (Summer), 53–60.

Hall, W. K. (1980), "Survival Strategies in a Hostile Environment," *Harvard Business Review,* 58 (September–October), 75–85.

Harrigan, K. P. (1980). *Strategies for Declining Industries.* Lexington, Mass: Lexington Books.

Hatten, K. J. (1974), "Strategic Models in the Brewing Industry," unpublished doctoral dissertation, Purdue University.

Hatten, K. J. and D. E. Schendel (1977), "Heterogeneity Within an Industry," *Journal of Industrial Economics,* XXVI, December, 97–113.

Hatten, K. J., D. E. Schendel, and A. C. Cooper (1978), "A Strategic Model of the U.S. Brewing Industry: 1952–1971," *Academy of Management Journal,* 21, 592–610.

Hatten, K. J. and M. L. Hatten (1985), "Some Empirical Insights for Strategic Marketers: The Case of Beer," in H. Thomas and D. M. Gardner (eds.), *Strategic Marketing and Management.* Chichester, John Wiley.

Hawes, J. M. and W. F. Crittenden (1984), "A Taxonomy of Competitive Retailing Strategies," *Strategic Management Journal,* 5 (July–September) 275–289.

Hayes, S. L. III, A. M. Spence and D. V. P. Marks (1983), "Competition in the Investment Banking Industry," Cambridge, MA: Harvard University Press.

Henderson, B. D. (1979). *Henderson on Corporate Strategy.* Cambridge, MA: Abt Books.

Hergert, M. (1983), "The Incidence and Implications of Strategic Grouping in U.S. Manufacturing Industries," unpublished doctoral dissertation, Harvard University.

Hofer, C. W. and D. E. Schendel (1978), *Strategy Formulation: Analytical Concepts*. St. Paul: West Publishing.

Howell, R. D. and G. L. Frazier (1983), "Business Definition and Performance," *Journal of Marketing*, 47 (Spring), 59–67.

Hunt, M. S. (1972), "Competition in the Major Home Appliance Industry 1960–1970," unpublished doctoral dissertation, Harvard University.

Iacocca, L. A. (1987), "The U.S.-Japan Trade Gap," *Journal of Business Strategy*, 7 (Spring), 4–6.

Johnson and Johnson (1986), *Annual Report*. New Brunswick, NJ: Johnson and Johnson.

Keen, P. G. W. (1986), *Competing in Time*. Cambridge, MA: Ballinger Publishing Co.

Kirkland, R. I. (1988), "Entering a New Age of Boundless Competition," *Fortune*, March 14, 40–48.

Kotler, P. (1986), "Global Standardization: Courting Danger," *Journal of Consumer Marketing* 3 (Spring), 13–16.

Kupfer, A. (1987), "Now, Live Experts on a Floppy Disk," *Fortune*, October 12, 69–82.

Lahti, A. (1983). *Strategy and Performance of a Firm: An Empirical Investigation in the Knitwear Industry in Finland in 1969–81*. Helsinki School of Economics, Helsinki.

Leonard-Barton, D. and J. S. Sviokla (1988), "Putting Expert Systems to Work," *Harvard Business Review* 66 (March–April), 91–98.

Levitt, T. (1983), "The Globalization of Markets," *Harvard Business Review*, 61 (May–June), 92–102.

Lieberman, M. B. and D. B. Montgomery (1988), "First-Mover Advantages," *Strategic Management Journal*, 9 (Summer), 41–58.

Lusch, Robert F., G. R. Lazniak, and W. D. Harris (1986), "Toward the Measurement of Competitive Structure: An Initial Empirical Assessment of Porter's Competitive Forces Framework," *Proceedings of the American Marketing Association Educator's Conference*, Chicago: American Marketing Association, 239–244.

Marakon Associates (1986), "The Ultimate Poison Pill: Closing the Value Gap," *Commentary* (San Francisco: Marakon Associates).

McFarlin, F. W. (1984), "Information Technology Changes the Way You Compete," *Harvard Business Review*, 62 (May–June), 98–103.

McGee, J. and H. Thomas (1986), "Strategic Groups: Theory, Research, and Taxonomy," *Strategic Management Journal*, 7 (March–April), 141–160.

Miles, R. H. (1982). *Coffin Nails and Corporate Strategies*. Englewood Cliffs, NJ: Prentice-Hall.

Moskowitz, M. (1987), *The Global Market Place*. New York: MacMillan.

Naisbitt, J. (1982), *Megatrends*. New York: Warner Books.

Newman, H. H. (1973), "Strategic Groups and the Structure/Performance

Relationship: A Study with Respect to the Chemical Process Industries," unpublished doctoral dissertation, Harvard University.

Newman, H. H. (1978), "Strategic Groups and the Structure/Performance Relationship," *Review of Economics and Statistics*, 60, 417–427.

Ohmae, K. (1982), *The Mind of the Strategist*. New York: McGraw-Hill.

Ohmae, K. (1987), "The Triad World View," *Journal of Business Strategy*, 7 (Spring), 8–19.

Oster, Sharon (1982), "Intraindustry Structure and the Ease of Strategic Change," *Review of Economics and Statistics*, LXIV, August, 376–384.

Parsons, G. L. (1983), "Information Technology: A New Competitive Weapon," *Sloan Management Review*, Fall, 3–14.

Petre, P. (1985), "How to Keep Customers Happy Captives," *Fortune*, September 2, 42–46.

Porter, M. E. (1973), "Consumer Behavior, Retailer Power, and Manufacturer Strategy in Consumer Goods Industries," unpublished doctoral dissertation, Harvard University.

Porter, M. E. (1980), *Competitive Strategy*. New York: The Free Press.

Porter, M. E. (1981), "The Contributions of Industrial Organizations to Strategic Management," *Academy of Management Review*, 6, 609–620.

Porter, M. E. (1985), *Competitive Advantage*. New York: The Free Press.

Porter, M. E. and V. E. Millar (1985), "How Information Gives You Competitive Advantage," *Harvard Business Review*, 63 (July–August), 149–160.

Porter, M. E. (1986), "The Strategic Role of International Marketing," *Journal of Consumer Marketing*, 3 (Spring), 18–22.

Primeaux, W. J., Jr. (1985), "A Method for Determining Strategic Groups and Life Cycle Stages of an Industry," in H. Thomas and D. M. Gardner (eds.) *Strategic Marketing and Management* , Chichester: John Wiley.

Ramsler, M. (1982), "Strategic Groups and Foreign Market Entry in Global Banking Competition," unpublished doctoral dissertation, Harvard University.

Ricks, D. A. (1983). *Big Business Blunders*. Homewood, IL: Dow-Jones Irwin.

Robinson, W. T. and C. Fornell (1985), "Sources of Market Pioneer Advantages in Consumer Goods Industries," *Journal of Marketing Research*, 22 (August), 305–317.

Rogers, E. M. (1986). *Communication Technology*. New York: The Free Press.

Ryans, A. B. and D. R. Wittink (1985), "Security Returns as a Basis for Estimating the Competitive Structure in an Industry," in H. Thomas and D. M. Gardner (eds.), *Strategic Marketing and Management*, Chichester: John Wiley.

Scherer, F. (1980). *Industrial Market Structure and Economic Performance*. Chicago: Rand-McNally.

Schnaars, S. P. (1986), "When Entering Growth Markets, Are Pioneers Better than Poachers?" *Business Horizons* (March–April), 27–36.

Shapiro, C. (1989), "The Theory of Business Strategy," *Rand Journal of Economics*, (Spring), 125–137.

Sheth, J. (1986), "Global Markets or Global Competition," *Journal of Consumer Marketing*, 3 (Spring), 9–12.

Simon-Miller, F. (1986), "World Marketing: Going Global or Acting Local?," *Journal of Consumer Marketing*, 3 (Spring), 5–7.

Smith, D. L. (1988), "Invasion of Booty Snatchers? Foreign Stores Opening U.S. Stores in Record Numbers," *Dallas Morning News*. February 22.

Taylor, A. (1987), "Who's Ahead in the World Auto War?" *Fortune*, November 9, 74–88.

Urban, G. L., T. Carter, S. Gaskin, and Z. Mucha (1986), "Market Share Rewards to Pioneering Brands: An Empirical Analysis and Strategic Implications," *Management Science*, 32 (June), 645–659.

Utterback, J. M. and W. J. Abernathy (1975), "A Dynamic Model of Process and Product Innovation," *OMEGA*, 3, 639–656.

Vanderwicken, P. (1974), "P & G's Secret Ingredient," *Fortune*, July, 75–78.

Vesper, K. (1979), "Strategic Mapping—A Tool for Corporate Planners," *Long-Range Planning*, 12, December, 75–92.

White, R. E. (1986), "Generic Business Strategies, Organizational Context and Performance: An Empirical Investigation," *Strategic Management Journal*, 7, 217–231.

Wind, Y. (1986), "The Myth of Globalization," *Journal of Consumer Marketing*, 3 (Spring), 23–26.

Wiseman, C. (1985), *Strategy and Computers: Information Systems as Competitive Weapons*. Homewood, IL: Dow Jones-Irwin.

Wissema, J. G., and H. W. Van der Pol, and H. M. Messer (1980), "Strategic Management Archetypes," *Strategic Management Journal*, 1, 37–47.

Wright, P. (1987), "A Refinement of Porter's Strategies," *Strategic Management Journal*, 8, 93–101.

Zeeman, J. (1986), "Technology and Marketing at United Airlines," presentation to the American Marketing Association Intercollegiate Conference, Chicago, April 18.

PART **III**

PERSPECTIVES FROM

CORPORATE FINANCE

CHAPTER 8

SUSTAINABLE

GROWTH

Introduction

Financial Strategy Concepts

Return on Equity

Sustainable Growth
    The Sustainable Growth Equation
    Coping with Sustainable Growth Problems
    The Rapid Growth/No New Equity Firm
    The Slow Growth Firm
    The Multibusiness Unit Firm
    The Rapid Growth Firm with Access to
      Equity

Sustainable Growth and Shareholder Value

A Concluding Note

References

INTRODUCTION

The advent of strategic market planning has required that senior marketing executives begin to appreciate the role of financial management concepts when making product-market and business unit decisions. In a series of interviews with top management in twenty-one major corporations, Webster (1981) noted that a major criticism was that "marketing managers do not understand basic concepts of financial management and are unable to consider the financial consequences of their decisions." Similarly, Anderson (1979) observed that:

> Too often marketing tends to focus on sales growth or market share, and it fails to recognize the impact of marketing decisions on such variables as inventory levels, working capital needs, financing costs, debt-to-equity ratios, and stock prices. To assume such factors are *purely* the responsibility of finance is to be guilty of a kind of marketing myopia not less damaging as (sic) that originally envisioned by Levitt (1960).

341

The purpose of this chapter is to review fundamental financial management concepts central to the practice of strategic market planning. Basic concepts from corporate finance are first introduced. This discussion is followed by an overview of the determinants of return on equity—the principal financial performance ratio used in industry (Walsh, 1984). Finally, an extended treatment of the sustainable growth concept is provided and linked to portfolio planning. This discussion augments the material in chapter two and provides a foundation for additional perspectives from corporate finance described in chapter nine: Value-Based Planning.

FINANCIAL STRATEGY CONCEPTS

Financial strategy decisions fall into two categories: *Investment decisions* focus on issues related to the financial resources needed. *Financing decisions* deal with how the firm provides the financial resources it needs (Harrigan and Wilson, 1986). As Boyd and Larréché note (1978), a firm's product-markets are its "*basic investment units* because the firm's income streams derive from coupling specific products with markets." Investment decisions in strategic market planning therefore concern how assets will be affected by decisions about which product-markets to add, delete, and keep. Financing decisions play a complimentary role. That is, once the necessary financing is identified, attention is turned to determining where the financial resources will come from. Three sources of funds are (1) profits from operations, (2) debt, and (3) new equity in the form of new issues of common and/or preferred stock.

A fundamental financing decision is the determination of whether to fund new investments with debt or equity. A decision to use debt will be dictated by a firm's corporate financial policies concerning a firm's acceptable debt-to-equity ratio and debt-to-total capital ratio. Funding from equity sources will be determined by corporate policies related to the issuance of new equity and the use or availability of retained earnings. The use of retained earnings, in turn, is influenced by the amount of such earnings given corporate policies on dividends paid to shareholders.

Corporate decision-making related to financial strategy can be summarized as follows (Harrigan and Wilson, 1986):

$$\Delta A = \Delta D + NI - D + \text{NE}$$

where

ΔA = changes in assets,
ΔD = change in debt,
NI = net income,
D = dividends paid, and
NE = new equity. (1)

This expression allows management to model the change in assets decision by manipulating the variables that affect it. For example, if the corporate financial policy contains a set debt-to-equity goal and dividend policy, then for a specified net income the amount of new equity can be determined. Such thinking was apparent at American Motors Corporation in the early 1980s. The company had incurred serious cash shortages owing to aggressive new product development efforts and continuing losses. Recognizing the need for $300 million in new assets (equipment and working capital), which could not be obtained from operating income, the company sought funds through the issuance of stock, increased debt, and other sources such as Renault, which owned a sizeable share of AMC stock (*Wall Street Journal*, 1983). Ultimately, AMC was acquired by the Chrysler Corporation in 1987.

RETURN ON EQUITY

Return on equity is the principal financial performance barometer used by firms. Its popularity arose because this measure shows the profits per dollar of owner capital, or the efficiency with which owner capital is employed.

The determination of return on equity is itself a useful tool of corporate finance. Figure 8.1 shows how a company's income statement and balance sheet accounts combine to produce a company's return on equity. This visual representation allows the manager to assess the effect of a change in one or more income and balance sheet accounts on return on equity.

Figure 8.1 can be simplified to:

$$\frac{\text{Net Income}}{\text{Shareholders Equity}} = \frac{\text{Net Income}}{\text{Sales}} \times \frac{\text{Sales}}{\text{Assets}} \times \frac{\text{Assets}}{\text{Shareholder Equity}}$$

$$\begin{pmatrix} \text{Return on} \\ \text{Equity} \end{pmatrix} = \begin{pmatrix} \text{Profit} \\ \text{Margin} \end{pmatrix} \times \begin{pmatrix} \text{Asset} \\ \text{Turnover} \end{pmatrix} \times \begin{pmatrix} \text{Financial} \\ \text{Leverage} \end{pmatrix} \quad (2)$$

where

Profit Margin denotes the profitability of a firm's operations,
Asset Turnover denotes a company's effectiveness in utilizing assets to generate sales, and
Financial Leverage denotes the use of debt to fund company operations.

This straightforward equation contains a powerful message. That is, there are three pathways for improving return on equity. A firm can increase the profitability of its operations, improve its asset utilization, and/or increase its debt.

The description of financial strategy concepts and return on equity provides the basis for assessing company growth objectives. For years, sales growth has been second only to earnings in the pantheon of corporate

FIGURE 8.1
Return on Equity Model

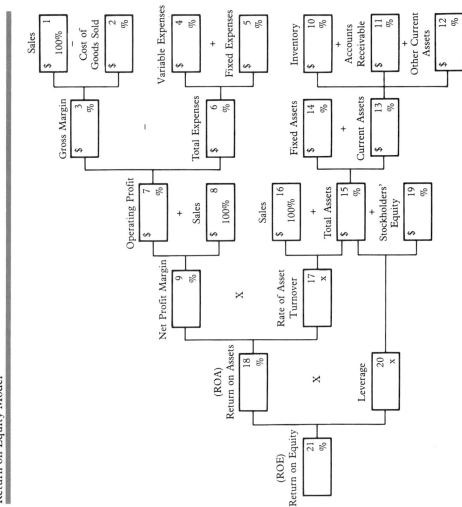

Item and Calculation	Source Statement
1. *Sales:* All revenues from the sale of products and/or services	Income
2. *Cost of goods sold:* Cost value of those sales which are made during a period	Income
3. *Gross margin:* Subtract 2 from 1	Income
4. *Variable expenses:* All expenses which change with changes in sales volume; short-run concept	Income
5. *Fixed expenses:* All expenses that stay the same over a wide range of sales volumes and a long time period	Income
6. *Total expenses:* Add 4 and 5	Income
7. *Operating profit:* Subtract 6 from 3	Income
8. *Sales:* A repeat of number 1	
9. *Net profit margin:* 7 divided by 8	
10. *Inventory:* Value of products in stock	Balance sheet and income
11. *Accounts receivable:* Gross value	Balance sheet
12. *Other:* Cash, etc., used in business	Balance sheet
13. *Current assets:* Add 10, 11, and 12	Balance sheet
14. *Fixed assets:* At original cost or investment	Balance sheet
15. *Total assets:* Add 13 and 14	Balance sheet
16. *Sales:* A repeat of number 1	
17. *Rate of asset turnover:* Divide 15 by 1	
18. *Return on assets:* Multiply 17 times 9	
19. *Equity:* Subtract total liabilities (debt) from total assets	Balance sheet
20. *Leverage:* Divide 15 by 19	Balance sheet
21. *ROE:* Multiply 18 times 20	

virtues. Balancing sales growth and earnings is a difficult task, however. To do so requires determining a company's sustainable growth.

SUSTAINABLE GROWTH

Sustainable growth represents the maximum sales or asset growth that a firm can support using both internally generated funds and debt. This concept has gained increasing prominence as a key financial and operating concept in recent years (Govindarajan and Shank, 1986; Donaldson, 1985; Higgins and Kerin, 1983; Ellsworth, 1983; Robinson, 1979; Fruhan, 1984; Varadarajan, 1983). However, little attention has been paid to this concept in the strategic market planning literature.

Sustainable growth problems in many firms have forced marketing and financial executives to coordinate activities much more closely than formerly, and have led to the realization that increased sales are not always a blessing. Executives who do not understand sustainable growth at least intuitively run the risk that company sales growth will create severe financial problems. At the extreme, failure to heed the lessons of sustainable growth can result in a firm literally "growing broke."

The Sustainable Growth Equation

Sustainable growth is a financial characterization of the old adage, "it takes money to make money." Suppose a company with annual sales of $\$S$ anticipates increasing sales by $\$\Delta S$ in the coming year. Increased sales require more assets in the form of increased inventories, accounts receivable, cash, and quite possibly, fixed assets, which often must be financed. Sustainable growth ties the buildup in assets created by sales increases to the company's ability to pay for these new assets on an ongoing basis.

When a company anticipates increasing sales by $\$\Delta S$ and when its *sales to assets ratio* is equal to T, the increased assets required are $\Delta S/T$. Thus, if ΔS is $\$10$ million and the sales to assets ratio is two, the new assets required equal $\$5$ million. T is also referred to as the firm's *asset turnover* and is an important indicator of the efficiency with which management employs the firm's assets.

The new assets, $\Delta S/T$, must be paid for, and there are three possible ways to do this: (1) through additions to retained earnings through profitable operations; (2) through new borrowing; and (3) through new common stock. Initially, assume the company is unable or unwilling to sell new common stock, and that it wants to maintain a stable, target *debt to equity ratio*, L. (Alternative assumptions are discussed in the following paragraphs.)

If the company's *profit margin* (profits/sales) is P, its profits are PS. Assuming the company pays dividends and has a dividend payout ratio (dividends/profits) of D, only a portion of profits comprise its retained earnings. This portion is $P(1 - D)$.

If the company wants to maintain a stable debt-to-equity ratio of L, this increase in retained earnings enables the company to borrow an additional $PS(1 - D)L$. Thus, if annual additions to equity are $5 million, and the target debt to equity ratio is 1.5, then debt can increase $7.5 million ($5 million × 1.5) without altering the company's capital structure.

Finally, assuming the company does not sell new common stock, its uses of cash required to increase assets must equal its sources of cash from increased retained earnings and accompanying new borrowing. Consequently, the total funds used must equal the total sources of funds:

$$\underline{\text{Uses of Funds}} = \underline{\text{Sources of Funds}}$$

$$\frac{\text{New}}{\text{Assets}} = \frac{\text{Added Retained}}{\text{Earnings}} + \frac{\text{New}}{\text{Borrowings}}$$

$$\Delta ST = PS(1 - D) + PS(1 - D)L. \tag{3}$$

Solving this expression for the growth in sales,

$$\frac{\Delta S}{S} = P(1 - D)(1 + L)T \tag{4}$$

This is one view of the sustainable growth equation. Other formulations of the sustainable growth equation are available (Table 8.1). While differences between the equations exist, the fundamental message remains unchanged.

To aid interpretation, let $\Delta S/S = g^\star$ and refer to $g^\star$ as the firm's sustainable percentage growth in sales. Note too that $(1 - D)$ is the firm's *retention ratio R* or the fraction of earnings retained in the business. If the company pays forty cents of each dollar earned as dividends, it retains $1.00 - 40$ cents, or sixty cents of each dollar earned. Finally, observe that $(1 + L)$ equals the company's *assets to equity ratio* which we will call $A[(1 + L) = (1 + \text{debt/equity}) = (\text{equity} + \text{debt})/\text{equity} = \text{assets/equity}]$. Incorporating these notational changes, sustainable growth can then be viewed as:

$$g^\star = PRAT \tag{5}$$

where

$g^\star$ = sustainable sales growth expressed as a percentage
P = profit margin after taxes,
R = retention ratio or reinvestment rate,
A = assets to equity ratio or leverage, and
T = sales to assets ratio or asset turnover.

This equation, given the assumptions noted above, says there is only one sales growth rate consistent with stable values of the four right-hand ratios. If the company increases sales at any rate other than its sustainable growth rate, one or some combination of these ratios must change. Accom-

TABLE 8.1
REPRESENTATIVE FORMULATIONS OF THE
SUSTAINABLE GROWTH EQUATION

Source	Formulation
Zakon (1971)	$G = D/E\ (R - i)p + Rp$ where: G = maximum sustainable long-term asset growth rate D/E = debt-equity ratio R = after-tax return on assets (adjusted for inflation) P = earnings retention rate ($= 1 -$ dividend payout ratio) i = after-tax current cost of debt
Ellsworth (1983)	$SG = (1 - p)(1 + D/E)[ROI - i(D/E)]$ where: SG = sustainable growth rate p = dividend payout ratio D/E = debt-equity ratio ROI = return on total invested capital after tax but before interest expense i = interest rate on corporate debt after corporate taxes
Donaldson (1985)	$g(S) = r[RONA + d(RONA - 1)$ where: $g(S)$ = growth rate of sales r = earnings retention ratio d = debt-equity ratio i = after-tax interest rate on debt $RONA$ = return on net assets (return on investment)

modating to, and planning for, these changes are at the heart of the sustainable growth problem in strategic market planning. For example, when Coca-Cola management planned for sizable sales and asset growth in the late 1980s, the company lowered its dividend payout ratio and added to its debt to finance its ambitious plans (*Wall Street Journal*, 1986).

Table 8.2 provides further insight into the relationship between the ratios that affect the sustainable growth rate. The table provides sustainable growth rate estimates for a sales-to-asset ratio of 2.0, an earnings retention ratio of 0.60, debt-equity ratios ranging from 0 to 1.00 in increments of 0.10, and an after-tax profit margin on sales ranging from 0.04 to 0.24 in increments of 0.02. Of course, other simulations could be generated by modifying the sales-to-asset ratio and the earnings retention ratio.

TABLE 8.2
SUSTAINABLE GROWTH RATE

ATMS	Debt/Equity Ratio										
	0.00	0.10	0.20	0.30	0.40	0.50	0.60	0.70	0.80	0.90	1.00
0.04	0.048	0.053	0.058	0.062	0.067	0.072	0.077	0.082	0.086	0.091	0.096
0.06	0.072	0.079	0.086	0.094	0.101	0.108	0.115	0.122	0.130	0.137	0.144
0.08	0.096	0.106	0.114	0.125	0.134	0.144	0.154	0.163	0.173	0.182	0.192
0.10	0.120	0.132	0.144	0.156	0.168	0.180	0.192	0.204	0.216	0.228	0.240
0.12	0.144	0.158	0.173	0.187	0.202	0.216	0.230	0.245	0.259	0.274	0.288
0.14	0.168	0.185	0.202	0.218	0.235	0.252	0.269	0.286	0.302	0.319	0.336
0.16	0.192	0.211	0.230	0.250	0.269	0.288	0.307	0.326	0.346	0.365	0.384
0.18	0.216	0.238	0.259	0.281	0.302	0.324	0.346	0.367	0.389	0.410	0.432
0.20	0.240	0.264	0.288	0.312	0.336	0.360	0.384	0.408	0.432	0.456	0.480
0.22	0.264	0.290	0.317	0.343	0.370	0.396	0.422	0.449	0.475	0.502	0.528
0.24	0.288	0.317	0.346	0.374	0.403	0.432	0.461	0.490	0.518	0.547	0.576

Sales to assets ratio = 2.00
Earnings retention ratio = 0.60
  ATMS = after-tax profit margin on sales.
  Cell entries are maximum sustainable growth rates computed using the following expression: maximum sustainable growth rate = (after-tax margin on sales) × (sales to assets ratio) × (1 + debt to equity ratio) × (earnings retention ratio).
  Multiply cell entries by 100 to express maximum sustainable growth rate as a percentage figure.

Coping with Sustainable Growth Problems

At least four classes of sustainable growth problems associated with four different company scenarios are possible. The first class is a company experiencing a growth in sales g greater than its sustainable growth $g^\star$. Furthermore, it is assumed the company is unwilling or unable to sell new common stock.

The Rapid Growth/No New Equity Firm   Consider a firm with a profit margin of two percent, a retention rate of sixty percent, an assets-to-equity ratio of 1.8, and a sales to asset ratio of two. Then, according to Equation (5), the company's sustainable growth is

$$g^\star = (.02)(.60)(1.8)(2) = 4.32\%$$

It is physically impossible for the company to increase sales at a rate greater than 4.32 percent per year without increasing the ratios on the right-hand side of the equation. Which ratios to increase and the impact of these increases on the company should be major managerial concerns.

Increases in the retention rate R or leverage A are financial solutions to the sustainable growth problem posed. A reduction in dividends, and the corresponding increase in R, increases retained earnings. An increase in debt (i.e., an increase in A) provides cash to finance new assets. It does this in two ways. In the long run, an increase in debt raises $g^\star$ by increasing leverage. In the short run, it provides cash immediately through new borrowings. This enables a company to increase sales above $g^\star$ in the year in which the new debt is raised. Increasing the retention rate and debt is what computer programmers would call the "default option." If management does not anticipate financing problems created by rapid sales growth and attempt to deal with them systematically, the company will find its cash balances running dangerously low. All too often, the only short run solution is to cut dividends or increase bank borrowings. If these solutions are not feasible, the company can literally go bankrupt for lack of cash to finance growth.

Even in the longer run, financial solutions to the problems posed imply costs as well as benefits. Increases in debt add to financial leverage, increasing interest costs, adding to the volatility of shareholder returns, and most important to management, heightening the chance of bankruptcy. The benefits of more rapid sales growth, therefore, are purchased at the cost of increased risk. At excessively high values of debt, the cost will exceed the benefit. Allegheny International, the maker of Sunbeam and Oster appliances, encountered these problems in 1988 and filed for bankruptcy (*Wall Street Journal*, 1988).

Increases in R reduce the dividend payout ratio received by shareholders. Their reaction will depend on the uses to which the retained earnings are put. If earnings are used to finance "profitable" sales growth, shareholders will respond positively to the increase in the retention rate, and there will be no cost of the strategy. Conversely, an increase in the retention rate to finance "unprofitable" sales growth will result in a decline in stock price, and this is a "cost" of an increased rate. It is also obvious that the retention rate cannot be raised without limit. Retaining more than the company earns is impossible, so the retention rate cannot exceed one.

Profitable sales growth occurs when the new assets accompanying the sales increase promise a discounted cash flow rate of return in excess of the company's cost of capital. The specifics of rate of return analysis and measurement of capital costs are beyond the scope of this chapter (see, for example, Brealey and Myers, 1987, and the discounted cash flow discussion in chapter nine). All that is necessary to observe is that for any company, there is an upper limit to the retention rate set by shareholders' perceptions of the profitability of future growth opportunities. Increases in the retention rate above this ceiling drive down stock prices.

Increases in the profit margin P and sales to asset ratio T in equation (5) constitute operating solutions to the sustainable growth dilemma. As was shown in Figure 8.1, the profit margin is a summary measure of management's income statement performance. Success in controlling operating costs and overhead is reflected in a higher P and higher sustainable growth.

Increasing P will be considered in the next paragraph. T measures management's balance sheet performance. To increase T, managers must use assets more efficiently. Because the product of P times T equals the *return on assets*, operational strategies to improve sustainable growth are equivalent to increasing the return on assets.

When operating and financial solutions to sustainable growth problems are inadequate, it may be necessary to consciously limit growth. The most direct way to do this is to raise prices across-the-board or on selected, high-turnover items. This action has two salutary effects: it reduces growth, bringing it more in line with $g^\star$, and it increases a firm's profit margin. Provided that management can keep asset turnover at least constant as profit margins rise, either by maintaining sales or reducing assets in proportion to the decline in sales $g^\star$ will rise.

An alternative way to reduce growth is to eliminate slowly turning inventory. This will reduce sales and increase T. Notice the perspective here: Sales growth is not necessarily good and, indeed, excessive growth is financially dangerous—so dangerous that it might be avoided, by, say, raising prices. Despite the financial validity of this perspective, it is not one that comes naturally to many firms.

When wrestling with sustainable growth problems, an important standard of comparison is the industry growth rate. When sustainable growth exceeds the industry growth rate, throttling back on actual growth to sustainable levels still implies an increasing market share. When industry growth exceeds the firm's sustainable growth, a cutback in sales increases to sustainable levels may only assure that the enterprise lives to fail another day, because it implies a steady diminution in the market share. In this situation, more fundamental remedies are necessary, including the sale of new equity or merger with another company. These possibilities are discussed below.

The Slow Growth Firm   The slowly growing firm has a much different set of sustainable growth problems. Instead of constantly scrambling for cash to fund growth, slow-growth companies have the problem of what to do with the cash generated by the company in excess of its investment needs. If the company does nothing, idle cash balances will accumulate, return on assets and return on equity will fall, and the firm's stock price will likely decline—all unwanted results. A note of urgency is added when one realizes that excess cash and a depressed stock price make a company vulnerable to takeover attempts. There are two common solutions to the sustainable growth problems of slow-growth companies. One is to reduce the retention rate by increasing dividends; the second is to purchase growth by acquiring other, more vibrant companies. This latter approach was presumably followed by Gould, Inc. in the last decade. The company transformed itself from a "smokestack" company with slow growth to a "high-tech" firm by acquiring numerous firms in such growth industries as defense electronics, industrial automation equipment, and medical equipment (*Business Week*, 1986).

Payment of higher dividends occurs in slower growth industries, but there appears to be a prejudice in the minds of many managers against dividends that are high by industry standards. One basic reason corporations exist is that professional managers are presumed to be more adept at investing individuals' money than the individuals themselves. The return of a large fraction of earnings to shareholders as dividends can be interpreted as a failure by management to fulfill a basic fiduciary responsibility. To avoid this onus, managers of mature or declining firms frequently pursue growth via acquisition.

The Multibusiness Unit Firm   The first two company types described— rapid growth, no new equity, and slow growth—have a natural affinity for one another. The former needs cash and the latter has more than it can productively use. A frequent outcome is merger and the creation of a multidivisional company. This outcome is consistent with the recommendations of portfolio strategists who argue that companies should maintain an array of products or business units such that the excess cash generated by mature products (business units) is available to finance the growth of new products and business units. In fact, much of product or business portfolio theory is a response to sustainable growth problems experienced by companies attempting to grow more rapidly than available financial resources permit (see, for example, Day, 1986; Larréché and Srinivasan, 1981; Hax and Majluf, 1984).

Cash user and cash provider business units can be defined using the concepts and notation developed previously. Consider a fully decentralized, multibusiness firm in which each business unit has its own profit margin P and asset to sales ratio T. To calculate a business unit's sustainable growth, $g_p{}^\star$, it is necessary to assign it a retention R and leverage A ratio. Assuming initially that these ratios equal company-wide ratios, then the sustainable growth for a business unit is

$$g_p{}^\star = P_p\, R\, A\, T_p \qquad (6)$$

where the subscripted variables are unique to business unit "p" and R and A equal company values. The comparison of $g_p{}^\star$ with the actual sales growth of a business unit (g_p) indicates which units are consuming cash and which are generating cash to finance growth elsewhere in the company.

A more informative way to assess the cash position of a unit is to calculate its financing gap or surplus. From equation 3 and using the subscript p to denote a division, the cash required to finance the growth of a business unit is $\Delta S_p / T_p$, while the cash available from a division is $P_p\, S_p\, R\, A$. The difference is the unit's financing gap or surplus, denoted as FG_p if positive and FS_p if negative.

$$\text{Financing Gap (Surplus)} = \$\Delta S_p / T_p = P_p\, S_p\, R\, A \qquad (7)$$

FIGURE 8.2
Company (Divisional) Growth Rate and Financial Gap (Surplus)

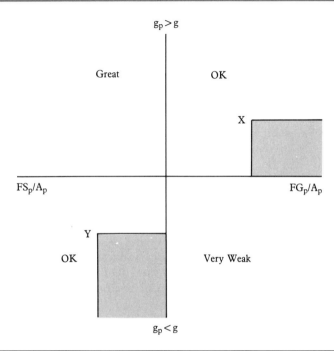

Further insight into the analysis can be gained by viewing Figure 8.2. Figure 8.2 shows a business unit's actual growth in sales less the overall company growth in sales and a unit's financing gap or surplus per dollar of assets. Treating cash used to finance growth as a scarce resource, the horizontal axis measures each business unit's use of, or contribution to, this resource. The vertical axis is a measure of the payoff to the company from the use of this investment cash, as indicated by the unit's sales growth relative to the company's.

The best possible location in Figure 8.2 is the upper left quadrant. Business units in this quadrant are growing faster than the company as a whole and are generating more cash than they consume. Conversely, units in the lower right quadrant are displaying terrible performance. They are consuming scarce cash and growing slower than the company as a whole. Unless improvement is anticipated, they are candidates for divestiture. Business units in the remaining two quadrants—those that are consuming cash, but are growing faster than the company average, and those that are growing more slowly than the company average, but are providing cash—are performing satisfactorily.

Three important caveats must be borne in mind when performing the analysis suggested in Figure 8.2. First, with rare exceptions, business unit cash flow and profitability are only accounting estimates and should not be treated as hard facts. Second, investment and divestiture decisions should be based on estimated consequences in the long-run. Consequently, Figure 8.2 is useful in making such decisions only to the extent that it represents enduring patterns. Third, in some instances it may not be appropriate to assign company values of R and A to a unit. In general, individual business units that are growing more rapidly than the company as a whole warrant a higher retention ratio than slower growth divisions. Similarly, one can argue that less risky units deserve a higher assets-to-equity ratio than riskier ones because they contribute more to the firm's debt capacity. Introducing these modifications considerably complicates the construction and interpretation of the future.

The Rapid Growth Firm With Access to Equity   If a company is willing and able to sell new equity shares, sustainable growth and product or business portfolio problems all but vanish. Management does not need to worry about the firm's growth characteristics because new equity capital is available whenever a financing gap arises.

For such companies, the sustainable growth concept is most useful as a means of estimating the amount of new equity required annually. Expanding equation (3) to include common stock financing yields

$$\Delta S/T = PS(1 - D) + PS(1 - D)L + F \tag{8}$$

where F is common stock financing plus new borrowing, which can accompany the increased equity. Assuming management wishes to maintain a debt to equity ratio of L on the newly raised capital, then

$$F = C + CL = C(1 + L) = CA \tag{9}$$

where C is common stock sold and, as before, A is the assets-to-equity ratio. Combining these expressions and simplifying

$$C = (g - g^\star)E \tag{10}$$

where g is the target sales growth rate and E is the firm's equity. To illustrate, if a company with equity of \$100 million wants to increase sales at fifteen percent a year without altering its capital structure when its sustainable growth rate is eight percent, it must raise \$7 million in new common stock annually [\$7 million = (15 percent − 8 percent) \$100 million].

Even though sustainable growth problems are minimized by selling new equity shares, this practice will make management more sensitive to capital market priorities. That is, by responding to product-market forces and priorities of growth, the sale of new equities often requires that greater attention be placed on return on equity and benefits to shareholders in the form of share appreciation and dividends (Donaldson, 1985).

SUSTAINABLE GROWTH AND
SHAREHOLDER VALUE

The cycle just described has prompted interest in the process and practice of value-based planning described in chapter nine. Attention to shareholder value creation is not too far removed from the sustainable growth concept.

Sustainable growth is closely related to return on equity. Rewriting equation two, sustainable growth equals the retention ratio times return on equity:

$$g^\star = \frac{\text{Net Profit}}{\text{Sales}} \times \frac{\text{Sales}}{\text{Assets}} \times \frac{\text{Assets}}{\text{Equity}} \times \text{Retention Ratio}$$

$$\quad (P) \qquad\quad (T) \qquad\quad (A) \qquad\qquad (R)$$

$$= \text{ROE} \times \text{Retention Rate} \qquad\qquad (11)$$

This correspondence between return on equity and $g^\star$ suggests a major reason for the popularity of ROE as a corporate performance measure: Companies with high ROEs also tend to have a high $g^\star$ and correspondingly fewer sustainable growth problems. Thus, a high return on equity indicates a high current return and high future growth capacity.

Research on the relationship between sustainable growth and a firm's market value of equity, while limited, suggests a positive relationship (Higgins and Kerin, 1983; Fruhan, 1979, 1984). What determines the market value of equity is a complex and much studied topic and certainly beyond the scope of this chapter. However, the linkage underscores the congruity among sustainable growth, return on equity, and share price. Executives who integrate operational and financial policies will produce profitable, sustainable growth and be rewarded in the stock market as well.

A CONCLUDING NOTE

An appreciation for the sustainable growth concept is a necessary first step in integrating strategic market planning and financial policy. The application of the concept, however, has not proven to be an easy task. The gulf between market-oriented and finance-oriented perspectives will be difficult to bridge, because financial policies and strategic market analysis originate in two very different worlds. Strategic market planning focuses on product-markets and the demand by business unit managers for capital to fuel strategies. Financial policies are typically driven by capital markets and the desire to preserve a firm's capital structure (Donaldson, 1985; Ellsworth, 1983). The mark of a well-managed company is balance in responding to both product and capital markets in the long run.

REFERENCES

Anderson, Paul (1979), "The Marketing Management/Finance Interface," *American Marketing Association Educators' Conference*. Chicago: American Marketing Association, 325–329.

Boyd, Harper and J. Larréché (1978), "The Foundations of Marketing Strategy," in G. Zaltman and T. Bonoma, eds. *Review of Marketing: 1978*. Chicago: American Marketing Association, 45.

Brealey, Richard and Stewart Myers (1987). *Principles of Corporate Finance*, Third Edition. New York: McGraw-Hill Book Company.

Business Week (1986), "McDonald's the Name, Fixing Gould is the Game," (July 28), 77–78.

Day, George S. (1986), *Analysis for Strategic Market Decisions*. St. Paul: West Publishing Company.

Donaldson, Gordon (1985), "Financial Goals and Strategic Consequences," *Harvard Business Review* (May–June), 55–66.

Ellsworth, Richard R. (1983), "Subordinate Financial Policy to Corporate Strategy," *Harvard Business Review* (November–December), 170–182.

Fruhan, William E. (1979), *Financial Strategy: Studies in the Creation, Transfer, and Destruction of Shareholder Value* (Homewood, IL: Richard D. Irwin).

Fruhan, William E. (1984), "How Fast Should Your Company Grow?" *Harvard Business Review* (January–February), 84–93.

Govindarajan, V. and John K. Shank (1986), "Cash Sufficiency: The Missing Link in Strategic Planning," *Journal of Business Strategy* (Summer), 88–95.

Harrington, Diana and Brent Wilson (1986), *Corporate Financial Analysis*, 2nd ed. Plano, TX: Business Publications, Inc.

Hax, Arnaldo and Nicolas Majluf (1984), *Strategic Management: An Integrative Perspective*. Englewood Cliffs, NJ: Prentice-Hall.

Higgins, Robert C. and Roger A. Kerin (1983), "Managing the Growth-Financial Policy Nexus in Retailing," *Journal of Retailing* (Fall), 19–45.

Larréché, J. and V. Srinivasan (1981), "STRATPORT: A Decision Support System for Strategic Planning," *Journal of Marketing* (Fall), 38–52.

Levitt, Theodore (1960), "Marketing Myopia," *Harvard Business Review* (July–August), 24ff.

Robinson, S. J. Q. (1979), "What Growth Rate Can You Achieve?" *Long Range Planning* (August), 7–12.

Varadarajan, Poondi (1983), "The Sustainable Growth Model: A Tool for Evaluating the Financial Feasibility of Market Share Strategies," *Strategic Management Journal* (October–December), 353–367.

Wall Street Journal (1983), "AMC is Raising $500 Million Via Loans, Stock Offer, Planned Sale of AM General," (March 24), 2.

Wall Street Journal (1986), "Profoundly Changed, Coca-Cola Co. Strives To Keep On Bubbling," (April 14), 1ff.

Wall Street Journal (1988), "Allegheny International Seeks Protection Under Bankruptcy Law in Surprise Move," (February 22), p. 3, 9.

Walsh, Francis J. (1984), *Measuring Business Performance.* New York: The Conference Board.

Webster, Frederick E., Jr. (1981), "Top Management Concerns About Marketing: Issues for the 1980s," *Journal of Marketing* (Summer), 9–16.

Zakon, Alan (1971), *Growth and Financial Strategies* (Boston: Boston Consulting Group, Inc.)

CHAPTER **9**

VALUE-BASED

PLANNING

Introduction
  Rising Interest in Value-Based Planning
  Importance of Cash Flow

Market-to-Book Ratio Model
  Determinants of Shareholder Value
  Prescriptions for Value Creation
  Implications for Strategic Market Planning
  Portfolio Assessment
  Acquisition and Divestment
  Profitability and Growth Trade-off
  Perspectives on the Market-to-Book Ratio
    Model

Discounted Cash Flow Model
  Determinants of Shareholder Value
  Shareholder Value Creation of a Business
    Unit
  Implications for Strategic Market Planning
  Portfolio Assessment
  Business Unit Strategy
  Perspectives on the Discounted Cash Flow
    Model

A Concluding Note

References

INTRODUCTION

The need to integrate perspectives from financial theory with strategic thinking is frequently advocated. Creating value for a firm's shareholders is one such perspective. While shareholder value creation is a widely accepted objective for the firm (e.g., Treynor, 1981; Anderson, 1981, 1982; Howard, 1983; Alberts and McTaggart, 1984; Kimmel, 1984; Buzzell and Gale, 1987), this perspective has been only recently incorporated into the

358

literature on strategic decision-making through what is termed value-based planning.

Value based planning relies on a set of conceptual and operational frameworks for assessing the economic returns produced by corporate and business unit strategies. Economic return is measured by the future cash flows from a given strategy discounted by the cost of capital of a firm or business unit. A firm or business unit creates (destroys) values when it pursues strategies that produce a return that exceeds (falls short of) its cost of capital. As will be shown in this chapter, value-based planning has important implications for strategic market planning in the areas of portfolio assessment, business unit evaluation, and acquisition and divestment decision-making. Indeed, value-based planning has been proclaimed as ". . . the Eighties' most important contribution to formal corporate planning" (*Fortune*, 1988).

From a practical perspective, knowledge of the conceptual and operational frameworks underlying value-based planning will become a necessary prerequisite for participation in the corporate strategy development process by marketers. As Day and Fahey (1988) note, ". . . once marketers understand the key relationships that determine how shareholder value is created, they will be better equipped to influence the strategy dialogue in the business."

The two value-based planning approaches described in this chapter have received the most attention in the academic literature and actual practice as compared to other such approaches. The first is the market-to-book ratio model advanced by Marakon Associates, a management consulting firm (Marakon Associates, 1980). Strategic Planning Associates (1981) also employs the market-to-book ratio model; however, specific aspects of this method differ from those of Marakon Associates' method. The second approach is the discounted cash flow model proposed by Rappaport (1986). Other approaches proposed by Naylor and Tapon (1982) and Reimann (1987b) are not explicitly addressed. The model proposed by Naylor and Tapon is similar in concept to Marakon Associates', whereas Reimann's approach complements Rappaport's.

This chapter illuminates the message of value-based planning and its implications for strategic market planning. Accordingly, conceptual and practical issues associated with its use are emphasized.

Rising Interest in Value-based Planning

Interest in value-based planning arose because of several developments in the 1980s:

1. large corporations such as Sears, Dart and Kraft, Time, Signode Industries, Combustion Engineering, Borden, NCR, and TRW have made value creation a central objective in the corporate planning process (Noyes, 1985; Brindisi, 1985),

2. traditional financial indicators such as earnings-per-share (EPS) have not proven to be reliable indicators of future returns to shareholders (*Fortune*, 1984; Stern, 1988),
3. growing concerns among corporate management that their company's stock was undervalued (*Business Week*, 1984a),
4. increased attention to linking top management performance evaluation and long-term compensation to shareholder returns (Merchant and Bruns, 1986; *Wall Street Journal*, 1987b),
5. heightened realization that shareholder wealth creation is important given the performance ratings published in the business press, e.g., *Business Week* and *Fortune* magazine's annual rankings of industrial firms (*Wall Street Journal*, 1988), and
6. the development of approaches for implementing value-based planning.

At the same time, academicians have considered value creation issues related to mergers and acquisitions (Rappaport, 1979; Kerin and Varaiya, 1985), divestiture decisions (Alberts and McTaggart, 1979; Arzac, 1986), business unit evaluation (Arzac, 1986; Reimann, 1986; Blyth, Friskey, and Rappaport, 1986), market strategies (Buzzell and Chussil, 1985; Buzzell and Gale, 1987; Day and Fahey, 1988), and company sales and asset growth (Fruhan, 1984; Higgins and Kerin, 1983; Rappaport, 1986).

Importance of Cash Flow

A brief comment on cash flow analysis is necessary before the two value-based planning approaches are described, since both incorporate this financial planning tool. Simply put, *cash flow* is the after-tax amount of cash generated or consumed by the firm over a certain period, typically an operating year.

Corporate Perspective The basis for this heightened interest in cash flow by corporations is that top-level executives have been grimly reminded of a simple fact: net earnings are not the same as cash on hand (see, for example, Gale and Branch, 1981; Stancil, 1987). Two examples illustrate this point. First, suppose a firm loses control of its accounts receivable by allowing customers increasingly long periods to pay, or suppose a firm produces more than it sells, thus building a high inventory. Even though profits are realized in an accounting sense, the firm may not be generating enough cash inflows to replenish the cash outflows needed for production and investment. Second, suppose a firm carefully manages its inventories and receivables, but rapid sales growth creates an ever-larger investment in these assets. This firm may again show earnings; however, its cash is absorbed in noncash assets, which will leave it with too little cash to meet its obligations. Neither case is unique. The U.S. automobile industry experienced the first situation in late 1986, when its production outpaced its sales, resulting in unmanageable inventories. The use of interest-rate incentives and "buy one (car) get one free" tactics became commonplace, which further exacerbated the profit and cash squeeze in the fourth quarter of 1986 (e.g., *Business Week*, 1986b; *Wall Street Journal*, 1987a). Endo-Lase, a distributor of medical lasers, illustrate the second scenario (*Forbes*, 1987). Company sales trebled in 1984; and significant earnings were recorded. However, accounts receivables increased at an even faster rate, which in turn consumed cash. The company soon found it necessary to write down its receivables, write up its inventories, and eliminate over 90 percent of its earnings. The company filed for bankruptcy in 1986.

Investor Perspective Interest in cash flow analysis has increased because it has become a valuation tool of investors as well (*Business Week*, 1987b). In an economic sense, investors (shareholders) calculate the present value of each of their investments by discounting the expected cash flow of each at their required rate of return. Their rate of return, or cost of capital, is presumed to be the sum of the current interest rate on "risk free" securities, such as government securities, plus a premium based on the estimated riskiness of the investment. The most common method for determining the cost of (equity) capital is the capital asset pricing model (CAPM) described in any basic finance textbook.

The present value of expected cash flow represents the economic value of a security to the investor. In the case of a bond or stock, an investor will examine the present value of expected cash inflows relative to cash outflows over time. Shareholder wealth occurs when the present value of forecasted equity cash flows (cash inflow versus cash outflow) exceeds the book value of the equity of the firm.

Unfortunately, how cash flow is determined and reported by corporations is a matter of debate. Numerous procedures are applied, each of which produces different figures for investors (*Forbes*, 1986; *Business Week*, 1987b). The Federal Accounting Standards Board (FASB) has taken steps to produce consistency in the reporting of cash flow (Ernst & Whinney, 1986). The results of this effort are expected to bear fruit in the 1990s.

Interest in cash flow, both from a corporate and an investor perspective, has also promoted the use of value-based planning. However, as will be shown, specific aspects of cash flow are applied differently for the two models described in this chapter.

MARKET-TO-BOOK RATIO MODEL

According to the *market-to-book ratio model*, shareholder wealth is created when the market value M of the equity invested in the firm by shareholders exceeds the book value B of their equity capital. At any point in time in a firm's history, the book value B approximately measures the value of the capital contributed (up to that point in time) by the firm's shareholders. The (warranted) market equity value M of the firm is, on the other hand, an estimate of the stock market's assessment of how effectively the firm utilizes that capital. The warranted market equity value is the discounted value of the equity cash flows the firm can be expected to produce over time given its overall strategy and its cost of equity capital. A firm's management creates value for shareholders if M is greater than B, destroys value if M is less than B, and sustains value if M equals B.

Determinants of Shareholder Value

According to the market-to-book ratio model, value for shareholders results from the determinants of cash flow and their present value. These determinants are the firm's expected return on equity (ROE), the firm's cost of equity capital (ke), the expected earnings growth rate of the company (g), and the period over which the firm is expected to maintain a positive spread between its return on equity and its cost of equity (i.e., ROE $-$ ke > 0).[1] A simple expression of these relationships is shown in Figure 9.1.

The cost of equity is of central importance in value creation. The cost of equity ke is the *minimum* return that shareholders of the firm demand

FIGURE 9.1
MARKET-TO-BOOK RATIO VALUE CREATION MODEL

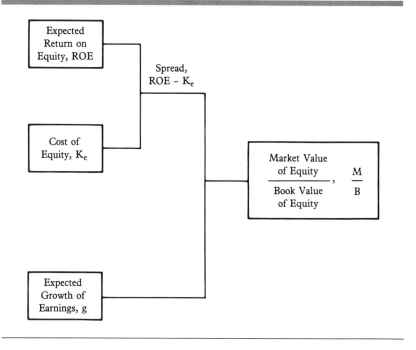

consistent with the riskiness of their investment in the firm (based on the capital asset pricing model). Consequently, value is created (destroyed) when a firm adopts strategies that produce a return that exceeds (falls short of) its cost of equity. Profitable strategic decisions are those that generate such positive spreads.

This perspective is in sharp contrast with the view that a positive ROE alone is indicative of a profitable firm or business unit. As Hax and Majluf (1984, p. 214) point out:

> It is economic, and not accounting, profitability, that determines the capability for wealth creation on the part of the firm. It is perfectly possible that a company is in the black, and yet its market value is way below its book value, which means that from an economic point of view, its resources would be more profitable if deployed in an alternative investment of similar risk.

Similarly, this perspective questions the singular preoccupation with earnings growth rate found in many companies (*Fortune*, 1984). Earnings, and particularly earnings-per-share, represent only one aspect of value creation. Indeed, Booz, Allen, and Hamilton reports that there is virtually no long-term correlation between earnings-per-share growth and return to shareholders (Brindisi, 1985). Accordingly, attention has been placed on the relationship between (ROE − ke) spread and the market-to-book ratio.

Marakon Associates has studied this relationship. One of their findings is shown in Figure 9.2 in which a positive association between (ROE − ke) spread and the market-to-book ratio is indicated. We should emphasize that the market-to-book ratio model does not specify the strategic influences on (ROE − ke) spread and growth (g) , or the dynamic interaction between them. Rather, it simply directs managerial attention to the levers that affect a firm's value.

Prescriptions for Value Creation

The market-to-book ratio model generates three prescriptions for corporate strategic decision making:

1. with the magnitude of the earnings growth rate held *constant g*, a strategy that generates a higher (ROE − ke) spread results in a higher valuation M/B,
2. with the magnitude of the (ROE − ke) spread held *constant*, a strategy that generates a higher earnings growth rate results in a higher valuation M/B, *provided* the spread is *positive*, and
3. with the magnitude of the (ROE − ke) spread held *constant*, a strategy that generates a higher earnings growth rate results in a lower valuation M/B, *provided* the spread is *negative*.

FIGURE 9.2
MARKET-TO-BOOK RATIO VERSUS SPREAD GRAPH FOR DOW
JONES INDUSTRIAL FIRMS: SEPTEMBER, 1987

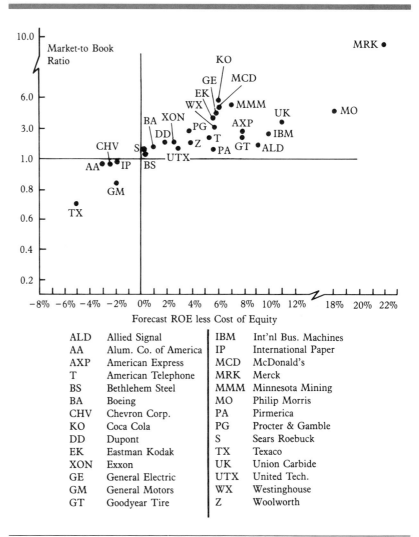

ALD	Allied Signal	IBM	Int'nl Bus. Machines
AA	Alum. Co. of America	IP	International Paper
AXP	American Express	MCD	McDonald's
T	American Telephone	MRK	Merck
BS	Bethlehem Steel	MMM	Minnesota Mining
BA	Boeing	MO	Philip Morris
CHV	Chevron Corp.	PA	Pirmerica
KO	Coca Cola	PG	Procter & Gamble
DD	Dupont	S	Sears Roebuck
EK	Eastman Kodak	TX	Texaco
XON	Exxon	UK	Union Carbide
GE	General Electric	UTX	United Tech.
GM	General Motors	WX	Westinghouse
GT	Goodyear Tire	Z	Woolworth

Source: James McTaggart (1988), "The Ultimate Takeover Defense: Closing the Value Gap," *Planning Review* (January–February), 28.

Little research has examined the empirical validity of these prescriptions. Woo (1984) reported empirical results that provided weak support for them. However, using a different methodology, Varaiya, Kerin, and Weeks (1987) concluded that (ROE − ke) spread and growth do influence shareholder value in the manner predicted; however, the relationships were conditional. In related work, Branch and Gale (1983) observed that return on equity and growth, coupled with research and development expenditures and the firm's interest coverage ratio, were the most important determinants of a company's market-to-book ratio.

Implications for Strategic Market Planning

This value-based planning perspective is likely to affect strategic market planning in three ways over the next decade. First, investment decisions concerning the present portfolio of product-markets or strategic business units will take into consideration the individual and collective contribution to shareholder value. Second, the acquisition and divestment of businesses will be considered in light of shareholder wealth consequences. Finally, business unit strategies will be assessed in terms of the implicit trade-offs between (ROE − ke) spread and growth. Each application is briefly considered below.

Portfolio Assessment   Valid concerns about the portfolio matrix approach for strategic market planning were raised in chapters three and four. Nevertheless, the multibusiness firm is a fact, and corporate performance standards for assessing the contribution of each business to the total corporate entity merit attention. The market-to-book ratio method views the contribution of each business unit (i.e., assets) in terms of value creation. Arzac (1986), Hax and Majluf (1984), and Alberts and McTaggart (1984) propose that the value created by a firm is simply equal to the sum of the values created (destroyed) by each of its businesses. The specifics of how this is done are beyond the scope of this discussion given the technicalities of the relationships between cash flow, cost of capital, and the effect of any synergy among individual business units (see Hax and Majluf, 1984; chapter ten).

Marakon Associates (1981) has developed a scheme for assessing the economic return of individual business units within the firm using what it refers to as "The Profitability Matrix." Figure 9.3 shows this matrix and assigns individual business units to specific locations based on their (ROE − ke) spread and growth. The cut-off points are the business unit cost of equity ke and the growth of the market in which it competes G. The diagonal separates business units into those that produce cash and those that do not.

A powerful message can be extracted from this matrix, since profitability as measured by (ROE − ke) spread and growth are clearly positioned against each other. When a firm's business portfolio is portrayed in this manner, it is clear that cash generation by itself is not always good and an optimum business portfolio is not necessarily balanced in a cash flow sense. Rather, by assigning business units to seven categories in terms of (ROE − ke) spread, cash flow, and changes in market share, it becomes clear that growth is desirable under economically profitable conditions and detrimental under economically unprofitable conditions. This message ac-

FIGURE 9.3
THE PROFITABILITY MATRIX

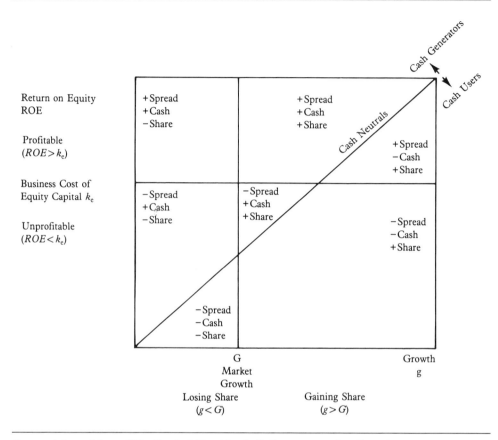

Source: Adapted from "The Profitability Matrix," *Commentary.* San Francisco: Marakon Associates, 1981.

cents the discussion in chapter three on the BCG matrix and in chapter eight on sustainable growth.

Acquisition and Divestment The influence of acquisition and divestment decisions on shareholder wealth creation should be of central concern given the restructuring of corporations apparent in the 1980s (Davidson, 1987). The acquisition decision in particular affects the acquiring firm in terms of the price paid for a new business and the operating performance postacquisition. According to an assessment of acquisition activity in *Business Week* (1987a), the stock prices of acquiring companies typically lose from one to seven percent of their value during the year following an acquisition. Moreover, this study reported evidence that acquiring firms experience an average cumulative loss in market value of sixteen percent over three years relative to market projections for the acquiring firm preacquisition.

These observations indicate that shareholder value considerations warrant serious consideration when acquisitions are planned. Kerin and Varaiya (1985) have applied the market-to-book ratio model in making such a determination. Using the offering price per share of common stock $\hat{M}$ and the value-sustainable spread (ROE* $-$ ke), they have identified the minimum permanent spread that the acquiring firm must be expected to generate postacquisition to preserve the preacquisition share price of the acquiring firm. Marakon Associates (1982) has developed a similar approach to this topic. In more direct terms, Salter and Weinhold (1981, p. 127) note: "The real question is not whether attractive (acquisition) candidates are available, but whether the company's potential to create value for the acquirer's shareholders is sufficient to justify the purchase price."

Arzac (1986) and Alberts and McTaggart (1979) have proposed value-based approaches for examining divestment decisions. In both approaches, the contribution of individual business units to company-wide value is assessed using the (ROE $-$ ke) spread and growth concepts. The technicalities and assumptions involved can become cumbersome and are therefore beyond the scope of this discussion.

Profitability and Growth Trade-off   The perspective emerging from the market-to-book ratio approach forces management to explicitly consider the trade-off between growth and profitability (e.g., the spread between ROE and ke). Growth and profitability cannot be treated separately. A firm's (ROE $-$ ke) spread and its earnings growth rate g are related in that, in general, efforts to increase growth are likely to decrease spread, and efforts that increase spread are likely to decrease growth. (A generalized representation of the relationship between spread, growth, and value is shown in Figure 9.4). Consequently, management's goal in strategic market planning is to identify options that result in the *combination* of growth and spread that produces the largest value of the firm's market-to-book ratio. Unfortunately, work on the market-to-book ratio method of value-based planning has not yet advanced to this level of sophistication.

Perspectives on the Market-to-Book Ratio Model

The market-to-book ratio model is a popular approach to value-based planning for three reasons. First, a firm's return on equity, cost of equity capital, and forecasted earnings growth rate are commonly used as financial indicators for measuring business performance (Walsh, 1984). Indeed, return on equity is one the most frequently used barometers of corporate

FIGURE 9.4
SCHEMATIC REPRESENTATION OF THE RELATIONSHIP
BETWEEN SPREAD, GROWTH, AND VALUE

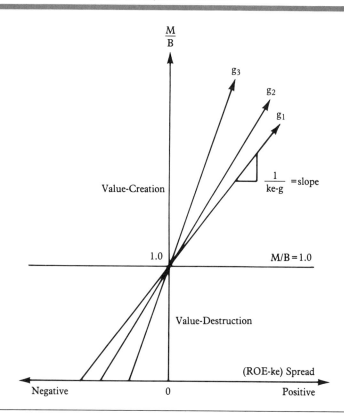

Note: Each line passing through the point $M/B = 1.0$, is a representation of the equation $M/B = 1 + ROE - ke/ke - g$ for different earnings growth rates, $g_1 < g_2 < g_3$. See Note 1 for further elaboration.

health and, along with growth, have been shown to be associated with market-to-book ratios (Branch and Gale, 1983). Therefore, existing financial reporting procedures mesh easily with this value-based planning approach. Second, the approach is based on the extant valuation theory in finance (Fruhan, 1979). Third, corporate executives can visualize the market value of common stock as an external scorecard gauging their performance. Thus, even though sixty percent of executives in the United States believe their companies are undervalued, eighty percent believe that equity markets are a healthy influence on management and the way it conducts its business (*Business Week*, 1984a).

However, the market-to-book ratio model is not without its detractors. Two major criticisms have been voiced, each based on the use of accounting data (Rappaport, 1983; 1986; Reimann, 1986a; 1986b; 1987a). First, it has been argued that the (ROE − *ke*) spread is based on an inappropriate comparison. That is, ROE is an accrual accounting ratio, whereas cost of equity *ke* is a market-based measure derived from the capital asset pricing model. Therefore, the two measures are not directly comparable. Second, the positive relationship between (ROE − *ke*) spread and the market-to-book ratio reported by Marakon Associates can be affected by accounting capitalization versus expense rules. For example, the smaller the total investment capitalized by a firm, the smaller the book value of investment, and hence, the higher the ROI and ROE. At the same time, the lower book value affects the market-to-book ratio by making it larger. Rappaport (1983) illustrates this point by showing that firms in industries such as cosmetics, pharmaceuticals, and computer software, which invest large amounts in noncapitalized assets (e.g., research and development and advertising), tend to have a high ROI and ROE.

DISCOUNTED CASH FLOW MODEL

A second value-based planning approach has been proposed by Alfred Rappaport and the Alcar Group, Inc., a management education and software company (Rappaport, 1986; Blyth, Friskey, and Rappaport, 1986).[2] This approach is based on discounted cash flow analysis. The *discounted cash flow model* estimates the economic return from an investment by discounting forecasted cash flows by the corporate or business unit cost of capital. These cash flows in turn serve as the foundation for shareholder returns from dividends and share-price appreciation. By focusing on cash flow, this approach overcomes the criticisms of the market-to-book model, since accounting-based ROE and book values are not used.

Determinants of Shareholder Value

The conceptual underpinnings of the value-based planning approach proposed by Rappaport (1986) are summarized in Figure 9.5. Seven factors affect shareholder value. Rappaport calls them "value drivers." They are (1) rate of sales growth, (2) operating profit margin, (3) income tax rate, (4) investment in working capital, (5) fixed capital investment, (6) cost of capital, and (7) value growth duration.

The first six "value drivers" are self-explanatory. However, value growth duration requires elaboration. Value growth duration represents management's estimate of the number of years over which investments can be expected to produce rates of return that exceed the cost of capital. This estimate is based on management's belief that a temporary position of

FIGURE 9.5
SHAREHOLDER VALUE CREATION NETWORK

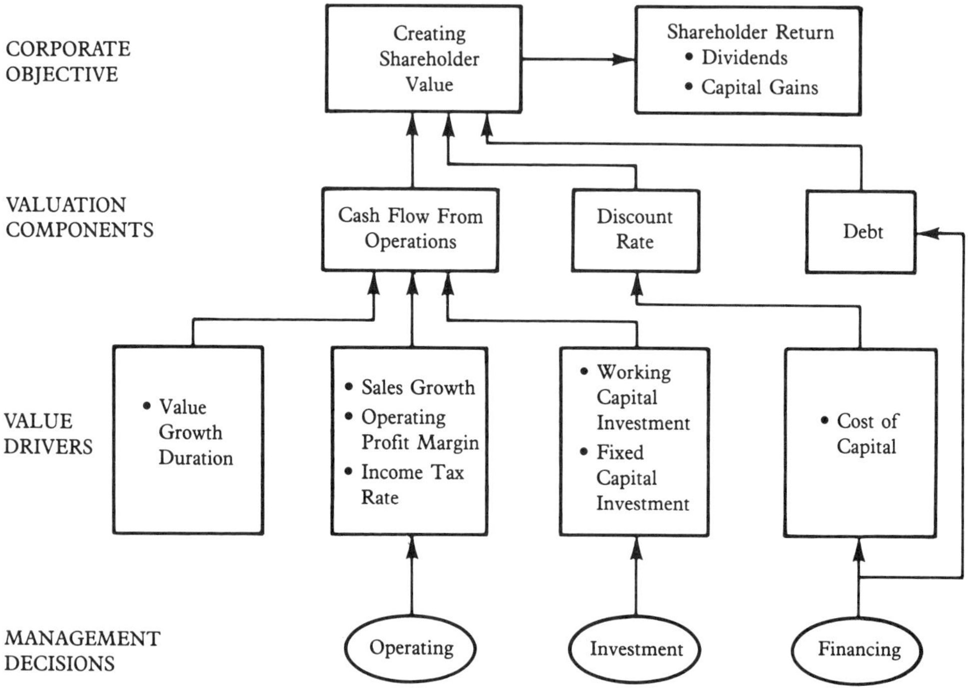

Source: Alfred Rappaport, *Creating Shareholder Value* (New York: The Free Press, 1986), p. 76.

competitive superiority will exist that will result in profitability levels higher than the cost of capital. Afterward, competitive superiority is lost, and profitability regresses to the cost of capital (which implies that the market value of the remaining or residual cash flow is equal to the book value of the firm's investments). An identical perspective lies at the foundation of the market-to-book ratio model (see note 1).

Shareholder Value Creation
of a Business Unit

While common in capital investment decisions, the use of discounted cash flow analysis is somewhat novel in its application to value-based planning. The application of discounted cash flow analysis to value-based planning for a business unit follows in an abbreviated form. For an extended discussion, the reader should consult Rappaport (1986) and the references listed in note 2.

The procedure typically begins with a forecast of annual operating cash flows for a business unit for a specific strategy and planning period, usually three to five years. In step 2, cash flows are discounted back to the initial time period (year) and summed to arrive at the present value of the forecasted cash flows. The discount rate for the cash flow stream is the weighted average cost of debt and equity capital. The residual value of the business unit (strategy) at the end of the planning period is estimated and discounted to its present value in step 3. The fourth step involves the calculation of the present value of the business unit (strategy), which is the sum of the present values of future cash flows and the residual value. After subtracting the market value of debt, this figure is termed "total shareholder value." Step 5 requires the calculation of the present value of the business unit in the initial time period (year). This figure is termed the "prestrategy shareholder value" and is determined by dividing the business unit's cash flow in the initial time period by its cost of capital. The final step is the determination of the shareholder value creation potential of the business unit (strategy). Shareholder value creation is the difference between "total shareholder value" developed in step 4 and the "prestrategy shareholder value" calculated in step 5. A summary of the six-step procedure is shown in Table 9.1.

A simple illustration of discounted cash flow analysis and shareholder value creation applied to a business unit (strategy) is shown in Table 9.2. This illustration, provided by Reimann (1987a), makes the following assumptions:

1. sales growth remains constant at ten percent per year,
2. gross margins and selling, general, and administrative expenses remain constant at twenty-five percent and ten percent, respectively,
3. asset turnover remains constant,
4. the discount rate is fifteen percent,
5. after-tax earnings in the initial period are equivalent to cash flow, since no "incremental" investment exists, and
6. the business unit has no assignable debt.

For this business unit adopting a specific strategy, the shareholder value creation is $6.98 million. This same analysis can be expanded to the corporate level. In this instance, marketable securities and corporate debt must be considered. By adding marketable securities and subtracting the market value of corporate debt, value creation by the corporation can be determined. Assume, for example, that the illustration in Table 9.2 applies to the corporation and not to a business unit, and the firm's marketable securities and market value of debt were $1 million and $4 million, respectively. The value creation potential for the corporation would be as follows:

Cumulative Present Value of Cash Flows	$16.94 million
Present Value of the Residual Value	+40.04
Marketable Securities	+ 1.00
Total Corporate Value	$57.98
Market Value of Debt	− 4.00
Total Shareholder Value	$53.98
Prestrategy Shareholder Value	−50.00
Value Created by Strategy	$3.98 million

Implications for Strategic Market Planning

This value-based planning perspective is likely to affect strategic market planning in two ways over the next decade. First, like the market-to-book ratio model, investment decisions concerning the present portfolio of product-markets or strategic business units will consider the individual and collective contribution to shareholder value. Second, the discounted cash flow model will focus attention on the value created by specific business units and their strategies. Each application is briefly described below. A specific application using the Coca-Cola Company as an example is found in Box 9.1.

Portfolio Assessment   The discounted cash flow model has a direct bearing on the assessment of a firm's portfolio of business units or product-markets. The present values of individual business units should equal the total value for the firm, as was described earlier—considering, of course, any synergies in the corporate portfolio. Such a review of business units should provide answers to questions such as (Rappaport, 1986, p. 106)

1. what business units in the portfolio are creating (destroying) value for shareholders?
2. which business units are cash flow producers, cash flow neutral, and cash flow drains?
3. which combination of business units (strategies) generates the highest total value for shareholders?

Answers to questions 1 and 2 provide useful insights into a firm's present portfolio. Question 3, by comparison, allows for an assessment of alternative business unit (strategy) moves and their effect on the portfolio of businesses. Blyth, Friskey, and Rappaport (1986) illustrate how this can be done with an extensive hypothetical example using alternate strategies.

Business Unit Strategy   Perhaps the clearest use of the discounted cash flow model lies in business unit (strategy) analysis, and particularly, resource allocation decisions. In this context, Rappaport (1986, p. 116–117; 1981) introduces a new criterion for evaluating investment decisions,

TABLE 9.1
COMPUTING SHAREHOLDER VALUE

STEP	Elaboration
Step 1: Forecast annual operating cash flows for the business unit (strategy).	Annual cash flow is defined as: Cash Inflow = (Sales)(Operating Profit Margin)(1-Effective Tax Rate) $(-)$ Cash Outflow = Incremental Fixed Costs + Working Capital Investment
Step 2: Discount forecasted cash flow at the weighted average cost of debt and equity capital	Discounted Cash Flow can be expressed as: $$PV = \sum_{t=1}^{T} \frac{C_t}{(1 + k_w)^t}, \text{ where}$$ PV = Present (market value) C_t = Forecasted incremental cash flow after taxes T = Project or planning period (C_T includes salvage value at end of the period) k_w = Weighted cost of debt and equity capital Weighted Cost of Debt and Equity Capital, K_w (Higgins, 1984): $$k_w = \frac{(1 - T)^k{}_d D + k_e E}{D + E}, \text{ where}$$ D = Debt Market Value E = Equity Market Value k_d = Expected Return on Debt (Cost of Debt) k_e = Expected Return on Equity (Cost of Equity) T = Effective Tax Rate
Step 3: Estimate the residual value of the business unit (strategy) and discount to its present value	$$\text{Residual Value} = \frac{\text{Perpetuity Cash Flow}}{\text{Cost of Capital}}$$
Step 4: Sum the present values of future cash flows and residual value to arrive at Total Shareholder Value	Total Shareholder Value = Cumulative Present Value of Cash Flow + Residual Value − Market Value of Debt
Step 5: Calculate the Prestrategy Value	Prestrategy Value = $$\frac{\text{Cash Flow Before New Investment}}{\text{Cost of Capital}} -$$ Market Value of Debt
Step 6: Compute the Value Created by Strategy	Value Created by Strategy = Total Shareholder Value − Prestrategy Value

TABLE 9.2
ILLUSTRATION OF DISCOUNTED CASH FLOW MODEL
IN VALUE-BASED PLANNING

	Current Values 1985	Income Statement Projections					Residual Value 1990 +
		1986	1987	1988	1989	1990	
Sales*	$100.00	110.00	121.00	133.10	146.41	161.05	161.05
Gross margin (= 25%)	25.00	27.50	30.25	33.28	36.60	40.26	40.26
S. & G. A. (= 10%)	10.00	11.00	12.10	13.31	14.64	16.11	15.11
Profit before tax	$ 15.00	16.50	18.15	19.97	21.96	24.16	24.16
Income tax	7.50	8.25	9.08	9.98	10.98	12.08	12.08
Net profit	$ 7.50	8.25	9.08	9.98	10.98	12.08	12.08
		Statement of Financial Position (Year-End)					
Net working capital	10.00	11.00	12.10	13.31	14.64	16.11	16.11
Depreciable assets	30.00	33.00	36.30	39.93	43.92	48.32	48.32
Assets employed	$ 40.00	44.00	48.40	53.24	58.56	64.42	64.42
Return on assets	18.8%	18.8%	18.8%	18.8%	18.8%	18.8%	18.8%
		Cash Flow Statement					
Net earnings	7.50	8.25	9.08	9.98	10.98	12.08	12.08
Depreciation	7.00	3.00	3.30	3.63	3.99	4.39	4.39
Capital expenditures		6.00	6.60	7.26	7.99	8.78	4.39
Increase in working capital		1.00	1.10	1.21	1.33	1.46	0.00
Cash flow		$ 4.25	4.68	5.14	5.66	6.22	12.08
PV factor (at 15% discount)		0.87	0.76	0.66	0.57	0.50	3.31†
Present value of cash flow		.3.70	3.53	3.38	3.23	3.09	40.04
Total present value		$56.98	(Annual cash flows + residual value)				
Current (preplan) value		50.00	(Year 0 net operating earnings/discount rate)				
Net present value		$6.98	= Shareholder value contribution				

*Sales growth: 10%

†"Perpetuity" assumption: PV factor/discount rate = 50/.15

Source: Bernard C. Reimann (1987), "Stock Price and Business Success: What Is The Relationship?" *Journal of Business Strategy* (Summer), p. 44.

namely, Value ROI or VROI, which is the amount of shareholder value created per dollar of investment:

$$\text{VROI} = \frac{\text{Value Created by Strategy}}{\text{Present Value of Investment}}$$

BOX **9.1**

VALUE-BASED PLANNING AT THE COCA-COLA
COMPANY

Some recent actions of the Coca-Cola Company provide
good illustrations of the value-based portfolio (VBP) approach. A VBP
portfolio analysis revealed that its Entertainment Business Sector was not
contributing its fair share to corporate value. A key reason was that the
business was very different in nature from Coke's other endeavors. In
particular, its performance was much more volatile, resulting in greater
risk, and, therefore, a relatively high cost of capital. Top management decided
to spin the entertainment business off as a separate unit by combining it
with its thirty-eight and six-tenths percent-owned Tri-Star Pictures Inc.
Coca-Cola will keep only a minority financial interest in the new company,
to be called Columbia Pictures Entertainment, Inc. Since this move will
reduce the Coca-Cola Company's risk considerably, the stock market reacted
very favorably to the news.

However, Coca-Cola used the VBP approach not only to decide which
businesses to divest from or acquire, but also to fix poorly performing
individual businesses. The VBP analysis uncovered a rather surprising fact:
its mainstay soda fountain business was actually destroying shareholder
value at a worrysome rate. This discovery came as quite a shock, since the
business had always been regarded as highly profitable. After all, there
weren't a lot of bottles or cans to fill, transport, and store. What
management had not realized was that, over time, the business had become
quite capital intensive. The return on capital was only 12.5%, while the
company's cost of capital was estimated to be 16%. Thus, every dollar
invested in this business was dissipating shareholder value.

The main culprit turned out to be an expensive, five-gallon, stainless steel
container used to transport the Coke syrup. The business switched to
disposable bag-in-a-box containers and to fifty-gallon containers for large
customers. Its return on capital rose to seventeen percent and, by increasing
its leverage, the company was able to reduce its cost of capital to fourteen
percent. Suddenly the business was turned into a strong contributor to
shareholder value.

Source: Bernard C. Reimann (1988), "Managing for the Shareholders: An Overview of Value-Based Planning," *Planning Review* (January–February), 10–22.

The value created by strategy is computed using the procedure described previously. The present value of investment is the net present value of the projected working capital and fixed capital investment required by the proposed business unit strategy. When the VROI equals zero, the strategy only yields the cost of capital. Hence, no increase in shareholder value should exist. If VROI is positive, the strategy produces a rate of return greater than the cost of capital, and shareholder value should occur. If the strategy results in a negative VROI, then shareholder value is destroyed. Thus, VROI is a measure of a strategy's potential for adding to shareholder value *relative* to the investment required.

Perspectives on the Discounted Cash Flow Model

The discounted cash flow model of value-based planning is appealing for four reasons. First, attention to cash flow in and of itself is on the rise, as was described earlier. Second, by not using accounting-based ROE and book value of investment, it is not subject to the limitations of the market-to-book ratio model discussed previously. Third, discounted cash flow analysis is a well-known technique. With advances in financial planning software, this technique is likely to gain in popularity (Blyth, Friskey, and Rappaport, 1986). Fourth, this model is particularly attractive to firms interested in evaluating individual business units. By broadening performance standards to include value created by business units, business unit manager attention is directed towards the long-term as opposed to short-term, quarterly earnings reports (*Business Week*, 1984b; Drucker, 1986).

Like the market-to-book ratio model, the discounted cash flow model is not without its critics. Two major concerns focus on estimating the residual value and the "prestrategy shareholder value" (Reimann 1986a; 1986b; 1987a). As shown in Table 9.2, residual value accounts for a sizeable portion of the total present value attributed to a business unit (strategy). In fact, it can account for between sixty and ninety percent of the total present value. Estimating the residual value is therefore a central task requiring managerial judgment. The simplest estimate assumes that long-term cash flows stabilizes at about the same amount projected for the final year of the planning horizon. Such an estimate was applied in Table 9.2. However, this assumption may be questioned on the grounds that businesses rarely sustain the same level of cash flow over an extended time period given competitive conditions. A more realistic approach would assume a pattern of growth rates and returns over a specific period beyond the planning horizon. Moreover, assuming that competitive superiority is lost or lessened over time, the profitability would regress to the firm's cost of equity capital. Further value gains would not be forthcoming.

How "prestrategy shareholder value" is estimated is also a matter of concern. "Prestrategy shareholder value" is determined by capitalizing the previous year's cash flow of the business unit by dividing the cash flow by the discount rate (see Table 9.2). However, two conditions make this practice suspect. First, the prior year profits of a business unit's could have been unusually low or nonexistent. Second, applying the capitalization approach in evaluating a new venture is suspect when historical figures are unavailable. In both situations, management judgment plays an instrumental role in the final assessment of the value creation potential of a business unit (strategy).

The role of managerial judgment in performing discounted cash flow analysis also applies for two aspects of the method itself. For example, Myers (1984) has raised serious questions about managers' ability to estimate the discount rate and the impact on other business unit performance or strategies. In short, whether the market-to-book ratio model or the discounted cash flow model is followed, one should consider the advice of Arzac (1986, p. 126): "Value creation analysis has been designed to complement rather than substitute for managerial creativity and good judgment."

A CONCLUDING NOTE

Value-based planning has clearly attracted the attention of the corporate and academic communities. Shareholder wealth creation as a corporate and business unit performance standard is likely to remain appealing for some time. Nevertheless, cautionary words are already being expressed. The most notable concern is the possibility that a balanced perspective on strategic thinking will be lost in light of the elegance of value-based planning frameworks (Day and Fahey, 1988). This view is represented by Bromily (1986, p. 6-6):

> Although financial returns are an important factor in evaluating an investment or a strategy, they are not the only factor. Thus, at the capital investment level, and much more at the strategic level, the challenge is to integrate financial criteria in a meaningful way with substantial business considerations and strategic possibilities.

Similarly, others (Day, 1986; Barwise, Marsh and Wensley, 1989) argue that any estimate of value creation must go beyond numeracy to ultimately consider whether the actions taken by the firm gain or sustain a competitive advantage. A more complete understanding of the value creation/ destruction process will necessitate linking value-based planning models with frameworks developed for assessing competitive strategy. Porter (1985, p. 4) argues that long-term profitability in an industry should be measured by "rates of return on investment in excess of the cost of capital." This recognition represents an initial attempt to mesh value-based planning with competitive strategy analysis, since they both have a common reference point. Unfortunately, the gap has yet to be bridged.

From a marketing perspective, if marketers are to engage in the strategy dialogue concerning the use of value-based approaches, they must be armed with insights into how the variables under their control can influence shareholder wealth. Results from the PIMS program (Buzzell and Gale, 1987; Gale and Swire, 1988a) suggest that the same strategic variables that produce a high ROI also create shareholder value. But Buzzell and Gale (1987) also voice a cautionary note. That is, a high incidence of new products, heavy spending on marketing and research and development, and improvements in relative quality each depress ROI in the short-run, but each is positively related to the long-term value enhancement. As yet, a comprehensive assessment of the role of marketing-related variables on shareholder value creation is not available.

A second concern relates to implementation. While value-based planning models make sense at a conceptual level, implementing them in practice is another matter. When value-based planning approaches are utilized, line managers might feel uneasy dealing with variables they feel are outside their control and considerable effort is necessary to tailor theory to practice (Chakravarthy, Loomis and Vrabel, 1988; Fahey, 1988). Moreover, a recent survey on the use of cost of capital techniques indicated that ". . . a significant gap between financial theory and practice remains" (Gitman and Mercurio, 1982, p. 29).

A third concern focuses on an inherent limitation of the value-based models currently used. Neither model considers value creation issues related to new ventures in product-markets (as opposed to acquisitions).

A fourth concern, and a matter for research by academicians and practitioners alike, is which if any value-based planning model best captures the value creation/destruction process. Only Gale and Swire (1988b) have examined this question, and they have only done so at the level of the corporation. They observed that value creation estimates using the market-to-book model outperformed the discounted cash flow model (based on the perpetuity assumption) using stock price appreciation plus dividends paid as a measure. Clearly, this question deserves further study.

In summary, value-based planning represents yet another stage in the evolution of strategic market planning. How it will improve decision-making has yet to be demonstrated through critical, scholarly research and corporate practice. Like other concepts (business portfolio analysis, experience curve dynamics, and so forth), the substance of value-based planning will be fleshed out with time; its potential contribution to strategic market planning has yet to be determined.

NOTES

1. Hax and Majluf (1984) and Fruhan (1974) provide a detailed description of these relationships. However, a brief summary might be instructive.

   Fruhan (1979) expresses the M/B ratio as

   $$\frac{M}{B} = \left(1 + \frac{ROE - ke}{ke - g}\right)\left[1 - \left(\frac{1 + g}{1 + ke}\right)^n\right] + \left(\frac{1 + g}{1 + ke}\right)^n,$$

   where

   ROE denotes the expected return per year on book equity investment,

   ke denotes the cost of equity capital (assumed constant),

   g denotes the expected annual rate of growth in earnings per year (assumed constant), and

   n is the number of years which the firm is expected to maintain its current ROE. Up to year *n*, ROE $\gtrless$ *ke;* thereafter ROE = *ke*.

   This equation can be viewed as a generic representative of a value-based planning model and will be designated the finite growth model. This equation states that the market-to-book ratio *M/B* is a function of three factors:

   1. the magnitude of the percentage spread (ROE − *ke*), expected to be earned,
   2. the volume of future investment opportunities as expressed by their rate of growth earning per year *g*, and
   3. the number of years *n* during which future investment opportunities will be available so as to enable the generation of exceptional spreads (ROE $\gtrless$ *ke*).

      When N = ∞, the equation represents the constant growth model of corporation finance

      $$\frac{M}{B} = 1 + \frac{ROE - ke}{ke - g}$$

   Equilibrium requires that *ke* < *g* (Miller and Modigliani, 1961).

2. Readers interested in following the development and application of this approach should consult Rappaport (1979; 1981; 1983; 1987a; 1987b).

REFERENCES

Alberts, William and James McTaggart (1979), "The Divestiture Decision: An Introduction," *Mergers and Acquisitions*, Fall, 18–30.

Alberts, William and James McTaggart (1984), "Value Based Strategic Investment Planning," *Interfaces* January–February, 138–151.

Anderson, Paul (1981), "Marketing Investment Analysis," in Jadgish N. Sheth, ed., *Research in Marketing*, Vol. 4 (Greenwich, CT: JAI Press), 1–37.

Anderson, Paul (1982), "Marketing Strategic Planning and the Theory of the Firm," *Journal of Marketing*, Spring, 15–26.

Arzac, Enrique R. (1986), "Do Your Business Units Create Shareholder Value?" *Harvard Business Review*, January–February, 121–126.

Barwise, P., Paul Marsh, Robin Wensley (1989), "Must Finance and Strategy Clash?" *Harvard Business Review*, (September–October), 85–90.

Blyth, Michael, Elizabeth Friskey, and Alfred Rappaport (1986), "Implementing the Shareholder Value Approach," *Journal of Business Strategy*, Winter, 48–59.

Branch, Ben and Bradley Gale (1983), "Linking Corporate Price Performance to Strategy Formulation," *Journal of Business Strategy*, Summer, 40–50.

Brindisi, Louis J., Jr. (1985) "Shareholder Value and Executive Compensation," *Planning Review*, September, 14–17.

Bromily, Philip (1986), "Shareholder Value and Strategic Management: Some Caveats," in William D. Guth (ed.), *Handbook of Business Strategy: 1986/1987 Yearbook* (New York: Warren, Gorham & Lamont), 6-1–6-6.

Business Week (1984a), "Companies Feel Underrated By the Street," February 20, 14.

Business Week (1984b), "Rewarding Executives for Taking the Long View," April 2, 99–100.

Business Week (1984c), "Borden: Putting the Shareholder First Starts to Pay Off," April 2, 100.

Business Week (1986a), "Borden's No. 1 Product: Contented Shareholders," July 28, 28–79.

Business Week (1986b), "GM is Acting as if There's No Tomorrow," September 15, 44–45.

Business Week (1987a), "For Better or For Worse?" January 12, 38–40.

Business Week (1987b), "The Savviest Investors are Going With the Flow," September 7, 92–93.

Buzzell, Robert D. and Mark J. Chussil (1985), "Managing for Tomorrow," *Sloan Management Review*, Summer, 3–14.

Buzzell, Robert D. and Bradley T. Gale (1987), *The PIMS Principles* (New York: The Free Press), Chapter 11.

Chakravarthy, Bala, Worth Loomis, and John Vrabel (1988), "Dexter Corporation's Value-Based Strategic Planning System," *Planning Review*, January–February, 34–41.

Davidson, Kenneth M. (1987), "Do Megamergers Make Sense?" *Journal of Business Strategy*, Winter, 40–48.

Day, George S. (1986), "Tough Questions for Developing Strategy," *Journal of Business Strategy*, Winter, 60–68.

Day, George S. and Liam Fahey (1988), "Valuing Market Strategies," *Journal of Marketing*, July, 45–57.

Drucker, Peter F. (1986), "If Earnings Aren't the Dial to Read," *Wall Street Journal*, October 30, 30.

Ernst & Whinney, "Statement of Cash Flows," October, 1986.

Fahey, Liam (1988), "The Westinghouse Shareholder Value Culture," *Planning Review*, January–February, 42–45.

Forbes, (1986), "Confusing Flows the Cash Flow," April 7, 72–75.

Forbes (1987), "Now You See It . . .," February 9, 70.

Fortune (1984), "Business Is Bungling Long-Term Compensation," July 23, 64–69.

Fortune (1988), "Corporate Strategy for the 1990s," February 29, 34–42.

Fruhan, William E., Jr. (1979), *Financial Strategy: Studies in the Creation, Transfer and Destruction of Shareholder Value*, (Homewood, IL: Richard D. Irwin), chapters 1–2.

Fruhan, William E., Jr. (1984), "How Fast Should Your Company Grow?" *Harvard Business Review*, January–February, 84–93.

Gale, Bradley and Ben Branch (1981), "Cash Flow Analysis: More Important Than Ever," *Harvard Business Review*, July–August, 131–136.

Gale, Bradley and Donald Swire (1988a), "Business-Unit Strategies that Create Shareholder Value," *Planning Review*, March–April, 6–13.

Gale, Bradley and Donald Swire (1988b), "The Tricky Business of Measuring Wealth," *Planning Review*, March–April, 14–17, 47.

Gitman, Lawrence J. and Vincent A. Mercurio (1982), "Cost of Capital Techniques Used By Major U.S. Firms: Survey and Analysis of Fortune's 1000," *Financial Management*, Winter, 21–29.

Hax, Arnaldo and Nicolas Majluf (1984), *Strategic Management: An Integrative Perspective*, (Englewood Cliffs, NJ: Prentice-Hall, Inc.), 209–242.

Higgins, Robert C. (1984), *Analysis for Financial Management*, (Homewood, IL: Richard D. Irwin), 204.

Higgins, Robert C. and Roger A. Kerin (1983), "Managing the Growth-Financial Policy Nexus," *Journal of Retailing*, Fall, 19–48.

Howard, John (1983), "Marketing Theory of the Firm," *Journal of Marketing*, Fall, 90–100.

Kerin, Roger A. and Nikhil Varaiya (1985), "Mergers and Acquisitions in Retailing: A Review and Critical Analysis," *Journal of Retailing*, Spring, 9–34.

Kimmel, George S. (1984), "Creating Shareholder Value: A Primary Financial Objective," *Forum*, June, 14.

Marakon Associates (1980), "The Role of Finance in Strategic Planning," Business Week Conference.

Marakon Associates (1981), "The Marakon Profitability Matrix," *Commentary*, April.

Marakon Associates (1982), "Growing Profitability By Acquisition," *Commentary*, June.

Merchant, Kenneth A. and William J. Bruns, Jr. (1986), "Measurements to Cure Management Myopia," *Business Horizons* (May–June), 56–64.

Miller, Merton and Franco Modigliani (1961), "Dividend Policy, Growth and the Valuation of Shares," *Journal of Business*, (October), 411–433.

Myers, Stuart (1984), "Finance Theory and Financial Strategy," *Interfaces*, (January–February), 126–137.

Naylor, Thomas H. and Francis Tapon (1982), "The Capital Asset Pricing Model: An Evaluation of its Potential as a Strategic Tool," *Management Science*, October, 1166–1173.

Noyes, Thomas E. (1985) "The Evolution of Strategic Planning at Signode," *Planning Review*, September, 10–13.

Porter, Michael (1985), *Competitive Advantage: Creating and Sustaining Superior Performance* (New York: The Free Press).

Rappaport, Alfred (1979), "Strategic Analysis for More Profitable Decisions," *Harvard Business Review*, July–August, 99–110.

Rappaport, Alfred (1981), "Selecting Strategies That Create Shareholder Value," *Harvard Business Review*, May–June, 139–149.

Rappaport, Alfred (1983), "Corporate Performance Standards and Shareholder Value," *Journal of Business Strategy*, Spring, 28–38.

Rappaport, Alfred (1986), *Creating Shareholder Value* (New York: The Free Press).

Rappaport, Alfred (1987a), "Linking Competitive Strategy and Shareholder Value Analysis," *Journal of Business Strategy*, Spring, 58–67.

Rappaport, Alfred (1987b), "Stock Market Signals to Managers," *Harvard Business Review*, November–December, 57–62.

Reimann, Bernard C. (1986a), "Strategy Valuation in Portfolio Planning: Combining Q and VROI Ratios," *Planning Review*, January, pp. 18–23ff.

Reimann, Bernard C. (1986b), "Does Your Business Create Real Shareholder Value?" *Business Horizons*, September–October, pp. 44–51.

Reimann, Bernard C. (1987a), "Stock Price and Business Success: What Is The Relationship?" *Journal of Business Strategy*, Summer, 38–49.

Reimann, Bernard C. (1987b), *Managing For Value*. (Oxford, OH: The Planning Forum.)

Salter, Malcolm and Wolf Weinhold (1981), "Choosing Compatible Acquisitions," *Harvard Business Review*, January–February, 117–127.

Stancil, James (1987), "When Is There Cash In Cash Flow?" *Harvard Business Review,* March–April, 38–49.

Stern, Joel (1988), "Think Cash and Risk—Forget Earnings Per Share," *Planning Review,* January–February, 6–9.

Strategic Planning Associates, Inc. (1981), *Strategy and Shareholder Value: The Value Curve,* Washington, D.C.

Treynor, Jack L. (1981), "The Financial Objective in the Widely Held Corporation," *Financial Analysts Journal,* March–April.

Varaiya, Nikhil, Roger A. Kerin, and David Weeks (1987), "The Relationship Between Growth, Profitability, and Firm Value," *Strategic Management Journal,* September–October, p. 487–497.

Wall Street Journal (1987a), "Buy One Car, Get One Free: Marketers Experiment with Freebies on Grand Scale," March 16, 21.

Wall Street Journal (1987b), "Firms Trim Annual Pay Increases and Focus on Long Term," April 10, 21.

Wall Street Journal (1988), "Wanted: A List of Value to Holders," April 8, 10.

Walsh, Francis J., Jr. (1984), *Measuring Business Performance.* (New York: The Conference Board).

Woo, Carolyn (1984), "An Empirical Test of Value-Based Planning Models and Implications," *Management Science,* September, 1031–1050.

PART **IV**

Perspectives from the

Organizational Sciences

A QUEST FOR

ORGANIZATIONAL EXCELLENCE

Introduction

An Overview of Studies of Excellent and Nonexcellent Companies
Traits of Excellence: America's Best-Run Companies
Traits of Excellence: The Corporate Stars of America
Traits of Excellence: America's Outstanding High-Technology Companies
Traits of Excellence: America's Midsized Growth Companies
Traits of Nonexcellence: The Case of Britain's Troubled Companies
Traits of Superior vs. Poor Performers: A Contrast of PIMS Businesses

Critique of Studies on Excellent Companies
Research Methodology
Criteria Employed for Inferring Superior Corporate Performance
Deterioration in Performance of Excellent Companies
Generalizability of Traits of Excellence

Implications for Strategic Market Planning
Impetus for New Research Directions
Choice of Product-Markets
Choice of Generic Strategy

A Concluding Note

References

INTRODUCTION[1]

"Excellence" entered the lexicon of business language in the 1980s. Attention to excellence seemed to be a direct result of the erosion during the 1970s of U.S. competitiveness in both the domestic and world markets and the rapid gains achieved by foreign competitors in several key U.S. industries. This loss of the leadership position by many U.S. firms prompted researchers to take a hard look at the practices of successful American and foreign companies to generate useful prescriptions for remedying the performance shortfalls of companies in general.

Studies of excellent companies focus first on identifying companies demonstrating consistently superior financial performance over an extended period of time, and then on uncovering the distinctive organizational traits, management practices, and strategies that were instrumental to their superior performance. For instance, it has been reported that emphasis on planning and a strong planning orientation are among the hallmarks of excellent companies (Gluck, Kaufman, and Walleck, 1980). Reinforcing this point of view, Goldsmith and Clutterbuck (1984) note that successful companies pay close—in some cases fanatic—attention to business planning. Excellent companies view planning as the basis for establishing competitive advantage, and excel in the thoroughness with which their managements link strategic planning to operational decision-making. This is largely accomplished in excellent companies by three mechanisms:

1. a **planning framework** that cuts across organizational boundaries and facilitates strategic decision-making about customer groups and resources,
2. a **planning process** that stimulates entrepreneurial thinking, and
3. a **corporate value system** that reinforces manager commitment to the firm's strategy (Gluck, Kaufman, and Walleck, 1980).

Among the strategic market planning issues examined in earlier chapters were: What product-markets should a firm compete in? What are the relative merits of diversifying into related versus unrelated new product-markets? How should an SBU compete in a particular industry or product-market domain? What are the sources of competitive advantage of an SBU? Studies of excellent companies provide valuable insights into these and other questions germane to strategic market planning. This chapter reviews the major findings of a number of studies of excellent and nonexcellent companies and their implications for strategic market planning. Chapter 11 considers issues in organizational renewal.

AN OVERVIEW OF STUDIES OF
EXCELLENT AND NONEXCELLENT COMPANIES

Six large-scale studies epitomize the work that has been done on organizational excellence. Each provides a different perspective. Two studies (Peters and Waterman, 1982; Loomis 1984a, 1984b, 1989a, 1989b) focus on excellent companies in general. Another two studies are more focused in scope—the distinguishing traits of excellent high-technology companies (Maidique and Hayes, 1984) and midsized growth companies (Clifford and Cavanagh, 1985). Finally, two studies compare the traits of excellent vs. nonexcellent companies (Goldsmith and Clutterbuck, 1984; Strategic Planning Institute, 1984).[2]

Traits of Excellence: America's Best-Run Companies

In a widely acclaimed book, Peters and Waterman (1982) identified eight traits that distinguish excellent companies. Their findings were based on a study of sixty-two companies that demonstrated consistently superior performance from 1961 to 1980. The sixty-two companies studied by Peters and Waterman (1982) were selected on the basis of six measures of long-term financial superiority:

Measures of Growth and Long-Term Wealth Creation:

- compound asset growth rate
- compound equity growth rate
- average ratio of market value to book value

Measures of Return on Capital and Sales:

- average return on total capital
- average return on equity
- average return on sales

According to the authors, the eight distinguishing traits of excellent companies are:

- **A bias for action, for getting on with it**—Excellent companies (ECs) share a do it, try-it, fix-it mentality that helps solve problems quickly.
- **Closeness to the customer**—ECs demonstrate a commitment to customer service, superior product quality, and reliability bordering on obsession.
- **An environment that fosters autonomy and entrepreneurship**—ECs create a work environment conducive to fostering many leaders and innovators throughout the organization, and to encouraging individuals to champion new products.
- **Productivity achieved through people**—ECs know how to motivate their employees. They see the rank and file of the organization as the

root-source of quality and productivity gains, not capital investment as the fundamental source of efficiency improvement.

- **Hands-on, value driven leadership**—The CEOs and other top executives of ECs strive to create an exciting work environment through personal attention, persistence, and direct intervention.
- **Simple organization form, lean staff**—The organization structures in ECs tend to be simple. A lean top-level staff—quite often fewer than 100 corporate staffers—are known to run multibillion dollar corporations.
- **Simultaneous loose-tight properties**—ECs tend to be highly centralized with respect to certain core values such as customer service and product quality. At the same time, they are also highly decentralized and push decision making and autonomy down to the shop floor or new product development team.
- **Stick to the knitting**—ECs resist conglomeracy. They tend to focus on the products, services, and markets they know best.

Traits of Excellence: The Corporate Stars of America

Loomis (1984a, 1984b) identified twenty-five superior financial performers—the corporate stars of America—using the following criteria: (1) an average return on equity (ROE) of at least twenty percent from 1974 to 1983; and (2) an ROE of at least fifteen percent during each year over the same period.

Four common characteristics shared by the thirteen U.S. manufacturing and twelve U.S. service companies were:

1. most are market leaders in one or more product-markets,
2. most are tight with a dollar and extremely cost conscious,
3. most believe in sticking to the businesses they clearly understand, and
4. most are disdainful of bureaucracy.

Two recent studies by Loomis (1989a, 1989b) focusing on the 21 most profitable companies in the *Fortune* Industrial 500 and the 9 most profitable companies in the *Fortune* Service 500 during the decade 1979 to 1988 reaffirm the findings of the earlier studies. Two other hallmarks of excellent companies highlighted in the recent studies are superior product quality and superior customer service.

Traits of Excellence: America's Outstanding High-Technology Companies

Based on a study of the strategies, policies, practices, and decisions of a select sample of high-technology firms, Maidique and Hayes (1984) reported that outstanding U.S. high-technology companies excel in the following six areas:

- **Business focus**—Excellent high-technology companies (EHCs) tend to be highly focused with respect to their product offerings, R&D activities, and corporate priorities, such as superior customer service, new product development, etc.
- **Adaptability**—EHCs evidence a willingness to adapt to and exploit changes in technology, markets, and customers served.
- **Organizational cohesion**—EHCs achieve organizational cohesion by encouraging open communication between divisions and with customers, following a policy of job rotation, creating multidisciplinary project teams, and committing to long-term employment and intensive training.
- **Entrepreneurial culture**—EHCs nurture an entrepreneurial culture by forcing decision-making down the hierarchy, keeping the size of divisions small, tolerating failure, providing a variety of funding channels to encourage risk taking, and providing sufficient time to allow employees to pursue speculative projects that do not necessarily constitute the mainstream activities of the company.
- **Sense of integrity**—ECHs do not knowingly promise what they cannot deliver either to their stockholders, employees, or customers.
- **Hands-on top management**—The CEOs and top management of EHCs tend to be actively involved in the innovation process.

Traits of Excellence: America's Midsized Companies

Clifford and Cavanagh (1985) focused on the traits of excellence of midsized companies. They studied one hundred companies with annual sales ranging from $25 million to $1 billion and achieved sales, asset and profit growth rates in excess of twenty percent from 1975 to 1980. The key findings of their study were:

Excellent mid-sized companies (EMCs) have a distinctive competitive position in the marketplace:

- EMCs strive for and achieve leadership in niche markets rather than competing in large markets.
- EMCs build on their strengths and spend more than their competitors on business functions (service, quality, etc.) critical to success in the niche markets.
- EMCs view innovation as a way of life, strive to continually improve their product/service offering, and tend to compete in terms of value rather than price.
- EMCs are proactive rather than reactive, view agility as more important than continuity, and are responsive to environmental changes.

EMCs have a focused organization:

- EMCs exhibit a sense of mission, shared values, and organizational discipline.
- EMCs are disdainful of bureaucracy, encourage risk taking, tolerate mistakes and failures, and frequently use task forces cutting across functional areas to solve problems.
- EMCs are people oriented, successful people motivators, and are close to their customers.

In EMCs, the CEO is both an architect and a builder:

- The CEOs of EMCs are perseverant, focused on organizational effectiveness, dedicated to learning, close to their customers, calculated risk takers, externally active and involved, and they encourage experimentation.
- The CEOs of EMCs take pains to communicate their strong sense of mission. They pay close attention to the firm's finances and operations and to the external forces that affect them, and are personally involved in every aspect of the business.
- The CEOs of EMCs place top priority on developing and motivating their employees.

Traits of Nonexcellence: The Case of Britain's Troubled Companies

A major methodological limitation of most studies of excellent companies is their exclusive focus on excellent companies. The reported traits of excellence cannot be viewed as unique to excellent companies unless it is empirically demonstrated that these traits are lacking in nonexcellent companies. Goldsmith and Clutterbuck's (1984) study of excellent and nonexcellent companies does suggest that nonexcellent companies indeed lack in traits commonly found in excellent companies. The following are among the traits of nonexcellent companies in the United Kingdom:

- **Poor leadership at the top**—Although top-level executives in troubled companies might be working harder and longer than their counterparts in successful companies, and may even do part of the work of their subordinates, a critical ingredient often missing is their failure and inability to lead.
- **Centralized bureaucracy**—Senior-level managers in troubled companies tend to centralize authority and surround themselves with many layers of management.
- **Ineffective controls**—Rather than the absence of controls, ineffective controls tend to afflict troubled companies.
- **Lack of sharing**—Troubled companies tend to be characterized by a reputation for low pay and lack of employee participation plans.

- **Scattergun approach**—Unsuccessful companies exhibit a tendency to spread themselves too thinly into areas unrelated to, or only remotely related to, their present business.
- **Lack of creativity**—Troubled companies stifle creativity and risk taking, and often operate under the false notion that their current successes will go on indefinitely.
- **Lack of concern for customers**—Troubled companies tend to be indifferent to concerns of their customers.
- **Lack of integrity**—An environment of distrust often prevails in troubled organizations owing to the general lack of clear objectives and performance standards.

Traits of Superior versus Poor Performers: A Contrast of PIMS Businesses

The fact that excellent companies differ from their nonexcellent counterparts is further substantiated by a PIMS (Profit Impact of Market Strategy) study by the Strategic Planning Institute (1984). This study compared four hundred and four excellent PIMS businesses with four hundred and thirty-eight poorly performing PIMS businesses. Businesses with a return on investment (ROI) and sales growth rate (SGR) greater than the sixtieth percentiles for all businesses in the PIMS data base were defined as excellent performers. Businesses with an ROI and SGR below the fortieth percentiles for all businesses in the PIMS data base were defined as poor performers. Significant differences between excellent and nonexcellent businesses were observed along the following dimensions:

A. Competitive position.
   In comparison to poorly performing businesses, excellent businesses (EBs):

   - have more product and process patents to their credit,
   - are more innovative, with a larger percent of their total sales accounted for by new products,
   - offer higher relative product quality for comparable prices, and
   - have higher relative market shares and lower direct costs.

B. Investment ratios and productivity.
   In comparison to poorly performing businesses, EBs have:

   - lower investment to sales ratios,
   - relatively newer plant and equipment,
   - higher operating effectiveness, and
   - higher value added per employee for a given level of investment per employee.

C. Structural characteristics.
   In comparison to poorly performing businesses, EBs:

- compete in more concentrated industries,
- are more vertically integrated,
- operate at higher capacity utilization rates,
- are less unionized, and
- compete in less concentrated end use markets.

CRITIQUE OF STUDIES OF EXCELLENT COMPANIES

Studies of excellent companies have not been free of criticism. As a case in point, consider the Peters and Waterman (1982) study, which is by far the most celebrated study focusing on excellent companies. Since its publication in 1982, *In Search of Excellence* and its translated versions in several languages have sold over seven million copies in both hardcover and softcover editions. Simultaneously, the book has stimulated a number of critical academic reviews and studies aimed at testing its provocative generalizations. The major criticisms lie in four broad areas:

1. research methodology,
2. the performance criteria employed to identify excellent companies,
3. the subsequent deterioration in performance of excellent companies, and
4. the generalizability of traits of excellence.

These issues are briefly discussed next.

Research Methodology

A major methodological limitation of studies focusing exclusively on excellent companies such as that by Peters and Waterman (1982) is that the reported traits of excellence cannot be viewed as truly unique to excellent companies unless it is empirically demonstrated that these traits are lacking in nonexcellent companies. In addition, the Peters and Waterman study, as well as most other studies of excellent companies, view excellence as a dichotomous construct. That is, a firm is designated either as excellent or nonexcellent. However, excellence is a matter of degree, and not something which a firm either does or does not possess. The Peters and Waterman study has also been criticized for its less-than-perfect research base and methodology and its failure to specify precisely how the excellent companies were analyzed and how the eight attributes of excellence were identified (Carroll, 1983).

Criteria Employed for Inferring Superior Corporate Performance

Another frequently voiced criticism centers around the criteria used by Peters and Waterman in defining "excellence" (Bettis and Mahajan, 1985;

Johnson, Natarajan, and Rappaport, 1985). Peters and Waterman's (1982) choice of sixty-two excellent companies for in-depth study was based on their superior performance evaluated in terms of three measures of growth and long-term wealth creation and three measures of return on capital and sales.

As part of a larger study, Bettis and Mahajan (1985) focused on a sub-sample of seventeen diversified firms that were common to their study and Peters and Waterman's list of excellent companies. On the basis of their study, they contend that Peters and Waterman did not adequately consider risk in evaluating performance in selecting their sample of excellent companies.

Johnson, Natarajan, and Rappaport (1985) contend that truly excellent companies are those that create shareholder wealth (dividends plus share price appreciation over a specified period of time). In their study, the authors demonstrate that the companies chosen as excellent by Peters and Waterman failed to show superior shareholder wealth creation.

Table 10.1 summarizes the findings of studies contrasting the performance of the Peters and Waterman sample of excellent companies with other samples of firms employing alternative economic/financial measures of excellence. The findings reported raise questions regarding whether the Peters and Waterman sample of firms would qualify as excellent based on these measures.

The economic performance criteria used by Peters and Waterman in selecting their sample of "excellent" companies have been criticized as being altogether inappropriate by others. Taylor and Paul (1986) suggest that such factors as job creation and employee productivity must also figure in the assessment of corporate excellence. Further echoes of this discontent with the use of narrow financial screens have been voiced by O'Toole (1985) and Tuleja (1985); both consider corporate social responsibility as the ultimate test of a firm's performance.

The eight criteria *Fortune* employs in its annual survey for selecting America's ten most admired companies is another example of an alternative perspective of corporate excellence (*Fortune* 1983–1989). Box 10.1 describes the eight attributes on which companies are evaluated and provides an overview of the *Fortune* annual survey on America's most admired corporations.

Deterioration in Performance of Excellent Companies

The continued performance of some of the companies praised for their excellence by Peters and Waterman has been studied as well. According to *Business Week* (1984), at least fourteen of Peters and Waterman's sample of excellent companies experienced a considerable decline in their performance in subsequent years. The fall from excellence of twelve of these fourteen companies was attributed to their failure to adapt to fundamental

TABLE 10.1
AN EVALUATION OF THE PERFORMANCE OF EXCELLENT COMPANIES USING ALTERNATIVE FRAMES OF REFERENCE

Study	Sample(s)	Purpose	Measures	Findings
Johnson, Natarajan, and Rappaport (1985)	1. Thirty-six publicly traded* firms of Peters and Waterman (P&W) 2. All New York Stock Exchange (NYSE) listed firms 3. *Fortune* 500 firms 4. List of competitor firms in the same industry as P&W firms (matched pairs)	Compare P&W excellent firms with NYSE firms, *Fortune* firms, and competitor firms on economic performance measures.	1. Stock market performance (see Johnson et al. 1985, p. 56) 2. Industry adjusted shareholder returns (see Johnson et al. 1985, p. 58) 3. Residual returns: creation of shareholder wealth (see Johnson et al. 1985, p. 59)	1. P&W firms clearly outperformed NYSE firms (stock market performance). 2. P&W firms did not outperform firms in their *Fortune* 500 industry groups (industry adjusted returns). 3. With the exception of one five-year period P&W firms did not outperform matched competitor firms (residual returns).
Aupperle, Acar, and Booth (1986)	1. P&W firms[†] 2. Firms from the upper quartile of *Forbes* 1000	To see if P&W firms scored above their respective industry averages on financial measures and compare P&W firms with *Forbes* upper-quartile firms	1. ROE, ROA, market valuation, sales growth	1. P&W firms scored above their respective industry averages on all four measures (compared to *Forbes* median industry values). 2. On market value and sales growth, P&W firms were outperformed by the *Forbes* firms (1973–1977). From 1978 to 1982, *Forbes* firms outperformed P&W firms on all four measures.

396

3. For "benchmark" value of the four criteria (Aupperle et al. 1986, 508), P&W firms were outperformed by *Forbes* firms for both time periods on tests of means and proportions.
4. Few P&W firms classified as upper-quartile firms on tests of proportions (Aupperle et al. 1986, p. 510).

Hitt and Ireland (1987)

1. P&W firms[‡]
2. One hundred and eighty-five industrials from *Fortune*'s 1000

Compare P&W firms to *Fortune*'s on market return and scale variables

1. Market return measures: Treynor Index (Hitt and Ireland 1987, p. 92)
2. Scale measures of: leadership; closeness to the customer; innovation, autonomy, and entrepreneurship; productivity through people (Hitt and Ireland 1987, p. 93)

1. No differences between P&W firms and *Fortune*'s on Treynor Index. (In the aggregate, P&W firms were outperformed by *Fortune*'s. In the aggregate, when strategy, diversification, and industry types were considered, no differences were found.
2. No differences between P&W firms and *Fortune*'s on the scale measures. Overall, weak correlations between the Treynor Index and scale measures were found.

*For the years 1964–1983 where data are available.
†For the years 1961–1980 where data are available.
‡For the years 1973–1977 and for 1978–1982 where data are available.
Source: Sharma, Subhash, Richard Netemeyer and Vijan Mahajan (1987), "A Scale to Measure Corporate Excellence," working paper.

BOX **10.1**

AMERICA'S MOST ADMIRED CORPORATIONS: THE FORTUNE ANNUAL SURVEY

A reflection of the interest in America's best-managed companies is the *Fortune* annual survey of America's most admired corporations published since 1983. For its annual survey, *Fortune* polls a sample of over six thousand executives, outside directors, and financial analysts. Subsamples of individuals who are knowledgeable about specific industries are asked to rate (on a scale of poor to excellent) the reputations of the ten largest companies in each of America's thirty largest industries on eight attributes:

1. Quality of management
2. Quality of products or services
3. Innovativeness
4. Value as a long-term investment
5. Financial soundness
6. Ability to attract, develop, and retain talented people
7. Community and environmental responsibility
8. Use of corporate assets

The mean ratings for each company on the eight attributes are computed and firms are ranked on each attribute at the industry level as well as the total sample level. Additionally, by summing up a firm's mean rating on the eight attributes, a composite score of *overall corporate reputation* is computed for each company. Firms are ranked for their overall corporate reputation at the industry level as well as the total sample level on the basis of their corporate reputation score. Companies that have made the ten most admired list on more than one occasion include: IBM, Coca-Cola, 3M, Merck, Johnson & Johnson, Dow Jones Publishing, Boeing, Hewlett Packard, and Anheuser-Busch.

The *Fortune* studies note that while the ten most admired companies rank high in all eight key attributes, the least admired companies are ruled by uncertainty about management, markets, and earnings. The studies also note that the most admired companies enjoy strong positions in high-growth markets, while the least admired companies share the bad luck of being in troubled industries.

changes in their markets. Such findings raise questions about the traits companies need to *sustain* excellence.

It has been reported that some of the excellent companies have found it necessary to abandon attributes of excellence for which they were praised and alter their ways of doing business. The 1984 *Business Week* article cited the case of Hewlett-Packard (identified by Peters and Waterman as one of the United States' excellent companies), whose technology-driven, engineering-oriented culture, in which decentralization and innovation were the religion and entrepreneurs were the gods, was giving way to a marketing culture and growing centralization. The article also emphasized the need for companies to adopt a flexible stance to continue to be superior performers. It pointed out that excellent companies that experienced a decline in their performance were strict adherents to certain practices and failed to react to broad economic and business trends or were inept in adapting to fundamental changes in their markets.

Generalizability of Traits of Excellence

Hitt and Ireland (1987) contend that some of Peters and Waterman's prescriptions for excellence are not completely consistent with contemporary management thought. As noted in chapter three, the contingency perspective views the appropriateness of alternative strategies and organizational structures to be dependent upon certain environmental and organizational conditions. Hitt and Ireland note that, in contrast to the contingency management approach, Peters and Waterman propose the same eight principles of excellence for firms competing in different environments.

IMPLICATIONS FOR STRATEGIC MARKET PLANNING

Impetus for New Research Directions

Despite criticisms of studies of excellent companies, it would be difficult to convincingly argue against the desirability of emulating some of the traits of excellent companies (for example, traits such as an action orientation, closeness to the customer, constant innovation, hands-on, value-driven leadership, etc.) Besides serving as a forum for the widespread dissemination of these and other corporate *traits* and *management practices* that are indeed conducive to superior performance, studies of excellent companies have been instrumental in shaping the research agenda in two respects:

1. Research and dialogue characterized by excessive preoccupation with strategy-formulation-related issues have given way to a more balanced interest in the study of a multitude of factors that determine the performance of the firms (for example, strategy implementation).

2. The controversy surrounding the measures of performance employed to identify excellent companies has triggered interest among researchers in developing alternative measures of corporate performance—both financial and nonfinancial in character.

Choice of Product-Markets

A reported trait of excellent companies that has far-reaching implications for strategic market planning is Peters and Waterman's (1982) assertion that: "excellent companies stick to the knitting and resist conglomeracy." They note that "businesses that pursue some diversification as a basis for stability through adaptation . . . [built on their core skills] tend to be the superior performers" (p. 295). They further argue that successful firms are those that diversify around a single skill. These firms are followed by firms that diversify into related fields. The least successful firms are those that diversify into a wide variety of fields. Other studies of excellent companies that reinforce this point of view are those done by Maidique and Hayes (1984), Goldsmith and Clutterbuck (1984), Loomis (1984a, 1984b, 1989a, 1989b) and Clifford and Cavanagh (1985).

This finding suggests a practical guideline for the addition of new SBUs to a firm's portfolio, as well as for the deletion of SBU from its portfolio. However, advocacy of related diversification and equally strong opposition to unrelated diversification in studies of excellent companies should be treated with caution. Although unrelated diversification has few advocates among Wall Street investment analysts, the cumulative body of evidence suggests that under certain conditions, it may be desirable for a firm to pursue this route.

To date, an extensive body of research focusing on the relationship between diversification strategy and performance has been published.[3] Although the findings are less than unequivocal, a sizeable body of literature suggests that related diversification is more conducive to superior performance than unrelated diversification.

Recent developments in the corporate business scene also seem to provide additional credence for the "stick to the knitting" philosophy. For instance, in recent years, the corporate world has been witness to the divestment of unrelated businesses by a number of firms. The divestment of shipping and energy businesses by R. J. Reynolds, Inc., of trucking and sporting goods businesses by PepsiCo. Inc., of financial services and car rental businesses by RCA, Inc. (before its merger with General Electric), and of baking operations by ITT, Inc., just to name a few, seems indicative of the "stick-to-the-knitting" mindset. Brooks (1984) attributes the recent spate of divestments of unrelated businesses by firms to the realization among business practitioners that diversifying into areas unrelated to a firm's core skills is generally unprofitable.

Davidson (1987) notes that the current spate of business divestitures reflects the growing belief among executives that there are limits to the number of businesses managers can understand and that businesses are worth more to managers that understand them because they can run them better. The trend toward divestitures of unrelated businesses coupled with the trend toward the acquisition of competing firms (Burger Chef by Hardees hamburger chain; Western Airlines by Delta Airlines; Fairchild Semiconductors by National Semiconductors), or the acquisition of firms whose product lines complement or broaden a firm's product line (Entenmann Bakeries by General Foods; Kentucky Fried Chicken by PepsiCo's Restaurant Division, whose other two restaurant chains are Pizza Hut and Taco Bell) also seems to reflect managers' misgivings about their ability to operate many unrelated businesses and their preference for focusing on few product-market domains.

Despite a large body of supportive evidence, it is important to realize that the decision to stay within narrowly defined business boundaries should be based on careful corporate deliberations, and not on blind faith in the popular "stick close to the knitting" philosophy. A review of evidence refuting the "stick to the knitting" philosophy highlights the risks inherent in such blind faith.

Four cases illustrate the opportunity costs that would have been incurred by some companies if they had chosen to blindly embrace the "stick to the knitting/resist conglomeracy" philosophy:

1. Until recently, the Singer Corporation derived a larger percentage of its revenues and profits from its aerospace operations than from sewing machines. In 1986, the company chose to spin-off its sewing machines division—its industry of origin—to its shareholders as a separate entity.
2. Gould currently derives a large percentage of its revenue from the high-growth semiconductor electronics industry and has exited from the low-margin, intensely competitive automobile battery industry—its industry of origin.
3. Companies such as NL Industries (formerly National Lead Company), and Insilco (formerly International Silver Company) are either no longer involved in their industries of origin, or derive only a very small percentage of their total revenues and profits from their industries of origin.
4. Greyhound Corporation, whose name is synonymous with intercity bus transport, sold its Greyhound Business division (United States) in 1987.

A relevant question to ask in these contexts is "what would have happened to Singer, Gould, NL Industries, Insilco, and other companies that have pursued similar courses of action had they chosen to resist conglomeracy and stick to the knitting?" Clearly, a more balanced perspective on the appropriateness of pursuing related versus unrelated diversification and the contingency variables that determine the appropriateness of alternative diversification strategies is needed. Ohmae's (1985, p. 4) word of caution in this regard is both timely and appropriate:

> It's become increasingly dangerous to ignore questions about the fundamental viability of a company's traditional business. For example, Brother realized that its basic industry—sewing machines—was shrinking as more and more Japanese women opted to buy ready-to-wear clothing. Relying on its expertise in precision machinery and its newly acquired microelectronics technology, Brother aggressively diversified into office automation equipment and became one of the world's largest electronic typewriter manufacturers.

Judgments regarding the appropriateness of diversifying into unrelated areas should also take into account the *impetus for diversification* and the *availability of industry alternatives into which to diversify.* In reference to the *concept of defensive diversification,* Weston and Mansinghka (1971) point out that firms located in product-markets that constrain corporate growth or profitability are the most likely candidates for diversification. Further, firms or businesses in low opportunity markets are likely to find a similar lack of opportunity in related markets that they could enter through *constrained diversification.* While studies by several industrial organization economists (Weston and Mansinghka 1971; Holzman, Copeland, and Hayya, 1975) indicate that unrelated diversification does not lead to higher corporate returns, Weston and Mansinghka (1971), note that defensive diversification (out of industries with low profitability into unrelated areas) enables firms to increase their profitability in relation to the status quo.

Leontiades' (1986) also provides a timely counterargument to the widely held view that unrelated diversified companies are not usually successful. He highlights the need for further research on conglomerate companies quite succinctly:

> For over three decades, diversification into unrelated businesses has been a strategy of business without a respectable body of scholarly opinion to support it. Since the strategy appears to be here to stay, one needs to try to begin to understand it (p. 81).

In this context, three questions merit further examination:

1. Is related diversification always desirable?
2. Is unrelated diversification always undesirable?
3. Could it be that the problem is not with the unrelated diversification strategy, but with the firm's approach toward managing unrelated businesses? For instance, is it conceivable that problems such as a mismatch between strategy and structure, a lack of controls, and so forth are the root cause of failed unrelated diversification strategies?

Choice of Generic Strategy

Cost leadership, differentiation, cost focus, and differentiation focus constitute the generic strategies available to firms (Porter, 1985), Studies of excellent companies seem to generally view differentiation as a more effective basis for achieving competitive advantage than cost leadership. For instance, Peters and Austin (1985) note that there are only two ways for a firm to create and sustain superior performance over the long run: (1) by taking exceptional care of its customers via superior service and superior quality; and (2) by constantly innovating. The authors note that excellent companies incorporate these two ways of sustaining strategic competitive advantage by listening, trusting, and respecting the dignity and creative potential of each person in the organization. Leadership (management by wandering around or MBWA) at all levels of the organization is viewed as the element that catalyzes the other three elements—caring for customers, constant innovation and turned-on people—in excellent companies.

A CONCLUDING NOTE

Excellent companies have been variously described as customer-oriented, proactive, aggressive, innovative, pioneering, flexible, and versatile. More importantly, their present state of excellence is attributed to the dedicated efforts of highly motivated and competent managers at all levels in the organization over a sustained period of time. All industrialized economies are characterized by a mix of excellent, mediocre, and poor companies. Although no magic formula or surefire steps for achieving corporate excellence exist, many of the action tendencies and behavior patterns of excellent companies identified in this and other studies might be worthy of emulation by other companies. However, the important question is "Which ones?" This is best answered by individual managers and companies functioning in specific contexts, and should be based on careful deliberation regarding the appropriateness of these actions in specific situations.

The controversy surrounding studies of excellent companies has been instrumental in stimulating a lively debate and research on two key issues:

1. What organizational traits and management practices are conducive to superior corporate performance or corporate excellence in the long run? To what extent are these traits universal and/or timeless?
2. What criteria should be employed to evaluate superior corporate performance? Should corporate excellence be evaluated solely on the basis of economic performance measures or based on a mix of economic and noneconomic performance measures?

Although a variety of issues remain unresolved, the various perspectives and viewpoints on excellent companies reflect the emerging consensus among academicians, practitioners, and consultants that the right strategy alone cannot help a company move forward. Corporate success in a competitive environment is increasingly viewed as determined by the joint effect of a number of factors. The McKinsey 7-S framework, for example, lists seven factors that interact with one another and the firm's environment in determining overall organizational effectiveness. In addition to strategy, structure, and systems (the hardware), the 7-S framework lists four other factors (staff, skills, style, and superordinate goals) as the soft-

TABLE 10.2
A SUMMARY OF THE SEVEN Ss

1. *Strategy.* A coherent set of actions aimed at gaining a sustainable advantage over competition, improving position vis-à-vis customers, or allocating resources.

2. *Structure.* The organization chart and accompanying baggage that show who reports to whom and how tasks are both divided up and integrated.

3. *Systems.* The processes and flows that show how an organization gets things done from day to day (information systems, capital budgeting systems, manufacturing processes, quality control systems, and performance measurement systems all would be good examples).

4. *Style.* Tangible evidence of what management considers important based on the way it collectively spends time and attention and uses symbolic behavior. It is not what management says is important: It is the way management behaves.

5. *Staff.* The people in the organization. Here it is very useful to think not about individual personalities but about corporate demographics.

6. *Shared values (or superordinate goals).* The values that go beyond, but might well include, simple goal statements in determining corporate destiny. To fit the concept, these values must be shared by most people in an organization.

7. *Skills.* A derivative of the rest. Skills are those capabilities that are possessed by an organization as a whole as opposed to the people in it. (The concept of corporate skill as something different from that of the summation of the people in it seems difficult for many to grasp: however, some organizations that hire only the best and the brightest cannot get seemingly simple things done, while others perform extraordinary feats with ordinary people.)

Source: R. H. Waterman, Jr., "The Seven Elements of Strategic Fit," p. 71. Reprinted by permission from the *Journal of Business Strategy,* Winter 1982. Copyright © 1982. Warren, Gorham & Lamont Inc., 210 South Street, Boston, Mass. All Rights Reserved.

ware of the organization. A summary of the seven Ss is presented in Table 10.2. These factors are hypothesized to interact with one another and with the firm's environment in determining a firm's degree of success. Pascale and Athos (1981) attribute the success of many Japanese companies to their meticulous attention to the soft Ss, which supposedly act as lubricants in the organizational machine and prevent the hard Ss from grinding each other away. Furthermore, the authors note that the prime determinant for outstanding U.S. companies is their management—their grasp of, and effective utilization of the seven Ss—and their ability to link corporate purposes and ways of realizing them with human values, as well as economic measures such as profit and efficiency. Chapter eleven provides a more detailed discussion of three other organizational variables—culture, leadership, and entrepreneurship—that play an instrumental role in strategic market planning.

NOTES

1. Sections of this chapter are adapted from Varadarajan (1983, 1989a, 1989b) and Varadarajan and Ramanujam (1989).

2. Other noteworthy contributions that may be of interest to readers include the writings of

   - Ouchi (1981) on the people orientation of excellent companies,
   - Deal and Kennedy (1982) on corporate culture,
   - Pascale and Athos (1981) on the art of Japanese management,
   - Chakravarthy's (1986) comparison of excellent and nonexcellent firms in the computer industry in terms of a number of financial, economic, and slack measures,
   - Hobbs' (1987) work on fourteen excellent U.S. companies that demonstrated consistently superior performance for from ten to twenty-five years,
   - Waterman's (1987) study of the traits of renewing companies—organizational attributes that are conducive to achieving and sustaining excellence,
   - Peters' (1987) prescriptions for thriving under chaos, which is based on the premise that sustaining excellence is almost impossible in an environment of intense competition and rapid change, and
   - *Business Month's* (previously published as *Dun's Review* and *Dun's Business Month*) annual special report titled, "U.S.'s Five Best-Managed Companies." Over the period from 1972 to 1987, seventy-nine U.S. companies have been honored by *Business Month's* editors for best exemplifying those qualities of management that a company needed to survive and prosper in a particular year.

3. See Ramanujam and Varadarajan (1989) for an extensive review of research on diversification and performance.

REFERENCES

Aupperle, Kenneth E., William Acar, and David E. Booth (1986), "An Empirical Critique of 'In Search of Excellence': How Excellent Are the Excellent Companies?," *Journal of Management*, 12, Winter, 499–512.

Bettis, Richard and Vijay Mahajan (1985), "Risk-Return Performance of Diversified Firms," *Management Science*, 31, July, 785–799.

Brooks, Geraldine (1984), "Some Concerns Find That the Push to Diversify Was A Costly Mistake," *Wall Street Journal*, October 2, 37.

Business Week (1984), "Who's Excellent Now?" *Business Week*, November 5, 76–88.

———— (1987), "How the Best Get Better," September 14, 98–120.

Carroll, Daniel T. (1983), "A Disappointing Search for Excellence," *Harvard Business Review*, 61, November–December, 78–88.

Chakravarthy, Balaji S. (1986), "Measuring Strategic Performance," *Strategic Management Journal*, 7, September–October, 437–458.

Clifford, D. K., Jr. and R. E. Cavanagh (1985), *The Winning Performance: How America's High Growth Midsize Companies Succeed*, New York: Bantam Books.

Davidson, Kenneth (1987), "Do Megamergers Make Sense?," *Journal of Business Strategy*, 7, Winter, 40–48.

Deal, Terrence E. and Allan A. Kennedy (1982), *Corporate Cultures*, Reading, Massachusetts: Addison Wesley.

Dun's Business Month (1981 to 1987), "The Five Best-Managed Companies," *Dun's Business Month*, December 1981, 59–78; December 1982, 47–61; December 1983, 37–51; December 1984, 35–49; December 1985, 31–43; December 1986, 25–37; December 1987, 22–37.

Dun's Review (1972 to 1980), "The Five Best-Managed Companies," *Dun's Review*, December 1972, 3, 33–41; December 1973, 51–61, December 1974, 43–56; December 1975, 41–57, December 1976, 39–50; December 1977, 47–61; December 1978, 29–44; December 1979, 45–60, December 1980, 39–51.

Fortune (1983 to 1989), "America's Most Admired Corporations," *Fortune*, January 10, 1983, 34–44; January 9, 1984, 50–61; January 7, 1985, 18–30; January 6, 1986, 16–27; January 19, 1987, 18–31; January 18, 1988, 32–52; January 30, 1989, 68–94.

Gluck, Frederick W., Stephen P. Kaufman, and A. Steven Walleck (1980), "Strategic Management for Competitive Advantage," *Harvard Business Review*, 58, July–August, 154–161.

Goldsmith, W. and D. Clutterbuck (1984), *The Winning Streak*, London: Weidenfeld and Nicholson.

Hitt, Michael A. and R. Duane Ireland (1987), "Peters and Waterman Revisited: The Unended Quest for Excellence," *Academy of Management Executive*, 1, May, 91–98.

Hobbs, James B. (1987), *Corporate Staying Power*, Lexington, Mass.: Lexington Books.

Holzman, Oscar J., Ronald M. Copeland, and Jack Hayya (1975), "Income Measures of Conglomerate Performance," *Quarterly Review of Economics and Business*, 5, Summer, 67–78.

Johnson, W. B., A. Natarajan, and A. Rappaport (1985), "Shareholder Returns and Corporate Excellence," *The Journal of Business Strategy*, 6, Fall, 52–62.

Leontiades, Milton (1986), *Managing the Unmanagable: Strategies for Success Within the Conglomerate*, Reading, Mass.: Addison-Wesley.

Loomis, Carol J. (1984a), "Corporate Stars That Brightened a Decade," *Fortune*, April 30, 224–232.

Loomis, Carol J. (1984b), "How the Service Stars Managed to Sparkle," *Fortune*, June 11, 156–166.

Loomis, Carol J. (1989a), "Secrets of the Superstars," *Fortune*, April 24, 50–62.

Loomis, Carol J. (1989b), "Stars of the Service 500," *Fortune*, June 5, 54–62.

Maidique, Modesto A. and Robert H. Hayes (1984), "The Art of High-Technology Management," *Sloan Management Review*, 26, Winter, 1–31.

Ohmae, Kenichi (1983), "Japan's Admiration for U.S. Methods is an Open Book," *The Wall Street Journal*, October 10, 23.

Ohmae, Kenichi (1985), "In Praise of Planning," *Planning Review*, November, 4.

O'Toole, J. (1985), *Vanguard Management*, New York: Doubleday.

Ouchi, William G. (1981), *Theory Z: How American Business Can Meet the Japanese Challenge*, Reading, Mass: Addison-Wesley.

Palia, Kyama A., Michael A. Hitt, R. Duane Ireland, and Yezdi H. Godiwalla (1982), *Grand Corporate Strategy and Critical Functions*, New York: Prager Publishers, Inc.

Pascale, Richard T. and Anthony G. Athos (1981), *The Art of Japanese Management: Application for American Executives*, New York: Simon and Schuster, Inc.

Pascale, Richard T. (1982), "Our Curious Addiction to Corporate Grand Strategy," *Fortune*, January 25, 115–116.

Peters, Thomas J. and Robert H. Waterman Jr. (1982), *In Search of Excellence: Lessons From America's Best Run Companies*, New York: Harper & Row.

Peters, Thomas J. and Nancy Austin (1985), *A Passion for Excellence*, New York: Random House.

Peters, Thomas J. (1987), *Thriving on Chaos: Handbook for a Management Revolution*, New York: Knopf.

Porter, Michael E. (1985), *Competitive Advantage: Creating and Sustaining Superior Performance*, New York: Free Press.

Ramanujan Vaeudevan and P. Rajan Varadarajan (1989), "Research on Corporate Diversification: A Review and Synthesis," *Strategic Management Journal*.

Sharma, Subhash, Richard Netemeyer and Vijay Mahajan (1987), "A Scale to Measure Corporate Excellence," working paper.

Strategic Planning Institute (1984), "In Search of Evidence: A P. S. to Peters and Waterman's Book," *Proceedings of the PIMS Conference '84*, Cambridge, Mass.: The Strategic Planning Institute.

Taylor, J. W. and R. N. Paul (1986), "The Real Meaning of Excellence," *Business*, 36, July–September, 27–33.

Tuleja, Ted (1985), *Beyond the Bottom Line*, New York: Penguin Books.

Varadarajan, P. Rajan (1983), "Content of Effective Organizational Strategies: An Analysis of *Dun's Review* Reports on U.S.'s Best-managed Companies," in P.E. Murphy et al., (eds.) *1983 AMA Summer Marketing Educators' Conference Proceedings* (Chicago: American Marketing Association, August 1983, 316–319.

Varadarajan, P. Rajan (1989a), "Pathways to Corporate Excellence in Retailing," Texas A & M University Center for Retailing Studies-Arthur Anderson & Co. *Retailing Issues Letter*, Volume 2 (February).

Varadarajan, P. Rajan (1989b), "Perspectives on Corporate Excellence in Retailing," in W. D. Darden (ed.) *Proceedings* of Symposium on Patronage Behavior and Retail Strategic Planning, Baton Rouge (May).

Varadarajan, P. Rajan and Vaeudevan Ramanujam (1989), "Strategic and Organizational Sources of Superior Corporate Performance," in H. E. Glass (ed.) *Handbook of Business Strategy: 1988/1989* Yearbook, New York: Warren, Gorham and Lamont, Inc.

Waterman, Jr., Robert H., Thomas J. Peters and Julian R. Phillips (1980), "Structure is Not Organization," *Business Horizons*, 23, June, 14–26.

Waterman, Jr., Robert H. (1987), *The Renewal Factor*, New York: Bantam Books.

Weston, J. Fred and Surenda K. Mansinghka (1971), "Tests of the Efficiency Performance of Conglomerate Firms," *Journal of Finance*, 26, September, 919–936.

CHAPTER 11

ORGANIZATION RENEWAL:

THE ROLE OF CORPORATE CULTURE,

LEADERSHIP, AND

ENTREPRENEURSHIP

Introduction

Corporate Culture
  Dimensions of Culture
  Manifestations of Corporate Culture
  Cultural Implications for Strategic Market
    Planning
      Product-Market Choice and Performance
      Portfolio Design and Acquisitions
      Portfolio Management
  Culture Maintenance and Change: Towards a
    "Marketing" Culture

Leadership
  A Look at Corporate Leaders
  Leadership and Vision
  Leadership and Strategic Thinking

Corporate Entrepreneurship
  Central Issues in Corporate
    Entrepreneurship and Innovation
      A General Management Perspective
      Integrating Institutional and Technical
        Processes
  Organizational Types and Entrepreneurship
  Institutionalizing Innovation and the
    Functional Role of Marketing

A Concluding Note

References

INTRODUCTION

The 1980s witnesses a rebirth of academic and practitioner interest in the functioning of the corporation. Stimulated in part by the views expressed in *In Search of Excellence* (Peters and Waterman, 1982), how firms are led and managed became a central concern of scholars and executives alike. In many respects, attention to corporate structure gave way to attention to corporate style and planning frameworks gave way to perspectives on people. Accordingly, the unifying theme of this chapter is organizational renewal, or attention to the behavioral factors that are instrumental in creating an organization that shapes rather than reacts to the events in its external environment. By implication, this chapter addresses the ever-present problem of "organizational drift," or the loss of corporate identity, opportunism, and ultimately, competitive advantage. Three subthemes are present in this chapter:

1. the literature on strategic market planning is distinguished by the conscious or unconscious omission of behavioral factors,
2. behavioral factors, such as culture, leadership, and entrepreneurship, have a place in the study and execution of strategic market planning, and
3. attention to organizational factors may be the needed stimulus to push strategic market planning to its next phase of development and practice.

This chapter focuses on three specific topics: (1) culture, (2) leadership, and (3) corporate entrepreneurship and innovation. These topics are inextricably related and an abundant and diverse literature exists on each. Surprisingly, however, academicians and practitioners have tended to view each subject independently. Moreover, research, commentary, and prescriptions on these topics have often raised more questions than they have answered. For example:

1. what role might corporate culture play in the choice of product-markets to add, retain, or delete?
2. how does leadership affect the strategic market planning process?
3. how can a corporation become more entrepreneurial in its orientation?

While no simple answers to these questions are given in this chapter, insights are provided that hopefully illuminate the potential contributions each can make to the future study and practice of strategic market planning.

CORPORATE CULTURE

Even though the notion of culture burst upon the corporate landscape in 1980 (*Business Week*, 1980), the concept itself is not new. Fifty years ago Chester Barnard (1938), in his classic treatise, *Functions of the Executive*, made frequent reference to an organization's informal organization, which contained many parallels with contemporary culture. For example, he observed that the direct effects of informal organizations are shared and communicated customs, mores, folklore, institutions, and social norms and ideals. This view is similar to the variety of definitions of culture used today. For example, organizational culture has been defined as:

. . . some underlying structure of meaning, that persists over time, constraining people's perception, interpretation, and behavior (Jelinck, Smircich, and Hirsch, 1983, p. 337);

. . . a pattern of beliefs and expectations shared by organizational members (Schwartz and Davis, 1981, p. 33);

. . . the system of . . . publicly and collectively accepted meanings operating for a given group at a given time. This system of terms, focus, categories, and images interprets a people's own situation to themselves (Pettigrew, 1979, p. 574);

. . . shared philosophies, ideologies, values, beliefs, expectations, and names (Kilmann and Saxton, 1983).

Dimensions of Culture

These definitions, including numerous others, have three commonalities. Most importantly, the idea of "meanings or understandings" permeates any and all discussions of culture. "Meanings" in this context relate to the frames of reference used by people to describe corporate action and often themselves. Often these frames of reference point toward heroic acts, symbols, how business is conducted, and company values, beliefs, or purpose. A second commonality is communication. In other words, meanings are communicated—verbally and symbolically through formal or informal codes of behavior. A third commonality is sharedness (Sathe, 1983). That is, culture exhibits itself in *shared things* ("We don't wear ties"), *shared sayings* ("We are customer-oriented"), *shared doings* (team efforts), and *shared feelings* ("We care").

The nuances of corporate culture are beyond the scope of this discussion.[1] However, it is instructive to at least consider the dimensions of a corporate culture. Reynolds' (1986) content analysis of the writings of Ansoff (1979), Deal and Kennedy (1982), Harrison (1972; 1978), Hofstede (1980) and Peters and Waterman (1982) uncovered fourteen dimensions of culture as shown in Table 11.1. These dimensions portray a firm's dominant culture.[2]

TABLE 11.1
DIMENSIONS OF CORPORATE CULTURE

1. *External Orientation* . . . . *Internal Orientation*
   (Focus on customers) (Focus on internal activities)

2. *Task Emphasis* . . . . *Social Emphasis*
   (Focus on work or job to be (Focus on personal needs of
   done) people)

3. *Safety* . . . . *Risk*
   (Cautious/conservative emphasis) (Emphasis on change)

4. *Conformity* . . . . *Individuality*
   (Focus on uniformity) (Focus on the idiosyncratic)

5. *Individual Rewards* . . . . *Group Rewards*
   (Focus on individual (Focus on team contributions)
   contributions)

6. *Individual Decision-making* . . . . *Collective Decision-making*
   (Individual choice and (Committee or group choice and
   implementation) implementation)

7. *Ad hocery* . . . . *Planning*
   (No guidelines, action) (Systematic planning)

8. *Stability* . . . . *Innovation*
   (Focus on known procedures, (Focus on novel solutions, prod-
   products, and services) ucts, and services)

9. *Cooperation* . . . . *Competition*
   (Fellow workers are colleagues) (Fellow workers are competitors)

10. *Simple Organization Structure* . . . *Complex Organizational Structure*
    (Simple informal and formal (Complex informal and formal
    structure and processes) structure and processes)

11. *Informal Procedures* . . . . *Formal Procedures*
    (Little formalization) (Detailed rules for behavior

12. *Centralized Decision-making* . . . *Decentralized Decision-making*
    (Focused sources of approval) (Multiple sources of approval)

13. *High Loyalty* . . . . *Low Loyalty*
    (Organization is focus of (Diffused focus of attention)
    attention)

14. *Intrinsic Commitment* . . . . *Extrinsic Commitment*
    (Commitment to firm based on (Commitment to firm based on
    opportunity for self-expression, financial rewards, association
    interesting work, etc.) with firm, etc.)

Source: Adapted from Paul D. Reynolds (1986), "Organizational Culture as Related to Industry, Position and Performance: A Preliminary Report," *Journal of Management Studies* (May), pp. 334–354.

Manifestations of Corporate Culture

Corporate culture manifests itself in the countless details of organizational life. The formal and informal management control systems employed by firms mirror its culture (Ray, 1986; Lebas and Weigenstein, 1986) as does its reward system (Kerr and Slocum, 1987). Thompson and Wildavsky (1986) describe how culture may affect the process by which information enters and is interpreted in corporate settings, and suggest that leadership itself is a function of organizational culture. In a similar vein, Sathe (1983) suggests that the decision-making process itself is influenced by culture, since organization members have consistent assumptions and preferences.

An illuminating case study of Texas Instruments (TI) and Hewlett-Packard (H-P) shows how cultural variables are manifested in a variety of organizational characteristics (Wheelwright, 1984). As shown in Table 11.2, TI and H-P evidenced very different cultures in the early 1980s. According to Wheelwright (1984, p. 28–29):

> . . . Texas Instruments tends to be driven by measures of financial performance and competition, and it values management for cost reduction; a primary role of top management is to decide the market strategy for products and to allocate the necessary resources; planning units are treated as largely autonomous and often differ significantly from the more integrated operating organization; performance evaluation is the basis for financial rewards for individuals . . .
>
> In contrast, (Hewlett-Packard) is built around a management style based on cooperation and team (family) effort. The CEO leads by example and emphasis, not fiat; product-market areas are selected and competitive advantages are preserved with products that are of better quality than competitors' or are unique to the firm and its resources; planning and operating are done by the same groups with line management responsible for both functions; . . . values and environment are more important than near-term financial goals.

While it is clear that differences and not similarities in cultural variables were emphasized in this illustration, the message is no less important. Corporate culture may manifest itself in corporate performance. As Wheelwright (1984) later documented, Hewlett-Packard's return on assets and operating profit exceeded those for Texas Instruments. This view is shared by Buzzell and Gale (1987, p. 21), who in their discussion of strategy related to the PIMS program, state: "No doubt companies differ in terms of culture, and such differences unquestionably affect performance." However, a word of caution is necessary. To conclude that the cultural description of Hewlett-Packard should be the prototype for any and all companies or that one culture fits all would be incorrect. Rather, the view expressed by Reynolds (1986, p. 343–344) would seem more plausible:

Relative success in a given industry may be associated with a distinctive organizational culture, but may be quite different from the culture found in successful organizations in other industries. To expect the same sociocultural system, cultural systems, and organizational participants to foster success in all industries seems quite naive.

TABLE 11.2
TEXAS INSTRUMENTS AND HEWLETT-PACKARD CULTURE COMPARISON (EARLY 1980s)

Texas Instruments	Hewlett-Packard
1. SKILLS SUPPORTED AND VALUED	
Engineering (Product and Process)	Product Development
Manufacturing	Marketing
Cost Reduction Management	New Products Management
2. TOP MANAGEMENT'S STRATEGY ROLE	
Strategist	People Development
Resource Allocation	Leadership on Values
Global View	Detailed (Tactical) Involvement
3. ORGANIZATION STRUCTURES	
Large Production Operations	Small Operating Units
Integrated Divisions	Autonomous Divisions
Corporate-Level Staff	Division-Level Staff
4. STRATEGIC PLANNING PROCEDURES	
Analysis by Staff	Analysis by Line
Evaluation of a Few Big Bets	Screening of Many Small Bets
Rational, Explicit, and Precise	Subjective, Implicit, and Imprecise
5. PERFORMANCE EVALUATION AND PEOPLE MOTIVATION	
Individual Evaluation	Team Evaluation
Competitive (Internally)	Cooperative (Internally)
Winners May Not Keep Earnings	Winning Teams Keep Earnings
Short-Term Rewards (Bonuses)	Long-Term Status (Stock Ownership)
6. THE FIRM'S EVALUATION OF ITSELF	
Competitive Status (External)	Organizational Health (Internal)
Organizational Innovativeness (Internal)	Technical Superiority (External)
Profits or Financial Returns	Long-Term Capabilities

Source: Steven C. Wheelwright (1984), "Strategy, Management, and Strategic Planning Approaches," *Interfaces* (January–February), p. 28.

Others would agree with this viewpoint, albeit from a different perspective. Barney (1986), for example, argues that culture can result in a sustained competitive advantage, and by implication, superior corporate performance, only when three conditions are met. First, the culture must be *valuable.* That is, a culture must enable the firm to perform in ways that add financial value to the organization. Second, the culture must be *rare;* it must possess qualities not common to its competitors. Third, the culture must be *imperfectly imitable.* This condition means that competitors cannot engage in culture change efforts that will replicate the firm's culture. If they try, they will be at some disadvantage (in reputation, or experience) when compared with the firm they are attempting to imitate.

Cultural Implications for Strategic Market Planning

The previous discussion would suggest that corporate culture, expressed in varied ways, should also affect company strategic market planning and performance. Unfortunately, little scholarly research has specifically addressed this issue (Despandé and Parasuraman, 1984; Despandé and Webster, 1989). Yet there are numerous examples from practice that would suggest that culture-related variables do surface in product-market choice and the design and management of product-market portfolios.

Product-Market Choice and Performance The most prevalent evidence of culture-related variables affecting strategic market planning lies in product-market choice. Gillette never took advantage of a market opportunity for feminine hygiene sprays in the 1970s even though the aerosol technology and experience in marketing feminine products existed. Why? Gillette executives could not bring themselves to discuss the subject in their business conversations (Corley, 1972). Texas Instrument's ill-fated efforts in the consumer electronics market have been attributed to its culture, which emphasized R&D initiated innovations rather than consumer-oriented product development (*Business Week*, 1982). Early, unsuccessful efforts by Apple Computer and Tandy to penetrate the corporate personal computer market have been attributed to the cultural underpinnings of both companies (*Business Week*, 1984a; *Business Week*, 1987).

Portfolio Design and Acquisitions Buzzell and Gale (1987, p. 233) note that "Companies that stray outside their domain of knowledge usually have difficulty developing . . . a 'culture' that accommodates all businesses in their portfolio. As one might expect, they have trouble trying to run high-tech businesses in tandem with low-tech businesses, or labor-intensive businesses alongside capital-intensive businesses." Such has been the case with Johnson & Johnson in its move to diversify its portfolio to include high technology businesses alongside its less technical consumer product businesses during the 1980s. According to one observer, "More than one successful CEO has found that changing his company's mix of businesses is a lot easier than changing managers' attitudes" (*Business Week*, 1984a).

The clearest example of culture affecting portfolio design and acquisition decisions rests in the acquisition of Electronic Data Systems (EDS) by General Motors (GM) in 1984. Merging EDS and GM was fraught with cultural difficulties resulting from differences in dress codes, business philosophy, and operating style (*Business Week*, 1985b). Ultimately, Roger Smith, Chairman of GM and H. Ross Perot, Chairman and Founder of EDS, became embroiled in a highly publicized confrontation over how GM should be managed. Perot and several of his lieutenants ultimately departed EDS.

Portfolio Management Despandé and Parasuraman (1986) have attempted to relate culture to business portfolio management practices. Based on the work of Deal and Kennedy (1982), they suggest a contingency approach to matching culture with product-market life cycle and industry evolution within the growth-share matrix developed by the Boston Consulting Group described in chapter three. Deal and Kennedy (1982) identified four generic cultures or "tribes" based on two dimensions: (1) degree of risk present in the firms' activities, and (2) the rate of feedback on the success or failure of business decisions or strategies. The four generic cultures based on risk and feedback are shown below (Despandé and Parasuraman, 1986):

GENERIC CULTURE	DEGREE OF RISK	RATE OF FEEDBACK
"Tough Guy/Macho"	High	Fast
"Bet Your Company"	High	Slow
"Work Hard/Play Hard"	Low	Fast
"Process"	Low	Slow

Despandé and Parasuraman (1986) argue that the culture must match the risk-feedback dimensions; otherwise, the likelihood of failure will increase. They propose the scheme and assignment of cultures shown in Table 11.3.

It is noteworthy that the contingency view of culture parallels similar thinking in the literature on leadership. Recently, management scholars have debated the appropriateness of assigning managers on the basis of product life cycle, business unit mission, and competitive strategy (Leontiades, 1982; Kerr, 1982; Szilogyi and Schweiger, 1984; Gupta, 1986; Kerr and Jackofsky, 1989). The merits of this action, like the notion of culture proposed by Despandé and Parasuraman (1986), represent an interesting area for inquiry. Indeed, the link between culture and leadership is discussed at greater length later in this chapter.

TABLE 11.3
MATCHING CULTURE AND THE FIRM'S BUSINESS PORTFOLIO

	Relative Market Share	
	High	Low
High Market Growth Rate	*Product Life Cycle Stage:* Growth *BCG Descriptor:* Star *Culture:* "Bet Your Company"	*Product Life Cycle Stage:* Introduction *BCG Descriptor:* Question Mark *Culture:* "Tough Guy/ Macho"
Low	*Product Life Cycle Stage:* Maturity *BCG Descriptor:* Cash Cow *Culture:* "Work Hard/Play Hard"	*Product Life Cycle Stage:* Decline *BCG Descriptor:* Dog *Culture:* "Process"

Source: Adapted from Rohit Despandé and A. Parasuraman (1986), "Linking Corporate Culture to Strategic Planning," *Business Horizons* (May/June), pp. 28–37.

Culture Maintenance and Change: Towards a "Marketing" Culture

The recognition that culture and strategy must be in concert has been recognized by scholars and practitioners alike (Smircich, 1983; Schwartz and Davis 1981; Uttal, 1983; Cooper, 1987). However, two important questions remain unanswered:

1. How is culture preserved?
2. How can a culture be shaped to be consistent with managerial purpose?

Surprisingly, little scholarly attention has been directed at either question. Fombrun (1986) suggests there are three characteristics of culture that insure continuity rather than change. The first of these is *reproduction*, which encompasses lineage systems or executive succession in a firm. According to Fombrun, one only has to look at the backgrounds of top executives to uncover the values and assumptions underlying strategic decisions and frame of reference. The second is the *institutionalization* of the behaviors, routines, systems, or policies that reinforce the expressed or implied values of the firm. Finally, a culture *legitimizes* or justifies the activities of the corporation. That is, success resulting from certain cultural behavior perpetuates the extant culture at a point in time. Stated in more succinct terms, John Sculley, Chairman of Apple Computer, Inc. notes (*Inc.*, 1987, p. 58):

> I think the concept of culture has been misused a lot. It tends to limit a company by putting too much emphasis on tradition, on yesterday's myths and rituals, whose sole value is that they derive from an earlier time. Culture is a feel good tool, a way for a company to remain comfortable with its habits. It is something that looks backward at the past rather than forward toward change.

These observations provide useful insights into culture change and the creating of a "marketing" culture. First, the lineage system in corporations might be circumvented. Indeed, many corporations have done so in recent years by recruiting top executives from outside the firm and promoting marketing professionals to CEO status (Heidrick and Struggles, 1987). Breaking entrenched institutionalized behaviors is a second means of altering a culture. In fact, these might be the most difficult behaviors to influence, at least in the short-run (Parasuraman and Despandé, 1984). Johnson & Johnson (J&J) faced this very problem when its chairman James E. Burke embarked on an effort to change the firm's management style and culture in the early 1980s (*Business Week*, 1984a). The company had long emphasized and rewarded autonomy among its one hundred and seventy business units engaged in the sale of consumer products, hospital supplies, and prescription drugs. However, Chairman Burke viewed a move toward medical technology, greater cooperation among business units, and less decentralization as a strategic imperative. This vision of the future and the resultant change in orientation have been difficult to implement. Part of the reason for the slow change at J&J might be that the firm's culture had been legitimized through past successes—the third impediment to change.

Companies in the late 1980s have faced the crisis of legitimacy in ever increasing numbers. "For those involved in a crisis, that may be the best time to understand their culture," says Fombrun (1986). Crisis may be also the needed incentive for exacting a change in culture. Apple Computer, Inc. is a case in point. The company had prospered under the entrepreneurial guidance and technical wizardry of its founder, Steven Jobs. However, in 1985, the home personal computer industry collapsed and, equally important, Apple's product-driven philosophy encountered reversals. A change in the company's orientation toward the marketplace was also deemed necessary given the rise of numerous competitors, the growth of computer networking, and greater buyer sophistication. The time was right for John Sculley to consider modifying Apple's culture (*Inc.*, 1987; *Fortune*, 1987). What was necessary was leadership—a second factor affecting organizational renewal.

LEADERSHIP[3]

An emerging theme in the 1980s that paralleled the attention to culture was leadership or the lack thereof in American corporations (Kiechel, 1983; Main, 1987). Like culture, the concept of leadership is not new. Over four thousand studies of leadership have been conducted in the last century, two thirds of which have appeared in the past twenty-five years (Van Fleet and Yakl, 1986).

The concept of leadership in the decade ahead will depart from what is now called management. Leadership has assumed a transformational quality whereby leaders are those individuals who act as change agents (Tichey and Devanna, 1986; Kozmetsky, 1985). According to Hosmer (1982, p. 55):

> A leader is an individual within an organization who is able to influence the attitudes and opinions of others within the organizations; a manager is merely able to influence their actions and decisions. Leadership is not a synonym for management; it is a higher order of capability.

This higher order of capability is reflected in the qualities of leaders and the techniques of leadership. It is therefore instructive to take a closer look at corporate leaders.

A Look at Corporate Leaders

The literature on leadership during the past decade represents an interesting mix of scholarship ranging from biographies (e.g., Lee Iacocca, *Iacocca: An Autobiography*, 1984; Robert J. Schoenberg, *Geneen*, 1985) to psychological profiles (Zaleznik, 1977). Contemporary research and commentary on leadership has tended to examine the unique qualities of leaders. Levison and Rosenthal (1984) identified five such qualities after interviewing the CEOs of six leading U.S. corporations (Citicorp, IBM, GE, NY Times Co., Monsanto, and AMAX Inc.) They concluded that a leader (1) is able to take charge, (2) has a strong self-image and a powerful ego ideal, (3) interacts with customers, employees, and other constituencies supportively, (4) provides permission to take risks, and (5) is a thinker as well as a doer. Garfield (1986) identified six qualities of leaders: (1) a strong sense of mission, (2) well-defined goals, (3) a capacity for self-observation and self-analysis, (4) an ability to bring out the best in others, (5) the mental agility to steer a "critical path" through complex situations, and (6) the foresight to anticipate and adapt to major changes without losing momentum.

Related research has focused on the techniques of leadership. For example, Bennis and Nanus (1985) have identified four common techniques used by successful leaders: (1) *manage attention* with a compelling vision; (2) *manage meaning* through communicating the vision and aligning individual's interests and actions with that vision; (3) *manage trust* through reliability or constancy; and (4) *manage self* through proper deployment of the leader's own resources.

This brief glance at corporate leadership is important in the sense that it highlights what leaders do in addition to the qualities they possess. Two central themes in corporate leadership that may affect strategic market planning are a leader's ability to (1) create and communicate a vision and (2) think strategically.

Leadership and Vision

Much of the work in strategic market planning described in the first five chapters of this book emphasized technique. Vision and leadership were noticeably absent or somehow treated as a given. Vision, however, will assume greater significance in the decade ahead (Westlay and Mintzberg, 1989). In fact, Donald M. Kendall, Chairman and CEO of Pepsico, Inc., has asserted that vision is the essence of leadership (Kendall, 1986):

> I believe the most important job of top management is to create a vision of the organization, a sense of purpose, and then to share that vision with others in the organization—so that everyone knows what it was that made the organization successful in the past and what it will take to ensure the continuation of that success. I think this is the essence of leadership—the sharing of vision.

If the vision is the essence of leadership, what then is the essence of vision? Several perspectives have been advocated (e.g., Morris, 1987; Bennis, 1986; Gluck, 1984; Hunsicker, 1986; Lewis, 1984). These perspectives share a common thread. *Strategic vision* encompasses a clear notion of which present and future product-markets the firm will compete in and specific concepts of how the firm will establish sustainable competitive positions in those product-markets.

Furthermore, vision emerges from understanding industry structure, competitive dynamics, and the firm's capabilities and potential. Consider, for example, James E. Burke's vision for Johnson & Johnson (*Business Week*, 1984). His vision for the company included a recognition that the firm's core businesses, while profitable, were maturing and had limited long-term growth. Moreover, advances in science and technology promised to revolutionize health care as it is now known. Therefore, he saw the need for J&J to venture into technologically based product-markets through acquisitions; otherwise, J&J "would be heading toward becoming just another company."

Hunsicker (1986) takes the notion of vision a step further by identifying five necessary abilities that contribute to creating a vision for the firm:

1. the ability to see and understand the pattern of forces underlying superficially unrelated events and phenomena,

2. the ability to know when to reassess or challenge assumptions that may have been part of the tradition of a company or industry for so long that they have been accepted as "givens,"

3. the ability to see the value—and the limitations—of insights derived from analogous situations in other fields,

4. the ability to recognize and understand "hybrid" behavior and avoid falling prey to the tyranny of averages in observing and dealing with it, and

5. the ability to balance quantitative and qualitative judgments (e.g., analysis and intuition/experience) in arriving at conclusions.

The role of vision in leadership and, specifically, strategic market planning has yet to be demonstrated in a systematic fashion. While the concept makes intuitive sense, implementing it is another matter. For vision to play an instrumental role in strategic market planning, it must be communicated and shared and the corporate rank and file must be empowered to act on the vision. In more straightforward terms, Jack F. Welch, CEO of General Electric, believes that once an individual is assigned leadership responsibility for one of GE's many business units, that person must "develop a vision" for that business and oversee a change in culture to accomplish it (*Business Week*, 1987c).

Leadership and Strategic Thinking

An implicit assumption in any discussion of leadership is that the leader is able to think strategically. Like vision, strategic thinking is a vague concept. Strategic thinking is not strategic planning as it is commonly practiced. Whereas strategic planning has often degenerated into frameworks for the systematic and comprehensive analysis of known options, strategic thinking involves creative and entrepreneurial insights into a company, its industry and its environment (Glueck, Kaufman, and Walleck, 1982). Strategic thinking is a creative process. It involves identifying possibilities, not simply evaluating known options. Consider, for example, Levitt's (1983, p. 138) perspective on strategic planning and the need for creativity:

Strategic planning can be mechanistically, and therefore incorrectly, defined as deciding how to allocate resources among the possibilities of what's to be done. This definition is incorrect, because it presumes that these possibilities are self-evident. They are not. It is wrong to say that the most important and creatively challenging act of corporate decision-making is about choices regarding what's to be done. The most important and challenging work involves thinking up the possibilities from which choices may have to be made. To select among stipulated possibilities is to make choices of preferences, not decisions about appropriateness. A possibility has to be created before it can be chosen. Therefore to think up the possibilities from among which choices might be made is to engage in acts of creative imagination.

Others such as Day (1984), Hunsicker (1980), Sheth (1985), and Kerin and Harvey (1987) have voiced similar views.

Creativity alone does not capture the essence of strategic thinking. Morrison and Lee (1979) note that the focus of effective strategic thinking is to gain a competitive product-market advantage. According to the authors, strategic thinking in the following six areas makes all the difference between mediocrity and competitive superiority:

1. identifying and emphasizing more effectively than competitors the key success factors inherent in the economics of each business,
2. segmenting markets so as to gain decisive competitive advantage,
3. basing strategies on the measurement and analysis of competitive advantage,
4. anticipating competitor's responses,
5. exploiting more, or different, degrees of freedom than competitors do, and
6. giving investment priority to businesses that promise a competitive advantage.

Strategic thinking also challenges the sometime preoccupation on return-on-investment evident in many firms by directing attention to the levers and buttons that ultimately affect probability. It does so by incorporating broadened measures of performance (Drucker, 1986). Table 11.4 lists a few of these performance barometers.

Irrespective of how it is conceptualized and implemented, *strategic thinking* involves creating product-markets by capitalizing on environmental opportunities and transforming threats into opportunities. In this respect, Drucker (1985) has prescribed four entrepreneurial strategies designed to convert threats into opportunities:

1. being "fastest with the mostest" (aim at leadership in, if not dominance of a new market or a new industry, but do not necessarily create a big business right away);
2. "hitting them where they ain't" (imitate an existing product creatively or exploit an existing product in another market that the original developer does not understand);
3. finding and occupying a specialized "ecological niche" (obtain a monopoly or control in a small area of expertise immune to competition and unlikely to be challenged);
4. changing the economic characteristics of a product, a market, or an industry.

For the most part, advocates of strategic thinking are like heralds crying for creativity, innovation, flexibility, and reasoned risk taking in strategic marketing planning. They have proposed new perspectives and recommend new measures for scoring the results of planning efforts. Their influence on the substance and practice of strategic market planning has yet to

TABLE 11.4
SELECTED BROADENED MEASURES OF PERFORMANCE

1. *Customer Value Creation*
   - What is the price/quality relationship of our product/services from a buyer's viewpoint?
   - Are there unique applications of our products/services for a particular buyer use?
2. *Liquidity and Cash Flow*
   - Are profits being achieved at the expense of a weakened liquidity and cash position?
   - Is the company *buying* rather than earning its sales volume (e.g., through generous financing of purchases by customers)?
3. *Innovation*
   - What are the firm's achievements as a successful innovator relative to direct competitors?
   - What have been the trends in innovation lead time (time between inception of an innovation and its successful launch)?
   - What is the ratio of successful innovations to failures?
   - What is the level of innovative activity by product-market served and specifically in product-markets with the greatest future growth potential?
4. *Market Standing*
   - Standing relative to direct competitors in product-markets served.
   - Standing trends over time.
   - Opportunity to improve or preserve market standing.
5. *Productivity*
   - Productivity trends with respect to all major factors of productivity—capital resources, human resources, etc.
   - Productivity trends within major factors of productivity by key segments [e.g.: *major factor:* human resources; *key segments of factor:* blue collar labor, clerical labor, managers, and service staffs.]
6. *Shareholder Wealth Creation*
   - Are the company's investment strategies building or destroying the wealth of its stockholders?
   - What combination of profitability and growth are most beneficial to stockholders?

---

be determined, apart from highlighting the importance of corporate entrepreneurship and innovation as sources of organizational renewal.

CORPORATE ENTREPRENEURSHIP

The third leg in organizational renewal is corporate entrepreneurship. Innovation is the key to this emerging theme as companies have implored their people to *create* product-markets and *lead* rather than follow competitors. A bevy of new challenges has been voiced by top management, all of which emphasize "being something": *Be* Market-Driven, *Be* Consumer-Oriented, *Be* Creative, *Be* Opportunistic. One challenge underlies each of these exhortations: *Be* Entrepreneurial! Unfortunately, little systematic work has addressed the synoptic question: How can a company become or remain entrepreneurial? (e.g., Stevenson and Jarrillo-Mossi, 1986; Rule and Irwin, 1988). A sampling of unanswered questions on corporate entrepreneurship is given in Table 11.5.

Central Issues in Corporate Entrepreneurship and Innovation

Interest in corporate entrepreneurship, like many of the emerging themes in strategic market planning, has spawned new terms and practices. One such term is "intrapreneuring," which describes the process by which individuals or groups assume direct responsibility for creating innovation

TABLE 11.5
SOME UNANSWERED QUESTIONS ON
CORPORATE ENTREPRENEURSHIP

1. What skills are necessary to succeed as an entrepreneur?
2. How does a person prepare for the role of an entrepreneur?
3. How can management distinguish between opportunities and blind alleys?
4. How much of the entrepreneurial process is based on instinct and how much on rigorous planning?
5. What factors are necessary to keep an organization entrepreneurial?
6. How can employees be motivated to identify opportunities?
7. What kind of management structure most effectively enables an organization to exploit opportunities?
8. What kind of managerial style encourages entrepreneurial behavior in organizations?
9. How should firms restructure themselves to make managers more entrepreneurial?
10. How can the risks associated with entrepreneurial failure be reduced?
11. What kind of financial reward system in an organization would facilitate greater entrepreneurial zeal?
12. Given that the primary strategic resource of enterprises has shifted from capital to the information, knowledge, and creativity only people can supply, what should managers do to adjust to such fundamental change?

Source: David E. Gumpert (1986), "Stalking the Entrepreneur," *Harvard Business Review,* (May–June), pp. 32–36.
The above questions adapted from Gumpert's article and summarized in tabular form are intended to highlight the dearth of research on corporate entrepreneurship.

within the confines of the corporate setting (Pinchot, 1985; Finch, 1985; *Wall Street Journal*, 1988). Bonoma (1986) has coined the term "marketing subversives" to describe people who operate outside company structures and policies to bring about innovation in products and practices. A new practice rests on the view that innovation or creativity centers can stimulate new ideas and entrepreneurial activity. Forerunners of this perspective include Hallmark's Technology and Innovation Center and Kodak's Office of Innovation (*Business Week* 1985a; Ward, 1985; Chandler, 1986).

A General Management Perspective While new terminology and practices provide an impetus for corporate entrepreneurship, what is necessary is a general management perspective on corporate entrepreneurship and innovation (Lewis and Minton, 1985). Van de Ven (1986) offers one such perspective. By viewing the innovation process as the development and implementation of new ideas by people who interact with others within an organizational context, Van de Ven implicitly draws the link between corporate entrepreneurship and innovation. Moreover, he identifies four challenges that require top management attention for an organization to "be entrepreneurial." The first of these challenges is to *manage the attention* of employees to focus on nonroutine issues and problems and trigger action where inertia prevailed. A second challenge is to *manage part-whole relations* by allowing entrepreneurial activity to flourish as a part of the larger corporate structure. These islands of innovative opportunity, referred to as "skunkworks" (Peters and Waterman, 1982, p. 211), often disrupt formal review and reporting policies and epitomize the tension inherent in managing part-whole relations. *Managing ideas into good currency* is a third challenge. This challenge involves shaping ideas into commercially successful ventures. *Providing institutional leadership and an innovative context* is the fourth, and perhaps most important challenge for top management. Leadership and context represent the lubricant enabling structure, systems, and staff to operate effectively to innovate.

Integrating Institutional and Technical Processes These challenges cast the innovation process in a different light by focusing on institutional processes as well as technical processes. By doing so, the manifestations of culture, leadership, and entrepreneurship emerge and interact to create the necessary context for stimulating innovation in organizations (Kiechel 1983; *Business Week* 1983a; 1983b; 1984; Pearson, 1988).

Lodahl and Mitchell (1980) compare and contrast the institutional and technical processes of innovation along five dimensions: (1) founding ideals, (2) recruitment, (3) socialization of people to serve those ideals, (4) leadership, and (5) formalization to shape and stabilize the organization (see Figure 11.1). The technical process of innovation begins with setting well-defined goals. People are recruited through impersonal and universal criteria and socialized by clear rules and procedures. Leadership is characterized by analytical and consensus-building activities and the innova-

FIGURE 11.1
INSTITUTIONAL AND TECHNICAL PROCESS IN INNOVATION

Institutional Processes	Idea	Technical Processes
Creation, Elaboration of Ideology	Founding Ideals	Statement of Organizational Goals
Use of Personal Networks; Selection Based on Values and Ideals	Recruitment	Broad Search; Use of Universalistic Criteria
Face-to-Face Contact with Founders; Sharing Rituals, Symbols	Socialization	Rules and Procedures Learned Through Colleagues
Charismatic, Mythic Images (Transforming)	Leadership	Problem Solving and Consensus Making (Transactional)
Ideals Paramount; Structure Tenative	Formalization	Early Routinization; Uncertainty Reduction

Source: Thomas M. Lodahl and Stephen M. Mitchell (1980), "Drift in the Development of Innovative Organizations," in John R. Kimberly, Robert H. Miles, and Associates, *The Organizational Life Cycle* (San Francisco: Jossey-Bass Publishers), p. 184–207, at p. 204.

tion process is formalized by routinizing activities to minimize uncertainty in new ventures.

Technical processes parallel the common stepwise procedure for new product development such as that proposed by Booz, Allen, and Hamilton (1982, p. 11). These steps are:

1. corporate objectives and business strategy,
2. new product strategy development,
3. idea generation,
4. screening and evaluation,
5. business analysis,
6. prototype development,
7. market testing, and
8. commercialization.

It is noteworthy, however, that adherence to technical processes alone does not differentiate successful companies from their less successful counterparts. Among the key findings by Booz, Allen, and Hamilton after studying seven hundred firms and thirteen thousand new product introduction efforts was the following (Booz, Allen, and Hamilton, 1982, p. 17):

> In many ways, companies successful in new product introductions look like their less successful counterparts. They introduce about the same mix of new products. They spend about the same amount of money (as a percent of sales) on R&D and promotion in support of new products. Both groups are as likely to use a formal new product process or formally measure new product performance. And both groups spend about the same proportion of total time and expense on the various steps in the new product process. . . . Important differences . . . between the two groups . . . are related to operating philosophy, organization structures, extent of experience with new product introductions, and management styles.

This finding suggests there is more to innovation than merely adopting similar procedures and allocating the same level of resources. Rather, the "operating philosophy" and "management style" evident at successful innovator companies indicates that institutional processes need attention.

Institutional processes are very different from technical processes. The creation and elaboration of an ideology serves as the basis for ideals. People are recruited on the basis of their values through personal networks and socialized by sharing rituals and symbols. Leadership is characterized by charismatic, almost mythical, images; values drive the structure and formalization of the innovation process.

The central focus in the institutional process involves people, not procedure, and again draws the distinction between leadership and management. Personal and shared norms and values become paramount and create a cultural context that fosters innovative activity. As Van de Ven (1986, p. 601) notes:

> By plan or default, this infusion of norms and values into an organization takes place over time, and produces a distinct identity, outlook, habits, and commitments for its participants—coloring as it does all aspects of organizational life, and giving it social integration that goes far beyond the formal command structure and instrumental functions of the organization.

The importance of an underlying ideology and, specifically, values in creating direction and meaning for people is best articulated by Selznick (1957), who argued that an organization does not become an "institution" until it becomes infused with values that serve as a source of direct personal gratification and as a vehicle for group integrity. A tangible example of this phenomenon is found in the Polaroid Corporation. Box 11.1 de-

BOX **11.1**

POLAROID CORPORATION AND EDWIN LAND:
LINKING LEADERSHIP, CULTURE, AND
ENTREPRENEURSHIP

The linkage between culture, leadership, and entrepreneurship is embodied in the history of the Polaroid Corporation, its founder Edwin Land, and instant photography. Land's vision and values created and shaped Polaroid's culture and produced nearly two thousand patented products and processes during his tenure as chief executive. He wanted to make Polaroid "a noble prototype of industry" by melding art and science. His vision focused on a single product-market (amateur instant photography) and innovation. His motto: "Don't do anything that someone else can do. Don't undertake a project unless it is manifestly important and impossible."

Land's vision and values created a Polaroid culture that gave employees "an ultimate sense of confidence, purpose, and permanence." According to one employee, during Land's tenure: "We felt we could do anything."

In 1977, Polaroid introduced the Polavision instant movie system for amateur photographers. While a technical breakthrough, the product was a commercial failure. The project was written off in 1979 at a cost of $68.5 million. Land resigned as chief executive in 1980, but his vision remained, the culture he nurtured lingered, and the entrepreneurial effort continued, although all were shaken. At the same time instant photography was in a slump given the growth of 35mm cameras. Even though his successors broadened the company's product-market scope and technology base through modest diversification, attention to instant photography, innovation, and the character of the company remained paramount. Polaroid reaped the dividends from these qualities in 1986. The company introduced the Spectra camera which produced 35mm-quality pictures instantly for the amateur photography market. This innovation produced record company earnings in 1987.

Land was interviewed in 1987 and asked what he thought of the success and his successors:

> For a while they were searching, but I think they've settled down to the full appreciation of what a wonderful field instant photography still is. They have come to appreciate the unique things the company has and to perceive that they are unique.

Source: Based on Subrata N. Chakravarty (1987), "The Vindication of Edwin Land," *Forbes* (May 4), pp. 83–84; William M. Bulkeley (1983), "As Polaroid Matures, Some Lament a Decline in Creative Excitement," *Wall Street Journal* (May 10), pp. 1, 22.

scribes how Edwin Land's legacy of leadership, the culture he nurtured, and the entrepreneurial zeal both engendered played a part in the successful 1986 introduction of the Spectra camera after the disaster of Polavision in 1979.

Organizational Types and Entrepreneurship

"Innovation is not the enterprise of a single entrepreneur" concludes Van de Ven (1986, p. 601). "Instead, it is a network-building effort that centers on the creation, adoption, and sustained implementation of a set of ideas among people who, through transactions, become sufficiently committed to these ideas to transform them into 'good currency.' " These observations would suggest that certain "types" of organizations are more likely to be innovative than others.

Interest in organization typologies has produced a number of descriptive models (e.g., Mintzberg, 1973; Miles and Snow, 1978; Miller and Friesen, 1982). The Miles and Snow (1978) typology has gained the most attention because it views organizations as complete, integrated, and self-organizing systems in dynamic interaction with the environment. A key factor in their typology is the organization's response to its environment, evidenced in the rate at which an organization modifies its products and markets (product-market scope) to assure an alignment with the environment. Four specific organization types exist in the Miles and Snow model. *Prospectors* continually search for new opportunities and experiment regularly with potential responses to emerging environmental trends. *Defenders* have a narrow product-market scope and do not search for opportunities outside this domain. *Analyzers* typically compete in two very different product-market domains: one rapidly changing, the other relatively stable. *Reactors* are unable to respond effectively to environmental change. They lack any semblance of a consistent strategy. Table 11.6 provides a more complete description of each type.

Burgelman (1983) suggests that prospectors and analyzers might be the most innovative type of organizations. Empirical research generally supports this view (McDaniel and Kolari, 1987; Conant, Mokway, and Wood, 1987).

The underlying theory of self-organizing systems, epitomized by the Miles and Snow (1978) typology, raises two important questions. First, how does each come about? Second, what is the long-term viability of each of these types? Both questions have particularly important implications for creating and preserving innovative organizations that create product-markets. Some insights into these questions emerge from the literature on institutionalizing innovation in companies.

Institutionalizing Innovation and the
Functional Role of Marketing

The phrase "institutionalizing innovation" would, at first glance, seem to be a contradiction in terms. However, there is a growing recognition that

TABLE 11.6
MILES AND SNOW ORGANIZATIONAL TYPOLOGY

Adaptive Cycle Components

	Characteristics	Defenders	Prospectors	Analyzers	Reactors*
			Management Styles		
Administrative Problems & Solutions	Product-Market Domain	Narrow and carefully focused	Broad and continuously expanding	Segmented and carefully adjusted	Uneven and transient
	Success Posture	Prominence in "their" product market(s)	Active initiation of change	Calculated followers of change	Opportunistic thrusts and coping postures
	Surveillance	Domain dominated and cautious/strong organizational monitoring	Market and environmentally oriented/aggressive search	Competitive oriented and thorough	Sporadic and issue dominated
	Growth	Cautious penetration and advances in productivity	Enacting product market development and diversification	Assertive penetration and careful product market development	Hasty change
Engineering Problems & Solutions	Technological Goal	Cost-efficiencies	Flexibility and innovation	Technological synergism	Project development and completion
	Technological Breadth	Focal, core technology/basic expertise	Multiple technologies/"pushing the edge"	Interrelated technologies/"at the edge"	Shifting technological applications/fluidity
	Technological Buffers	Standardization, maintenance programs	Technical personnel skills/diversity	Incrementalism and synergism	Ability to experiment and "rig solutions"

Entrepreneurial Problems & Solutions	Finance and production	Marketing and R&D	Planning staffs	Trouble-shooters
Dominant Coalition Planning	Inside/out . . . control dominated	Problem and opportunity finding/campaign (program) perspective	Comprehensive with incremental changes	Crisis oriented and disjointed
Structure	Functional/line authority	Product and/or market centered	Staff dominated/matrix oriented	Tight formal authority/loose operating design
Control	Centralized and formal/financially anchored	Market performance/sales volumes	Multiple methods/careful risk calculations . . . sales contributions	Avoid problems/handle problems . . . remain solvent

*Conventionally, reactors have been presented as a "residual" style lacking consistent response characteristics.

Source: Adapted from Jeffrey S. Conant, Michael P. Mokwa, and John J. Burnett, "Pricing and Performance in Health Maintenance Organizations: A Strategic Management Perspective," *Journal of Health Care Marketing*, March, 1989, pp. 25–36.

innovation can be institutionalized in the manner proposed by Lodahl and Mitchell (1980) and outlined in Figure 11.1. Case studies of 3M and Merck & Co., two acknowledged innovative firms, illustrate the institutionalization process (Peters and Waterman, 1983; *Business Week*, 1987b). These companies share a number of important qualities. First, both benefit from an ideology that stimulates innovation. At 3M, the Eleventh Commandment is: "Thou shalt not kill a new product idea." Second, top management plays a critical role in the strategic recognition of opportunities. For example, Roy Vegelos, Merck & Co. Chairman, targets key areas for special attention and allows people to act on their ideas within these areas. Third, both companies give product champions and venture teams an opportunity to develop ideas *and* commercialize them. In neither instance are these teams "assigned membership." Rather, they emerge from the shared values and ideals of prospective members. Finally, both companies have "routinized the vision" of their leaders.

Institutionalizing innovation also involves transforming the planning-budgeting process from simple resource allocation to one in which opportunity seeking becomes important as well (Quinn, 1979). In this respect, portfolio planning can play a role in directing attention toward key product-market areas for entrepreneurial effort (Kamm, 1986).

It would seem that the marketing function should play a central role in institutionalizing innovation in corporations. Simmons (1986, p. 488) argues that the functional role of marketing in the firm can be described as *organized rational innovation*. He adds that marketing

> . . . is organized innovation because it is the marketer's specific organizational function to identify the opportunity for change, and to induce the change within the organization. It is rational in the sense of reasoned, because marketers must identify from the subset of innovations which are possible and which are wanted. . . .

Unfortunately, the corporate marketing function has not performed this role, at least in the eyes of top management (Webster, 1981). The reasons for lack of performance are unclear. One might hypothesize that marketing has been relegated to "downstream" status in the value-chain (Porter, 1985) or business system (Buaron, 1981) approach to competitive strategy (see chapter seven). Such labeling by definition commits marketing to the realm of tactical activity, not of strategic action. Another hypothesis is that marketing has been absorbed by the strategic planning *staff* function. As a consequence, there is little recognition of the role of marketing as an innovating and adaptive *line* function in the organization (Day and Wensley, 1983). A third hypothesis is that purposeful intraorganizational linkages between marketing and other functions (e.g., R&D) is weak or nonexistent. Research addressing this hypothesis is only now emerging, as are prescriptives for building these relationships (e.g., Rueckert and

Walker, 1987; Gupta, Raj, and Wilemon, 1986). A fourth, and more troubling hypothesis, is that marketing function and marketing professionals have abdicated responsibility for innovation (Mauser, 1980). Whatever the reason for the present status of the functional role of marketing in innovation, the need for a "marketing perspective" has never been greater. One of the major qualities looked for in chief executives of the 1990s is that they possess a marketing vision for the firm and are able to effectively communicate this vision to operating management (Bassler, 1986).

A CONCLUDING NOTE

The role of organizational factors in strategic market planning is likely to assume greater significance as companies struggle for renewal in an increasingly complex and competitive environment. Marketing scholars and practitioners alike would benefit from closer attention to these factors (Channon, 1985). Admittedly, this discussion has provided only a pen-and-ink sketch of corporate culture, leadership, and entrepreneurship—the essence of each lies in the shadings.

Several conclusions and cautionary thoughts are warranted given this brief look at the place of behavioral factors in strategic market planning. Each relates to the promise and reality of culture, leadership, and entrepreneurship in corporate settings, and specifically strategic market planning.

Smircich (1983, p. 346) has suggested that "culture may be another lever or key by which strategic managers can influence and direct the cause of their organizations." Such views represent the promise of culture and particularly culture change as a source of renewal. The reality is that culture is not easily changed because culture is not just something that a company has, but what it is. Thus, the intellectual commitment to "being something" discussed earlier is not only an aspect of entrepreneurship, but a facet of cultural change. Unfortunately, not enough is known about culture to systematically effect its change despite highly publicized efforts to do so. (Webster, 1988; Guyon, 1987). Moreover, ethical and legal issues in managing and changing corporate culture are also a matter of recent concern (Drake and Drake, 1988).

Leadership is the one behavioral factor that seems to be central to culture change and, particularly, to efforts to stimulate corporate entrepreneurship and innovation. In fact, the promise of leadership is that certain kinds of individuals can act as driving forces to mobilize organizations. Such individuals possess vision, think strategically, and can infuse positive values and empower others to act through charisma, advocacy, and passionate involvement. Not surprisingly, Roy Vegelos (Merck & Co.), Lee Iacocca (Chrysler Corporation), and Jack Welch (General Electric) are seen as epitomizing these qualities by their fellow CEOs (Heidrick and Struggles, 1987). But again, a word of caution is necessary. Based on the works of Marx and Wood (1975) and Etzioni (1971), Soeters (1986) suggests that mobilization of organizations is often momentary and charismatic activation generates a flurry of activity, but only for a short time. This idea is repeated by McGill (1988) who challenges the notion of "Messianic Leadership" which pervades the popular business literature today.

The concept of leadership and, specifically, transformational leadership, however, should not be dismissed outright, but rather, should be assessed with respect to its purpose. Leadership is a catalyst. And leaders, according to Levitt (1988, p. 7)

> . . . establish order and discipline, and simultaneously foster skepticism, incredulity, experimentation, and change. They encourage the generation of new forms and actions that may have neither precedent or accustomed approval. They inject creative enzymes into the system, with results that can be destabilizing and disorderly and are rarely parametric. They know that to achieve more and better results, more resourcefulness is as important as more resources.

Given almost two decades of research on and application of strategic market planning models, the time may be right to consider the dimensions of leadership no matter how elusive the concept might be. (See for example Noel, 1989; Shrivastava and Nachman, 1989).

Corporate entrepreneurship and its hoped for derivative, innovation, is the most alluring of the behavioral factors. The promise of entrepreneurship is that it will create new products and markets for corporations. Entrepreneurship is a synonym for achievement and action, a touchstone for creativity, and the remedy for the lack of competitiveness in many corporations. It is the celebration of the individual, such as Art Fry, who developed Post-It notes at 3M, Chuck House, who pioneered new markets for oscilloscope technology at Hewlett-Packard, and Jack Kilby, who created the first integrated circuit while a young research analyst at Texas Instruments.

Increasingly, however, there is growing recognition that corporate entrepreneurship results from corporate culture and leadership (Van de Ven, 1986) and that collective efforts, not just individual initiatives, produce innovations (Reich, 1987). Efforts to stimulate creativity in organizations (*Business Week*, 1985a), while welcome, represent only a first step. Unless these efforts are coupled with culture-building activities and leadership at the highest levels of the organization, they have the potential to be dismissed as passing fads.

The role of organizational factors in the study and practice of strategic market planning has been overlooked much too long. Many of the concepts, issues, and processes described in this chapter are not new. It would seem that the old questions have not been answered—they only went out of style. Perhaps it is necessary to again consider what is meant by strategy formulation and consider the thoughts of Andrews (1983, p. 9):

> It is part of the *comprehensive* concept of strategy that leaders of a company must be dedicated to the durable core of a company's character . . . while encouraging innovations that will bring about or respond to the changes taking place in its surroundings.

Another look at these old issues might provide the new perspectives necessary to guide strategic market planning research and practice in the 1990s.

NOTES

1. Research and commentary on culture appears in three special issues of scholarly journals: *Administrative Science Quarterly* (September, 1983); *Organizational Dynamics* (Autumn, 1983), and *Journal of Management Studies* (May, 1986). Popular books on this topic include Deal and Kennedy (1982), Peters and Waterman (1982), Peters and Austin (1985), Ouchi (1981); and Pascale and Athos (1981). For an insightful review on culture from a marketing viewpoint, see Despandé and Webster (1989).
2. The term "dominant culture" is used advisedly. Within a corporate setting, multiple cultures can exist that go by various names, such as tribes, clans, sects, subcultures, and countercultures. For an examination of cultural traits and related issues, see Saffold (1988).
3. For recent research and commentary on leadership, see the special issue in *Strategic Management Journal* (Summer 1989) titled "Strategic Leaders and Leadership."

REFERENCES

Andrews, Kenneth R. (1983), "Strategic Planning of Mice and Men," *Across The Board*, November, 6–9.

Ansoff, H. Igor (1979), *Strategic Management* (New York: John Wiley & Sons).

Barnard, Chester (1938), *Functions of the Executive* Boston: Harvard University Press.

Barney, Jay B. (1986), "Organizational Culture: Can It Be a Source of Sustained Competitive Advantage?" *Academy of Management Review*, Vol. 3, No. 3, 656–665.

Bassler, John (1986), "Companies Want CEOs with Strong Marketing Vision," *Marketing News*, May 23, 17, 36.

Bennis, Warren (1986), "Leaders and Visions: Orchestrating the Corporate Culture," in Melissa A. Berman (ed.), *Corporate Culture and Change* (New York: The Conference Board).

Bennis, Warren and Burt Nanus (1985), *Leaders: The Strategy for Taking Charge* (New York: Harper & Row).

Bonoma, Thomas V. (1986), "Marketing Subversives," *Harvard Business Review*, November–December, 113–118.

Bower, Joseph L. (1982), "Solving the Problems of Business Planning," *Journal of Business Strategy* Winter, 32–44.

Booz, Allen, & Hamilton, Inc. (1982), *New Product Management for the 1980s* (Chicago: Booz, Allen, and Hamilton, Inc.).

Buaron, Roberto (1981), "How to Win the Market Share Game? Try Changing the Rules," *Management Review*, January, 8–17.

Burgelman, Robert A. (1983), "Corporate Entrepreneurship and Strategic Management: Insights from a Process Study," *Management Science*, December, 1349–1364.

Business Week (1980), "Corporate Culture: The Hard-to-Change Values that Spell Success or Failure," October 27, 148–160.

Business Week (1982), "An About-Face in TI's Culture," July 5, 77.

Business Week (1983a) "Big Business Tries To Imitate the Entrepreneurial Spirit," April 18, 84–89.

Business Week (1983b), "Here Comes the 'Intrapreneur,' " July 18, 180–90.

Business Week (1984a), "Changing a Corporate Culture," May 14, 130–138.

Business Week (1984b), "Can Apple's Corporate Counterculture Survive?" January 16,

Business Week (1985a), "Are You Creative?" September 30, 80–84.

Business Week (1985b), "How Ross Perot's Shock Troops Ran Into Flak at GM," February 11, 118–119.

Business Week (1987a), "Tandy Finds a Cold, Hard World Outside the Radio Shack," August 31, 68–69.

Business Week (1987b), "The Miracle Company," October 19, 84–90.

Business Week (1987c), "Jack Welch: How Good a Manager?" December 14, 92–103.

Buzzell, Robert D. and T. Gale Bradley (1987), *The PIMS Principles* (New York: The Free Press).

Chandler, Colby H. (1986), "Eastman Kodak Opens Windows of Opportunity," *Journal of Business Strategy*, Summer, 5–9.

Channon, D. F. (1985), "Strategic Management: Key Concepts and Future Directions," in A. H. G. Rinnooy Kan (ed.), *New Challenges for Management Research* (Amsterdam: North Holland), 115–137.

Conant, Jeffrey S., Michael P. Mokway, and Steven D. Wood (1987), "Management Styles and Marketing Strategies: An Analysis of HMOs," *Health Care Management Review*, Vol. 12, No. 4, 65–75.

Cooper, Michal R. (1987), "Managing Cultural Change to Achieve Competitive Advantage," in Haig Babian and Harold E. Glass (eds.) *Handbook of Business Strategy, 1987/1988 Yearbook* (Boston: Warren, Gorham & Lamont), 11-1–11-21.

Corley, W. (1972), "Gillette Co. Struggles as its Rivals Slice at Fat Profit Margins," *Wall Street Journal*, February 2, 1ff.

Day, George S. and Robin Wensley (1983), "Marketing Theory with a Strategic Orientation," *Journal of Marketing*, Fall, 79–89.

Day, George S. (1984), *Strategic Market Planning* (St. Paul: West Publishing Co.)

Deal, Terrence E. and Allan A. Kennedy (1982), *Corporate Cultures* (Reading, MA: Addison-Wesley).

Despandé, Rohit and A. Parasuraman (1984), "Organizational Culture and Marketing Effectiveness," in P. Anderson and M. Ryans (eds.), *Scientific Method in Marketing* (Chicago: American Marketing Association).

Despandé, Rohit and A. Parasuraman (1986), "Linking Corporate Culture to Strategic Planning," *Business Horizons*, May–June, 28–37.

Despandé, Rohit and Frederick Webster, Jr. (1989), "Organizational Culture and Marketing: Defining the Research Agenda," *Journal of Marketing*, January, 3–15.

Drake, Bruce H. and Eileen Drake (1988), "Ethical and Legal Aspects of Managing Corporate Cultures," *California Management Review*, Winter, 107–123.

Drucker, Peter F. (1985), *Innovation and Entrepreneurship* (New York: Harper & Row).

Drucker, Peter F. (1986), "If Earnings Aren't the Dial to Read," *Wall Street Journal*, October 30, 30.

Etzioni, A. (1971), *The Active Society: A Theory of Societal and Political Processes* (New York: The Free Press).

Finch, Peter (1985), "Intrapreneurism: New Hope for New Business," *Business Marketing*, July, 32–40.

Fombrun, Charles (1986), "Of Tribes and Witch Doctors: The Anthropologist's View," in Melissa A. Berman (ed.), *Corporate Culture and Change* (New York: The Conference Board).

Fortune (1987), "Sculley's Lessons From Inside Apple," September 14, 109–117.

Garfield, Charles (1986), *Peak Performers* (New York: William Morrow).

Glueck, Frederick (1984), "Vision and Leadership," *Interfaces*, January–February, 10–18.

Glueck, Frederick, Stephen P., Kaufman, and A. Steven Walleck (1982), "The Four Phases of Strategic Management," *Journal of Business Strategy*, Winter, 9–21.

Guyon, Janet (1987), "Culture Class: GE's Management School Aims to Foster Unified Corporate Goals," *Wall Street Journal*, August 10, 25.

Gupta, Aril (1986), "Matching Managers to Strategies: Point and Counterpoint," *Human Resource Management*, Summer, 215–234.

Gupta, Ashok K., S. P. Raj, and David Wilemon (1986), "A Model for Studying R&D—Marketing Interface in the Product Innovation Process," *Journal of Marketing*, April, 7–17.

Harrison, R. (1972), "Understanding Your Organization's Character," *Harvard Business Review*, May–June, 19–128.

Harrison, R. (1978), "Questionnaire on the Cultures of Organizations," in C. Handy (ed.), *Gods of Management* (London: Souvenir), 83–88.

Heidrick and Struggles (1987), *Chief Executive Officer* (New York: Heidrick and Struggles, Inc.).

Hofstede, Geert (1980), *Culture's Consequences: International Differences in Work-Related Values* (Beverly Hills: Sage Publications).

Hosmer, LaRue T. (1982), "The Importance of Strategic Leadership," *Journal of Business Strategy*, Fall, 47–57.

Hunsicker, J. Quincy (1980), "The Malaise of Strategic Planning," *Management Review*, March, 25–35.

Hunsicker, J. Quincy (1986), "Vision, Leadership and Europe's Business Future," *The McKinsey Quarterly*, Spring, 22–39.

Inc. (1987), "Corporate Antihero: John Sculley," October, 49–59.

Jelinek, Mariann, Linda Smircich, and Paul Hirsch (1983), "Introduction: A Code of Many Colors," *Administrative Science Quarterly*, September, 331–338.

Kamm, Judith (1986), "The Portfolio Approach to Divisional Innovation Strategy," *Journal of Business Strategy*, Summer, 25–37.

Kendall, Donald F. (1986), "The Four Simple Truths of Management," *Vital Speeches*, May 15.

Kerin, Roger A. and Michael G. Harvey (1987), "Strategic Marketing Thinking: A Game Perspective," *Journal of Business and Industrial Marketing*, Spring, 47–54.

Kerr, Jeffrey (1982), "Assigning Managers on the Basis of the Life Cycle," *Journal of Business Strategy*, Spring, 58–65.

Kerr, Jeffrey and Ellen F. Jackofsky (1989), "Aligning Managers with Strategies: Management Development Versus Selection," *Strategic Management Journal* (Summer), 157–170.

Kerr, Jeffrey and John W. Slocum, Jr. (1987), "Managing Corporate Culture Through Reward Systems," *Academy of Management Executive*, May, 99–108.

Kiechel III, Walter (1983), "Wanted: Corporate Leaders," *Fortune*, May 30, 135–140.

Kilmann, R. H. and M. J. Saxton (1983), *Kilmann-Saxton Culture-Gap Survey* (Pittsburgh: Organizational Design Consultants).

Kozmetsky, George (1985), *Transformational Management* (Cambridge, MA: Ballinger Publishing Company).

Lebas, Michel and Jane Weigenstein (1986), "Management Control: The Role of Rules, Markets and Culture," *Journal of Management Studies*, May, 259–272.

Leontiades, Milton (1982), "Choosing the Right Manager to Fit the Strategy," *Journal of Business Strategy*, Fall, 58–69.

Levison, Harry and Stuart Rosenthal (1984), *CEO: Corporate Leadership in Action* (New York: Basic Books).

Levitt, Theodore (1988), "The Innovating Organization," *Harvard Business Review*, January–February, 7.

Lewin, Arie Y. and John W. Monton (1986), "Determining Organizational Effectiveness: Another Look and an Agenda for Research," *Management Science*, May, 514–538.

Lewis, Walker W. (1984), "The CEO and Corporate Strategy in the Eighties: Back to Basics," *Interfaces*, January–February, 3–9.

Lodahl, Thomas M. and Stephen M. Mitchell (1980), "Drift in the Development of Innovative Organizations," in John R. Kimberly, Robert H. Miles and Associates, *The Organizational Life Cycle* (San Francisco: Jossey-Bass Publishers), 184–207.

Main, Jeremy (1987), "Wanted: Leaders Who Can Make A Difference," *Fortune*, September 28, 92–102.

Martin, Joanne and Caren Siehl (1983), "Organizational Culture and Counterculture: An Uneasy Symbiosis," *Organizational Dynamics*, Autumn, 52–64.

Marx, G. T. and J. L. Wood (1975), "Strands of Theory and Research in Collective Behavior," *Annual Review of Sociology*, Vol. 1, 363–427.

Mauser, Ferdinand F. (1980), "The Marketing Fraternity's Shortfall," *Journal of Marketing*, Fall, 97–98.

McDaniel, Stephen W. and James W. Kolari (1987), "Marketing Strategy Implications of the Miles and Snow Strategic Typology," *Journal of Marketing*, October, 19–30.

McGill, Michael G. (1988), *American Business and The Quick Fix* (New York: Henry Holt, Inc.).

Miles, Robert E. and Charles C. Snow (1978), *Organizational Strategy, Structure and Process* (New York: McGraw-Hill).

Miller, D. and P. H. Friesen (1982), "Innovation in Conservative and Entrepreneurial Firms: Two Models of Strategic Momentum," *Strategic Management Journal*, January–February, 1–25.

Mintzberg, H. (1973), "Strategy-Making in Three Modes," *California Management Review*, Vol. 16, 44–53.

Morris, Elinor (1987), "Vision and Strategy: A Focus for the Future," *Journal of Business Strategy*, Fall, 51–58.

Morrison, J. Roger and James Lee (1979), "The Anatomy of Strategic Thinking," *Financial Times*, July 27, 21.

Noel, Alain (1989), "Strategic Cores and Magnificent Obsessions: Discovering Strategy Formation Through Daily Activities of CEOs," *Strategic Management Journal* (Summer), 33–49.

Ouchi, William G. (1981), *Theory Z* (Reading, MA: Addison-Wesley).

Parasuraman, A. and Rohit Despandé (1984), "The Cultural Context of Marketing Management," in R. W. Beek, et al. (eds.) *1984 American Marketing Association Educators Conference* (Chicago: American Marketing Association).

Pascale, R. T. and A. G. Athos (1981), *The Art of Japanese Management* (New York: Warner).

Pascale, R. (1984), "Fitting New Employees in the Company Culture," *Fortune*, May 28, 28–41.

Pearson, Audrall (1988), "Tough-Minded Ways to Get Innovative," *Harvard Business Review*, May–June, 99–106.

Peters, Thomas J. and Robert H. Waterman, Jr. (1982), *In Search of Excellence* (New York: Harper & Row).

Peters, Thomas J. and Robert H. Waterman, Jr. (1983), "Corporate Chariots of Fire," *Across The Board*, May, 49–47.

Peters, J. and Nancy Austin (1985), *A Passion for Excellence* (New York: Random House).

Pettigrew, Andrew M. (1979), "On Studying Organizational Cultures," *Administrative Science Quarterly*, December, 570–581.

Pinchot III, Gifford (1985), *Intrapreneuring* (New York: Harper & Row Publishers).

Porter, Michael E. (1985), *Competitive Advantage: Creating and Sustaining Superior Performance* (New York: The Free Press).

Quinn, James B. (1979), "Technological Innovation, Entrepreneurship and Strategy," *Sloan Management Review*, Spring, 19–30.

Ray, Carol A. (1986), "Corporate Culture: The Last Frontier of Control," *Journal of Management Studies*, May, 287–297.

Reich, Robert B. (1987), "Entrepreneurship Reconsidered: The Team as Hero," *Harvard Business Review*, May–June, 77–83.

Reynolds, Paul D. (1986), "Organizational Culture as Related to Industry, Position and Performance: A Preliminary Report," *Journal of Management Studies*, May, 334–345.

Ruekert, Robert W. and Orville C. Walker, Jr. (1987), "Marketing's Interaction with Other Functional Units: A Conceptual Framework and Empirical Evidence," *Journal of Marketing*, January, 1–19.

Rule, Erik G. and Donald W. Irwin (1988), "Fostering Intrapreneurship: The New Competitive Edge," *Journal of Business Strategy*, May/June, 44–47.

Saffold, Guy S. (1988), "Culture Traits, Strength, and Organizational Performance: Moving Beyond 'Strong' Culture," *Academy of Management Review*, October, 546–558.

Sathe, Vijay (1983), "Implications of Corporate Culture: A Manager's Guide to Action," *Organizational Dynamics*, Autumn, 5–23.

Schwartz, Howard and Stanley Davis (1981), "Matching Corporate Culture and Business Strategy," *Organizational Dynamics*, Summer, 30–48.

Selznick, Philip (1957), *Leadership and Administration*. New York: Row, Peterson.

Sheth, Jagdish N. (1985), *Winning Back Your Market* (New York: John Wiley & Sons).

Shrivastava, Paul and Sidney A. Nachman (1989), "Strategic Leadership Patterns," *Strategic Management Journal* (Summer), 55–66.

Simmons, Kenneth (1986), "Marketing as Innovation: The Eighth Paradigm," *Journal of Management Studies*, September, 479–500.

Smircich, Linda (1983), "Concepts of Culture and Organizational Analysis," *Administrative Science Quarterly*, September, 339–358.

Soeters, Joseph L. (1986), "Excellent Companies as Social Movements," *Journal of Management Studies*, May, 299–312.

Stevenson, Howard H. and Jose Carlos Jarrillo-Mossi (1986), "Preserving Entrepreneurship as Companies Grow," *Journal of Business Strategy*, Summer, 10–24.

Szilogyi, Andraew D. and David M. Schweiger (1984), "Matching Managers to Strategies: A Review and Suggested Framework," *Academy of Management Review*, Vol. 9, 626–637.

Tichey, Noel M. and Mary Anne Devanna (1986), *The Transformational Leader* (New York: John Wiley & Sons).

Uttal, Bruno (1983), "The Corporate Culture Vultures," *Fortune*, October, 66–72.

Van De Ven, Andrew H. (1986), "Central Problems in the Management of Innovations," *Management Science* (May), 590–607.

Van Fleet, D. D. and G. A. Yaki (1986), "A Century of Leadership Research," *Academy of Management Conference*.

Wall Street Journal (1988), "Consumer-Product Giants Relying on 'Intrapreneurs' in New Ventures," April 22, 21.

Ward, Bernie (1985), "Centers of Imagination," *Sky Magazine*, June, 72–80.

Waterman, Jr., Robert H. (1987), *The Renewal Factor: How the Best Get and Keep the Competitive Edge* (New York: Bantam Books).

Webster, Frederick E. (1981), "Top Management's Concerns About Marketing: Issues for the 1980's," *Journal of Marketing*, Summer, 9–16.

Webster, Frederick E. (1988), "Rediscovering the Marketing Concept," *Business Horizons*, November–December, 29–39.

Westley, Frances and Henry Mintzberg (1989), "Visonary Leadership and Strategic Management," *Strategic Management Journal* (Summer), 17–32.

Wheelwright, Steven C. (1984), "Strategy, Management, and Strategic Planning Approaches," *Interfaces*, January–February, 19–33.

Zaleznik, Abraham (1977), "Managers and Leaders: Are They Different?" *Harvard Business Review*, May–June, 67–78.

INDEX

A

Abell's generic strategy framework, 309–310
Acquisition
  corporate culture and, 415
  shareholder wealth creation and, 366–367
Admired corporations, Fortune's annual survey of, 398
Aging industry, defined, 78
Alcar Group, Inc., value-based planning and, 369
Allied-Lyons, global markets and, 327
Allied Signal, Inc., 31
Alternative programs, 22
  evaluation of, 22–23
  marketing, 22
American Airlines
  distinctive competence and, 10
  Sabre reservations system and, 322–323
Apollo reservations system, 322–323
Arm & Hammer, market penetration and, 234
Arthur D. Little, Inc., life cycle matrix and, 77–80
Assets, preemption of scarce, market entry and, 156–157

B

Backward vertical integration, 245
Baskin-Robbins, global markets and, 326–327
Bausch & Lomb, use of experience curve, 124
Bayer AG, strategic business units and, 11–13
BCG matrix, 101–103
Bendix Corporation, 31
Bic Corporation, distinctive competence and, 10
Black & Decker, experience curve usage, 124

Book value, 157
Booze, Allen & Hamilton
  product innovation spectrum and, 226–227
  technical processes and, 426
  technology development guidelines, 88, 89
Boston Consulting Group
  growth-share matrix, 39–40
  strategic business unit (SBU)
    assumptions, 63–65
    grouping by, 41–44
  strategic market planning and, 23
  strategic market unit, cash flow outlook matrix, 50
Briggs & Stratton, experience curve usage, 124
Bunker Ramo Corporation, 31
Business environment, monitoring of, 20–21
Business experience, pooled, 25
Business portfolio matrices, strategic market planning, 23, 25
Business screen portfolio matrix, 73–77
  assessing business strength, 76
  assessing industry attractiveness, 76
  factors checklist, 73, 75–76
  illustrated, 74
Business system gaps, 99
Business unit
  level, defined, 13
  performance, vertical integration and, 247–248
  PIMS strategy and, 145
  shareholder value creation and, 370–372
  strategy, 13–15

C

Campbell Soup Company
  new geographic markets and, 238
  product reformulation and, 239
Capability gaps, 99–101

Capability gaps—(*continued*)
  refraining from closing, 100
Capital intensity, 157, 159
Cash flow
  discounted model, 369–377
    perspectives on, 376–377
    shareholder value creation, 370–372
    shareholder value determinants, 369–370
    strategic market planning and, 372, 376
  importance of, 360–361
  market share decisions and, 59–65
  SBUs and, 49–52
  strategic influences on, *147*
Cash Management Account (CMA), 323
Coca Cola
  global markets and, 326
  value-based planning at, 375
Competition
  generic strategies and, 303–313
    Abell and Hall frameworks, 309–310
    business definition and alternative, 311
    Porter's framework for, 303, 306–309
    strategic market planning and, 310, 312–313
    topologies of, 304–305
  global markets and, 326–330
  moderating factors, *286*
  pioneer market dominance and, 292–293
  profit and, product substitutes and, 290
  profit potential and, 283–294
    buyers and, 289–290
    existing firms and, 284, 286–287
    industry suppliers and, 287–288, *289*
    potential entrants and, 287, *288*
  strategic groups, 294–302
    empirical studies on, 297–298
    formation of, 294, 296, 299, 300–301
    strategic market planning and, 299, 302
    two dimensional view of, *299*
  strategic market planning and, 290–291, 294
  trends in, 317–330
    global markets and, 326–330
    information technology and, 318–325

    value chain and, 313–317
    strategic market planning and, 314, 317
Competitive advantage, 4, 10–11
  attributes
    differentiation in important, 98
    product/delivery, 99
  capability gap, 99–100
  conditions of, 98
  cost leadership and, 10
  defined, 7
  differentiation and, 10
  footprint in the market, 99
  key buy criterion, 99
  sustainable, 10, 98–101
Competitive analysis, strategic market planning and, 25
Competitive positions, defined, 78
Competitive strategic models, 98–108
  competitive advantage, sustainable, 98–101
  McKinsey strategic gameboard, 103–107
  new BCG matrix and, 101–103
  Strategic Planning Associates and, 107–108
Complementary related diversification, 257
Corporate culture, 411–418
  defined, 411
  dimensions of, 411–412
  institutionalizing innovation and, 429, 432–433
  maintenance and change, 417–418
  manifestations of, 413–415
    Hewlett-Packard, 413, *414*
    Polaroid Corporation, 427–429
    Texas Instruments, 413, *414*
  organizational types and, 429
  strategic market planning implications and, 415–417
  typology of, 430–431
Corporate entrepreneurship, 423–433
  issues in, 424–427, 429
    general management and, 425
    institutional and technical process integration, 425–427
  strategies of, 422
Corporate objectives, determination of, 20

Corporate strategy, strategy levels, 13
Cost advantage, achieving competitive, 123–124
Cost and demand interrelationships, 58–59
Cost leadership
    competitive advantage and, 10
    generic strategies and, 303
Costs
    experience curves and, 115–116
    switching, market entry and, 157
Cross-sectional data pooling, 170
Culture *see* Corporate culture
Customers
    new geographic markets, reaching, 236
    present geographic markets, expanding, 236–237

D

Data bases, PIMS, 25
Defensive supplemental diversification, 257
Differentiation
    competitive advantage and, 10
    generic strategies and, 303, 309
Directional Policy Matrix, 80, 83–86
    illustrated, *83*
    prospect analysis, *85*
    strategic options and, *84*
Distinctive competence, 6, 7, 10
Diversification
    benefits of, 253–254
    conceptualization of, 252–253
    defined, 252
    direction of, 254, 256–258
    motives, 254
    tests, 260
    typologies of strategies of, 255
Diversification growth strategies, 224, 225–226, 249–268
    benefits of, 253–254
    conceptualization of, 252–253
    definition of, 252–253
    direction of, 254, 256–258
    evolution of, 252
    firm performance and, 261, 264–265, 267–268
    investment community influence and, 262–263

mode of, 261
    alternative, *264*
    motives, 254
    synergy and, 258, 260
    typologies of, 255
Diversified firms, evolution of, 252
Divestment, shareholder wealth creation and, 366–367
Dominant competitive position, defined, 78
Douglas Aircraft Co., experience curve usage, 124
Downstream vertical integration, 245
DuPont, experience curve usage, 124

E

Economics of scale, 287
Eltra Corporation, 31
Embryonic industry, defined, 78
Emerging product markets, competition and, 291, 294
Emerson Electric, experience curve usage, 124
Entrepreneurship *see* Corporate entrepreneurship
Environment, monitoring of, 20–21
Equipment, market entry and, 157
Equity costs, value creation and, 362
Esprit, global markets and, 326
Excellence
    critique of studies of, 394–395, 399
    evaluation of, 396–397
    Fortune's annual survey of, 398
    generic strategy choice and, 403
    planning and, 388
    strategic market planning implications, 399–403
    superior versus poor performers, 393–394
    traits of, 389–392
        America's best run companies, 389–390
        America's corporate stars, 390
        America's high technology companies, 390–391
        America's midsized companies, 391–392
        Britain's troubled companies, 392–393

Excellence—(*continued*)
    generalized, 399
Excellent companies *see* Excellence
Experience advantage, neutralizing, 132–133
Experience curves, 115–122
    anticipating future developments with, 124–125
    assumptions validity, 135–136
    cost components and, 128–129
    cost reduction sources and, 119–121
    estimating future unit of output with, 121–122
    examples of, 118
    exogenous progress and, 119
    experience accumulation rate, 123
    experience effects and, 120–121
    focus of, 117
    future unit of output and, 121–122
    plotting, 115–117
    product life cycle and, 126–128
    scale effects, 119–120
    shared experience and, 129–131
    slope of, 123
    strategic implications of, 123–134
        anticipating future developments, 124–125
        competitive cost advantage and, 123–124
        experience advantage and, 132–133
        product life cycle and, 126–128
        shared experience and, 129–131
        technology life cycles and, 131–132
    strategy based on, 128
        appropriateness of, 15
    technology life cycles and, 131–132
    time required to accumulate, *126–127*
    total cost and, 115–116
    types of, 117
Experience effects
    market entry and, 156
    measurement and prediction of, 121–123

F

Favorable competitive position, defined, 78
Financial goals, market share growth and, 60–63

Financial planning system, 17, 19
Financial strategy, 342–343
Firm, defined, 313
Fisher Scientific Company, 31
Florida State Citrus Commission, product promotion and, 234
Focus, generic strategies and, 309
Fortune, annual survey, admired corporations, 398
Forward vertical integration, 245
Functional strategy, 15–16

G

Gap Inc., global markets and, 326
GE/McKinsey portfolio matrix *see* Business screen portfolio matrix
General Electric, strategic business units and, 11
General Foods, new geographic markets and, 237–238
General Motors, portfolio design and, 416
Generic strategies, 303–313
    Abell and Hall frameworks, 309–310
    business definition and alternative, 311
    Porter's framework for, 303, 306–309
    strategic market planning and, 310, 312–313
    typologies of, 304–305
    value chain and, 313–317
Geographic market expansion, 236–238
Gerber, new market segments and, 237
Global markets, emergence of, competition and, 326–330
Gould, Inc., sustainable growth and, 351–352
Groups, strategic *see* Strategic groups
Growth industry, defined, 78
Growth opportunities
    alternative, 224
    assessing, 225–231
        market structure profile and, 227–229
        product innovation spectrum and, 226–227
        product-market growth matrix, 230–231
Growth-share matrix
    assumptions concerning, 45, 48
    Boston Consulting Group, 39–40
    portfolio analysis and, 39–45, 48

matrix dimensions, 39–40
strategic business unit,
  grouping of, 41–44
  representation of, 40
Growth strategies, 224–225
  diversification, 249–268
    benefits of, 253–254
    definition and conceptualization of,
      252–253
    direction of, 254, 256–257
    evolution of, 252
    firm performance and, 261, 264–265,
      267–268
    investment community influence and,
      262–263
    mode of, 261, *264*
    motives for, 254
    synergy and, 258, 260
    typologies of, 255
  integrative, 244–249
    alternatives to, 249
    benefits and cost, 245–246
    business unit performance, 247–248
  intensive
    market development and, 235–237
    market penetration, 232, 234–235
Growth, sustainable *see* Sustainable
  growth

H

Hall's generic strategy framework, 309–
  310
Heineken, geographic expansion and,
  236–237
Hershey Foods Corp., new customer
  groups and, 236
Hewlett-Packard, corporate culture and,
  413, *414*
High-growth markets, perils of, 90–92

I

IBM
  competitive advantage and, 11
  global markets and, 326
Individual product-market level, 227–228
Industry growth rate (IGR), defined, 41
Industry maturity, stages of, 78
Industry, types of, 157–158
Information technology

competition and, 318–325
  changing balance of using, 320, 322–
    325
  creating competitive advantage, 319–
    320, 322
  value chain and, 321
  growth of, 318
  new market creation and, 324, *325*
  strategic market planning and, *319*, 320
Innovation, institutionalizing, 429, 432–
  433
Institutional processes, corporate
  entrepreneurship and,
  425–427, 429
Integration, economics of, *247*
Integrative growth strategies, 224, 225–
  226, 244–245
  vertical integration and,
    alternatives to, 249
    benefits and cost, 245–246
    business unit performance and, 247–
    248
Intensive growth strategies, 224, 225–226,
  232–244
  market development and, 137–138,
    235–237
  market penetration and, 232, 234–235
  product development and, 238–244
Investment intensity and, profitability
  and, 157–159, 178–181
Investment ratio, return on investment
  and, 157, 159

J

Johnson & Johnson
  corporate strategy and, 13, *14–15*
  global markets and, 326
  portfolio design and, 415

K

Kodak, global markets and, 326

L

Leadership, 419–423
  strategic thinking and, 421–423
  vision and, 420–421
Lean Cuisine, global markets and, 327
Learning curve, 115
Level of analysis, PIMS and, 169–170

Life cycle portfolio matrix, 77–80
  identifying strategies with, 81
Life cycle portfolio matrix model, chart
  of, 79
Linear regression analysis, PIMS and, 160
Long-range planning systems, 19

M

M&M, new customer groups and, 236
McDonald's, global market and, 326
McKinsey & Co.
  business screen portfolio matrix and,
    73–77
  excellence studies, 25
  global markets and, 326
  strategic gameboard, 103–107
  technology development guidelines, 88
Malaysia, competitive advantage and, 10
Management reports, PIMS and, 165–168
Managerial quality gaps, 100
Market complexity, 35–36
Market development, intensive growth
  strategies and, 235–237
Market entry, PIMS and, 153, 156–159
Market growth rate see Industry growth
  rate
Market mix, growth opportunities and,
  230–231
Market penetration, intensive growth
  strategies and, 232, 234–235
Market position, profitability and, 146–
  148
Market share
  measuring, 44, 46–47
  multidimensional nature of, 44
  PIMS and, 153, 156–159
  profitability and, 173–178
Market share growth
  financial goals and, 60–63
  sales volume growth and, 59–60
Market share strategy decision, 49
  cashflow outlook and, 59–65
Market structure profile (MSP), growth
  strategies and, 227–229
Market-to-book ratio model, 361–369
  perspectives on, 367–369
  shareholder value determinants, 362–
    363

strategic market planning and, 365–367
  value creation prescriptions, 363–365
Marketing, institutionalizing innovation
  and, 429, 432–433
Marketing mix, growth opportunities and,
  230–231
Marketing programs, generating
  alternative, 22
Markets
  emerging product, 291, 294
  geographic expansion, 237–238
    new users and, 236–237
  global, competition and, 326–330
  high growth, perils of, 90–92
  pioneer dominance of, 292–293
  poor performers, turning around, 93
  strategic field, Proctor and Gamble, 95
  technology relatedness and, 259
Mars, new customer groups and, 236
Mature industry, defined, 78
Merrill Lynch, Cash Management
  Account and, 323
Mission assignment decisions, SBUs and,
  49, 51–52
Mobility barriers, new products and, 302
MSP see Market structure profile
Multifactor portfolio matrix models,
  72–86
  business screen, 73–77
    assessing business strength, 76
    assessing industry attractiveness, 76
    factors checklist, 73, 75–76
    illustrated, 74
  Directional Policy Matrix, 80, 83–86
    illustrated, 83
    prospect analysis, 85
    strategic options and, 84
  life cycle portfolio matrix, 77–80
    chart of, 79
    identifying strategies with, 81

N

Narrow vs. broad spectrum
  diversification, 257
Nestle Co.
  global markets and, 327
  new customer groups and, 236
New product development strategy, 243–
  244

O

Offensive supplemental diversification, 257
Operating complexity, *35–36*
Optimum strategy report, 166
Organizational culture, defined, 411
Organizational gaps, 100
Output, unit of, estimating cost of, 121–122

P

Par report, 165–166, 167
PCU *see* Planning and control unit
PIMS, 25
  business unit strategy measures, 145
  competitive position measures, 145
  competitive strategy paradigm, 143, 144
  cross-sectional data pooling, 170
  data,
    confidentiality of, 143, 146
    security of, 143, 146
  data base, 143
  description of, 141
  excellence and, 393–394
  format of reports reported, 171–172
  independent variables and, 171
  investment intensity, profitability and, 178–181
  level of analysis and, 169–170
  management reports and, 165–168
  market entry and, 153, 156–159
  market environment measures, 145
  market share and, 153, 156–159
  market share and profitability
    relationship, 173–178
    low market businesses and, 174–175
    market share definition and, 176–177
    moderating effects, 174
    pooling issues and, 175
    spurious relationship, 177–178
  measurement and scaling, 172
  objectives of, 142
  operational definitions of constructs, 173
  performance measures, 145
  philosophy, 168–169
  questions from data forms, 188–220
    competitive cost profile, 202–203
    corporate relationships, 203–204
    customers, 194
    feasible strategies, 219–220
    financial statements, 212–217
    internal sales, 206–207
    market diversity, 197–198
    new products, 208–211
    number of customers, 195–196
    product description, 191–194
    production process, 207–208
    purchase and sales in the corporation, 205–206
    quality profile, 198
    quality profiling sheet, 199–202
    shared resources, 204–205
    strategy analysis assumptions, 217–219
  regression models, 159–162, 165
  research findings, 146–153
    market share and profitability, 146–148
    product value, market share, and profitability, 153
    product/service quality and profitability, 148–152
  start-up businesses and, 162
  strategic decision making and, 162, 165
  strategic value of findings, 173
  time frame of data, 170–171
  unit of observation in, 142
  utilization of, 141–142
  variables of, 143, 146
  vertical integration and, 247–248
Pizza Hut, product promotion and, 234–235
Planning and control unit (PCU), 33
Planning systems
  characteristics of, 16, *17*
  defined, 16
  evolution of, 16–20
  financial, 17, 19
  long-range, 19
  strategic, 19
  strategic management, 19–20
  types of, 18
Planning, value based *see* Value based planning
Plant, market entry and, 157
PMU *see* Product market unit

Polaroid Corporation, institutional
processes and, 427–429
Porter's generic strategy framework, 303,
306–309
Portfolio analysis, 225
assumptions, validity of, 63–65
balanced and unbalanced, 57
basis for, 36–37
competitors', 55–56
conceptual framework for, 37–39
developments in illustrated, 86
growth-share matrix, 39–45, 48
matrix dimensions, 39–40
imbalance analysis, 55, 57
organizational context and, 33
prescriptions of, 48–52
product, 86–89
product portfolio trajectory analysis
and, 53–55, 57
served market and, 33–36
shared momentum analysis and, 52–53
strategic business unit and, 33
strategic implications of, 48–52
Portfolio assessment, 22
value-based planning and, 365–366
Portfolio decisions, 22
Portfolio management, corporate culture
and, 416
Portfolio matrices
business screen, 73–77
assessing business strength and, 76
assessing industry attractiveness and,
76
factors checklist, 73, 75–76
illustrated, 74
classifying businesses into, 96
comparison of standardized, 97
Directional Policy Matrix, 80, 83–86
life cycle, 77–80, 81
limitations of, 92–98
strategic market planning, 23, 25
using, 90–92
Position gaps, 100
Proctor and Gamble
emerging product markets and, 291
new geographic markets and, 237–238
strategic field markets, 95
Product complexity, 35–36

Product development
intensive growth strategies and, 238–
244
additions strategy, 242
line extension strategy, 242–243
new product strategy, 243–244
problems and challenges of, 244
quality improvement, 239–241
reformulation, 238–239
Product feature additions strategy, 242–
243
Product innovation spectrum, growth
strategies and, 226–227
Product life cycle, experience curve
strategies and, 126–128
Product line extension strategy, 242–243
Product market unit (PMU), 33
Product-market growth matrix
growth opportunities and, 148–152, 233
growth strategies and, 230–231
Product portfolio
analysis, 86–89
trajectory analysis, 53–55
Product promotion, 234–235
Product quality
improvement strategy, 239–241
profitability and, 148–152
Product reformulation strategy, 238–239
Product replacement strategy, 243
Products
choice of
corporate culture and, 415
excellence and, 400–402
global markets and, 326–330
assessment of, 328, 329
new, mobility barriers to, 302
Profit
competition and, 283–294
buyers and, 289–290
existing firms and, 284, 286–287
industry suppliers and, 287–288, 289
potential entrants and, 287, 288
product substitutes and, 290
Profit Impact of Market Strategies see
PIMS
Profit Impact of Market Strategy data base
see PIMS

Profitability
    determinants of, 163
    investment intensity and, 157–159,
        178–181
    market/industry factors and, 159, 160–
        161
    market position and, 146–148
    market share and, 173–178
    "par" and, 167
    product quality and, 148–152
    service quality and, 148–152
    source of, high share businesses and,
        150–151
    strategic influences on, *147*
Profitability matrix, 365–366

Q

Quality, dimensions of, *240–241*
Quality improvement strategy,
    formulating, 154–155
Quality profiling sheets, PIMS, 199–202

R

R. J. Reynolds, Inc., divestment and, 400
Ratio of investment, 157
Regression models, PIMS and, 159–162,
    165
Regulatory/legal gaps, 100
Related ratio, 265
Relative market share (RMS)
    defined, 42
    profitability and, 146
Report on "Look-Alikes" (ROLA), 166
Research and development, market entry
    and, 156
Resource allocation
    decisions, 49, 51–52
    portfolio matrices and, guidelines for,
        94
Resource constraints, portfolio matrices
    and, 94
Retention/deletion decisions, strategic
    business units and, 37–39, 49,
        51–52
Return on equity, 343–346
    model, *344*
Return on investment (ROI)
    investment ratio and, 157, 159

PIMS and, 146
product/service quality and, 151
as profitability indicator, 363
regression analysis and, 159–162, 165

S

Sabre reservations system, 322–323
Sales volume growth, market share
        growth and, 59–60
SBS *see* Strategic business segment
SBU *see* Strategic business unit
Scarce assets, preemption of, 156–157
Served market, portfolio analysis and,
        33–36
Service quality, profitability and, 148–152
Share momentum analysis, 52–53
Shareholder value
    computing, 373
    creation of as a business unit, 370–372
    determinants of, 369–370
    sustainable growth and, 355
Shell Chemicals, Directional Policy
        Matrix and, 80
Singapore, competitive advantage and, 10
Situation audit, 21–22
Space, preemption of, market entry and,
        157
Specialization ratio, 265
SPI *see* Strategic Planning Institute
Start-up businesses, PIMS findings on,
        162
State Farm Insurance, information
        technology and, 324
Stick to the knitting philosophy, 400–402
Stouffer, global markets and, 327
Strategic analysis report, 166
Strategic business segment (SBS), 33
Strategic business unit (SBU), 11–13
    Boston Consulting Group, 39–40
    business screen portfolio matrix and,
        73–77
    cash flow outlook and, 49–52
    charting, 48
    grouping of, 41–44
    interdependency among, 94
    life cycle portfolio matrix and, 77–80
    mission assignment decisions, 49, 51–
        52

Strategic business unit—(*continued*)
    multifactor portfolio matrix models
        and, 72
    perspectives of, *34*
    PIMS and, 142
    portfolio analysis and, 33
    representation of, 40
    retention/deletion decisions, 37–39, 49,
        51–52, 57–59
Strategic decisions, PIMS and, 162, 165
Strategic groups, 294–302
    empirical studies on, 297–298
    formation of, 294, 296, 299, 300–301
    strategic market planning and, 299, 302
    two dimensional view of, *299*
Strategic management planning system,
    19–20
Strategic market planning
    business portfolio matrices, 23, 25
    competition and, 290–291, 294
    competitive analysis and, 25
    corporate culture and, 415–418
    defined, 4–5
    excellence and, 399–403
    generic strategies and, 310, 312–313
    McKinsey excellence studies, 25
    organizational renewal and, 25–26
    pooled business experience analysis, 25
    process, 20–23
    strategic groups and, 299, 302
    strategic marketing planning and, 5
    value-based planning and, 365–367,
        372, 376
    value chain and, 314, 317
Strategic marketing planning, strategic
    market planning and, 5
Strategic models
    competitive, 98–108
        competitive advantage, sustainable,
            98–101
        McKinsey strategic gameboard, 103–
            107
        new BCG matrix and, 101–103
        Strategic Planning Associates and,
            107–108
Strategic planning
    described, 421
    responsibility of, 5

Strategic Planning Associates, strategic
    models and, 107–108
Strategic Planning Institute (SPI), 140
    PIMS data base and, 143
Strategic planning systems, 19
Strategic thinking, leadership and, 421–
    423
Strategic thrusts, families of, 80
Strategic vision, 420
Strategy
    concept of, 6–7, 10–16
        distinctive competence, 6, 7, 10
    definitions of, 8–9
    generic *see* Generic strategies
Strategy levels, 7, 11–16
    business unit strategy, 13–15
    corporate strategy, 13
    functional strategy, 15–16
Strong competitive position, defined, 78
Supplementary related diversification, 257
Suppliers, profit impact of, 287–288
Sustainable competitive advantage, 10,
    98–101
Sustainable growth, 346–355
    equation, 346–349
    problems of, 349–354
        multibusiness unit firm and, 352–354
        rapid growth firm/easy equity access,
            354
        rapid growth/no equity firm, 349–351
        slow growth company and, 351–352
    shareholder value and, 355

T

Taiwan, competitive advantage and, 10
Technical processes, corporate
    entrepreneurship and, 425–427,
    429
Technology development, guidelines for,
    88–89
Technology leadership, market entry and,
    156
Technology life cycles, 131–132
Technology portfolio matrix, 86, *87*
Tenable competitive position, defined, 78
Texas instruments, corporate culture and,
    413, *414*
3M, new customer groups and, 236

Touchstone Pictures, 4
Toys "R" Us, global markets and, 326

U

Unit of output, estimating cost of, 121–122
United Airlines
    Apollo reservations system and, 322–323
    distinctive competence and, 10
Upstream vertical integration, 245

V

Value activities, 314
    generic categories of, 315
    support, generic categories of, 316
Value-based planning, 358–383
    cash flow and, 360–361
        model of, 369–377
    interest in, 359–360
    market-to-book ratio model and, 361–369
        shareholder value determinants, 362–363
        strategic market planning and, 365–367

value creation prescriptions, 363–365
Value chain
    defined, 313–314
    generic strategies and, 313–317
    information technology and, 321
    strategic market planning and, 314, 317
Value creation, market-to-book ratio model and, 363–365
Vertical integration strategies, 244–245
    alternatives to, 249
    business unit performance and, 247–248
    defining characteristics, 246
    strategic benefits and costs of, 245–246
Vertical ratio, 265
Vision
    leadership and, 420–421
    strategic, 420

W

Wal-Mart, 287
Walt Disney Pictures, 4
    market change, strategic response to, 6–7
Weak competitive position, defined, 78